THE AMERICAN LIBRARY

10, RUE DU GÉNÉRAL CAMOU
75007 PARIS

American Library
in Paris
Book Award
2013 Submission

GARDENS OF STONE

STEPHEN GRADY

and Michael Wright

HODDER &
STOUGHTON

First published in Great Britain in 2013 by Hodder & Stoughton
An Hachette UK company

3

Copyright © Stephen Grady 2013

Map by Rodney Paull

The right of Stephen Grady to be identified as the Author
of the Work has been asserted by him in accordance with the Copyright,
Designs and Patents Act 1988.

A CIP catalogue record for this title is available from the British Library

Hardback ISBN 978 1 444 76059 0
Trade Paperback ISBN 978 1 444 76060 6
Ebook ISBN 978 1 444 76061 3

Typeset in Sabon MT by Palimpsest Book Production Limited,
Falkirk, Stirlingshire

Printed and bound by
CPI Group (UK) Ltd, Croydon, CR0 4YY

Hodder & Stoughton policy is to use papers that are natural,
renewable and recyclable products and made from wood grown in sustainable forests.
The logging and manufacturing processes are expected to conform to the
environmental regulations of the country of origin.

Hodder & Stoughton Ltd
338 Euston Road
London NW1 3BH

www.hodder.co.uk

GARDENS
OF STONE

To my friends and comrades in the Resistance,
and the brave people of northern France,
who risked their lives for freedom.

They shall grow not old, as we that are left grow old

Laurence Binyon

*Every man thinks meanly of himself for not having been
a soldier*

Samuel Johnson

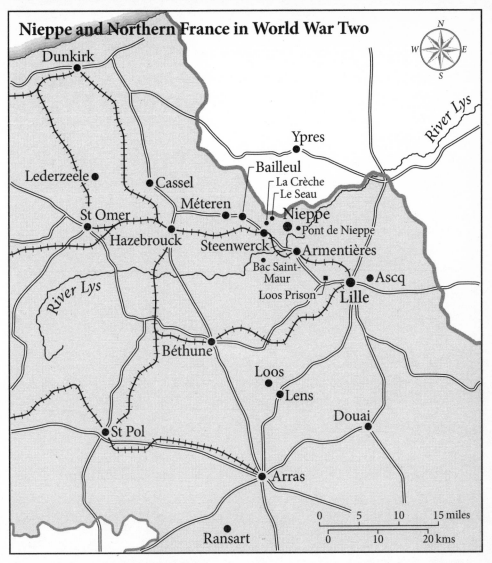

Nieppe and Northern France in World War Two

Dunkirk

River Lys

Ypres

Lederzeele

Cassel

Bailleul
— La Crèche
— Le Seau

Méteren

St Omer

Nieppe

Pont de Nieppe

Hazebrouck

Steenwerck

Armentières

Bac Saint-Maur

Ascq

Loos Prison

Lille

River Lys

Béthune

Loos

Lens

Douai

St Pol

Arras

Ransart

0   5   10   15 miles

0   10   20 kms

Ghent

Dunkirk

Calais

Ypres

Boulogne

Nieppe

BELGIUM

River Lys

Lille

FRANCE

Mons

Arras

The 'Forbidden Zone' of the Nord/Pas-de-Calais, attached to the German Military Command in Brussels

January 2012 – Halkidiki, Greece

I can't say why I didn't begin this story until today. I suppose I didn't dare. Besides, there was always something more pressing to do. A garden will not weed itself, my father used to say as we stood in one of his cemeteries, a man of forty-four and a boy of five, gazing at the rank upon rank of white headstones.

Nothing had been left standing in our part of northern France after the First World War. Our whole neighbourhood was a battlefield. The front lines were still visible in the scarred countryside. I played marbles with balls of shrapnel. The locals pegged out their garden lines with bayonets.

My father worked as a gardener for the Imperial War Graves Commission. His job was to create and tend the graves of the fallen. At first these were simply marked with wooden crosses. Then the permanent headstones arrived; I can remember how my mother screamed to see my father stuffing the wooden crosses, some of them still caked with earth, into the wood-burning stove. She clicked the beads on her rosary and begged him to stop. She said she was worried we would all go to hell.

'Hell can't be any worse than this,' I heard my father mutter. Because, of course, none of us had any idea what lay ahead.

Eighty-two years later, on a terrace overlooking the Aegean, I am sitting in a white plastic chair to enjoy my eleven o'clock smoke as I wait for a guest to arrive. I like to have a little puff when I am gazing out over the lighthouse point, over this same view that has helped to soothe my mind for so long. I never have more than one cigar, except on difficult days, when the memories swarm like flies.

My memory is still good, unfortunately. That's why the nightmares have not stopped. Nothing helps memory as much as fear. And I lived in terrible fear when I was growing up: fear of being caught by the Germans; fear of being tortured by their police. Fear so intense that I have never been able to obliterate it.

I have tried everything. God helps; whisky, too. My garden is booby-trapped with tripwires, and a wing mirror screwed to the wall helps me keep an eye on anyone approaching the house. The police don't need to know about the shotgun beneath my bed.

I have been on several pilgrimages to the monasteries of sacred Mount Athos. On one of these retreats, I met a huge Russian monk with wild hair and a big black beard, who had prayed in the great monastery of St Panteleimon for twenty years. Father Vitali and I became friends, and now he comes to stay from time to time.

Heavy footsteps, clumping up the hill. That will be him now.

'This place is still a fortress, Stephanos,' booms the monk, panting from the effort of climbing up my drive in his heavy black robes. 'Ah, the eleven o'clock smoke. Are you busy?'

'Only with staring out to sea.'

He pulls up a chair and we both sit in silence for a while, enjoying the distant rumble of the waves.

'The funny thing is,' he says at last, 'that your Russian neighbour has this same view from his house. But it looks different from yours.'

I shrug and take another puff on my cigar.

'Your terrace is prettier, too. Where did you get all this marble?'

'They're gravestones – it's a long story.'

Another silence.

'What do you think about, Stephanos, while you're sitting here like this?'

I don't take my eyes off the horizon. I like Father Vitali but I don't like interrogations.

'Still going over the past?' he asks.

I hesitate. 'My son keeps hounding me to write it all down. He bullies me. He won't let me off the hook.'

Vitali looks straight into my eyes, with a gaze so unwavering that it goes right through me. And I know what he's thinking. He's thinking my son is right.

7 July 1930

I am five years old. Dad is weeding his graves as usual, while I play hide-and-seek among the headstones of a war cemetery in northern France. This is my favourite game, even though it is quite tricky to play by yourself. How cool the grass feels beneath my feet.

Today I have an especially dangerous mission. I am planning to ambush my father. He is kneeling just over there, digging with his red trowel. I can see the veins on his forearms as he works.

'Bang, bang, you're dead, I'm not,' I shout, jumping out from behind a gravestone.

'Very funny,' replies my father. 'Now get your dirty great feet off that grave. That's someone's brother or son you're standing on, right there.'

I take a step back, gazing at the imprint of my toes in the grey earth.

'But, Dad, I thought you said they were dead soldiers.'

'They are dead soldiers,' he says, now with the hint of a smile. 'But look: you see those flowers that someone has left over there?'

I nod.

'Well, that means that, for someone, whoever is buried there will live forever.'

I think very hard about this, and however hard I try to think, it still doesn't make any sense. Something about my father's words frightens me. What I love about his cemeteries is that they are all so grassy, so peaceful, so perfect for playing hide-and-seek. I don't like to think that some of those soldiers' bodies buried underground are somehow still alive.

18 June 1933

'Is he coming? Is he coming?'

Sitting on the front step of our house, Elizabeth is so excited that she has to yell the question twice. Mind you, little Elizabeth has to say everything twice: Lou-Lou, bread-bread, gun-gun. And now it's a warm Saturday evening and Dad-Dad is expected home any minute.

Eight of us live all squashed in here, at number 6, rue du Sac, a little house on the outskirts of the village of Nieppe, right on the border between France and Belgium. A customs barrier just up the road reminds us that we live on the edge of someone else's world.

Everything in our house is painted lime green. Green is the standard paint colour of the Imperial War Graves Commission, and my father brings home any half-finished pots going spare. Bit by bit, he has turned everything green: green bedsteads, green bikes, green walls.

'I've got green fingers, me,' he likes to joke, creeping up behind my mother and pretending he is going to give her a hug. Except that he never does.

Grandmother, whom we call Mémère, shares one bedroom with Auntie Val and my sisters Rosemary, eleven, and Elizabeth, three. My parents sleep in the other bedroom, along with me and my younger brother Francis, whom I call Kléber. My nickname is Lou, because I was as hairy as a wolf – *un loup* – when I was born. My father also calls me Lighting, because I'm not the quickest to do what I'm told. I am eight years old.

Our house is divided in half by a passage that runs from

the front door to the back. There are two large rooms to the right, and two to the left. We mostly live on the left. The right-hand front room houses Auntie Val's knitting machines, and the back room is a kitchen with two hand pumps, one for pumping water from a shallow well, the other for pumping rainwater from a cistern on the roof. All the water tastes of cat. A glass-covered veranda runs along the back of the house, with a washroom at one end and an earth closet full of flies and a horrid stink at the other. Beyond the veranda is the garden, where my father grows his spuds.

Tonight, a stub of candle has been lit in the front room. My big sister Rosemary has brushed her hair, Auntie Val is wearing a cardigan she only finished knitting this afternoon, and even Grandmother, Mémère, has put in her teeth. My mother, in a green dress that matches the skirting boards, keeps tiptoeing over to the window and squinting out, as if she hopes to spot my father wobbling up the road on his army bicycle. And every time she does so, it sets Elizabeth off again.

I can feel her watching me, mouth agape, as I sit out on the front step in my shirtsleeves, taunting gendarme beetles with a twig. Behind us, my brother Kléber gallops up and down the passage. None of us can believe he has been allowed to stay up so late.

In other words, tonight is just another Saturday evening at our house in the rue du Sac. Saturdays are when my father dresses up in his town suit, a white silk scarf and a trilby, and pedals off on his bicycle to Armentières, five kilometres away. The first time I saw him looking so smart, I asked my mother if he was going to church. Auntie Val laughed, but Mummy wrung her hands. No, she explained, he was going to drink beer and play snooker with his English chums; men who, like him, fell for French girls while on leave from the trenches and stayed on in northern France at the end of the war. Now that the work of killing is finished, their task is to look after the gardens of graves that cover so much of the flat countryside.

'It's my one escape,' my father once told me, when we were sitting among his graves, and I'd asked him about Saturdays. 'You've no idea what it's like to live in a house full of French women.'

'But I do,' I protested. 'It's the same for me.'

'Lou, you're only eight years old, and you speak their lingo. That's not the same thing at all.' He gazed for a while at the line of headstones in front of us. 'You'll understand one day, Lou. A man needs to belong to something bigger than his family. And on Saturday evenings, I almost feel I do.'

My father would be amazed to witness all the fluffing up of feathers that goes on in his house full of French women, when my mother, aunt and grandmother want him home. In the week, they cook for him, clean for him and largely ignore him. They chat among themselves about French people he doesn't know, and mop the floor beneath his chair as if he isn't there. Although he insists that we all speak English at mealtimes, most meals are conducted in silence. And an English silence, I have learned, is much the same as a French one. Yet, come Saturday, and the women are like a bunch of hens without a cockerel: they become quite tense until he reappears.

I do my best to pretend I am different; not simply that I am English, but that I am immune to my father's charm. He can be very strict, after all, and only last week gave me another clip around the ear for pelting Monsieur Faure's shutters with mud balls. He didn't seem to care that Faure is a horrible old man, with warts all over his face, and deserves to be pelted. Dad said it wasn't the mess I'd made that he minded. It was the fact that I'd allowed myself to get caught.

'I didn't get caught,' I replied, aggrieved. 'It was that rascal Chabin who told on me. And he was supposed to be my friend.'

From the way my father shook his head, I knew the subject was closed. 'Just mind you never tell tales, Lou. Keep it under your hat.'

Tonight, I have skewered every beetle on the front step by

9

the time the church clock in Nieppe chimes nine and Elizabeth starts jumping up and down.

'Look, here he comes,' she shouts. 'And he has *two* bike-bikes with him.'

In the twilight, my father slowly cycles towards us in his trilby and his white silk scarf, with one hand on his own handlebars, and the other on the handlebars of a second machine, smaller than the first.

'*Quel bel homme*,' murmurs Mémère.

'Welcome home, my heart,' says my mother, as if he has been away for a week. 'Did you have a good moment?'

He nods; tuts at her grammar; brushes her kiss aside. 'I've got something for you,' he says, swaying as he blinks down at me.

I can hardly bring myself to glance at the metal shape that glints beside him, in case I am deceived. I know we are very poor, that I will be lucky ever to inherit my sister Rosemary's bashed-up green bicycle, let alone have one of my very own.

'Is it . . .'

'It's a bicycle' interrupts Kléber, his voice at once steely with envy and wobbly with awe. Out of the corner of my eye, I watch my brother stroke the leather saddle. I want to tell him to take his dirty hands off. I can't help thinking of all the new tricks I shall be able to play, now that I have a means of escape.

'How did you get it?' murmurs my mother.

'I won most of it, and one of the cousins came up with the rest.' My father can barely contain himself. 'I told you all that snooker practice would pay off in the end, Berthe.'

'You did,' she replies, running her fingertips over the bicycle. My bicycle.

My father starts to tell us about how hard it is to ride two bicycles at once, but nobody is listening.

'Well, go on then, Lou,' orders Auntie Val, appearing on the step. 'Let's see you ride it.'

Five minutes later, I am sitting with my leg up on the kitchen table, and everybody is admiring my wound. My mother feels a field dressing is required, but my father is calling for amputation.

'Stretcher bearers!' he keeps yelling, which I don't think is very funny at all.

'I can't believe you allowed Lou, of all people, to ride a bicycle in the dark with no brakes,' says Auntie Val, pushing him out into the passage.

'Is my bicycle all right?' I wonder aloud.

'Don't you think we should call Dr Vanuxeem?' I hear my mother whisper to her sister. 'I do have a little money put aside.'

'Oh, don't be ridiculous. The boy will be fine,' pronounces Auntie Val, who has appointed herself the family medic.

It is far too expensive to call out Dr Vanuxeem, with his bowler hat and his motor car, for anything less than a preventable death. Instead, it is Auntie Val who spoons the cod liver oil down our throats every morning, and who sends us out with a clove of garlic tucked under our tongues if flu has been reported. Constipation I never dare admit, ever since I watched her wedge a piece of toilet soap the size of a hazelnut up Kléber's back passage. And now she is examining the gash in my leg.

'It really doesn't hurt,' I lie.

'Hold still,' she nods. And with that she tips a teaspoon of salt into the open wound.

'I was only joking about the amputation, you know,' yells my father, dashing in to see what all the noise is about. '*Salt?* I can't believe you just did that.'

'It works for curing pork,' replies Auntie Val, flatly. 'So why not?'

'He's a human being, not an animal.'

'Is there a difference?'

'It hurts now,' I gasp, reaching for my mother's hand.

A little later, when the pain no longer roars but throbs, I hear someone playing the piano in the front room. But for once it is not Rosemary, tormenting us with her arpeggios. No, this time it is my father, bashing away.

Auntie Val glances at my mother. Rosemary must have goaded him into sitting down to play some of his English tunes, the old songs with which he wooed my mother in 1917, when he was a gunner in the Royal Artillery and she was running a café with Auntie Val, after the start of the war.

The pain in my leg forgotten, I slip off the kitchen table and hurry into the front room. My father cannot read music as Rosemary can, but he has rhythm and sometimes he even hits some of the right notes. He uses the piano a bit like a drum kit, and the effect is noisy and hilarious. I love the way he can sing without taking his cigarette out of his mouth. Even Mémère taps her battered clogs.

Ma'm'selle from Armentières, parlez-vous
Ma'm'selle from Armentières, parlez-vous
Ma'm'selle from Armentières,
Hasn't been kissed for twenty years,
Inky pinky parlez-vous.

I love it, too, when my parents talk about the olden days, as my father calls them. And tonight is one of those nights.

'Dad, tell us about how you met Mummy,' says Rosemary, sitting beside him at the piano. 'Tell us the story again.' With her glossy black hair tied back, and a severe pair of spectacles on her nose, my big sister already looks like a schoolmistress. She has a habit of speaking in imperatives. And she is only eleven.

'Oh, you don't want to hear about that.'

'Yes, we do,' says Auntie Val, entering the room with my mother. 'Don't we, Berthe?'

So my father describes how he would come in off duty with his artillery battery and start bashing out songs on the piano in the *Café du Centre*, his ears still ringing with the din of the Evening Hate, as he calls it.

'You should have seen how the beer and wine flowed,' nods Auntie Val, raising her eyebrows at Rosemary. 'At first your mother and I couldn't understand a word the Tommies were saying. *"Qu'est-ce que vous désirez, monsieur?"* we'd ask. And they didn't have a clue. But we did a roaring trade.'

My mother dabs her eyes. 'All those poor boys,' she adds, 'spending their last few pennies, sometimes their very last night, on earth.'

'You made it better for them,' murmurs my father.

'Did we?'

'It wasn't just the beer and the Bombardier Fritz. You gave them warmth, made them feel that someone cared.'

'Egg and chips.' My mother nods, smiling to herself. 'And then I fell for the piano player.'

'You were born lucky,' he replies.

'No, she wasn't,' corrects Auntie Val, glaring at my father. 'You were.'

I listen, doing my best to picture the scene: tankards swinging in a sea of khaki; the air thick with sweat and smoke; frightened young faces in the flickering lamplight, wondering if they'll still be alive to sing the same songs tomorrow night. And in the midst of it all, two young French women, doing their best to understand.

It is so hard to believe that my mother was ever young. Once upon a time, Mummy ran her own business on the side, delivering English newspapers to the troops in the trenches. She would gallop out at dawn with a horse and trap and a team of twenty boys. But as I gaze up at the fragile middle-aged woman who now stands beside the piano, her head bowed and her eyes misty with tears, I cannot picture her as the 23-year-old dynamo my father describes.

My mother's eyesight is fading fast. There is so much that she misses these days. That's why Mémère and Auntie Val moved in with us last year.

'You must have been so brave, Mummy,' says Rosemary, stroking my mother's arm with her fingertips.

'You were brave in those days, Berthe,' whispers my father, turning to gaze at her.

'I didn't *feel* brave,' she replies. 'But it's true that the world doesn't feel so frightening when you're young.'

'Even in the middle of the worst war in history?' Rosemary wrinkles her nose.

'I suppose you don't value your life in the same way when you're young. The less you know, the braver you can be.'

'Just look at Lou,' says Auntie Val, 'cycling headfirst into ditches in the dark.'

'I knew where I was going,' I retort.

My mother smiles. She explains how she and Auntie Val were living with Grandma at the time, above the café where they worked.

'It was a coven,' says my father.

'It was heaven,' retorts Auntie Val. 'We were in Pont de Nieppe, not far from here, and just a few miles from the lines.'

'That's why your mother liked my singing,' he adds. 'It drowned out the rumble of the guns.'

'And then the tocsin sounded . . .'

'The tocsin?' asks Rosemary.

'They used to ring the heaviest bell in the village church to warn us of danger, if they were expecting a bombardment. And I remember the bell just kept ringing and ringing in 1917. It went on going until the church was just a pile of dust. In the shelling, everyone lost everything. This house, this street: it was all built out of the rubble of the war.'

And as I listen to her talking, I see my mother as if for the first time: a poppy in the shadow of a thousand graves.

'This place,' continues my father, suddenly serious, 'is an up-yours to the Kaiser and the Krauts. It says you can be as cruel and vile as you like, but you'll never drive us out.' He lights another cigarette. 'And that's the one good thing about living in this hellhole. They say lightning never strikes in the same place twice. Let's hope not, eh?' He ruffles my hair and I growl, pretending to resist.

23 March 1936

Nothing ever happens in Nieppe. And in the rue du Sac, where we live, even less happens than anywhere else. The garden behind the house is entirely given over to my father's vegetables. Indoors, any game noisier than tiddly-winks is strictly forbidden. Kléber spends hours playing jacks by himself, bouncing a red India rubber ball. Rosemary practises the piano. And I lose count of how many times Elizabeth makes me recite 'Two Little Dicky Birds', with a couple of postage stamps stuck to my index fingers. Her eyes widen with wonder just the same, every time I make them reappear.

From 1931 to 1936, I attend the Catholic boys' school in Nieppe. The École Saint Louis takes boys from the ages of six to fourteen, and is run by Monsieur Ruckebusch, a fierce disciplinarian with a face like a thundercloud and a kick like a drayhorse, who prepares us for the Certificat d'Études. Where we sit in the dark classroom is determined by how well we have done in our tests: top scorers sit in the front row, with the lazy dunderheads at the back. I cannot say whether Monsieur Ruckebusch's strictness encourages me to wildness, rather as the molecules of a gas become livelier when compressed, or whether it is thanks to his ferocity that I have not yet gone off the rails entirely. All I know is that I am in trouble most of the time.

I am a winter sinner, more than a summer one. In winter, it is already dark by the time Ruckebusch lets us out of school. And, thus cloaked, a few of us like to play tricks on the sniffier, snootier residents of the church square.

At first, we just knock loudly on their front doors and scarper. Then I introduce a new element: we make neat packages of horse dung and deliver them through the letter boxes.

On the way back up the rue du Sac, I do my best to wipe my hands clean in the dewy grass, before patting them dry on the seat of my shorts. But when I get home one Friday night, the house is full of smoke and Auntie Val is hard at work in the kitchen. Friday nights are what my father calls our special treat night, when we have egg and chips. So it's Bombardier Fritz all round, and a glass of watered beer on the side for him. He is in cheerful spirits right now, telling my mother and Mémère about a new *estaminet* that has opened in the town where nothing ever happens.

It seems that the old *Café du Commerce*, a grey and cheerless place, has been sold. It has now been renamed *Au Petit Galopin* – the little rascal's place – and is run by two young ladies who, according to my father's awed description, are unusually glamorous for Nieppe.

'They even wear make-up on their faces, and everything.' He sends a big wink in my direction. 'You'd think they were fine ladies of Paris.'

'Or dancers,' huffs my mother, crossing herself.

'Or actresses,' adds Mémère with a grimace, 'which is worse.'

'Well, naturally, you won't catch me going into a place like that,' declares my father. 'The sort of fellows who go in there are only after one thing, and someone ought to teach them a lesson.'

'What *are* they after, Dad?' I ask.

'Never you mind, Lou,' says Mémère, shooting him a look. 'But they're up to no good.'

'Liquorice,' says my father. He folds his arms and smiles at Mémère. 'What they're after, Lou, is liquorice.'

I am intrigued by this information and want to see for myself what these ladies look like, who wear make-up on their faces. And, naturally, I very much want to know what sort of bad men frequent *Au Petit Galopin,* and why they are so fond of liquorice.

Just up the road from our house is another bar called *Au Repos des Cyclistes,* an *estaminet* where textile workers who have crossed the border from Belgium like to pause for a Pernod or gin. Spirits are banned in the pubs on the other side, so a French one for the road makes a popular chaser on the journey home.

This place becomes a target for me and my friends. It is just so tempting to see all those bicycles lined up in the rack outside the bar, while their owners knock back the spirits inside. We let the tyres down. We loosen all the saddles. And then, one moonlit night, inspiration strikes.

Nipping across to the *Repos des Cyclistes* with my pal Roussel, I haul out one of the parked bicycles from the rack, grip the front wheel between my knees and give the handlebars a sharp twist.

'There, that should do it,' I whisper. We do the same thing to all the other bikes in the rack.

The result of this small improvement exceeds our expectations. Behind the hedge, the two of us stand bent double, holding our sides and shaking uncontrollably as victim after victim sways out of the pub, mounts his bicycle and – wobble, wobble, *merde* – finishes up in the water-filled ditch across the road. One heroic soul in plus fours goes beyond the call of duty: determined to give value for money, he hauls himself from the ditch, examines his dripping bicycle, scratches his head, and then repeats the process all over again. When we hear the second splash, we have to lie down. It hurts too much.

Afterwards, Roussel and I head over to the *Petit Galopin,* hoping for a glimpse of the ladies with make-up on their faces. I have already told him about the unwholesome liquorice-lovers who frequent this place. A number of them come and go as we hide nearby. We giggle at the din they make as they relieve themselves into the fifty-gallon oil drum outside the door. Mostly the men are thick-set lorry drivers in sooty overalls, or commercial travellers in brown suits with sleeves that are too short. All of them look shifty and uneasy to me, as if they know a secret they wish they didn't, and the ones going in seem somehow more cheerful than the ones coming out.

Roussel says he wants to show me something else and leads me on a route that takes us past the house of Monsieur Bossu, the electrician. None of us likes Bossu, because when we kicked a football into his garden once, he stuck his screwdriver into it and punctured it. And then he kicked it back at us. So my eyes widen when Roussel points out Bossu's brand-new bicycle, leaning against the porch. What catches my attention are the tyres. Fat and white and lustrous in the moonlight, these things are moulded out of cream-coloured rubber, thick as a well-stuffed *andouillette*. I have heard people talking about balloon tyres before, but never actually seen the things on a bicycle. And now here they are, marked BRENNABOR in big black letters.

'German tyres' whispers Roussel.

'I thought they smelled bad,' I nod. 'Shall we give it a test ride?'

'Better not. You know what Bossu is like with his screwdriver.'

'*D'accord*. So maybe we should just let down his tyres for him?'

Suddenly the front door opens, and a soft light from the house slants out into the street. Ducking away from the porch, we both hide behind a cart until we hear the door close, and then sprint off down the road. But I can feel a familiar itch inside me. I am not yet ready to call it a night.

In class next morning, we are using our compasses to construct triangles, isosceles and equilateral, when the door flies open and a small figure in dark blue uniform marches in, the heels of his boots making drumbeats on the bare wooden floor.

We all jump to our feet.

'*Bonjour, les enfants,*' snaps Monsieur Houvenagel, the local policeman, clicking his heels together with a nod towards Ruckebusch at his throne-like desk.

'*Bonjour, Monsieur Houvenagel,*' we chant.

'Sit down,' he replies. 'I have something to show you.' Slowly he brings out what he has been hiding behind his back. Black, limp and dangling, at first I think it is a dead viper. But the object in Houvenagel's hand comes, he says, from inside one of the tyres of Monsieur Bossu's brand-new bicycle. He and the headmaster exchange knowing glances.

'And someone has made a number of holes in it with a sharp object,' he cries. 'With, perhaps, a compass such as this one?' Houvenagel suddenly leaps forward and plucks a compass from off the desk of Pierre Blanquart, a quiet, studious boy who lives in the centre of Nieppe.

Blanquart looks stricken. 'It wasn't me,' he pipes, in a small voice.

'Perhaps not. But it could have been someone *like* you.' Now Houvenagel takes a sharp sidestep until he is standing in front of Roussel's desk. He leans forward, as if to examine him more closely.

Roussel does not look up. I know I should keep my head down, too. But I have had enough of Houvenagel's posturing.

'And perhaps,' I say quietly, 'Monsieur Bossu cycled over a few nails in the road. Tyres are easily punctured, you know.'

'*Mais oui,*' he replies, pressing his particulars against Roussel's desk. 'Tyres are punctured. But not eighty times. Eighty times, I tell you!'

I dare to glance across at Roussel. I can see his lip beginning to quiver. The muscles in his cheeks and eyelids are desperately clenched. His shoulders are beginning to shake.

Houvenagel pauses. 'There are exactly eighty individual puncture holes in this rubber tube,' he declares. 'Eighty holes!' Now I can feel myself beginning to go, too. My stomach muscles are starting to wobble. I bite the inside of my cheeks;

dig my fingernails into my legs. If I laugh now, all is lost. 'I know this, because I have counted them myself. And I mean to winkle out the miscreant, so that he may pay for his crime.'

Reaching for my compass, I jam the sharp point into my leg.

And then we all just sit there, electrified, waiting for the axe to fall. Slowly, ever so slowly, Monsieur Ruckebusch takes off his spectacles and rises at his mighty desk, before stomping down the three wooden steps to stand next to Monsieur Houvenagel.

'Tears of remorse, Grady?'

'No, sir,' I gasp, blinking.

'Well, what then?'

'I suppose I was just feeling sorry for the bicycle.'

'Silence!' he roars, as the class erupts into peals of laughter. 'You, Grady,' he whispers. He leans forward, his face very close to mine. 'If you wish to live among us, I suggest you grow up fast. I don't care what you do in England. But in this country, we value maturity armed with wisdom and good judgement, not facetious little troublemakers armed with catapults and practical jokes. Do you understand me?' He straightens up. 'Right,' he says at last, raising his voice. 'Who was it?'

Silence.

'I repeat: *c'était qui?* I ask the culprit to own up. If not, the entire class will pay.'

So it is all for one, or one for all. I smart at the injustice of this, more than at the pain of the slow puncture in my thigh. Outside, the church clock strikes the hour.

'Last chance,' says Ruckebusch, hands behind his back. I hold my breath.

'Remember what Jesus said: the truth will set you free.'

Nobody even blinks.

'Let me put it another way. Either someone tells me who committed this wanton vandalism, or else every single one of you will be heavily punished on their behalf.'

'Even me, sir?' asks Blanquart, timidly.

'Yes, Blanquart, especially you,' snarls the headmaster, rounding on his favourite pupil. I bite my lip as Blanquart begins to sob.

'No one has the courage to step forward? To take the consequences on behalf of their friends?'

We all sit, fiddling with our compasses, staring at our desks. Houvenagel peers at his watch. And then Roussel clears his throat. Before he can speak, I raise my hand.

'*Oui, Grady?*' Ruckebusch steps forward a couple of paces. 'You have something more to say?'

'I just wondered why you are so sure that it must be someone from this class.'

'Because I can *smell* it,' snaps the headmaster. 'And because all the worst troublemakers just happen to be in this room.' He stares at me. 'Mentioning no names, Grady.'

Still no one speaks. I can hear the leather of Monsieur Houvenagel's boots creaking, as he bobs up and down on his toes.

'Right, that's it,' says Ruckebusch. 'With your silence, you have asked to be punished. For your false loyalty to your friends, you are all condemned. The entire class will sit here on Thursday afternoon, doing lines. Five hundred of them for each of you. Pens out; copy this down: *"I must not act without considering the consequences of my actions upon others."* And Blanquart . . .'

'*Oui, monsieur?*'

'Do stop snivelling. Isn't your father Henri a war veteran?'

'*Oui, monsieur.*'

'Well, don't make him ashamed of you.'

In the schoolyard afterwards, Roussel saunters over to me, hands in his pockets, and winks. Eyes wide, I pretend I have no idea what he means.

The weeks pass. Autumn hardens into winter, and the fields begin to glitter with frost. It is high time Roussel and I paid another visit to the *Petit Galopin*. I have been thinking about the place for a while, and at last an idea comes to me. I handpick a team of five for the operation: me, Roussel and three of the burly farming lads from the back row of the class, who have that careless disrespect for authority which comes from knowing you are about to leave school forever at the end of term.

Off we go, on a moonless night that is perfect for our secret purpose. It is only a short walk to the *Petit Galopin,* where an oil lamp glimmers through a chink in the curtains as we hide behind the fence. Taking it in turns, we peek at the extraordinary scene within. Men and women, lounging on sofas and chaises longues, appear to be wrestling slowly with each other, as if underwater. We have already pulled our scarves up over our mouths. And, once more, I explain the finer points of the plan to my section. Four of us will carefully manhandle the fifty-gallon *pissoir* into position. Roussel will open the door. And then we launch our assault.

Chaos. Absolute chaos. Despite Monsieur Ruckebusch's droned instructions about how to use pi to calculate the volume of a cylinder, I had no idea quite what fifty gallons of ancient urine, flecked with cigarette butts, would look like as it splashes and cascades over the feet of the drinkers in a small bar. I certainly didn't know what it would smell like, which is quite a lot worse than our earth closet at home, even in high summer. A cat jumps out of the window. Grown men scream. I have an inkling of what it might be like to be in the brig of a ship sinking in a typhoon.

Next day, Houvenagel is back at the school, his boots creaking more than ever. There are more lines to write in detention. And when I pass Monsieur Faure's house on the way home, I am surprised to see that he has left his best shoes out to dry.

I am still elated by the success of our mission when I awake the following morning. My father is already out of bed, getting ready for work, and he and I have the kitchen to ourselves. While he sips his sergeant-major's tea from a tin mug in silence, I gnaw on a crust of bread dipped in some sour grey sludge which Auntie Val calls her special apple jam.

The truth will set you free, I remind myself, as I summon up the courage to talk to him. I'm not owning up, exactly. I just feel I should tell him what we've done. After all, he said those men needed to be taught a lesson.

My father's face darkens and he grips the table with both hands. I think this is a bad sign.

'How dare you,' he whispers. 'How *dare* you?'

'I'm sorry, Dad. I thought you said they needed . . .' Terrified, I attempt to hold his gaze.

'Do you understand, Lou? If you've gone and got yourself into trouble . . .'

'I'm not in trouble, Dad. They didn't catch me. I just thought . . .'

'I do not want to know. Not now, not ever. Keep it under your hat, Lou. Do you understand? I do not want to know.'

'No, Dad. I mean, yes, Dad,' I reply, biting my lip. 'I think I do.'

1 August 1937

The quayside at Calais Maritime heaves with people, all pushing and shoving in different directions. Far above our heads, the port-side lamp of the steamer, the *Maid of Kent*, glows red through the mist of cigarette smoke. England, here we come.

Seagulls shriek as I struggle towards the gangplank with our suitcases. Elizabeth, her eyes as wide as coffee cups, clutches the sleeve of my jacket. Rosemary hurries just ahead of us, fists clenched, shoulders hunched.

'Ugh, smell that stinky fish,' says Elizabeth. But all I can smell is sweat and cheap perfume as we plough onwards, hoping the others are somewhere behind us in the crowd. And then we're at the gangplank, and someone is spitting a torrent of French into my ear, ending with the words '*dix francs*'. I turn to see a brass disc glinting above the peak of a battered cap.

Appalled, I begin to wrestle our bags from the scarecrow who stole them. But Rosemary is already waving a ten-franc note at him. The porter grabs it and vanishes.

'Why did you do that?' I demand.

'Sometimes, Lou, you have to know when *not* to fight,' she says, firmly.

Suddenly my father appears out of nowhere with Kléber. 'Everyone still alive?' he bellows, above the din. 'What have you done with Mummy?'

'We thought she was with you.'

'There she is,' trumpets Elizabeth, jumping up and down and pointing at the next gangplank, perhaps fifty yards further down the ship.

'Oh, crikey,' mutters my father. 'How did that happen?' He cups his hands and yells at my mother to stay where she is. But she is being blindly borne along by the crowd, and vanishes into the ship. 'Right, fix bayonets,' he says.

'What?' asks Elizabeth.

'When you hear my whistle, we all go over the top, right?'

'It's a joke, dear,' tuts Rosemary, patting our little sister on the head.

'Come on,' shouts my father, dragging Kléber behind him. And with that, we are swept aboard.

We make a trip to England like this every two years, our passage paid by the Imperial War Graves Commission. But today's crossing feels different, because I will not be coming back with the others in a fortnight's time. No, I am to be billeted at Briar Villa, my English grandmother's bungalow in Pegwell Bay, and packed off to St George's School in Ramsgate.

My father dropped this bombshell about a month ago. I felt a jolt of excitement, but my mother went quite pale at the news. She whispered that I must make my father change his mind; she begged me to do whatever I could to persuade him to let me stay with her in France. I nodded, wondering why I find it so hard to say no to her. Sometimes I think she forgets that I am twelve years old.

Before school the following day, I went with my father to the Pont d'Achelles cemetery. He was scrubbing the brickwork of one of the two bastions that stand on either side of the Cross of Sacrifice, and I helped him by holding the bucket while he climbed the ladder.

'Do you think I'll be all right at school in England, Dad?' I asked him. 'I mean, are you sure it's a good idea?'

He frowned down at me, his brush poised in midair.

'Of course I'm sure. And besides, I've already bought you a one-way ticket.' He went back to his scrubbing. 'I suppose your mother put you up to this, did she?'

'No,' I squeaked. My voice has begun to do this quite a lot recently. 'No,' I repeated, in a manlier tone.

'Don't get me wrong, Lou,' he chuckled. 'I think the school in Nieppe is fine. It's just that the people round here can be so blinkered and inward-looking. A lot of the locals have never even been to Lille, let alone Paris or London. Whereas you and I are British; we see the bigger picture. Look at me. I've served in Hong Kong and Singapore, and now I'm working in France. You'd never catch your mother so far from home, doing what I'm doing, would you?'

I thought of my mother in the war, driving her horse and cart through an artillery barrage to deliver newspapers to the boys at the front. I gazed at the headstone in front of me. It marked the grave of an infantryman: Private C. J. Ryan, of the 55th Battalion, Australian Infantry, who died on 27th November 1917, aged 21. He was a long way from home, too.

In the silence, with the sun beating down, we both considered our Britishness.

'We're an island race, too, aren't we?' said my father, after a while. 'I suppose it changes your viewpoint, if you're always looking out to sea, and wondering what lies just over the horizon.'

'Yes, but what's over the horizon from England is France.'

'Look, the world is a big place, Lou, and you're a clever boy. Sometimes a bit too clever. But, whatever happens, I don't want you to get stuck here in Nieppe. You'll end up like me, weeding graves for the rest of your life. You need to be with the living, not the dead.'

I had kept my promise to my mother. It was time to share my secret with my father. 'Dad, I want to be a soldier in the British army,' I declared, grinning up at him. But his face darkened.

'Tell me you're not serious,' he said, slowly. 'Do you have any idea?' He began to climb down the ladder. And then I heard him mutter: 'I wonder if there's still time.'

'What do you mean?'

'I mean your mother may be right, for once. I mean we

need to buy another ticket. I mean you'll be safer here in France.'

'But, Dad, I'm not going to join the British army tomorrow. I'm only twelve years old. And besides, you said yourself that there isn't going to be another war.' My father pondered this for a while. And then he nodded to himself, clambered back up the ladder, and the subject was closed.

In Calais, the gangplank on to the *Maid of Kent* is a bridge between two worlds. When we cross it, the heaving, bellowing crowd melts away. Now people are speaking in hushed voices, and someone says 'sorry' to me in English. I can smell tea and bacon and Virginia tobacco. The chipped paint of the quayside has given way to polished brass and teak. Kléber and Elizabeth fling out morsels of bread for the lime-white gulls following the boat. My mother lies down on a wooden bench inside.

It's the same when we board the gleaming Southern Railway train that will take us from Dover to Ramsgate. Compared with the clanking, jolting discomfort of the Calais–Basle, you can hardly feel this one pull away. There is a carpet on the floor. The seats are cushioned and uphol-stered. There is even a lavatory in our carriage with a varnished wooden seat.

'It's another world, isn't it, love?' says my father, smiling to himself, as he takes my mother's hand in his. Surprised, Rosemary and I exchange glances.

'Everything feels so soft,' nods my mother, her half-blind eyes closed as she gently rocks with the rhythm of the train. 'I like it.'

'So do you think you could ever imagine living here, in England? You know how much that would mean to me.'

Her face flickers. 'No,' she says, 'because I would never feel at home.'

My father pulls away his hand. 'So how do you think I feel,' he asks, coldly, 'every single day of my life?'

* * *

England makes me wish I were truly English, every time we come. The roads feel so smooth after the dust and cobbles of northern France, with a friendly policeman directing the traffic, and AA scouts ready to help anyone who breaks down. There is a huge shop called Woolworth's, with electric lights and a machine full of money that goes *ping* when the man presses a button to open the drawer. In another shop called Marks and Spencer, you can buy whatever clothes you want and wear them the same day, just like that. My mother says she wishes Auntie Val could see it, but my father says it's probably a good thing she can't.

On the beach at Ramsgate, we hunt for cockles and winkles and razor clams, and watch the other children having donkey rides. My father and I peer at the horizon, trying to see France. We all laugh as a squadron of biplanes zooms low over the beach, making us duck, and one of the pilots waves. My father says they must be training for something. Then he buys himself a small brick of ice cream wrapped in waxed paper and lets me have a bite. We also visit Dreamland in Margate, which I think must be what heaven is like, if you can afford to go on any of the rides. Rosemary says watching is just as much fun, but I don't agree.

One day, she and I wander down to the beach by ourselves. The tide is out and we have to walk for what seems like miles over the soft sand to reach the sea. Suddenly, Rosemary screams.

'Lou, Lou, I'm sinking,' she yells. 'Please help me.'

I stumble over to her and grab her arms. But soon I am up to my knees, too, as the sand gives beneath my feet. I throw myself flat on the sand, until I can lever myself out. Then I race away up the beach.

'Lou, stop!' shouts my sister, with fear in her voice. 'Come back. Help!'

I can hear her voice growing fainter behind me, begging me not to leave her there. I scan the sand with mounting panic. Where was it? Where the hell did I see it?

A minute later, I am lying prone on my plank of driftwood beside Rosemary. By now she is well and truly stuck, and her glasses are steamed up. She strains. I heave. She screams. I roar. But no matter how we struggle, we cannot shift her from the wet cement. Over her shoulder, I can see the tide coming in. Please, God, release her. I screw up my eyes, stiffen every sinew and make one final, desperate heave. And, all at once, the sand releases her with a squelching sigh. Rosemary falls on top of me, shaking. Exhausted, we lie like that for a few seconds.

'I didn't think you were coming back, Lou,' she sobs.

'Of course I came back.'

'I'm lucky to have a brother like you. I know I can be a bossy old stick sometimes. But I do care about you, Lou, you know I do.'

'Tide's coming in,' I mutter. 'We'd better make a move.'

At my new school, it takes me several weeks to adjust to the strange world of English education: to rods and firkins; the nightmare of compound interest in pounds, shillings and pence; and the difference between words like *heedless* and *insouciant*. But I don't mind, because I am learning to be British. My classmates laugh at my woollen undergarments, knitted by Auntie Val. Some of them call me Froggy. So I call them Mr John Bull in return. And, little by little, I begin to feel at home in this strange new land, with its milkmen and its dustcarts, its crumpets, condensed milk and bread baked in tins. So it comes as a blow when I receive a terse letter from my parents, summoning me back to Nieppe at the end of my third term.

30 April 1938

The house in the rue du Sac feels smaller and darker than when I left it, and France seems absurdly primitive after Kent. At Briar Villa in Ramsgate, my grandmother has her own flushing lavatory, with a roll of tissue paper on a wooden axle at the side. In Nieppe, we have a hole in the ground and wipe ourselves with newspaper as best we can.

I can tell that my father is furious that his dream of having at least one truly English child has been squashed. He spends every evening, except Saturdays, glued to the Home Service on his wireless set. This is a very early model, with blue and yellow valves flickering on top, and a speaker which emits mostly whistles and hisses, interrupted from time to time by a distant human voice. Last month, according to my father, the voice said that the German army had invaded Austria. This month, it says that Don Bradman scored 258 against Worcestershire, and Preston North End have beaten Huddersfield Town in the final of the FA Cup. His brow knotted, my father presses his ear against the Bakelite speaker, while the distant voice gurgles the news from London, or croons the latest tunes on the Light Programme.

My mother floats around the house like a ghost, a white stick in one hand and her rosary in the other. Auntie Val and Mémère mutter in the kitchen. I can't tell what they're saying, because I appear to have forgotten all my French. This is a worry. But when I explain the problem to my father after lunch one day, he slaps me on the back so hard that it hurts.

'That's my boy,' he says. And then he switches off his wireless for a moment, so that he can go and tell my mother the good news. 'Don't touch,' he mouths, pointing at the set.

Now I am sent off to Eton. This is what my father likes to tell his friends at the snooker club, anyway. But according to the faded sign outside my new school, its real name is the Ypres Memorial School. Most of the other children are, like me, the sons and daughters of employees of the Imperial War Graves Commission. We have all grown up in the cemeteries.

'The Eton Memorial School was founded in remembrance of all the Old Etonians killed in the battle of Ypres, little more than twenty years ago,' announces Mr Yorath, the young headmaster, at roll call on the first day. 'Some of those men, just a few years older than yourselves, died right here, on the very spot where you are standing. Your fathers will have buried some of them in their cemeteries. Others, blown to pieces, will never be found. But their blood enriches the earth beneath your feet.'

I can feel my chest swelling with patriotism as Yorath speaks. 'In all, 250,000 men died here at Ypres,' he continues, in a sing-song accent I cannot place. 'And while your fathers care for their mortal remains, your task, ladies and gentlemen, is to make yourselves worthy of their memory.'

Yorath pauses. 'So let me ask you this. Look around you. Turn to the person next to you, and look into their eyes.' We all turn nervously, wondering what this is all about. I find myself looking into the pale blue eyes of a small blonde girl with a ribbon in her hair. She is very pretty, must be about my age, and looks absolutely terrified. 'Do they look as if they have what it takes?' continues Yorath. 'Do you think they have the courage to stand up against evil; to make them-selves worthy of the memory of those who died for us?'

I blink, and my eyes widen. For the blonde girl is smiling and nodding at me. We stare at each other. And something clicks inside me, as if she has given me a gift that is worth more than all the rides in Dreamland. So I repay the gesture, nodding back at her with a sheepish grin. Oh, crikey. Her eyes are welling up with tears, and she hides her face in the crook of her elbow.

'Are you all right?' I whisper.

'So happy,' she mouths, blinking back her tears. 'Nobody's ever thought I might be brave before.'

The Eton Memorial School was set up to provide a British education for the children of IWGC workers in Belgium and France. And the red-brick building does indeed look much the same as my old school in Ramsgate. The uniform is very English, too. Even the disinfectant smell in the corridors is just the same. Now, however, there are girls as well as boys in my class, and one of them turns out to be the little blonde girl with the ribbon in her hair. Lilian Wilkins helps me find my way around the place. Although we never speak, I soon find myself looking out for her at the start of every day. If we lived nearby, I might offer to walk her home.

But Ypres is almost twenty miles from Nieppe. It might as well be in another country and, sure enough, being on the far side of the Belgian border, it is. In the winter, I travel there and back by tram. When the weather is fine, I cycle to school, and park my bike alongside all the bright green bicycles in the racks. I make some new friends. Yet they all live so far away. There is precious little opportunity for after-school pranks.

The arrival of a stranger in the rue du Sac changes all that.

One afternoon in May, as I am parking my bicycle outside our house, I am suddenly struck on the shoulder by a ball of mud. From the sting of the impact, it can only have been fired from a catapult. Annoyed, I spin on my heels, expecting to see Kléber scuttling away in panic. Instead, I come face to face with a boy of roughly my age, with wire-rimmed spectacles and sandy hair, who just stands there, catapult in hand, grinning at me.

'*Bonjour*,' he says. '*Ça va?*'

Stunned by his brazenness, I burst out laughing.

'I'm OK.' I rub my shoulder. 'Nice shot, for a beginner.'

'Thanks,' he chuckles, with a hint of relief, 'but actually I'm an expert. We've just moved into the farm on the corner.'

And that's how I get to know Marcel Lombard. Before long the two of us are thick as thieves. I spend all my free time at his father's farm at number 14, just opposite Boulet's shop, a *café-épicerie* on the Belgian side of our street, where farmers congregate to play cards, and Auntie Val buys ham and cheese and fruit in tins.

Papa Lombard teaches me how to use a short-handled scythe to mow a field of grass, and how to cut the borders of a wheat field to allow horse-drawn machinery to pass. I learn to flail wheat, to prune and weave hawthorn and hazel, to bake bread from home-ground flour. I learn the secrets of trapping hares and partridges, how to use a winch to lop a tree, and a thousand other things that feel far more useful to me than all the history and geometry I have learned at school. Afterwards, when the farm work is done, Marcel and I go out on long cycle rides, looking for adventure and half-buried weapons.

'You two are like a pair of dogs,' says Papa Lombard one afternoon, as we are about to pedal off in the direction of Steenwerck. 'It worries me.'

'What do you mean?' I ask, leaning on my handlebars.

'Well, look at Mirza over there,' he replies, gesturing at his flea-bitten Border collie, lazing in the sun. 'She's good as gold when she's by herself; almost an angel. She'd certainly never touch a chicken in the yard. But let her fall in with another dog, and the pair of them will be off round the houses in no time, getting up to no end of tricks. They lead each other astray, do dogs; come home with blood on their chops. And I look at you two boys, and I just hope that whatever it is you get up to when you're off on your bicycles doesn't end in tears.'

'It won't, Monsieur Lombard,' I assure him. 'We'll be fine.'

'Perhaps it would be good if I met your father, Stéphane, even so. I often see him digging in the cemetery over there.

Why don't you bring him round for an *apéro* one evening?'

I shift uneasily on the seat of my bicycle.

'I'm afraid my father doesn't speak much French, monsieur.'

Papa Lombard raises his eyebrows and glances at Marcel. 'But how long has he been in France?'

'About twenty years.'

'As long as that,' he nods. 'Well, in that case, perhaps we'd better just stick to waving at each other over the fence.'

One day, while out catching frogs in a drainage ditch, we make an exciting find: a Lee Enfield rifle and some unspent cartridges from the last war. We strip down the gun and grease it with oil drained from my father's ancient motorbike. Then we snap the copper-clad tip off one of the bullets, push the cartridge into the breach and pull the trigger.

Nothing happens.

Worse still, the cartridge is now jammed in the breach. After Marcel has tried to free it with various tools, I hit upon the brilliant idea of attempting to dislodge it with a length of stiff wire poked down the barrel. This is wonderfully effective. After a couple of sharp taps, the cartridge explodes, shooting the wire straight out of the barrel. The steel dart grazes my head. Marcel appears to find this funnier than I do.

What I begin to notice about our mischief is that whatever we did yesterday never seems quite enough today. There must always be a riskier trick, a heftier weapon, a more dangerous game. So now Marcel proposes that we drive two sturdy chestnut fence posts into the grass verge, with an old bicycle inner tube stretched between them, making a giant catapult. This is what I like about my new friend. He is so full of ideas. Sometimes I feel as if we have known each other all our lives.

On Thursdays, a group of retired farmers like to meet for a drink at Boulet's shop across the road in Belgium, because the beer is cheaper there than it is in France. The mud ball now becomes a formidable projectile, guaranteed to sting the recipient, and possibly even knock him off his bike. I know this is going a little too far, and Marcel tells me as much. But it's just so tempting. So it comes almost as a relief when one of the farmers has a quiet word with Papa Lombard and the old man puts a stop to our escalating violence.

'One day, you're going to kill someone, if you go on like this,' he warns, wagging his finger at me. It's all we can do not to laugh.

The Lombard farm makes a wonderful playground, after a war cemetery. Marcel and I can sit for hours in his hayloft, chatting about tanks and guns, or discussing our dreams for the future. He wants to join the French air force and fly fighter aircraft. I want to join the British army and fire guns, like my dad. And then we'll wander into the house, where the table is already laid, and sometimes Madame Lombard asks me to stay to lunch.

The Lombards have fresh bread and grilled chops, and one truly amazing luxury: a gleaming knob of creamy yellow butter melting all over a dish of boiled spuds.

At number 6, just up the road, our life is frugal by comparison. We have enough food to eat, but no luxuries. Meat is always from the cheaper cuts – pigs' feet, belly pork and cows' udders – although my father keeps a few chickens and rabbits for the Sunday pot. He drinks the weak local beer with a splash of water in it. The rest of us drink coffee at home, because this is the only way of making the water from the kitchen pumps taste as if it hasn't come straight out of a cat.

In winter, the one source of heat is the *cuisinière,* a coal-burning stove in the kitchen. On the coldest nights, Mémère places a few bricks in the oven, then wraps them up in newspaper to warm our feet. It's not much, but it helps. Kléber and I share one bed, Rosemary and Elizabeth another. Often we wake to find ice frosting the inside of the window panes.

Saturdays I dread in particular, for this is when Auntie Val heats a cauldron of water on the stove and pours it into the zinc tub she has made me bring in from the shed. I don't know why she bothers to heat the water, because it's always stone cold by the time anyone gets into it: Elizabeth and Kléber first, then Rosemary, then me. By rights Rosemary should be the last, as she's the oldest. But Auntie Val says I have to go at the end because I'm a boy. And boys don't mind water that is dirty grey.

'Besides,' she assures me, 'it'll harden you up.'

Harden me up for what? That's what I want to ask. But instead I just submit to the icy murk, gasping as my privates shrivel and grateful that no one can see.

My father never goes to church. But the rest of us have to attend: it is my mother's unbending rule. On Sunday mornings, Auntie Val and my siblings head out to the *Grande Messe* at eleven o'clock, often with asthmatic Roger Rioual from number 12 wheezing along behind. Elizabeth says Roger is sweet on Rosemary, which I find hilarious.

My mother and I have to set out in complete darkness at 5 a.m. to be on time for the 6 a.m. Mass. The early start is brutal, but it leaves me more time for messing about with Marcel before lunch. And there's another enticement: the shapely Marie-Louise Boulet – the daughter of Monsieur Boulet, the shopkeeper – comes too.

Together we walk, arm in arm, to church, with her on one side of me and my half-blind mother on the other. Even though Marie-Louise is already twenty and far too old for me, I like the way she smells of soap and apples, the click of her polished heels, and how soft her arm feels through the rough felt of her purple coat.

Recently, she has come up with a secret game for us to play, too. Her stepmother is unkind to her, she says. So, in revenge, Marie-Louise smuggles bars of chocolate out of the shop for me. The fun part comes when she tucks the chocolate bar down into the generous bosom of her dress. Warmed between her breasts, this chocolate is the most delicious thing

I have ever tasted. My poor, blind mother, anxious about slipping on the cobbles, is none the wiser as I tear off the foil and cram the skin-softened squares into my mouth.

A few months later, I turn fourteen. The summer holidays have just begun and I am looking forward to helping out with the various harvests – wheat, oats, haricot beans, potatoes, turnips, mangels and clover – on the Lombard farm. But my mother has a surprise in store for me. She has often said that I ought to learn a trade and, according to her, a good butcher is never out of work. I used to think she was joking. But, no: she has arranged for me to be apprenticed over the summer to Monsieur Bossart's butcher's shop and slaughterhouse in the centre of Nieppe.

'But it's the holidays,' I protest.

'Quite so,' she replies, 'and this will keep you out of trouble.'

So that's it. They're worried about my friendship with Marcel. And my mother wants to put a stop to our shenanigans.

'When do I start?' I ask. 'And am I to be paid anything for my pains?' I've gutted the odd chicken and rabbit before. But the thought of killing anything bigger makes me want very much to be somewhere else.

'We'll be paid in sausages and pâté,' says my mother brightly. 'And you start first thing in the morning.'

'Ah, wonderful.'

'Yes, isn't it? And Madame Bossart says you're going to begin by slaughtering a pig.'

1 September 1939

The summer is long and hot. Wasps and hornets bat themselves against the grubby windows in the veranda, buzzing and fizzing for freedom. My father says that Germany has invaded Czechoslovakia, and Italy has invaded Albania. Marcel and I spend our evenings working in the fields, after I have finished learning how to make sausages that won't explode in the pan.

'What the hell is that?' I ask, putting my finger to my lips. The holidays are coming to an end, and Marcel and I are sitting in his hayloft, planning our military careers, when an unfamiliar sound silences us both.

We both listen. 'Church bells,' he shrugs. 'Someone must have died.'

'I know what it is,' I whisper. 'It's the tocsin.'

When we race outside, however, there is nothing to be seen or heard. No sign of enemy tanks rumbling in our direction; no sound of distant machine-gun fire. Mirza the dog is still lazing in the sun, just the same as ever. The only unusual sight is my father, cycling back up the road from one of his cemeteries long before he is due home.

'What does it mean, Daddy?' I call.

'It means,' he yells, 'that you'd better come home.'

'Because why?'

Now my father stops his bicycle with a groaning of brakes. 'Because we must be at war with the Fritz. Again.'

Marcel and I turn to face each other.

'C'est la guerre?' My friend's eyes are sparkling with excitement. I can feel shivers of electricity running up and down my spine. And I know we are both thinking the same thing: *at last*.

Next day, as I cycle into Nieppe to learn how to make *boudin noir* at the butcher's shop, there are posters with tricolour borders all over town, announcing which men are to report to the mobilisation centre in Hazebrouck. One of our neighbours is among them, the lucky chump. I can't help smiling as I watch his wife and daughters weeping on the doorstep. I suppose they wish the army wanted them, too.

Marcel comes with me to the eleven o'clock Mass on Sunday, so that we can enjoy the tense atmosphere in town. Last week, Monsieur le Curé used his sermon to brief the congregation on the worsening news. This week, the picture is more serious, with Poland already overrun by the Fritz. We say prayers for an end to the hostilities that have yet to begin.

Seigneur, écoute nous. Seigneur, exauce nous.

Seated at the back of the church with Roussel and some of my old friends from the École Saint Louis, Marcel and I have armed ourselves for the forthcoming conflict with mini catapults made of stiff wire. These we keep hidden until the sermon is in full flow, And then we launch salvo after salvo of dried haricot beans, concentrating our fire on the most pompous members of the congregation, specifically targeting the backs of their ears. There are yelps of outrage, but we manage to get several shots away before people start turning round. Alerted by the commotion, a big man in a black cassock comes marching down to the back of the church and demands to know who the culprits are. I hold my breath. But no one snitches.

Days later, a few French soldiers appear. They have come to finish the fortifications which are meant to prevent a war. The unit, the 208th Infantry Regiment, look like old men to me. Marcel and I dare each other to poke our heads into their tents, to see their long rifles and to smell the gun oil mingled with the musty pong of leather equipment stiff with sweat.

'I'll bet you can't wait to take on the Boche,' says Marcel, when a couple of the soldiers let us have a closer look at their rifles.

'*Bof,* I might have said the same thing when I was your age,' replies the older of the two, puffing on a cigarette. A tall, bony figure with huge cauliflower ears, he reminds me of a lamp post. 'But now I have a wife and children, and that changes everything. I'd rather be growing cider apples in Normandy.'

'So why did you sign up?' I ask, amazed at his lack of fighting spirit.

The lamp post smiles; he glances at his friend. 'I signed up for a pension, not a war.'

Beside him, his friend nods. 'Who wants to get killed, fighting our neighbours? It's not as if the Germans are evil. I've got friends in Alsace, and they say they're just the same as us.'

'So what will you do when the fighting starts?' asks Marcel.

'We have our essential supplies,' says the lamp-post man, lifting his water bottle to his lips and taking a big swig. 'This stuff makes the French army invincible. It carried us through the last war, and it will carry us through the next.'

Before I can question this, the man thrusts the water bottle at me. 'Here,' he rasps. 'Men's wine. You try it.'

I really don't want to drink from the man's tin canteen; almost retch at the fumes that come wafting out of it. But I raise the metal to my lips and take a sip. My tongue shrivels. My throat burns. The liquid tastes more like battery acid than wine, with a cart-horse kick that makes my eyeballs lurch in their sockets.

'*C'est bon,*' I nod, wiping my mouth with the back of my hand. The two men laugh.

'No, it's not good. It's terrible,' says the lamp-post man. 'But it does the job.' He squints at Marcel. 'Here,' he adds, leaning towards him. 'Your turn.'

But Marcel shakes his head. 'It's time we were going,

Stéphane,' he says. '*Au revoir, messieurs.*' And, without even shaking their hands, he ducks and exits the tent.

After this first brush with the French army, I am cheered to hear that the British Expeditionary Force has landed in France and will soon be pitched against the Germans. I assure Marcel that this will change everything. Yes, the Alleyman advance, as my father calls it, has been fearsomely quick. But the Tommies will turn the tide.

Word has it that some of the British are stationed in La Bassée, just a short cycle ride from Nieppe. So Marcel and I head over there one afternoon and are rewarded with our first glimpse of real live Tommies in a convoy of Bren-gun carriers and Morris 1500cwt trucks. The sight of these British troops in their pressed uniforms, with weapons gleaming and their camouflaged vehicles in perfect order, makes my chest swell. I want to wave and shout that I am English, too – that I am one of them. Rule Britannia and God Save the King. I am in love with a country I hardly know.

One or two of the vehicles stop by the roadside. Marcel pushes me forward.

'Go on then, *Rosbif*,' he says, grinning. 'Now's your chance to show off your English.'

The Tommies eye me suspiciously as I approach a small group of them. One, a small man whose hair is so blond as to be almost white, reaches for his rifle.

'*Bong-jour*,' he says, with visible effort.

'Hello,' I reply, in English. 'Do you need any help?'

The man's eyes widen and he laughs. 'You're a long way from home, ain'tcha, sonny?'

'I'm English, but I live here in France. Are you on your way to kill some Fritz?'

The man turns to grin at his companions, who are watching with amusement.

'That's about the size of it, son. We're off to give Mr Hitler a jolly good spanking.'

'Wizard,' I reply.

'Careful, Sid,' says one of them.

'What do you mean?'

'You know the score. Best to keep mum.'

Sid rolls his eyes; takes a step towards me. His eyelashes are as white as his hair. 'Look,' he says, lowering his voice. 'Do you know where we can get some of that French wine everyone talks about?'

'I think there's a café not far from here,' I reply, glad that Marcel cannot understand much English. 'But my friend and I can bring you some beer if you want.'

'Sid!'

'All right, I'm coming,' growls Sid, over his shoulder. And then he grins at me. 'That's kind of you, sonny, but on second thoughts it won't be necessary. Here, take a couple of these for you and your friend. You're a bit young to smoke, but it'll help put some hair on your chest.'

'Are you going off to war right now?'

'Right now, we're still waiting for our orders,' he says, under his breath. 'But I think we've got a date with Adolf that some of the other boys don't want to miss. Cheerio, sonny. Maybe we'll see you on our way back.'

The blond soldier has given me two Craven A cigarettes. Clutching my war trophies, I dance back to Marcel and proudly hand one of them to him.

'*Et voilà*,' I announce. 'This is for you. They say they're just going to go and defeat the Boche, and they'll see us on their way back.'

'Not bad,' murmurs Marcel, whistling as he gazes at the unfamiliar cigarette.

After this first meeting, the British seem to vanish. All we see is the occasional military vehicle, speeding down the main road. Pale faces grin out of the back as they overtake me on my bicycle.

I have changed schools yet again. Each day, I now cycle the eight kilometres to the St Charles Catholic boys' school in

Armentières, on the far side of Nieppe. Being back in the French system means that I get to feel stupid all over again. In Ramsgate, the English children crowed about Trafalgar and Waterloo. In Armentières, the French children blame me for the weather and for burning Joan of Arc. I don't mind this one bit. At least I'm not German, I tell them. And, very soon, they stop.

One evening, I am sitting in the kitchen when there comes a loud knock on the front door. My father is glued to his wireless in the front room, so Auntie Val goes to answer it.

'Lou, go and fetch Dad,' she whispers, hurrying in to me. 'Tell him there are British soldiers, and they're asking for him.'

Tiptoeing into the front room, scarcely daring to glance at the soldiers as I pass them, I touch him gently on the arm. With a scowl, he waves me away. But when I blurt out the news, he leaps up from his chair so fast that he almost knocks over the lamp. For a second he hesitates, all in a dither. Then he adjusts his tie in the mirror, squares his shoulders and marches out into the corridor at the double.

'Come on, Berthe, Val,' he yells, a moment later, his voice buzzing. 'Bring us some sherbet, will you? Chop, chop. What does a fellow have to do to get served around here? There are Tommies out here, dying of thirst.'

And now it's as if my mother and aunt have turned into a pair of giddy schoolgirls, racing around, fetching this and dropping that, primping their hair, wiping their hands on their aprons, both in a terrific flap. The rest of us creep out into the corridor for a glimpse of the soldiers. But my father has already ushered them into the front room. So we have to content ourselves with spying through a crack in the door, until Auntie breezes past us with a tray of beer and water on her shoulder and my mother clutching on to her apron strings. Taking our cue from Rosemary, who has removed her glasses, we follow smartly in their wake.

'That's more like it,' says my father, sitting himself down

at the piano, as we gawp at the men: real live soldiers, right here, in our house. 'There, Val, it's just like the old days for you and Berthe, isn't it?'

The following day, six soldiers turn up for a singalong around the piano. They explain that our house is already known among the Tommies as The English House. To my surprise, my father does not look thrilled at this news. But he still goes through all the old favourites: 'Keep the Home Fires Burning', 'Take Me Back to Dear Old Blighty' and, of course, 'Ma'm'selle from Armentières, Parlez-vous'. My mother and Auntie Val look quite misty-eyed, but I don't think anyone else notices. The next day, there are a dozen of them. The soldiers bring a box with them, too, and we all marvel at the gifts inside: Shippam's paste, Bovril, Typhoo tea, a tin of bully beef and a packet of English biscuits.

My father's enthusiasm is faltering – I hear him mutter to my mother something about liberties – although he hides this from the soldiers.

'The first biscuit in the packet is always broken, isn't it?' he declares, in a loud voice, as Auntie Val hands round the custard creams. 'I've never understood why the makers don't just leave that one out.' Everyone roars with laughter. But I'm not sure that he means it as a joke.

Soon he has taught Elizabeth how to warble 'Loch Lomond' and 'Kiss Me Good Night, Sergeant Major', and he stands her on the dining table to sing while he bashes out the accompaniments on the piano, casting wary glances over his shoulder at the men. Tumultuous applause ensues, and shouts of 'encore!'. So they go through it all over again.

Elizabeth is rewarded by the men with a packet of wine gums and a pocketful of butterscotch. So now my father tells Rosemary to play her Chopin polonaise. One of the men whistles as she settles herself on the piano stool and my father glares at him. There are more wolf whistles mixed in with the polite clapping at the end of her piece, which lasts almost as long as one of Monsieur le Curé's sermons. There is a lot more glaring from my dad, too. I think he is worried about our neighbours.

'Right, that's it,' he announces. 'Rosemary, you'd best go to your room and stay there.'

'But Dad . . .'

'No buts, Rosemary. Upstairs, *now*. And that's an order.'

Judging from the wistful sighs of the men as she leaves, they appreciate Chopin a lot more than I do.

'Why does Rosemary have to stay upstairs whenever the soldiers come, Dad?' I ask him one morning in the cemetery.

'Because boys will be boys,' he says, shifting from one foot to the other.

'Oh, I see,' I reply, even though I don't.

9 May 1940

One cool, bright Thursday morning, I am lying in the vegetable patch behind the house, gazing up into a perfect blue sky. In a few minutes, I must attack my favourite task of emptying the stinking earth closet into which the eight of us relieve ourselves each day and pouring the contents on to the vegetable patch. The dirtiest jobs around here always seem to fall to me. But for now, with my father over at the Trois Arbres cemetery, I take a moment to roll myself a cigarette amid the young potato plants. The luscious Marie-Louise has begun to hide a little pouch of tobacco in her bosom for me on Sunday mornings, in place of softened chocolate. This suits me. And I deserve a smoke in peace.

The sun is so bright that I can barely see the flame of the match as I hold it to the tip of my roll-up and watch the tobacco crinkle from the heat. Breathing the smoke deep into my lungs, I gaze across at the boundary wall of the Pont d'Achelles cemetery and the ranks of white headstones beyond. It's hard to believe there's a war on. My eyes are drawn to the bronze broadsword embedded in the Cross of Sacrifice between the cemetery's two bastions. Strange, I think to myself, to put a weapon on a cross, like that.

In the distance, I can hear the rising drone of a machine approaching at speed. There it is: glinting just above the cemetery. It is heading straight for me, and for a moment I wonder if the rue du Sac is about to be bombed. But the aircraft roars overhead, heedless, insouciant, and low enough for me to see the black crosses under its wings. I recognise the plane as a Messerschmitt 109. I have seen pictures of these futuristic fighters in the newspaper. I recognise the black crosses, too, distant cousins of the stone one in the cemetery beneath.

After lunch, we all gather around my father's wireless to hear the latest news whistling from London. Belgium and Holland have been overrun by the Germans, and a man called Mr Churchill (or Monsieur Sharsheel, as Mémère calls him) has taken over from Mr Chamberlain.

'What does it mean, Dad?' asks Kléber, in his squeaky voice.

'It means that the war is coming closer,' he says, glancing out of the window.

'I'm scared,' shivers Elizabeth, cuddling up to Auntie Val.

'Oh, we should be all right,' declares the man who assured us, not so long ago, that there would never be another war. 'Driving a few tanks into Holland is not the same thing as crossing the Maginot Line, particularly when the British army is waiting for you on the other side.'

'And the French,' adds my mother. 'They say they have even more tanks than the Germans.'

My father shakes his head, smiling to himself. 'Yes, but do they know how to drive them in any direction except reverse?'

'*Ingrate!*' Now it is my aunt's turn to challenge him.

'Look,' says my father, raising his hands, for her eyes are glittering with anger. 'You've seen the fighting spirit of those Tommies. They're just itching to have a crack at the Krauts. Whereas I really don't think a few Frogs driving tanks on the wrong side of the road are going to worry Mr Hitler too much. Besides, at the first sight of any Germans, they'll all run away and hide. Isn't that right, Lou?'

'You should be ashamed of yourself,' says Auntie Val. 'Where's your patriotism?'

'About a hundred miles that way.' My dad grins at me, pointing his finger in the direction of the front door, and Dover.

'Come along, Berthe,' snaps my aunt, grabbing my mother's hand. 'Let us go and chop carrots. It'll make us feel better. Especially the small ones.'

Next day, high in the sky, I spot a formation of German aircraft, this time with twin engines and pencil fuselages. I think they are Messerschmitt 110s, but Marcel assures me they are Dorniers, off to bomb Britain. My mother weeps, clutching her rosary, much of the time. The house is unusually dark and silent. Lorry-loads of British troops come roaring down the main road, but we have no idea where they are heading. Conflicting reports on the radio do not help. No one seems to know what is happening, or how close the German advance has come.

A platoon of British soldiers appears in the rue du Sac, and they station themselves in the Lombard farm. Auntie Val says this makes her nervous. But Marcel and I are in clover, for the soldiers are armed with Bren guns mounted on tripods, and set up a Boys anti-tank rifle in a trench alongside Pont d'Achelles. That should give the Krauts something to think about.

By 20 May, it is obvious that things are going wrong. French troops start pouring down the road from Belgium. They look haunted and hungry, their carts loaded not just with military equipment but with looted civilian goods. Some soldiers are limping, many are bandaged, some lie prostrate on stretchers. When yet another quartet of German aircraft flies overhead, one quick-thinking soldier lets fly with his rifle, attempting to shoot them down. But his comrades leap upon him, forcing him to lower his weapon.

'*Quoi, putain?* You want to get us all killed?' one of them shouts, over the jingling of the harnesses and the clip-clop of hooves on the cobbled road.

Overnight, the British soldiers stationed in the Lombard farm disappear, leaving behind them a couple of 1500cwt trucks and a pair of motorcycles, all smashed up beyond repair. They must have sabotaged them with grenades. Dozens of greatcoats and webbing packs are strewn in the barn, along with mess tins, medical equipment and a shiny brass fire extinguisher. These, Marcel and I pick over, sort and stash with considerable relish.

Now civilian refugees appear from Belgium. They make a pathetic sight: the men walking; the women and children riding on horse-drawn carts, bicycles and prams, with every available space stuffed with possessions, from mattresses and mangles to frying pans and fruit. Auntie Val tells us not to watch. So I tiptoe upstairs to peek out of the window of our bedroom; I hear the cries of a frightened little girl being dragged along by her elbow and glimpse someone's grandma, strapped to a kitchen chair on top of a cart.

'And what about us?' My brother makes me jump as he creeps up behind me. 'Shouldn't we be going, too?'

'I don't know, Kléber,' I reply. 'Someone's got to stay and fight.'

'Oh, yes?' he snorts. 'One family against the entire German army. And we are to fight them with what? Your catapult?'

I want to protest. I want to twist his arm for talking to me like that. I'm certainly not about to tell him about the Lee Enfield, still hidden deep in the hay in Papa Lombard's barn.

Rumours, fear and panic are now spreading like bindweed. When I head outside, in search of first-hand news, everyone has a more lurid snippet. The Germans are coming, they say. Stormtroopers are shooting civilians and burning down everything in their path. Stukas are bombing schools and hospitals. Paratroops are sneaking into France, posing as refugees, or disguised as Catholic nuns. You can spot them, they say, because they all carry a red blanket, like that eighty-year-old crone in a wheelchair over there. She could be a killer, if you ignore her wooden teeth.

In the kitchen, Mémère and Auntie Val have begun to whisper about fleeing south towards Carcassonne. Rosemary wonders why we can't all go and spend a few weeks in Ramsgate with Grandma, until the fighting is over. My father puts a stop to this talk. He has been instructed by the Imperial War Graves Commission to remain at his post until the local mayor gives the order to evacuate.

'And orders is orders,' he says, with a swagger. 'Besides, I'm not going to get far with a blind wife and four children in tow, am I?'

'Charming,' replies Auntie Val, who is folding up a pile of red tablecloths and blankets that she has scavenged, discarded by terrified refugees. 'Isn't that right, Mémère?'

My grandmother sucks her teeth. I can see what she is thinking. She has been through one war in Nieppe. She is ready to see out another.

Two days later, my father looks quite pale when he receives a message from someone who used to work in the IWGC head office in Arras.

'They've all gone, Lou,' he says, in a hollow voice. He lights himself a cigarette, struggling to steady the flame. 'All the section heads. They told us not to desert our posts. But they've already taken a boat back to Blighty. The director left for England days ago, without telling anybody. With nine suitcases.'

'That's the British for you,' says Auntie Val, with a wink at Rosemary.

My father stares at her. And then he opens a beer and drinks it, just like that: from the bottle, without adding any water. I think this is a bad sign.

Elizabeth tries to climb into his lap. But he pushes her away. My mother burns a candle to Saint Rita, patron saint of desperate causes, and sticks lumps of the melted wax above the front door, because she says this will keep the Fritz out. And I suddenly have a morbid premonition of my own death: a strange, cold conviction that I must escape France before the Germans arrive, or else.

Now, once again, the British army begins to roar along the Dunkirk–Lille road. Only this time they are travelling in the wrong direction. At least they're still marching in step – left, right, left, right – unlike the French. Nauseous at the thought of the British army in retreat, I cannot even face seeing Marcel.

There is a knock on the door. Our neighbour Louis Rioual announces that he is planning to try his luck and make for the coast with his son Roger. Now Papa Rioual is an ex-submariner from the Great War, so he knows a thing or two about survival. And he seems to think they could use my help. Flattered, because I am barely fifteen, whereas Roger is eighteen, I agree. I leap at the chance to join their attempted escape. Anything, to stay alive.

My parents are not enthralled. My father says I'll end up carrying both Riouals, and he does not want to see our family split up. My mother turns quite pale when I tell her where I am going, and with whom. But everything is happening so fast. And when I confess to them my deep fear that, if the Germans come, I may well do something for which I must pay with my life, they relent.

'If you must go, then go quickly,' says my mother, burying her face in her apron. I want to leave straightaway, but Papa Rioual would prefer to wait until first light.

'Please don't tell the others you're going,' says my father, under his breath, when he returns from a chat with Papa Rioual, 'or they'll all want to come too. Give my regards to Grandma, and tell her we'll see her soon.' He extends his hand. I dare not look into his eyes.

25 May 1940

The three of us – Papa Rioual, Roger and I – leave the following morning at dawn. A light mist hangs over the fields. The plan is to head for Calais on our bicycles, keeping to the minor roads as far as possible. Dive bombers have been attacking the main routes. But the narrow lanes are already choked with refugees pushing wheelbarrows and handcarts, and by lunchtime progress is too slow even to cycle. From time to time, a French armoured car comes grinding along in our midst, making everyone yell and scarper for fear of getting squashed.

I'm not sure who hears the aircraft first. Roger grabs my shoulder and points into the sky behind us. I can just make out the flat 'W' shape of an aircraft with cranked wings heading straight for us. Then it drops like a stone.

Stuka.

'*Vite, Papa! Vite!*' shouts Roger, as the rising wail of the dive bomber scatters the traffic. A clatter of guns behind us. Women shrieking. Babies screaming. Bullets pinging off granite. The three of us dive for the ditch. Bodies flatten. Faces flinch. And then the walls of the ditch explode. A scalding blast of air punches my ears. Everything goes black.

When I awake, I am spattered with blood and earth. Am I already dead and buried, then? Something squirming beneath me makes me want to pick myself up. But my legs are too wobbly to stand, so I crawl to the edge of the ditch. I am relieved to see both Riouals watching me from the other side.

'*Ça va?*' mouths Papa Rioual, who looks suddenly much

older than he did a moment ago. All I can hear is ringing. I point to my ears and shrug. He nods. '*C'est normal*,' I see him say. He puts his arm around Roger's shoulders, because his son is shaking so much.

On the road, I can see people still sprawled where they have fallen. And then, as my blurred vision begins to sharpen, I glimpse things I want to forget: an army boot with a stump of bloodied bone sticking out of it; a woman kneeling with the body of a limbless child in her arms; a horse with both eyes blown out, flailing to get back on its feet.

We press on. Progress is slower than ever now, what with all the abandoned vehicles and the parents yelling for children they have lost. Roger's asthma is troubling him, too, and he says he needs to have frequent rests.

'It's not me, you know. It's Mummy who insists.'

By the time dusk falls on the first day, we have only travelled about thirty kilometres, with Calais another seventy kilometres further on. My balance is still precarious, but my hearing has returned. Papa Rioual has retreated into his own world. Every farmhouse we pass is already packed with refugees and people yell at us to move on. But somehow we find shelter at last in a cattle shed near Hazebrouck, just outside the village of Borre. Here Roger and I sleep on a bed of wet straw, woken every few minutes by the arrival of another few desolate refugees, and by the burping and farting of the cows. Papa Rioual does not sleep. He just stands in the doorway of the cattle shed, staring up at the sky.

By the end of the next day, we must be nearing the outskirts of Calais. It looks as if an air raid is going on, and the road is clogged with bombed-out vehicles and traffic fleeing the town. I do my best to ignore the twisted bodies, but the salty-sweet stench takes me back to my worst days in the butcher's shop in Nieppe. The sounds and stink of war are all around us now; the crump of distant explosions, and that smoky reek that catches at the back of your throat.

'Be careful,' says Roger, as I pick through the baggage in an abandoned Hispano-Suiza, looking for food. 'It may have been booby-trapped by Fifth Columnists.'

It is all I can do to keep Papa Rioual pedalling onwards. The old sea dog says he made a mistake; that we were damn fools to evacuate.

By Sunday morning, both Riouals say they cannot go on. We have been sleeping out in the open, and our options are looking bleak. I tell them that we must follow the soldiers and try to make Dunkirk. But having pushed our bikes for two hours amid utter pandemonium, Papa Rioual suddenly pulls off the road and shakes his head.

'That's it,' he mutters. 'I'm finished.'

'Then we have to go back,' I announce.

'Back to Calais?' Aghast, Roger looks back up the cratered road in the direction we have come. We have not eaten in thirty-six hours.

I shake my head. 'Back to Nieppe.'

'There is nowhere else,' nods Papa Rioual, almost brightening.

For several seconds, the three of us let this sink in.

'*D'accord*,' says Roger, whose legs have been cramping all morning. I can see him doing his best to be brave.

And so we begin our weary ride home. In Cassel, two gendarmes bar our route. They say that French artillery is about to be brought to bear on Armentières, where the Germans are digging in.

'Let's hope the guns hit my school,' I whisper to Roger, who allows himself a faint smile.

'I wish I was as brave as you, Stéphane,' he says, under his breath.

'I'm not brave. I'm just stupid.'

'I would do more, but I have my asthma, and Mummy says I mustn't.'

'You know what you need to do if you want to be brave, Roger?'

He looks shyly across at me. I can see him wondering if this is going to be one of my jokes at his expense.

'You've just got to say: bugger it. I'm going to do this thing come what may, and to hell with Mummy and my asthma. Maybe you die. Maybe you survive. But at least you'll know what it feels like to be brave.'

'Is that what you do then, Stéphane?'

I shake my head. 'I already told you: I'm not brave. I'm just immature. That's what old Ruckebusch always used to say, anyway. But perhaps it comes to the same thing.'

Now we must make a huge loop around the French position, straining to find some energy in our spent bodies. After another night in the open, we arrive back in the rue du Sac at last. I drop back to allow Papa Rioual to lead us in. It is Monday morning. Though our journey has taken only four days, I feel as if we have been away for a year. Everyone is amazed to see us. My mother says it is a miracle that we are safe. She lights an extra candle to Saint Rita to give thanks.

'What did you see, Lou?' asks Kléber, breathlessly. 'What did you see?'

I think of the things I have witnessed: the bombed-out houses, a soldier on fire and children blown to bits. I want to tell all him this. But when I open my mouth to speak, all that will come out is: 'Kléber, I saw the sea.'

'I knew you wouldn't leave us, Lou,' says Rosemary, emerging from the house once the Rioauls have disappeared into theirs. She gently clasps my arm. 'I told them you always come back.'

I do not have the strength to speak any more. Unhooking her arm from mine, I stumble upstairs to my room and sleep until the sun is high in the sky.

'Thank goodness you're back,' says Marcel, when I knock on his door. 'Just wait till you see what I've found.'

He leads me into the pasture beside the Pont d'Achelles cemetery. I blink. A British 3-ton truck is parked beneath the trees. Two soldiers in kilts are standing behind it, each holding a bottle of wine, much of which – to judge from their swaying and their laughter – they must already have consumed. Two French girls I do not recognise are watching, wide-eyed, on the grass. And all this, with the sound of bombs and shelling still rumbling in the distance.

I cast a casual glance into the back of the truck. It is littered with boxes of wine, champagne and various aperitifs, including Pastis, Salers and Cinzano – alcoholic luxuries almost unheard of in Nieppe.

'Parlay vous beer?' announces one of the soldiers, attempting to focus on Marcel.

I step forward and ask the man, rather sternly, what he wants.

'Jeepers, you's a Brit,' he exclaims. 'Och, laddie, all we're wanting is a little beer for the ladies here. They will nae touch a drop of what we've got.'

Marcel and I have a whispered discussion. And then it is agreed: the soldiers will give us as many bottles of champagne and Cinzano as we can carry, in exchange for half a dozen bottles of beer.

Under normal circumstances, my father would be appalled at such a transaction, especially with soldiers of the British army. But the voice on the radio says that Belgium has surrendered to Germany. And none of us can think as far as tomorrow, let alone the day after that. So we hand over a crate of booze apiece to him and to Papa Lombard, taking care to keep back a few bottles for ourselves. Most of these we hide in the hedge at the back of the cemetery.

On 29 May, everyone in the rue du Sac takes to their cellars, because Stukas are attacking Armentières and Bailleul, the town where Marcel goes to school. There is a frightful flap on, because my friend and I have gone missing, and what if we have been hit?

As it happens, Marcel and I have indeed been knocked to the ground by a mighty force. But not by a bomb dropped by the Germans. No, our nemesis is a bottle of Cinzano donated by the Scots. Side by side, we lie face down in the pasture behind Pont d'Achelles, woozy with wine and wishing the clouds would stop spinning above our heads. I hoped my first experience of drunkenness would bring a kind of happy oblivion, that it might wipe away my Dunkirk nightmares about having to pedal across a muddy, bloody battlefield which wants to suck me underground. It didn't occur to me that the oblivion in question might whirl like a fairground ride that never stops.

In the distance, I can hear bombs exploding, and I could swear I feel the ground tremble beneath me from time to time. But this doesn't seem to matter. Besides, there's no way I could find my way down into a cellar right now, even if I wanted to. And I can see from his giggling attempts to crawl towards a tree for a leak that Marcel is completely blotto, too.

'Over here, bombs!' I yell, waving at the sky. 'Come and get us.'

'Shhhhh!' hisses Marcel, shaking with laughter, his finger to his lips. 'They'll hear you.'

30 May 1940

I shall never forget today, and not just because I have the most magnificent headache in France. No, it's also because I have never known the world so quiet. You'd think a thunderstorm was about to break, from the tension in the thick air. The stream of refugees has disappeared from the rue du Sac, and the French customs officer has finally left his post. All Allied traffic on the main road has ceased. Even the birds have stopped singing.

Our house is silent at the best of times, but this is worse than that. My father locks and bolts all the doors. News that Ypres fell to the Huns yesterday has hit him hard. So many of his fellow gardeners from the War Graves live there, and he says the town is a sacred place for us Brits. I wonder if any of my old chums from the Eton Memorial School managed to get away. Last night the sky above Armentières was red. Inky pinky parlez-vous.

Inside, we all creep around in the shadows, while the sun beats down outside. My parents wish me a terse happy fifteenth birthday – I'd almost forgotten it was today – but none of us has the stomach to sing. I think they're still cross about yesterday.

And then, late in the afternoon, the world changes. Out of the silence comes the low buzz of approaching hornets. The clicking of my mother's rosary intensifies.

Two German motorcycles with sidecars appear in our street, at the bend in the road near the cemetery.

The riders must be sweating like pigs beneath those dusty leather greatcoats. My flesh creeps at the sight of their goggles and guns.

We watch through gaps in the shutters, holding our breath. A machine gun is mounted on each sidecar. Should we be lying on the floor? But after one slow pass up and down the rue du Sac, the motorcycles turn back towards Belgium and are gone.

'Was it them?' asks my mother.

'I feel as if we've been burgled,' replies Auntie Val.

Next day, a company of German infantry appears. I watch in awe as perhaps fifty soldiers install themselves in the Lombard farm, where the straw in the barn still bears the imprint of the Brits. According to Marcel, from the bloody state of their feet the Germans must have been marching for days. At number 12, Papa Rioual is forced to make up a bed for a lieutenant. Other officers are billeted in private houses elsewhere. For now, we are spared.

'You see?' gasps my mother, out of breath. She is stretching up to press more melted wax above the front door. 'Now do you see?'

The Germans are not as evil and ugly as I was expecting. But I hate them in my guts, even so. They are correct and distant, and speak in a meaningless language that sounds to me as if they are gargling spanners. Emboldened by their lack of violence, Marcel and I take to hiding in the hedge on one side of the street, armed with the shiny brass fire extinguisher that the Tommies left behind. Pump the handle hard enough and it shoots out a jet that really stings at close range.

We wait until one of the Germans wanders past our position, and I give him a couple of squirts.

'Aaarghhh,' he shouts, as if he has been shot. And then, glancing down at the stain on his uniform, he shouts again, even louder: 'Aaarghhhhh.'

Now he goes absolutely berserk, shouting and cursing as he tries to find a way through the hedge to get at us. I have to hold my nose to stop myself laughing, but Marcel looks almost as furious as our Kraut. I don't think he really believed I was going to do it.

Abandoning the fire extinguisher, we sprint off down a narrow lane into the fields. And now, at last, I feel alive again. My whole body buzzes with adrenaline, giddy with elation at not being caught.

'Why the hell did you do that?' pants Marcel as we crouch down, hidden in a field of young maize.

'I've no idea,' I shrug, grinning at him.

After a week of oiling their weapons in the sunshine, the Germans finally accept that nothing ever happens in the rue du Sac. They toss their fag ends into the street, clamber back into their grey lorries and depart.

Now columns of bare-headed prisoners, British and French, appear on the Dunkirk–Lille main road, escorted by helmeted Germans with machine guns slung around their necks.

Marcel and I stand in silence on the corner of the rue du Sac to watch them pass: rank after rank, mile after mile, step after painful step. Gone are the smiling faces that I saw grinning at me from the back of British trucks. Gone the well-pressed uniforms and the weapons glinting in the sun. Now every man looks shabby and shrivelled, grey with dust or darkened with sweat. Some of them march without boots, their feet raw and bloody in their threadbare socks. The day is the hottest of the year so far, with a fierce sun beating down on their necks. Half-marching, half-stumbling, they make heavy weather of the road I take almost every day into Nieppe.

'I can't believe it,' whispers Marcel beside me.

I shake my head.

'Why did they surrender?' he asks.

Again I shake my head. I only wish there were something we could do.

But all we can do is stand there, helpless, mesmerised by the grim embarrassment of it all. My sisters appear and Elizabeth slips her cool hand into mine. For minutes on end, none of us speaks. What is there to say?

'They look so thirsty,' whispers Rosemary at last.

'What does it mean, Lou?' asks Elizabeth. 'What does it mean?'

'I honestly don't know.' I cannot bring myself to tell her that the Germans must have won.

'It means,' says Rosemary, 'that things are going to get a whole lot worse before they get better. Stay here with Lou, Elizabeth.'

Marcel and I both turn to look at her, but she is already walking back down the street. A few minutes later she returns, carrying two buckets of water. We all watch, open-mouthed, as Rosemary waits for one of the German guards to pass before staggering forward with the buckets. She goes right to the very edge of the column of prisoners and carefully sets them down on the cobbles, a few feet apart.

One or two prisoners stop to drink. They reach their hands into the buckets and splash their mouths and faces with the cool water. Then comes a shout from our left. A German guard hurries forward. He kicks the buckets over, glaring menacingly at the four of us. I give Elizabeth's hand a squeeze as we stand to attention, eyes front, pretending we haven't heard.

Now other bystanders begin to break away and run to their houses. They must be scared at what they have seen. But soon they are back, bringing more buckets of water, with which they line the route. I fill ours again, too. The Germans kick them over. But not before a few of the prisoners have managed to slake their thirst.

On the edge of a section of French prisoners, I happen to notice one man who appears taller and even more shambolic than the rest. Something about him looks familiar to me. And then I spot his huge cauliflower ears, and I can scarcely believe it. For he is the man like a lamp post; the soldier of the 208th Infantry who invited me to drink men's wine from his canteen. The one who wanted to be growing apples in Normandy just now. How much the world has changed since we met.

'Ho,' I call softly, pointing at one of our buckets. 'Over here.'

The man turns his head and stares at me for a few moments. I grin back, and wave. But it's as if he were looking straight through me. Expressionless, he shambles on.

The Germans look expressionless beneath their helmets, too. But they carry themselves differently to the prisoners. From the way they stroll and swagger, shoulders back, kicking at chippings on the cobbles, you'd think they owned the place.

Suddenly Rosemary gasps. A young prisoner in the French ranks has fallen to the ground, visibly exhausted, clutching his thigh. The others behind him carry on marching, stepping over him. Two guards stride over to where he is lying and one of them kicks him, hard, in the back. Now they are both shouting at the fallen man, and the second guard is reaching for the holster on his hip. Surely he isn't going to . . .

We all turn our heads away, but it's too late. I saw how the man's body twitched when the pistol shot rang out. Someone has dropped a broken doll in the street. The prisoners march on. Left, right, left. Rosemary puts her hands over Elizabeth's eyes. Beside me, Marcel looks deathly pale. I can feel him staring at me. But I dare not catch his eye.

The columns of despair trudge on down the main road, day and night, for a week. And then the old silence returns to the rue du Sac. Even the Germans have gone. There are no soldiers and no swastikas. The war appears to be over. We all shut ourselves up in our houses, waiting for whatever is going to happen next.

With nobody to run things, nothing functions any more. In Nieppe, there is no school, no police, no trams or buses, no telephone, no postal service, no nothing. Everything comes to a standstill. My father has taken to spending the entire day with his ear pressed to his wireless. For us children, the atmosphere is at once ghostly and heavy with expectation. Even Auntie Val's knitting machines have stopped. When

Marcel and I cycle out into the countryside, I feel as if we are the last boys on earth.

Like a pair of magpies, we begin to comb the woods for any shiny stuff left behind by the retreating armies. And the pickings are rich. There are wagons loaded with ammunition, tools, clothing, sugar, coffee and flour. There are accordions, clarinets and trumpets, too. One day I bring home a drum for Rosemary, which she says will be jolly useful for her band. We also find a field telephone unit with a hand-cranked electrical generator. But it is the rifles, flares and grenades which bring the loudest whoops of delight when we discover a new addition to our arsenal. We're not planning to *use* all these weapons, exactly. It just gives us a kick to know that they are ours.

Marcel wants us to be scientific in our approach. So we collect the best two rifles of each model that we can find: two Fusils Lebel, two Mousquetons, two Fusils Gras and two Modèles 1936, complete with incorporated bayonets. We also find a Zulaika Ruby pistol and a French light machine gun in a case. With all these guns and their accompanying ammo, along with a decent haul of grenades and flares, we sneak back to the Lombard farm and hide our treasures beneath the straw at the back of the barn.

'What if someone finds them?' I whisper, as we attempt to see our hiding place through Papa Lombard's eyes.

'No chance,' replies Marcel. And then, after a pause, he adds: 'But what if we blow up my dad's best barn?'

'No way. It'll be fine.'

'You're right,' he nods. 'It'll be just fine.'

At dawn the next day, we move the machine gun and grenades into a hole we've dug at the bottom of the Lombard pasture, having first greased everything with goose fat to keep the water out. As for the Zulaika Ruby, I persuade Marcel that I should keep the pistol in the eaves above my bed, for emergencies.

Our most exciting find is yet to come. One afternoon, we

are cycling through a wood near Steenwerck when Marcel skids his bicycle to a halt. He lets out a low whistle.

'Do you see what I see?' he says, under his breath.

I glance around me. I can see nothing except oaks and chestnuts, and the sun streaming through the leafy canopy above our heads. Grinning, Marcel proffers his spectacles and points into the woods on our left. And that's when I spot them: two small, squat tanks, hidden amid a thicket of brambles perhaps sixty yards away, their gun barrels pointing straight at us.

'Germans?' I mouth.

'French,' he replies. 'Probably abandoned weeks ago.'

'Bagsy I man the gun turret,' I yell, over my shoulder, already racing for the tanks.

'Then I'll drive,' he puffs, just behind.

Of all the fairground rides that I did not get to go on at Dreamland in Margate, none of them could compare to this. For here I am, standing in the gun turret of a real live tank, with Marcel's head sticking out of the driver's hatch in front of me, wondering whether we should blast the Boche with our 37mm cannon or simply squish them beneath our caterpillar tracks. Driver, I think we'll do both.

Marcel announces that the tanks are a pair of old Renault FT17s.

'How on earth can you tell?' I ask, awe-struck. One day I am going to find something that my friend *doesn't* know.

'It says so here,' he shrugs, pointing to some lettering on the side of the hatch.

Our ammunition lockers and fuel tanks are empty. But in all other respects, this brute of a machine, whose interior smells of oil and diesel and cordite, appears to be ready for action. Its crew must have been in a hurry to leave, for the floor of the cramped turret is strewn with maps and papers.

Having blasted the German army to smithereens several times over, we come to a painful conclusion: we must sabotage the tanks, rather than let the Boche get their hands on them.

Yet bashing up a tank turns out to be easier said than done. Even after ten minutes of trying to chip bits off with a pickaxe, we've done little more than scrape the paintwork.

'Right, that's it,' I declare. 'What we need here is a grenade.'

This suggestion has a galvanising effect upon Marcel.

'I think I've cracked it,' he announces, his voice echoing up from the bowels of the tank. 'We just have to remove the breach blocks from the guns.'

'What does that mean?' I ask. Shouldering the pickaxe, I lean down into the hatch.

'It means that, by removing a couple of pins, we can put both guns out of action.'

'Sometimes, Lombard, you can be such a kill-joy.'

'Sorry,' he says, grinning as he pops his head out of the turret. 'Pass me that *clé anglaise* we found.' So I pass him our shiny new adjustable spanner and, a few minutes later, he hands me a heavy lump of metal. 'At least now we'll have spoiled the Boche's fun, too.'

It is not only the French who dropped everything and ran. The British have left things behind as well, and I manage to kit myself out with a complete service uniform in the regulation itchy khaki. I also bring home several other bits of battle dress and present them to Auntie Val. Her eyes light up at the sight of shirts and long johns discarded in the heat of retreat, and she immediately sets about dyeing everything dark blue. Elizabeth watches her, without rapture. My ten-year-old sister cares very much about what she wears. The next day, Auntie makes her go to school in a red pinafore cut from one of the sheets dumped by the refugees, and a pair of blanket trousers.

'But the other children already say I look like a gypsy,' she wails. 'They call me *la pauvre Anglaise*. Nobody wants to play with me because they think we're so poor. And now they'll hate me even more.'

'We *are* poor,' shrugs Auntie Val, 'and you are half-English. So they're right about that. But they only tease you because you're so pretty, and they're jealous. Isn't that right, Lou?'

'I don't know. I've never been teased, myself.' I gaze down at my knickerbockers, and at the thick green tunic my aunt knitted me for Christmas.

'That's because you're so ugly,' sneers Kléber, waving his crust of bread at me. I shall make the little devil pay for this later.

'At least we have food to eat, and that's the main thing,' says my mother from the corner, making me jump. She is so quiet that I sometimes forget she is there. 'And Elizabeth, I think you look lovely. You always do.'

'Yes, but Mummy,' Kléber trills, 'that's because you're blind.'

Mouths open, Elizabeth and I stare at each other. Auntie Val presses her finger tightly to her lips.

'I think you look jolly pretty, Elizabeth,' I lie. With the backs of her hands, she wipes her eyes.

Not to be outdone, Marcel has acquired a uniform, too. But his is a German one, snaffled from one of the soldiers billeted in his father's barn, who made the mistake of leaving his wet kit out to dry after a thunderstorm. My fearless friend hid it under a hay bale, for safekeeping.

'I dare you to wear it to school,' I tell him, one afternoon, when we are playing behind a hedge with the field telephone unit we found, cranking the handle and making sparks jump between its electrodes. But Marcel isn't really listening.

'One moment,' he says, raising his finger. 'I've had an idea.'

A couple of minutes later, on the grass verge in front of the Lombard farm, a pristine adjustable spanner marked SHEFFIELD STAINLESS glints in the afternoon sun. It looks as if someone has just dropped it there, on top of a pile of leaves. Only someone with very sharp eyes could spot the two brown wires which emerge from the leaf pile and run under the hedge in front of the house. And that someone is not old Pioffret, the woodcutter, who is even now sauntering down the rue du Sac towards us.

'Hold . . . hold . . . hold . . .' murmurs Marcel, peering through the hedge at our target as Pioffret approaches the grass verge, his attention clearly caught by the chromed tool glittering in the sunlight. 'And . . . NOW!' On command, I crank the handle of the field telephone for all I'm worth. We hear a gargled yelp from Pioffret.

'*Aaargh! P'tain! C'est quoi, ça?*' With a dull clang, he drops the spanner on the cobbles, and we have to hold our sides as, wounded and bewildered, he goes shuffling onwards, clutching his wrist and shaking his head.

After a happy afternoon of giving electric shocks to anyone gullible and greedy enough to pick up our spanner, including Kléber, Marcel invites me to stay and have supper with his family. My parents even give me permission to stay over. We are meant to be sleeping in the hayloft above the cows in the Lombard barn. Yet as the poplars lining the rue du Sac throw their long shadows in the moonlight, Marcel and I stand in the Pont d'Achelles cemetery, doing a spot of digging.

We are not digging graves. No, it is guns, not bones, that we need to bury underground. For days we have been scouting for a safe place to hide our arsenal. And at last I think I have found one, beneath one of the two bastions which flank the Cross of Sacrifice in the Pont d'Achelles cemetery, each lined with a low box hedge. My father would have a fit if he knew what we have in mind. But he has barely set foot in his cemetery since the Germans arrived. And so, this moonlit night, having clambered in over the hedge planted around the perimeter of one of the squat bastions, we begin to dig.

Even in the coolness of the early hours, when the dew dampens our clothes and the earth smells rich as mushrooms, this digging is hot work. We take it in turns, one of us hacking away with the shovel, the other making repeated trips with an old wooden cider crate to remove the earth. Marcel is worried the shovel may hit an unexploded shell, but I am more concerned about the bones we keep turning up; not from bodies buried in any grave, but from those in need of one. If we find dog tags or a skull, I shall have to tell my father.

Night after night, we dig down inside the bastion, working by feel, without a lamp. Before long, we are lying prone beneath the bastion wall itself, carving out the earth with a trowel. It is difficult to know when to stop. But by the time we have hollowed out a pit roughly the size of a small dining table, I call a halt. The bastion may collapse on top of us. So now Marcel brings wooden pickets from Papa Lombard's fencing store, with which we line the pit, roofing it with a sheet of corrugated iron. There is just room for a boy to crawl or crouch beneath. The only problem is how to clamber in or out, without being spotted.

Once again, Marcel has a solution. So now we begin to dig all over again: a tunnel this time, beginning beneath the cemetery's boundary wall, and aiming – we hope – at the bastion.

'I'm glad I'm not a mole,' coughs Marcel, when his head finally appears in the pit, from the tunnel mouth.

'I don't like it,' I reply, facing him on all fours. The earth seems to swallow our voices. 'It feels as if it could collapse at any moment.'

'If it does, we'll dig it again,' he replies. But I know he knows what I mean.

At last, our work done, we cover the roof of our pit with earth, and do the same with the wooden board which covers the tunnel mouth on the outside of the boundary wall. The camouflage is effective. Unless someone steps right on to the thing, they will never guess it is there.

When I creep back into the house, shortly after midnight, I am almost blinded by a torch shining in my eyes. Straightening up, I squint into the beam.

'Where the hell have you been?' asks my father, lowering his work lamp. 'And why are you covered with earth?'

'You honestly don't want to know, Dad,' I reply.

There is a long silence.

'No, you're right. I don't want to know,' he mutters at last. 'Keep it under your hat.'

'Good night then, Dad.'

'Good night.' He turns to climb the stairs, then hesitates. 'You haven't killed anyone, have you, Lou?'

'Of course not,' I reply, with a nervous laugh.

Elizabeth is in tears at the breakfast table once again. Auntie Val has her by the hand and is demanding to know why the nuns have punished her.

'Because I didn't have my pinafore,' sobs Elizabeth, flinching at her touch.

'The red one? But you went to school wearing it,' says Auntie Val, confused. 'I tied the straps myself.'

'I took it off,' says Elizabeth quietly. 'I hid it in my desk.'

'And you preferred to be beaten rather than wear the clothes I made for you?'

'Sometimes I just wish,' whispers Elizabeth, her eyes shut, 'that we could be like everyone else.'

Marcel and I are itching to try out our weapons. Though most are stashed in our newly dug cache in Pont d'Achelles, we have kept back a couple of rifles in the Lombard barn. My friend is adamant that these will be too noisy to risk firing them, but I manage to persuade him that we can try a few underwater shots in the Lombard pond, and that letting off the odd flare cannot do any harm in daylight.

And so, one fine Sunday morning, with most of my family away at the *Grande Messe*, we are both kneeling in the Lombard pasture, gazing down at the small metal canister we have placed between us in the grass. It has what looks like a wick sticking out of it.

'Are you sure this is a good idea?' asks Marcel.

'Aren't you always telling me that experimentation lies at the heart of all scientific progress?'

'Fancy a bike ride instead?'

'All right, stand to,' I announce. 'I'm going to light this thing.'

I touch my lighter to the wick and we both scarper, head down, in the direction of the trees. For a few seconds, nothing happens. Then dense clouds of bright red smoke begin to billow out of the canister.

'*Sacre bleu*,' murmurs Marcel.

'*Sacre rouge*,' I gulp, taking a step backwards. 'It's not mustard gas, is it?'

Before long, there is enough red smoke to hide a couple of tanks. Then a small house. Then a medium-sized castle. And still the stuff is spewing out of the tin.

'This is not good,' groans Marcel, pulling out his handkerchief and pressing it over his nose and mouth. By now, our smoke cloud is about the size of Ramsgate Pier. The Lombard farm has vanished. So, too, the rest of the rue du Sac, and most of northern France.

'It must be an artillery smoke flare,' he coughs. 'They'll be able to see us from Nieppe.'

'Are you joking?' I reply. 'They'll be able to see us from Dover.'

Marcel allows himself a brief grin, before his expression changes. 'And what if a German aircraft spots us?' he demands. 'You lit it, Stéphane. You put it out.'

I am just wondering how to achieve this when the canister stops spewing out scarlet, and a gust of wind begins to blow the smoke into Belgium.

'Oh, cripes,' I mutter. 'Now what do we do?' In the fields on the far side of the rue du Sac, two farmers are waving and shouting. They begin to run towards us.

'Run,' yells Marcel, and we both scarper into the deep ditch that was meant to keep out the Germans.

A minute later, however, and a faint pink tinge in the sky is all that is left of our scarlet smokescreen. The farmers must have thought better of coming to investigate. We both gaze in awe at the blackened empty canister.

'Right, what's next?' I say, pulling another tin from my pocket.

A few days later, a mysterious hole has appeared in the guttering of the Lombard farm. It looks as if the zinc has melted. Marcel's big sister, Cécile, is convinced that she saw a blinding white light up there, and unfortunately my mother gets wind of this from Madame Lombard. No doubt she is now convinced that the Virgin Mary has visited the rue du Sac.

A second apparition, unconnected with the Madonna, bothers us more. A wooden sign attached to an iron picket materialises overnight, right opposite Papa Rioual's house at number 12. The sign says LANGSAM FAHREN in black Gothic script.

We have no idea what this means. But we both take an instant dislike to the sign. So, one warm evening, when the sun has gone down, we resolve to attack it. Using all our combined strength, we manage to bend the metal picket in half. Shoulders back, standing tall, we glance nervously at what we have done, congratulating ourselves on our defiance.

Papa Rioual is not amused. He says he will be arrested if the Boche come back to find that their shiny new sign has been vandalised.

Next day, after a brief discussion, the two of us gouge a bullet hole in the eagle emblem of Marcel's German uniform. It looks amazingly realistic, too, by the time we've singed the edges with a match. Then we take the doctored tunic round to Papa Rioual's house. Roger answers the door, with his head in a bandage that goes right round his chin.

'Have you been shot?' I ask.

'Toothache,' he replies, sheepishly. 'I didn't want a bandage, but Maman insisted.'

'Well, look, we have shot a German soldier and buried him in one of the Lombard pastures.' As I speak, Roger's eyes widen. 'So you can tell your old man he needn't worry about the Boche any more. We're bumping them off, one at a time.'

Roger falls for it. He turns quite pale and his bottom lip takes on a life of its own. He stares at the bullet hole with an expression of appalled awe. It's pathetic, really. And hilarious, too.

'I'll tell my father,' he whispers, shutting the door with care.

Despite our bravado, the state of the bent-over LANGSAM FAHREN sign begins to give us the willies. It looks so *provocatif*, as Marcel puts it. We certainly don't want any of the Riouals to be arrested. And so, cowed by Roger's father's warnings about the threat of German retribution, we creep out at dead of night, dig the iron picket out of its concrete base and fling the whole thing into the Lombard pond.

As we watch the hateful object sink into the still black waters, I can tell from the way Marcel stands, spine erect and shoulders back, that we are both thinking the same thing. It may only be a road sign, and not a battleship, that we have sunk. But our days of schoolboy pranks are over. Now we are taking on the Wehrmacht.

23 June 1940

Outside the *mairie* in Nieppe, a small crowd has gathered around the notice board. I crane my neck, attempting to see what they're all looking at. It is a list of new laws, written in French and adorned with a large black Maltese cross. One sentence leaps out at me: '*Whoever commits acts of sabotage at installations or property of the German army or its members, who will be found in possession of arms of any type, will be condemned to death.*'

I read the sentence again. I begin to feel a familiar hollowness in the pit of my stomach. Can we be shot for lifting the LANGSAM FAHREN sign? Even if not, our cache of weapons in the cemetery is a good enough reason for condemning us to death. And our families, too.

Lost in thought, I pedal slowly down the main street towards the bicycle repair shop. My bicycle has been groaning in bent-sprocketed protest ever since my abortive trip to the coast with the Riouals. If only we had got away. There would be no cache of weapons waiting to incriminate us in Pont d'Achelles. And, as for that sign, if only I could turn the clock back, put the sword back into the stone. I know I must not act without considering the consequences of my actions. God knows, I've written the words out enough times. But what if my actions have consequences I couldn't possibly have guessed?

Francis André, the son of the owner, is standing on the pavement outside the bicycle shop when I grind to a halt. Arms folded, eyes tight shut, he appears to be sunbathing, his head tipped back to receive the afternoon sun full on his face.

'That doesn't sound good,' he says, not even bothering to open his eyes.

'I think it got run over by a tank,' I reply, peering down at my bicycle.

'Ah, Grady, it's you.' He reaches out for a hand to shake. 'Lovely day for a war, isn't it?'

'*Bonjour, Francis.*'

'Why the long face?' he asks, opening his eyes in surprise. 'It's not like you to be down in the dumps.'

'I've just seen that poster outside the *mairie*.'

'I know.' He glances up and down the street. 'Don't breathe, or we'll chop off your dick. All potatoes, whether boiled, chipped or fried, henceforth belong to Hitler. And don't fart in front of a German, because it might put us off all the champagne we've nicked from you. All that shit.'

I laugh, in spite of myself. 'That's the one,' I nod.

Francis works on my bicycle while I wait. He says the chainring is bent, which is why the chain keeps falling off. While he does his best to straighten the metal with an adjustable spanner, we chat in low voices about the war and what it means to us. A year older than me, but with a laconic savoir-faire that makes the gap seem wider, Francis is hoping to study engineering at the University of Lille.

'Or at least I was, before all this nonsense kicked off,' he says. 'But who knows if we'll all be here next week, let alone next year.'

'I tried to escape back to England,' I murmur. 'Because at least there I could join an army that still wants to fight.'

'Good for you,' he says, studying my face. He lowers his voice. 'My dad heard a radio broadcast last week by some French general with an unlikely name. Apparently he's trying to gee us all up to stand up to the Germans. I doubt anyone round here is going to heed the call, because they're all too busy panicking to fight. But I'll tell you this: if someone can tell me how I can be more useful to the Allied war effort than doing subtly crap repairs to German army bicycles, then I'll be there.'

'Me, too,' I reply. We grin at each other and, as I push my bicycle towards the sunlit doorway, I feel as if a weight has been lifted from my chest. I have the fleeting thought that perhaps Nieppe in 1940 is not such a bad time and place in which to be living, after all. Roughly three seconds later, as a vast German troop carrier comes thundering down the main road, almost taking off my front wheel, order is restored. Living in this place was always purgatory, I remind myself. These days, it is more like hell.

'Have you noticed,' whispers Francis, standing just behind me, 'that the Verdigris manage to make their lorries sound three times louder than the French and English ones that came down here a few weeks ago? Now why is that?'

'Probably it's because we don't want them here,' I shrug. 'I have the same problem with my little brother.'

'No, it's not that,' he chuckles. 'It's a technical thing. I think their fuel is missing something.'

He leans close to my ear and whispers a single word.

'Seriously?' I laugh. 'Sugar?'

He nods. 'Forms an emulsion with the petrol and clogs up the carburettor something wicked. Makes even the noisiest motor run perfectly silent, if you know what I mean. You should try it for yourself some time. Works a treat.'

'Perhaps I will.'

Back in the rue du Sac, I am just leaning my bike against the low wall outside our house when a shout from behind me makes me jump.

I spin on my heels and my heart jolts at the sight of the grey-green uniform of a German soldier, right here in our street. So soon? Have they come for me so soon? I open my mouth to speak; stare at the cobbles; am surprised to see that the German soldier is wearing clogs.

And now he is doubled up in pain.

No, not in pain. The man is laughing. He is laughing so

much that his forage cap falls off. And – oh, you vile piece of work, you rotting mashed potato – it's only that smelly rascal, Marcel.

'Are you crazy?' I ask, still too shaken to see the funny side. 'Have you any idea of the penalty for impersonating a German soldier?'

Marcel can hardly speak. 'You should have seen your face,' he manages to say at last, wiping his eyes. 'Anyone would think you'd seen a ghost.'

'That's what you'll be, if they catch you dressed like that.'

'Pretty cool even so, isn't it?'

'Yes, you make an excellent Boche.'

'Not jealous, by any chance, are we?'

'Well, you should see the poster they've just put up outside the *mairie*. And . . . *hélas* . . . too late. They're already coming for you.'

A low drone throbs in our ears and we both crane our necks to look up at the sky. The pale blue backdrop is dotted with small black crosses arranged in straight lines, each cross a bomber flying at low altitude, bound for England. We have been seeing more and more of these formations overhead, especially on the clearest days. But none as big as this one.

'Heinkel 111s,' says Marcel, squinting into the bright sky.

'They turn my stomach, whatever they are,' I reply. 'Now I do wish you'd go and change.'

'You were going to tell me about a poster outside the *mairie*.'

'Marcel, you're making me nervous.'

'*Jawohl*,' he grins, giving me a Nazi salute. Casually, he begins to stroll back to his house. And then, when he thinks I'm no longer watching, he sprints.

14 October 1940

We now have three British soldiers hiding in our attic. I don't know anything about them, except that one of them is called Sergeant Miles, and that they are stragglers from the British Expeditionary Force. Taken prisoner by the Germans at Dunkirk, they managed to escape from one of the columns of POWs we saw shambling along the road.

This afternoon, I am keeping guard in front of the house and pulling the legs off a beetle, when an imposing man on a bicycle swings off the main road and into the rue du Sac. To my alarm, he pulls up just beside me.

'*Bonjour, jeune homme,*' he says, and to my relief it is Monsieur Houcke, the mayor. I didn't recognise him at first, because we don't get a lot of official visitors in the rue du Sac.

'*Bonjour, monsieur,*' I announce. Don't say my father is in arrears with his *taxe foncière* again. 'Can I help you?'

'I was looking for Monsieur Stéphane Grady.'

'*C'est moi,*' I reply, cautiously.

The mayor narrows his eyes; glances down at the beetle in my hands. 'Pardon me for saying so, monsieur, but you look very young for someone who is supposed to be fifty-five.'

'I eat a lot of vegetables.'

He laughs. 'Ah, but of course,' he nods, lowering his voice. 'It is the English sense of humour.'

'I am Stéphane Grady.'

'And your father: isn't his name Stéphane, too?'

'*Non.*' And this is not really a lie. My father can't stand it when anyone tries to Frenchify his name.

Mayor Houcke gives me a long, hard look. 'It is good that you are cautious,' he says, at last. 'We must all be cautious. But I ask you to trust me, for I have not come to arrest your father.'

'Is there a problem with our *taxe foncière*?'

'Not that I'm aware of,' he chuckles. 'But I can look into it, if you like.'

'No, no, thank you,' I blurt. 'I'll just go and see if my father's in.'

'Please be kind enough to tell him that Mayor Houcke is here to see him. And that it's not about the *taxe foncière*.'

Glancing up at the attic, I make a lot of noise as I storm back into the house. Mayor Houcke is a good man; I know his reputation. Even so, it's probably best if he doesn't meet our house guests.

My father looks grave as he shakes the mayor's hand. The pair of them remain shut in the front room for only about ten seconds, before my father shoots out again.

'Lou, go and fetch Auntie Val,' he says, in a whisper. 'Tell her I need her at once. And see if Mémère will spare some coffee and sugar for the mayor.'

'But I can translate for you, Dad.'

'Lou, get me Auntie Val, now.'

When the three of them emerge, they all look very tired. Something is wrong. Mayor Houcke leaves in a hurry, shaking hands with my mother and Auntie Val on the way out, and then Elizabeth climbs into my father's lap. I stand by the window, keeping an eye on the empty street.

'Are you going to have to be a soldier again, Daddy?' she demands, fiddling with his tie.

'Are you in trouble with the police, Daddy?' asks Kléber, who is doing his best to knot my father's shoelaces together.

My father hangs his head.

'Oh, my heart,' says my mother, suddenly, from the doorway. Clutching her rosary in one hand, she leans on Rosemary with the other as she comes into the room. 'Are we going to be all right?'

'I don't know, love,' he says, pursing his lips. 'But Mayor Houcke is a good man, for a Frog, and he says he wants to help.'

'Help with what?' asks Rosemary. 'It's not the *taxe foncière* again, is it?'

'I wish it was.' My father runs his hands through his hair; lights himself a cigarette. 'Houcke says the Fritz have been sniffing around the town hall, wanting to know if there are any Brits in Nieppe.'

'Has he told them about us?' I shift uneasily from foot to foot.

'No, he just gave them a lot of smoke. But they'll be coming back. So I may have to lie low for a while.'

'The rest of you have nothing to worry about,' explains Auntie Val, 'because you have French papers and can blend in.'

'If you call blanket trousers and a red tablecloth blending in,' huffs Elizabeth.

'Apparently *"Deux bières, s'il vous plaît mam'selle"* may not be quite enough to convince Fritz that I'm a Frog,' chuckles my father, tickling her under her chin. 'Although I can't for the life of me think why not.'

'So we owe Mayor Houcke a huge debt of thanks, for offering to give your father French papers,' continues Auntie Val. 'But if the Germans ever find out that he is really British, then we will all be in big trouble. Including the mayor.'

'*Deux bières, s'il vous plaît, mam'selle*,' repeats my father to himself.

'But aren't the Germans at war with France as well as Britain?' asks Elizabeth. 'Why does it matter that Daddy is English?'

'Irish,' corrects my father.

'In a way you're right, Elizabeth,' explains Auntie Val, patiently. 'But Daddy may have to go into hiding, just for a short time.'

At this, my sister's eyes light up. 'How about we *all* hide?' she says. 'I know lots of good places.'

Suddenly a loud bump from upstairs makes us all stand very still, listening. My father raises his hands to the ceiling. Eyes wide, he stares at Auntie Val, then at Rosemary, then at me. The room is silent apart from the clicking of my mother's rosary beads, as we all consider the three men hiding upstairs.

At last, my father snaps his fingers, breaking the spell. 'Well, go ahead, Lou. Fetch down our Tommies. They'd better stay here for one more night, and we'll see if we can find them a better hide-out in the morning. It looks like I'll be needing one myself.'

And then, his face lighting up, he turns to Auntie Val.

'On reflection,' he says, 'you'd better make that *quatre bières, s'il vous plaît, mam'selle*. And get your pretty sister to help.'

We all turn to look at the frail little blind woman doing her rosary in the corner. Blushing, smiling, she is already on her feet.

The following day, with my father's tacit blessing, I move the men to the tool shed of the Grand Beaumart cemetery near Steenwerck. This windowless place is dark and airless by day, but should be comfortable enough at night, if they don't mind the whiff of oil and petrol and grass clippings which is, I think, my favourite smell in the world.

Sergeant Miles asks if they can stay for a month or so, until things quieten down, and then make their way up to the Channel and try to steal a boat. But after a fortnight, they have had enough of the sweet-smelling shed and set off on foot for the coast.

Other British soldiers are still being sheltered in Nieppe. One of them, a young Gordon Highlander called Jack Grassick, has shacked up with a local girl and her daughter in Pont de Nieppe and even been spotted in the *estaminets* of Armentières. Another is being sheltered at the home of Maurice Leblon – a stocky, pugnacious socialist who happens to be a complete Anglophile – a few streets away.

A few days later, Mayor Houcke returns. I am in the street, helping Elizabeth collect sheep droppings for the *potager*, when he arrives and disappears into the house. A few moments later, my father comes to the front door. His face in shadow, he gestures for me to join them.

Big news. Aged fifteen, I am to be given a job. And not just any job, either. When my father goes into hiding, he will be unable to work and the family will have no income. Houcke's suggestion is that I should take over my father's work in the cemeteries, for which I am to be paid a small wage by the *mairie*. My duty will be to keep the Pont d'Achelles cemetery in order, along with the War Graves sections of the two civilian cemeteries in Nieppe and Pont de Nieppe, where my father's neat planting and perfect turf have created a haven of ordered Englishness amid the jumble of Gothic crosses and tombs. There must be fifty war graves in Nieppe, and perhaps 150 in Pont de Nieppe. I am also to assist the municipal labourers as required, and maintain a small French military plot.

From now on, I shall be the family breadwinner. I glance at my father. He is staring out of the window, lost in thought.

My mother helps me get ready for my first day at work. Feeling her way around the kitchen, she fills a Thermos flask with tea, and makes a sandwich with a thin slice of cheese in it for my lunch.

'Special treat for the worker,' she says.

'It's amazing you can do all this, in the dark,' I remark, wrapping a scarf around my neck. For the shutters are still closed and she has not lit the lamp.

'Well, why not? I've done it every day, just the same, for the last twenty years.'

Then she fetches my father's work satchel and tucks the sandwich and flask inside, while I button up my coat and wonder if I've forgotten any tools. I'd ask my father, but he seems to have vanished. Probably he has gone for a smoke.

I hang the leather satchel around my neck, and stand to attention in front of her.

'Right, I'm just going off to work,' I announce, with a proud smile. My mother leans forward as if she is about to give me a kiss, and then changes her mind, hurriedly patting her hair.

'Oh, my brave warrior,' I hear her sigh, as I march out of the front door.

The works department at the *mairie* have told me to report to the civilian cemetery in Nieppe at eight o'clock to join a working party. It is a frosty morning and I try to keep warm by jogging on the spot, sheltering from the biting wind behind one of the big family tombs. How gothic and chaotic the place feels, beside the calm serenity of Pont d'Achelles. My father always says that death makes equals of us all. Well, you wouldn't think so to look at these graves; some jagged, some ornate; some ring-fenced and some studded with gaudy plaques. But there, on one side, is his little patch of England, with its immaculate turf and ranks of perfect white headstones, uniform as a well-drilled platoon. I am in charge here now. That grass is mine to tend. I shiver, and not simply because I'm cold.

Around half past eight, four ancient figures in dusty blue overalls appear, looking so decrepit that I am half-expecting to see four open graves, recently vacated. But these are my fellow workers.

'We heard that a youngster would be joining the team,' one of them rasps, his breath making a cloud in the cold air. 'We didn't expect it to be a child.'

'I'm almost sixteen.'

'Exactly,' he says, with a shrug.

After we have all shaken hands, he wanders away and returns with five hoes. Our task is to weed the alleyway that bisects the cemetery. So I set to work, while the others stand shivering and chatting in the corner of the cemetery.

Perhaps twenty minutes later, the first man shuffles up behind me.

'What are you doing?' he asks.

'Hoeing, like you said.'

'If you work at that rate, *mon petit*, we'll finish this job in a couple of days. And then what?'

I shrug.

'Look, chum, take a break. See if your hoe doesn't need a long and complicated repair. And stop using it as if it were a tool for removing weeds.'

'Isn't that what it is?'

'Of course not,' he replies. 'A hoe's main purpose is to provide a support upon which its operator may lean. And that's official French municipal policy.'

'*D'accord*,' I nod, confused.

A surprise awaits me when I come home from my first day at work. My father calls me into the front room. Taking a deep breath, he announces that I am now going to be allowed to smoke. He holds out his cigarette case.

Awe-struck, I reach out to take a cigarette, and then hesitate.

'Don't worry, Lou,' he says, watching my face. 'I know you've been puffing away in secret. But I think it's better we have it out in the open, don't you? So go ahead; help yourself.'

'Thanks, Dad,' I reply, my head spinning. 'But do you mind if I fetch my own?'

Dashing upstairs, I reach up into the eaves above my bed, feeling along the ledge with trembling fingers for the familiar coldness of my pistol and, behind it, for the soft packet of Gold Flake which one of the Tommies gave me months ago.

Back in the front room, I roll myself a cigarette and marvel at the sight of my own father lighting it for me. My first offical fag. Next he lights his own cigarette and we stand like that for a while, puffing away, glancing at each other from time to time.

'So what did you learn today, Lou?' he asks.

'Not much,' I shrug, watching the smoke curl up towards the ceiling. You'd think I had never seen smoke before. I know my father is annoyed that I have started in the civilian cemetery, when there is so much work to be done on his beloved war graves. 'I think I learned that doing nothing is far more tiring than doing something.'

He ponders this for a while. 'When you're a soldier,' he says at last, rolling the tip of his fag in the ashtray to make it a perfect cone, 'it's not the bullets that kill you. It's the waiting.'

'Mm.'

'Doing nothing is the death of a man. It eats you up inside.'

I cannot think of anything to say to this. So we stand there for a while longer, drawing on our cigarettes.

Rosemary appears in the doorway. 'Do you mind if I practise the piano?' she asks, coughing. 'I go back to school tomorrow, and I have my exam next week.' She stares at the foreign object smouldering between my fingers.

'Go ahead,' says my father, without looking up. He waves his hand at the piano. Rosemary begins to play one of her Chopin nocturnes, more quietly than I have ever heard her play before. Night falls outside. My father is deep in thought. And I wish this cigarette between my fingers would last until the end of time.

1 December 1940

The war is still going on, the house feels like ice, and food is becoming very scarce. But my mother is having one of her cheerful days today. And no wonder: Elizabeth has just signed up for catechism classes with Monsieur le Curé. She is to have her First Communion and confirmation in a few months' time. That's if the church is still standing and we haven't all been beheaded by the Fritz.

My father is bemused that his favourite daughter is being, as he puts it, led astray. He says he can't understand it, and wouldn't it be better if she spent a bit more time collecting grass for the rabbits, or gleaning the farmers' fields for any spuds left over after the harvest?

He and I are out in the vegetable patch, digging the hardening soil for winter, while Elizabeth and Kléber scamper about in their overcoats, collecting worms for the chickens. A quartet of twin-engined Messerschmitt 110s flies over and we all peer up at them, except my father, who lifts his arm to cover his face.

'Is it still there, Auntie?' asks Elizabeth, hopping up and down when Auntie Val emerges from the veranda, looking weary after a trip into Nieppe. She needs wool for her knitting machines. 'Is it still there?'

'Is what still there?' demands my father. 'Nieppe?'

'It's a piece of fabric that Elizabeth has spotted, in the window of Madame Houcke's shop,' says Auntie Val, flatly. 'And she thinks it would make a very pretty dress for her First Communion.'

'Oh, does she now?' My father narrows his eyes. 'Well,

Elizabeth, if you want to learn the whole blooming catechism for the sake of a pretty dress, good luck to you.'

'Does that mean I can have the fabric, Daddy? Can I have a dress? Please, Daddy?' She wraps her arms around his knees and gazes pleadingly up at him.

'That's not what I said,' he says, with the hint of a smile. But the smile quickly fades as another thought strikes him. 'Besides, if you need money for a dress, it's Lou you should be speaking to, not me. He's the big breadwinner around here.' He picks up his spade again, and attacks the earth so hard that the sound bounces off the back wall of the house.

I want to remind him that I don't have a centime of my own money. My wages go straight to Auntie Val, who rewards me with one small packet of Belgian tobacco per week. Which is probably not enough to barter for a handful of buttons, let alone a dress.

'Aren't you coming in for a cup of tea, Steve?' asks Auntie Val, wringing her hands. 'It's so cold out here.'

'Changed my mind about the tea break,' he replies, through gritted teeth.

Quite suddenly, the throb of massed engines droning in the distance makes us all look up into the sky again. Another huge formation of bombers, far above us, is silhouetted against the darkening heaven.

'Bastards,' yells my father, shaking his fist. But I recognise those silhouettes, because Marcel has taught me all about them. They are not Heinkels or Dorniers, but Halifaxes from Britain, probably on their way to bomb the industrial zone on the outskirts of Lille.

'It's all right, Dad,' I tell him. 'Those ones are ours.'

'British planes bombing France?' asks Auntie Val. 'It doesn't seem right somehow.'

'But it's factories they attack,' I reply. 'Not people.'

'People work in factories.'

Exasperated, I do my best to explain that the factories must be destroyed, because they are making munitions and other equipment for Germany. But Auntie Val is having none of it. Casting me a look of icy disdain, she stiffens and storms back inside.

Sunday morning, and I am alone in the house when there is a knock at the door. My father is being sheltered by friends in Bailleul, and everyone else is at Mass. Peering down from an upstairs window, I can see the hateful grey-green of a Verdigris uniform. I smile to myself. I recognise that forage cap, and that sandy hair imperfectly hidden beneath it. I can even spy a pair of non-regulation brown shoes that are almost certainly clogs. That pesky Marcel is not going to catch me out again.

After a quick glance up and down the street to check that there aren't any real Germans about, I fling open the window and lean out.

'You dirty, filthy Boche!' I yell.

Marcel takes a couple of steps back, puts his hands on his hips and stares up at me. And the laughter sticks in my throat. Because it's not Marcel.

'Would you like to come downstairs, please?' says the German soldier, with a cold smile, in perfect French.

For a second, it goes through my head to sprint out of the back door, jump over the wall, and flee across the fields. But then they will search the house and find evidence of my father.

'I'm so, so sorry,' I pant, as I open the front door and wait to be shot. 'I thought you were someone else.'

'A different filthy Boche?'

'No, no, I . . .'

'Don't worry,' he says. 'I am not going to shoot you, although I could if I wanted to.'

'Mm.'

'We all make mistakes.'

'*Oui.*'

'But, you see, not all Germans are monsters.'

'*Non.*'

'Actually, I came to ask if you have any eggs.'

My whole body is shaking with adrenaline as I rush down the corridor and out into the garden. Ducking into the chicken coop, I put the four biggest, cleanest eggs I can find into a bowl and run back to the German. This serves me right, I think to myself, for not going to the *Grande Messe* with the others. The chickens hardly lay at all in the winter, and those eggs would have fed all of us, or been valuable currency to barter for a scrap of cheese or salted meat.

'You can keep the bowl, monsieur,' I blurt, as he strolls away.

When there comes another knock at the door, a few minutes later, I almost don't want to answer it. A lady in a grey hat is standing there, holding a neatly wrapped parcel in her hands. She says she won't come in, but that she has brought something for my aunt.

'We all have to help each other out, don't we?' she says, handing me the parcel with a brisk smile.

'Why, yes,' I reply, 'Madame . . .'

'Madame Houcke. I'm the mayor's sister.'

'Thank you, Madame Houcke. It's kind of you to come all this way.'

'Ah,' she nods. 'We never forget the debt we owe.'

'You owe something to us?' I ask, mystified.

'To your country,' she whispers. 'For standing up.'

'Thank you,' I say, as I softly close the door.

Auntie Val looks blank when I give her the parcel. And then, when she opens it, her face falls. For there, held up between her outstretched hands, is a shimmering expanse of sky-blue fabric, even bigger than Monsieur Ruckebusch's map of the world.

'I don't believe it,' whispers Auntie Val. 'Come, Berthe, come touch this chintz that Madame Houcke has given us for Elizabeth's First Communion. It feels almost as soft as silk.'

'It is a gift from the Virgin,' murmurs my mother, touching the corner of the fabric to her cheek.

My father marches in from the veranda to see what all the commotion is about. Auntie Val takes a step back, because he is streaked with mud.

'What's the matter with Elizabeth?' he demands. 'And what's all this about virgins?' He kneels down beside my sister. 'Why are you crying, love?'

'I'm crying because it's so beautiful,' she sobs. 'And because I'm going to have a dress that I won't feel embarrassed to wear.'

'And do you honestly believe that people will like you more, just because of what you're wearing?' he says, with a grin in the direction of Auntie Val. 'Do you really think it matters that much?'

Elizabeth looks up at him, her eyes brimming with tears.

'Yes, Daddy,' she says in a clear voice. 'I'm afraid I do.'

17 May 1941

In the Pont d'Achelles cemetery, I am mowing the grass yet again. It needs doing so often at this time of year, and my father's ancient hand mower – a Qualcast Model H, with a 14-inch cutter – takes a lot of elbow grease to shift.

Day after day, I cycle between my three cemeteries, and do my best to keep them tidy. With Pont d'Achelles I make a special effort, because I know my father can see it from the window of his prison upstairs. Mostly he just sits up there, winding his little wheat grinder, or else he stands alone in the vegetable garden with his potatoes, pulling off the *doryphores* and squidging them between his fingertips. Auntie Val says he is in mourning for his Saturday nights with the boys. But he has been unsettled, too, by the news that the IWGC cemetery at Gorre, near Arras, was badly damaged during the British retreat last year.

'To think that they made that cemetery a battlefield,' he keeps whispering to himself. 'They tried to hide behind the graves.'

Only Elizabeth can make him smile these days. On the rare occasions when my father ventures down to sit with us in the front room, she will climb up on to his lap and sing one of the songs he has taught her, gazing up at him until he joins in. Usually just a couple of lines of 'Little Sir Echo' are enough to have my father humming along, gazing out of the window, his chin resting on top of her head.

I find I don't really know how to talk to my father any more. Perhaps I never did. The last proper conversation we had was on the veranda a few weeks ago. Head bowed, he presented me with his bag of tools, the precious ones that none of us is ever allowed to touch. He said he thought it was about time I had them – that he wouldn't be needing them any more.

'But what about after the war?' I reminded him. 'You'll have your old job back then.'

'Will I?' he said. He was squeezing his beloved secateurs. 'And what if the war never ends?'

'You told me yourself that the British will be back. I'm sure it can't be long now.'

'Oh, really? Hark at the expert.' And with that he stomped out into the garden, leaving me holding the tools.

In Pont d'Achelles, I have just reached the end of the last row of graves and am emptying the grass box on to the disguised roof of our cache when I freeze. A German motorcycle and sidecar has stopped outside the entrance to the cemetery. Motionless, I watch two soldiers with rifles come marching into the graveyard, heading straight for me and the bastion that harbours our cache. Their boots make no sound on the soft grass. Can they hear the thundering of my heart?

Lowering the grass box, I pick up my hoe; scrape at the nearest border as if I am in the middle of weeding it. My shaky blade makes little impression on the dry earth.

The Germans stop. They must be looking at the headstones. A few moments later, they begin to wander towards me. I can feel them watching me. They are scrutinising my work. One of them taps me on the back and I turn around. I feel a sudden chill in my chest. He must know about the cache.

'*Das ist gut, gut,*' he says, smiling at me. I open my mouth, confused.

He points at the graves I have been pretending to weed, and we all gaze at the headstones. Each bears a name, a few numbers and a Maltese cross. Both men remove their forage caps. For the graves belong to a handful of German soldiers who died here after being taken prisoner in 1918. I had almost forgotten they were any different to the rest. My father warned me I would, when he was mowing the grass in Pont d'Achelles on a day just like today and I was sitting atop the pile of soft, warm cuttings in the wheelbarrow. He said that death makes equals of us all.

'Now back to work,' orders the second German, straightening his cap.

After the soldiers have gone, I light a cigarette and lean on the edge of that same wheelbarrow, wondering how much longer my luck can last.

4 June 1941

A few days after my sixteenth birthday, Marcel and I are lying on the grass behind his father's hay barn, gazing up at the vapour trails etching the sky. It is a dazzling afternoon and my legs prickle with sweat. But this itchiness is a small price to pay for the long trousers that my parents are finally allowing me to wear, in place of my horrid knickerbockers. Poor Marcel is still in shorts. This is not his fault. While I spend every day mowing and weeding in my father's cemeteries, he has to sit in front of a blackboard, doing his arithmetic.

I have just been reading to him from *Le Courrier de l'Air,* a leaflet I found in a hedge when I was doing some weeding earlier today. It must have been dropped by the RAF in one of the daylight raids on Lille. According to the leaflet, the Allies are making progress against Hitler in a lot of places we have never heard of. But Hitler, in turn, has now invaded Greece and Yugoslavia. So the war is a spreading bonfire, not one which can easily be put out. This news digested, I smoke a cigarette while we deliberate one of our favourite questions: what would you eat right now, if you could eat anything in the world?

'*Une bonne blanquette de veau,*' Marcel declares, 'with lashings of cream in the sauce. And a huge bowlful of profiteroles, oozing Chantilly cream. And a mug of hot milk on the side. And a croissant to dip in the milk.'

I blow a smoke ring into the air and whistle. 'Right now, I think I would have a big pot of *pâté de lapin* that I could eat with a spoon,' I reply. Marcel laughs. He shakes his fingers as if he has burned them. But I haven't finished yet. 'And shepherd's pie, and a bar of Cadbury's chocolate in a purple wrapper, like the one my grandma once gave me in England. And fish and chips, all salty and greasy, and a steaming great vat of your mother's boeuf bourgignon.'

'She knows how to cook, Maman,' agrees Marcel. 'Or at least she did when we still had some meat in the house. But what about your Aunt Valentine's crêpes? I could eat a dozen of those right now.' He rubs his hollow belly at the thought.

The trouble with this conversation is that it is like scratching an itch. As long as you keep a picture of the food in your mind, you can forget your hunger for a moment. But as soon as you stop concentrating, you feel emptier than ever.

'I want to be a pilot, when I leave school,' says Marcel, changing the subject. 'Just imagine if we were up there now, in a couple of those Spitfires, zooming through the clouds and firing eight Brownings at once.'

'That would be amazing,' I agree, watching the swirling white arabesques above our heads. 'But I'd still rather be a soldier in the British army. Up there, they're killing one Boche at a time, if they're lucky. I want to machine-gun a whole lot of them, all in one go.' I shut one eye and hold up my fists, sweeping a hail of tracer fire across a Fritz-filled trench.

Thinking about the future helps to blot out the present. We know that the war could go either way, and so could our lives. I want to be a soldier, but my mother still wants me to become a butcher. Elizabeth wants to be a hairdresser, but my mother is adamant that she should train to be a teacher. Rosemary is training to be a teacher, but what she really wants is to become the pianist for the Radio Lille concert band. Goodness knows what Kléber will do if he ever grows up.

I am about to ask Marcel if he wants to go and hunt for some frogs to fry. But suddenly there is a drumming roar, louder than anything we have ever heard before, and a fighter plane flashes over our heads at tree-top height. It is so low that I can see the oil stains on its yellow nose cone and pick out the individual rivets on the underside of its wings. There is no mistaking the sinister black markings, either.

'*Merde!*' gasps Marcel, diving for cover.

Two seconds later and the red, white and blue roundels of an RAF fighter streak across our view in another ear-splitting din of over-revved valves and pistons.

'Spitfire!' I yell, as if it were another expletive.

'Hurricane,' corrects Marcel, who knows every plane in the sky. Even I can feel the hairs on my arms stand on end at the sound and fury of these machines, which passed right over our heads, almost low enough for us to feel the heat of their exhausts. We jump to our feet.

'I wonder if he'll get him,' says Marcel, fists clenched. 'I think it's a 109.'

'Of course he will.'

For a few moments both planes, Messerschmitt and Hurricane, are out of sight. And then we hold our breath as first one and then the other reappears, pulling up in an almost vertical climb, machine guns chattering with a sound like tearing fabric. I see one or two fragments fall off the leading plane, but there is no smoke. And now it flicks over, as if attempting to double back on its adversary and catch it from behind. Round and round go both planes, spiralling after each other like Mirza chasing her own tail, so that we cannot tell who is the pursuer and who the pursued.

And then it is all over. We hear the stutter of a faltering engine just to our right. A dark shape is coming down fast in the direction of Ploegsteert, dragging a trail of black smoke behind it. I'm sure I glimpse a flash of yellow, though this may be a trick of the setting sun. In the distance, we see a parachute billow into a tiny white half-moon.

'*Merde.* Is it the Hurricane?' asks Marcel, craning his neck.

'No way,' I reply. I throw my cigarette butt into a bush and grab my bicycle. 'Come on.'

'Where are we going?' For a bright boy, sometimes Marcel can be so dense that you just want to whack him.

'Finders keepers,' I yell over my shoulder. Coming upon abandoned French tanks after the retreat to Dunkirk was exciting enough. But the prospect of being able to pick over the bones of a crashed enemy aircraft promises an even bigger thrill.

Following the aircraft means heading deeper into Belgium, another step closer to Germany. I hesitate at the start of the rue de la Clef d'Hollande, waiting for Marcel to catch up. But instead of braking hard and giving me a lecture about how this is yet another of my very bad ideas, he sails straight on past, spewing machine-gun sound effects at me.

'*Fénien!*' he adds, hurling an insult I usually aim at him.

There is no column of smoke to tell us where the plane has come down. But after cycling for perhaps six or seven minutes, Marcel back-pedals so sharply that his bicycle stops as if he has jammed a stick into the spokes. He points over the low hedge of the potato field on our right. And there, glinting amid the spuds, is our prey.

'*Et voilà,*' he says. 'A fish on a dish.'

A real German fighter plane, right there in front of us, with a gaggle of spectators already ringing the aircraft. Wide-eyed, Marcel and I glance at each other.

'Are you thinking what I'm thinking?' he whispers.

'Marcel, it's way too big to fit in our cache.'

'Come on, *Rosbif,*' he laughs. 'Souvenir time.'

Tucking our bicycles into the hedge, we follow an earthen track towards the aircraft, hands in our pockets, sauntering along as casually as if we are in search of dandelions for salad.

With its undercarriage folded up under the wings, the Messerschmitt looks smaller than I was expecting. But as we come closer, it grows and grows, until it reminds me of a harpooned whale I once saw hauled up on the quay in Calais. Even as I recoil from the menacing crosses and dancing swastika on its tail, I am struck by the beauty of this stricken creature, the curves of its olive-green fuselage still graceful despite being sprayed with mud.

It is riddled with bullet holes. The propeller blades are twisted and bent like the leaves of a withered onion. But the plane is intact. I gaze at the sinister gun muzzles poking out from the leading edges of the wings; at the sleek scoops carved out of the egg-yolk yellow cowling for the cannon. The cockpit is open, and there are tyre marks on the earthen track. The pilot, dead or alive, must already have been driven away.

We stop, perhaps twenty paces from the aircraft. This is when I notice the two grey-green figures among the spectators, each with a sub-machine gun tucked under his arm as casually as a baguette. My mouth goes dry.

'Just look normal,' whispers Marcel. 'We haven't done anything wrong.'

'Not yet,' I murmur. We grin at each other. We will come back, with tools, at first light.

5 June 1941

I cannot sleep. I am too excited about the Messerschmitt; too worried that the Germans will already have taken it away for repair.

Dawn comes as a relief. Shivering in the early morning air, we are overjoyed to discover that our aircraft is still there, its camouflage paint tinged pink by the rising sun. No sign of any Boche, either.

'Bingo,' I whisper, in English.

'*Quoi?*' asks Marcel, behind me.

I chuckle and shake my head. From the leather bag on my handlebars, I pull two screwdrivers, some pliers, a hammer and a hacksaw, all pilfered from my father's tool box at home. And then we are skulking towards the aircraft, and I wonder if Marcel's heart is beating as fast as mine.

We are a pair of urchins about to rob a sweet shop as, side by side, we stand on one of the wing roots, peering into the cockpit.

'How do you open this thing?' I wonder aloud, struggling to prise open the cockpit lid. Someone has shut it since yesterday. But Marcel finds the catch and, with one foot in a stirrup set into the fuselage, he manages to raise the canopy. While I support the Perspex greenhouse with both hands, he climbs over the side of the cockpit and tumbles in. All I can see is a pair of flailing bare legs, like someone doing a handstand in a pond.

And then he reappears, the right way up, wearing a smile I have never seen before. Marcel is lost in another world, as he signals for me to lower the canopy. Through the glass, I can see him waggling the control column, flicking all the switches and twiddling the knurled knob on the gunsight in front of him.

'Souvenirs,' I remind him, lifting the canopy just enough to pass him one of the screwdrivers. But Marcel shakes his head.

'Your turn,' he announces, signalling for me to let him out. For a few seconds we both listen for sounds of vehicles approaching. But it is still only 6 a.m. The Boche will be sleeping off their stolen French wine for a while to come.

When I take my turn in the Messerschmitt, my head spins. The abandoned tanks we found last year felt like coffins with plumbing. But this machine is a fantastical riot of wires and needles and gauges, straight out of Jules Verne. Yes, it smells of oil and leather. But there are other smells, too. Electricity? Boche sweat? Germany?

These Boche pilots must be big brutes, I think to myself. I am tall for my age and even so can barely see over the instrument panel. It doesn't occur to me that the pilot would have a bulky parachute for a seat cushion. Almost without thinking, I jab the button at the top of the control column with my thumb; press the curved lever on its side. A click from the wing roots makes Marcel spin around. I freeze. There must have been a pressure lock in the hydraulic lines. Thankfully, the guns do not fire.

Again I scan the instrument panel. Marcel hands me one of the screwdrivers and, while he works on removing whatever bits and pieces he can from the fuselage, I begin to undo the four brass screws that hold each instrument in place, surprised at how easy they are to extract.

'Still all clear?' I call. I yank the hoses and wires from the back of a pair of instruments.

'*Dépêche-toi!*' urges Marcel, taking the instruments from me. He glances over his shoulder at the earthen track.

Only yesterday, a German pilot was sitting where I am sitting, attempting to shoot British aircraft out of the sky.

Right here, in this seat. Now I just want to smash everything in sight. And with my father's tuppenny hammer, that's exactly what I do: switches, gauges, throttle knobs, radio, warning lights, the lot.

This is fun. I turn to ask Marcel if he is sure he doesn't want to have a pop, but he shakes his head. He looks quite pale.

'Hurry up,' he repeats, more urgently this time. So now I use the pliers to cut any wires I can find, until something catches my attention: a flash of colour amid the grey of the metal cockpit. And there, tucked behind a set of levers which may be for the undercarriage, I am surprised to find a small photograph, little bigger than a postage stamp, of a smiling woman in a yellow dress. I mean to cut this up with the pliers, too. But I have never seen a colour photograph before, and the woman in yellow reminds me of someone. My sister Elizabeth? Whoever it is, she is very pretty, for a German. So I put the photograph back where I found it and attack the gunsight instead. Then I climb out on to the wing and, taking firm hold of one of the screwdrivers, begin to decorate the fuselage. For a moment I hesitate, taking stock of the possibilities. And then I etch a message in large letters down the entire length of the aircraft: '*VIVENT LES AVIATEURS ANGLAIS QUI ONT ABATTU CE SALE BOCHE*'. Which, roughly translated, means 'Long live the English airmen who shot down this filthy Kraut'.

Marcel watches in silence.

'Are you sure that's a good idea?' he asks.

'Of course.' I stare at my handiwork, wishing I had made the letters just a little bit smaller. *I must not act without considering the consequences of my actions upon others.* My father always says that everyone in France has the same handwriting. I hope nobody recognises mine today.

Marcel is now desperate to leave. 'Please, Stéphane,' he begs. 'We've done enough. We have to go.'

But the huge black crosses on the Messerschmitt's wings

are calling to me. How can we leave without such a perfect trophy, to remind us of our kill?

'Come on,' I urge. 'Give me a hand with these rivets.'

'But there are hundreds of them.'

'Not scared, are you?'

Marcel purses his lips. I can see how badly he wants to be brave.

'We'll be twice as fast if we work together,' I tell him.

He turns and stares hard at the road, and we both listen again.

The silence is chilling: a cold breeze is getting up, and even the birds have stopped singing.

Together, we kneel on the wing and start sawing and hammering away at the rivets as fast as we can.

'This is crazy,' grunts Marcel, glancing over his shoulder at the road. 'Come on, Stéphane, let's leave it now.'

'We'll get there. Look, there's another rivet gone. Just give it a little longer.'

But Marcel has a point. The wing does not want to come apart.

All the time, the sun is rising higher in the sky.

'Stéphane, please.' I can hear the tension in his voice. 'We have to go.'

'Just keep at it.' Head down, Marcel does not reply.

Now the wind is beginning to whip around us, whispering in the potato plants. We're just a couple of boys. Hunting for souvenirs is hardly the worst crime in the world, I tell myself, as I fumble with the rivets.

My screwdriver slips, gashing the soft flesh between my finger and thumb. A dark red droplet falls on to the white outline of the black cross.

'Where the hell are we going to put this thing, even if we do manage to get it off?' demands Marcel, scanning the road again.

'I don't know,' I reply, sucking my hand. 'Piss on it?'

'*Merde*,' he hisses, leaping to his feet.

My skin prickles. Someone is coming. Out of nowhere, a black staff car has appeared. It comes bumping on to the far end of the earthen track, no more than 200 metres away.

We slide to the ground. The ominous shape purrs slowly towards us. With the sun glinting on its windscreen, we cannot see how many people are inside.

'Marcel, I'm so sorry,' I whisper.

'Me, too.'

A huge grey lorry, belching smoke, rumbles in the staff car's wake. Too late now to run away.

All we can do is drop our tools, without a word between us, and walk into the wind, towards the advancing vehicles.

Sick as I feel, I still cannot bring myself to leave our precious souvenirs. Instead, I sling the leather bag over my shoulder. I have seen my dad do the same thing a thousand times, with his sandwiches and flask of tea.

We walk straight ahead, two boys out for an early morning stroll.

Less than fifty metres away, our adversary is still approaching like a knight at a joust; lance and visor lowered, pennants fluttering, proud hooves stamping the earth.

Don't look at him, I tell myself. Pretend you're just out picking dandelions.

Now the staff car is upon us. I can hear its tyres crunching; the flapping of its swastika pennants in the breeze.

A glimpse of grey uniforms and pale faces as we draw alongside.

And then it is behind us. The black knight has missed. My heart soars. It is typical Grady luck. We are in the clear.

At the end of the track, we calmly climb on to our bicycles. And then we are pedalling away, cycling for our lives: a pair of child outlaws, too quick for grown-ups to chase. Dizzy with excitement, I glance over my shoulder at the Germans, wishing I could see their sick faces when they discover my handiwork and laughing aloud at the thought. We did it, Marcel. The French and the English beat the dirty Boche.

But the laughter catches in my throat.

With a sinking heart, I watch the staff car describe a graceful semicircle, its tyres kicking up a flurry of dust. The black knight is wheeling for a second pass.

Marcel is pedalling like fun just ahead of me, his blond hair flying in the breeze. He has no idea.

I long for him to be spared. I want to turn back the clock. Or at least stop it, right now. But the hands are spinning too fast.

My lungs are bursting. My legs are on fire. Behind us, the staff car is accelerating hard.

A swish of tyres as it passes. Don't look up. They're not interested in us, after all.

Across the flat landscape, the tall spikes of the church spires stand like bayonets stabbing the sky.

Ahead of us, in a cloud of brown smoke, the car screeches to a standstill. All four doors open and four soldiers, each about eight feet tall, jump out.

'*Halt!*' snaps a voice like a gunshot. Another, deeper voice starts barking at us. I haven't a clue what the words mean, but it doesn't sound complimentary.

Grey-green giants, advancing upon us.

Suddenly the first giant pulls out a shiny black pistol, his hand shaking with rage.

I am shaking, too. Still astride my bicycle, I put my hands in the air, hoping they do not notice them trembling.

I need to hide my bag.

Marcel is breathing hard beside me. We both stand as still as we can.

'*Là! Là!*' the man barks, waving his gun at the ditch beside the road. While the others wear helmets like coal scuttles, he has a stiff-peaked officer's cap, with a bull's-eye cockade on the front. '*Sie gehen là.*'

So this is it. Dropping our bicycles, we stand side by side, staring into the ditch.

'*Nein, non, tournez, tournez.*'

Mechanically, we turn around to face the officer with the gun. How shiny his boots are. My head throbs with the force of the blood pumping round my body.

Another shout, and one of the soldiers hurries forward; rips the bag from my shoulder. I hope this is just a precaution, in case I am armed. If they open the bag now, we really are dead. And not only Marcel and me: they will come for our families, too. My father drummed this into me years ago: the Fritz always make you pay compound interest.

The soldier glances at my bag.

He hands it to the officer, who sniffs it and frowns.

A metallic eagle glints; a scarlet ribbon blazes against the drab grey-green of his jacket. He looks bored with the bag; is about to drop it on the ground at his feet. Then he changes his mind and pretends to toss it into the ditch. Without a shred of amusement, he grins.

He flicks at the clasp.

Everyone stands very still.

He is opening the bag.

A gust of wind blows up, making us squint against the dust. When it dies down, the German officer steps forward, very slowly and deliberately, and tips out the contents at our feet.

We all just stand there, gazing down at the objects glinting in the early morning light.

A single word forms in my head: Mummy.

Two sharp clicks from the direction of the car announce that the soldiers have cocked their machine guns.

This breeze on my face. Marcel, I'm so sorry. This sunshine.

'*Was ist das?*' murmurs the officer, pressing his nose almost against mine. His face is waxy and clean-shaven, but the stench of his breath is overpowering, as if he has been eating rotting flesh. So this is what a Kraut smells like, I think to myself. And then he whispers the same thing very slowly again, straight into my ear: '*Was . . . ist . . . das?*'

I have no idea what the words mean, let alone how to reply. So I just pull a stupid grin and shrug, as if I am up in front of old Ruckebusch again.

Something goes bang in my ear and I tumble to the ground. Dazed and squinting, I can just make out two blurry, ghoulish versions of myself, inches from my nose, reflected in the polished toes of the brute's boots.

Then his legs flex as if he is about to jump on me, and there is a sharp crack followed by a groan as he thumps Marcel, too.

The shiny boots retreat. Beside me, I can hear Marcel gulping back his tears. And then all four giants advance upon us.

'*Levez-vous*,' barks the deeper voice I heard earlier, in heavily accented French. 'Stupid children, you will suffer for this.'

We stagger to our feet. Deep-set eyes shadowed by the brim of a dark green helmet. The soldier doesn't seem to have any lips. Just yellow teeth set into a scowl; rocks in a cave. He grabs us both by our shirt collars and twists his fists, so that the fabric half-throttles us. 'To sabotage an aircraft of the Reich is a very grave offence.'

Is that what we have done, then: sabotage? Unable to breathe, my vision beginning to blur, I am aware that the German is still talking to us, but the words he is uttering belong to someone else's life.

I try not to flinch when he hits me, but he uses the back of his hand and is wearing a heavy gold ring. A stinging taste of salt in my mouth.

The German is rubbing the back of his hand. I spit a warm gobbet of blood into the ditch; check my teeth with my tongue; feel one of the molars wobble.

Next they bundle us into the staff car and drive us back into the field. We wait while the Messerschmitt's wings are removed and the fuselage is winched on to the back of the recovery lorry. Under guard in the car's hushed interior, I gaze at the cushioned leather seats; at the thick grey carpet beneath our feet. A dull ache throbs in my jaw. I try to catch Marcel's eye. Puffy-faced and bloodshot, he just keeps staring at the floor.

Perhaps an hour later, we are told to climb up into the back of the lorry and are driven towards Nieppe. I think I am going to be sick. Our bikes have been lobbed in with us and a helmeted hulk sits facing us, his finger hooked around the trigger of a machine gun, as we sit with our shoulders juddering against the lorry's steel side. We stop in the red-brick main square, between the church and the *mairie*. The minutes tick by.

I know this part of town backwards, but today it looks all new to me. The hulk with the gun tuts as I twist left and right, desperate to catch sight of anyone I know. It is past breakfast time. Our parents will be wondering where we are. Yet despite the sunshine, the streets are even more deserted than usual. The Germans have that effect on people: wear the right uniform, do the right march, and you can make an entire community vanish in seconds. It works even better than letting off a stink bomb at a party. The only person I recognise is beastly old Faure, mincing along the pavement in his best suit, begging to have his shutters pelted with mud balls yet again.

Suddenly I flinch. *Nom de Dieu*. My copy of *Le Courrier de l'Air* is still folded up in my trouser pocket. That scrap of RAF paper alone is worth a prison sentence. Add it to a charge of sabotage and it will be a blindfold at dawn.

I look at the guard and force a smile. Narrowing his eyes, he stares back at me.

Whistling tunelessly, I slip my hand into my right pocket, empty apart from my tobacco pouch. I stare up at the spire of the church; clench my hidden fist; pull my hand out of my pocket.

The German picks his nose.

I repeat this movement again and again, as if it is a nervous tic. Still no reaction. So then I swap hands, feel for the leaflet in my left pocket and, squeeze by silent squeeze, crumple it into a tight ball.

To our right, two old nuns waddle out of the church, heading in the direction of the *mairie*.

'Madeleine's looking very pretty today,' I say to Marcel, pointing at the nuns and hoping that our guard knows enough French to understand. The dozy Kraut leans forward to see what I am pointing at. I flick the ball of paper over my other shoulder. The sound it makes when it lands on the cobbles seems to echo around the square. But the German is too busy growling at me to notice.

By now the nausea has worn off and I am very hungry. Not just the normal, gnawing hunger, but a yawning, awful emptiness that makes me feel as if I am hollow as a drum, and that the drum is filled with clawing rats, and the rats are clamouring to be fed. I am also dying for a smoke; my lungs feel hollow, too.

At last the other soldiers return to the lorry from their office at the back of the church. Probably they have been drinking coffee and eating confiscated pastries in there. At least now that their bellies are full, they will drive us home to the rue du Sac. But no: the lorry continues along the long, straight road from Nieppe into Armentières, where all the brick buildings are the colour of fresh offal. Here, we pull into the yard of a requisitioned house with a swastika pinned roughly above the gateway, and Marcel and I are made to stand to attention beside the lorry. Our guard is replaced by a younger and scrawnier version of himself, whose helmet looks several sizes too big for him. He draws up a wooden chair, flips it round and sits astride it, his machine gun pointing straight at us.

It must be mid-afternoon by the time a fat little Boche officer with close-cropped blond hair, balding on top, comes out to us. He looks like the sinister German cousin of the Three Little Pigs. After exchanging a few words with our guard, he inspects the wingless aircraft on the lorry.

Now Herr Piglet goes completely berserk. I have never seen anything like it, especially from a soldier in uniform. Spinning on his heels, he starts to kick and punch and scream at us, blurting over and over again: 'You have written "Dirty Boche" . . .That is not kind!'

Even as I am doing my best to protect my head from his fists, I can't help laughing at how ridiculous he sounds. And then he stops beating us and delivers the sucker punch: 'For this you will be sent to a disciplinary camp in the Fatherland, where you will learn to respect the German army.'

I stand very still. I am conscious that people have started to disappear from Nieppe, though no one ever mentions them. Are we about to disappear, too? Just to remind me how stupid I have been, he repeats his favourite phrase, in his comedy accent: '*Vous avez écrit "Sale Boche"* . . . *C'est pas gentil, ça!*'

I want to tell him that it was I, not Marcel, who wrote that slogan. But the words will not come.

Soon we are in yet another staff car, bouncing along the pot-holed road towards Lille. I just hope we don't turn off the main road, into the forest.

'Where now?' whispers Marcel beside me.

'Silence,' barks the guard in the front seat, shaking the barrel of his pistol at us. I wobble my loose tooth with my tongue. It isn't ready to come out yet.

I am a caged beast as I peer out at the countryside, and at the people on the city pavements. If only one of them, just one, would catch my eye. But nobody looks up as we pass. The war has done this to France, I reflect. The less you know the better. So do not look. Do not listen. Vanish into your private world, where it is cold and dark and secure as a prison. Stay alive, say your prayers, and perhaps the angel of death will pass you by or will hit some other unlucky soul, such as that hollow-eyed boy peering out of the back window of that German car.

I wonder if Marcel is as hungry as I am. He and I have

still spoken barely a word to each other since our arrest, except for a whispered '*Ça va? Ça va*' to check we are both in one piece. But his presence gives me strength. I know that as long as we are together, we will be all right. We will find a way out in the end.

'*Blanquette de veau*,' I whisper, under my breath.

'Fish and chips,' he mouths, in English. But the joke doesn't seem funny any more.

5 June 1941

The car comes to a halt in the boulevard de la Liberté. We are met by guards of the *Feldgendarmerie*, or German police, and a deeply unsettling silence.

I am grateful not to be hit again. But at least when people are whacking you about the head, you know you're still alive. You feel that a bell will ring and the round will end. Whereas the bottomless silence in this place, where I cannot even hear the ticking of a clock, unnerves me. I wonder if I will ever see my family again.

We are led into a stuffy white room. The walls are bare save for a large RAUCHEN VERBOTEN – DÉFENSE DE FUMER notice. And a surprise is waiting for us: fellow human beings.

Pitiful as they look, it is hard to describe what a relief it is to see these two French civilians. One of them is a young man, a few years older than us, who says he is accused of spitting on the German flag. I don't need to ask how he came by his black eye. The other is a middle-aged woman in a floral print dress, sobbing into a handkerchief. She says they kicked her in the stomach, but it is her heart that she is clutching. Wringing her hands, she tells us she is accused of tearing a German poster from a wall.

'It was a list of names, of men they want to catch. It promised a reward if anyone would denounce them,' she explains. Now that I look at her, I see that she cannot be more than twenty-five. Her face is lit from within, with full lips and skin as smooth as fruit.

'It was brave of you to tear it down,' I reply, very quietly.

'It wasn't brave.' She shakes her head; looks up at me with her dark, dark eyes. 'One of the men on that list was my father.'

'Do the Germans know that?' I glance at the young man. He could be here to denounce us. The woman shakes her head.

'Tell no one,' I whisper. 'It will be better for you that way.'

'And you?' she asks. To my surprise, she reaches out and takes my hand. 'You're just a boy. What are you supposed to have done?'

I look at Marcel and then at the woman.

'We've done nothing,' I shrug, pulling away my hand. 'We just picked up a couple of souvenirs that had fallen out of the sky.'

It is growing dark by the time a soldier unlocks the door of the room.

'Grady, Stefan. *Komm*.'

With a quick glance at the others, I stand up and follow him. I am expecting an interrogation. Instead, he marches me out to a dank courtyard at the back of the building.

'*Attend ici*,' he tells me. Then he disappears.

I stand shivering in the silence, and wait. Is this how the Christians in the Colosseum felt, just before the lions were released? I am dying to relieve myself in the corner of the courtyard but fear for what may happen if I do.

Thankfully I resist, for a tall German officer strides into the yard, looks me up and down and gives me a mighty mule kick in the leg. I gasp at the lightning bolt of pain that shoots right up into my spine. Next he starts shouting at me in bad French, and pummelling me about the ears with his fists. I feel a sinking sense of déjà vu, only this time I am facing not a piglet, but a wolf. And this time, I am alone.

'Don't run away from me, you little French bastard. I'm here to teach you a lesson. You understand?'

Running and hobbling, lolloping and jinking, I do my best to evade him. The courtyard is a jumble of damp firewood, old fencing and other junk, so there are places I can hide for a few moments, while the stomping of his boots echoes off the walls, making it seem as if he is in three places at once. At last I chance upon the narrow entrance to a coal hole and manage to conceal myself inside. I almost think the Big Bad Wolf has given up on me. But the shouting starts up again a few minutes later and I hear poor Marcel cry out: he is now receiving his share of attention.

Hours later, we are both taken to a cell that smells of sour mushrooms and are locked inside it, in the dark, for the night. No food, no water, nowhere to relieve ourselves.

'Do you think we'll get out of here alive?' whispers Marcel. Feeling our way around the damp floor of the cell, we have found a pair of straw mattresses upon which we lie, staring up into the darkness.

'Of course we will.' I cross my fingers. 'They just want to frighten us, that's all.'

We consider this for a while. If they search my house, they will find my father hiding upstairs. I have a pistol tucked under the eaves above my bed. In the Lombard barn, there are all the rifles and ammo we have stuffed beneath the hay. The discovery of any one of these will mean a bullet for us all. I wish to God we could warn them; pray that my father is away at the safe house in Bailleul where he sometimes sleeps.

'We need to get our story straight,' says Marcel.

'They're bound to interrogate us separately,' I nod, in the darkness.

'*Tout à fait.* So here it is: we went to see the Messerschmitt on the day of the crash, and came back a day later to hunt for the odd souvenir. But the plane had already been smashed up by someone else. It was they who must have scrawled that hateful slogan.'

'That vile graffiti.'

'That noxious slander, which was there when we arrived.'

For a few moments, as I weigh up this version of our crime,

I feel almost cheerful. And then I shiver. In the silence, I could swear I just heard a woman scream.

'Did you hear that?' I ask.

'Hear what?'

'Nothing.'

'Did you hear something?' Marcel sits up on his mattress, listening.

'No, no. I don't think so. How are you feeling?' I ask him.

'I feel,' he intones, 'as if this is the worst day of my life.'

'Snap.'

'I'm just so glad you're here, Stéphane.'

'I wish you weren't. If I hadn't insisted on trying to get that bloody cross . . .'

'You never listen to me, do you?'

'I'm sorry, Marcel. I'm so, so sorry.'

'I know. And now we're here. And at least things can't get any worse. I know it's ridiculous, but I just keep thinking there's going to be a knock on the door, any minute now, and my parents will be there, waiting for us. They'll explain to the Germans that there's been a mix-up and scoop us up, and we'll all go back to Nieppe together on the tram.'

I fall silent, suddenly wishing that Marcel's parents were mine, too. His mum and dad seem so glad to be alive. The only way my father can help me now is by staying away. And all my mother can do, all my mother has ever done, is pray.

And then I feel ashamed for having these thoughts and, as I think about how much I love and miss my brave, hopeless parents, who have struggled so hard to bring up their ungrateful, wayward son, I can hold the tears back no longer. Mouth open, eyes closed, I begin silently to weep. Perhaps Marcel hears me, because before long he is crying, too. It has been such a long, long day.

Please, Lord Jesus, deliver Marcel Lombard and me from this abyss into which we have slipped.

Forgive us our trespasses, as we forgive those who trespass against us.

My mother (who was French) standing second from right, with
Auntie Val (fourth from left) and her team of paperboys who delivered
English newspapers into the trenches during the First World War.

My parents on their wedding day in 1918.

Ramsgate, with Dad and Rosemary (right) in the 1920s.

My grandmother
(Mémère) with Rosemary,
me, Francis – known as
Kléber – and Elizabeth.

Belgian refugees fleeing the German Blitzkrieg in 1940. I remember them pushing carts and prams laden with their possessions.

Captured French and British soldiers in June 1940. In stifling heat, the columns filed past the end of our street. Local people brought water in buckets for them, but the Germans kicked them aside.

When Marcel and I were sent to Loos Prison after the Germans caught us taking souvenirs from a crashed Messerschmitt, I made these drawings from memory, to take my mind off the tension and terror in cell 54. The top one is of our house in the rue du Sac (second from right); beneath it is the Lombard farm.

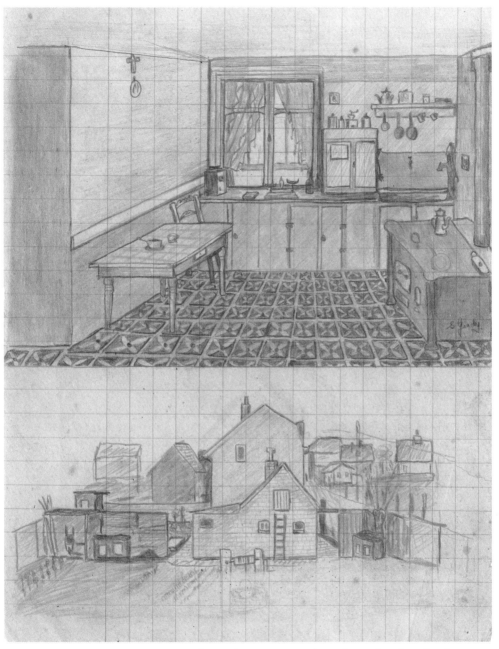

Drawn in prison in 1941, this is how I remembered our kitchen in the rue du Sac. Note the coffee grinder on the cupboard beside the window. I still use it, even now, in Greece. The second picture is of the back of the Riouals' house, seen from Pont d'Achelles.

Aged fourteen, Eton Memorial School, Ypres.

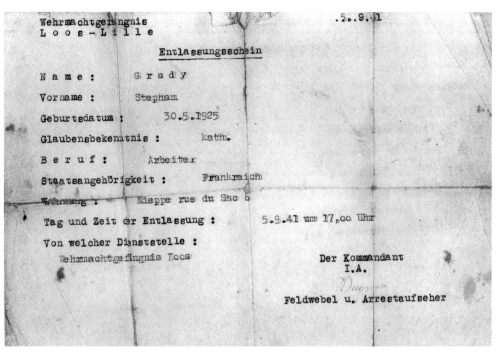

My precious discharge slip from Loos Prison. When it was first handed to me by a German officer, I had no idea what it meant.

The Pont d'Achelles cemetery. We hid our cache of weapons under the left bastion (arrowed).

My Resistance identity card, issued in the crazy belief that the Germans might treat us better if we could claim to be soldiers of a secret army, rather than civilians, when captured. This one even gives away my code name: Iroquois.

Captain Michael Trotobas of the SOE, known to us as Capitaine Michel. Trotobas was an inspirational leader, brilliant saboteur and the bravest man I ever knew. Although his name was put forward for a posthumous Victoria Cross, without the presence of a senior officer to witness his valour, the award was refused.

The Germans buried Capitaine Michel in an unmarked grave, but the Resistance discovered what had happened, dug up his body and reburied him. This monument in Lille is dedicated to his memory.

Except the Boche, obviously.
And deliver us from evil, Amen.
Suddenly there is a loud knock at the door.
We both sit bolt upright in the darkness.
'Papa?' says Marcel.
'Who's there?' I shout.
'Papa, is it you?'
A burst of gruff laughter outside the door; booted foot-
steps, creaking away.

6 June 1941

In the morning, we are given permission to use the lavatory and interrogated separately. With two armed soldiers standing behind me, I am questioned by a young German in a smart civilian suit. The man is almost polite as he sits in the pool of light thrown by a grey gooseneck lamp on the desk beside him. He allows me to smoke a cigarette and even addresses me as *vous,* not *tu,* as if I am a grown-up. He asks me where I live and what I have to say for myself, and accompanies my replies with the clacking of his typewriter. I notice that he mouths words in German as I speak. Then he hands me a gold pen and tells me to sign at the bottom of the sheet. I have no idea what he has typed. It is all in German. It could be anything.

The man leans back in his chair. I hesitate. Behind me, one of the guards nudges me with his rifle. And, in a shaky hand, I sign with the heavy pen.

Later, we are taken under guard to yet another small courtyard and ordered into the back of a van. I register the musky smell, the matted straw. This thing is meant for transporting condemned sheep to the abattoir.

I wonder if I look as rough as Marcel. One of his eyes is closed up, grey and swollen as a poached egg. His skin, red in places, suddenly seems a size too big for him. If it were not for his famous corduroy shorts, I don't think I would recognise him.

'*Ça va?*' I croak. We have been given no water since yesterday morning.

He twitches. '*Toi?*'

'We've survived, haven't we?' I smile; try to sound cheery.

'I wish we knew where they are taking us next.'

'I've always wanted a guided tour of Germany.'

'Are they allowed to . . . ?' Marcel's eyes widen. 'Aren't we too young for that?'

'They can do what they want, Marcel. Either way, we're *foutus*.'

My friend closes his eyes. A stocky German officer with a clipboard marches up and padlocks the doors of the van from the outside.

'Let's hope this thing doesn't end up in the river,' I mutter.

'If so, I'll drink it dry.'

The officer stops, his head just a few inches from us. I hold my breath. His hair is so severely cropped above his ears that he must have had it newly shaved this morning. I see a muscle flicker in his jaw; notice a shiny pink imprint on his nose, as if he usually wears spectacles. Thank goodness for these metal bars. I am not in the mood for being smacked again.

'*Vous zwei*: Grady, Lombard.' I am by now getting used to this bastardised argot, half-German, half-French. He neither looks at us, nor raises an eyebrow at my English-sounding name. 'You are to be taken to . . .' There is a long pause, as he holds his clipboard at arm's length. Marcel and I stare at each other, braced for the axe to fall. 'One moment. *Ja, ja, das ist gut.*' He nods cheerfully, as if he has just tasted an excellent wine and wants the waiter to fill his glass to the brim. 'We take you to the prison at Loos. For a time indefinite.'

'*Quoi?*' gasps Marcel, turning to stare at me.

'Loos Prison,' repeats the German, smacking his lips. It really is so delicious, this wine. 'You know the place?' He grins, exposing white teeth, perfect as a military cemetery. 'I hear it is *excellent*, if you happen to like rats and homos and misery. Should be fun for you lads, *nein?*' He leers at me. 'Especially you, pretty boy.'

I have no idea what he means. Besides, my head is

swimming. If the officer could just find his spectacles? I remember hearing about Loos Prison before the war. It had a reputation as a disease-ridden cesspool, where the murderers and debtors of the city were left to rot to death, if they hadn't killed each other first. Whereas we are just a couple of country boys who scrawled a silly message on a plane.

I can feel the German officer interrogating us with narrowed eyes. I put my head in my hands. And now the soldier's voice softens. 'You boys are young for Loos. But there's nowhere else. Why were you arrested, anyway?'

Sensing a chink of hope, we pour out our story once again. It wasn't sabotage, we plead, it was just beachcombing without a beach. Perhaps we may yet be spared, if this German takes pity on us. But then we hear approaching footsteps, and he silences us with a sweep of his clipboard.

'Everybody denies having done anything, but it doesn't make any difference,' he snaps, raising his voice. 'Sabotage is a very grave offence and, even if you happen to be innocent, you must pay on behalf of those who are guilty.' With the palm of his hand, he brushes at the shoulders of his tunic, before adding more quietly: 'Someone always must pay: this is only fair, *nein*?'

Then he raps on the side of the van and we swing out of the courtyard gate.

The journey to the prison may be short or long. I cannot tell. I am in a daze; a kind of dream. Marcel and I do not speak. What is there to say? I was so happy to be alive, once. And now it is finished. I try not to think about whether I will ever see my family again. The sunlight hurts the backs of my eyes as it flashes through the bars of the van.

Are we invisible? People in the street turn away as we pass. But just once, when we pause in a narrow lane, a woman in a ragged black dress is standing there on the pavement and she looks straight at me. I try to smile, because she looks so bereft. But she puts her hand over her mouth, as if she has seen a ghost.

And then everything goes dark. Loos Prison towers above us, its sinister black walls crested with a froth of barbed wire. I feel as if we are about to be swallowed by a monster.

An enormous searchlight above a forbidding steel gate. Cold eyes peering at us from beneath metal hats. I squint back up the road behind us. There is my past, where the green grass grows between the graves and there is mist at dawn in the rue du Sac. There is where my mother used to hold my hand against her cheek beside the stove, and my sisters pulled my hair until I yelled, and my father sang the old songs from a war that was meant to make the world a better place.

I take my last, desperate gaze at the scrubby grass, at the childhood which now lies in tatters at my back. I contemplate the iron gate before me. And my shoulders slump. Old Ruckebusch always said that my silly pranks would end in grief.

Outside the van, muttered exchanges appraise the meat inside. Marcel glances across at me with his one good eye. The gate swings open. The temperature drops by several degrees. And the darkness swallows us up.

Corridors, dank and clanking, and a stench that stings my eyes. Nothing I have ever smelled before in my life – not the rotting carcase of a flystruck sheep, or even the reek of the earth closet in high summer – has prepared me for this savage prison stink. The only thing that comes close to it was the smell of my English school in Ramsgate.

Honest odours of excrement or putrefaction I could bear, but here in Loos the air hangs heavy with the whiff of some sulphurous disinfectant that may be intended to mask the infernal pong, but somehow merely amplifies it, like a band playing at a feast and making all the guests shout louder. As we stand to attention in a dripping corridor, I can feel myself inhaling grey-green pestilence, more like soup than air.

Someone prods me in the back with his rifle and marches

us down yet another echoing corridor, until we arrive in a large circular hall with grey doorways all around it. Above us, on either side of the main hall, I am dimly aware of two wings of cells, each on three or four storeys, accessed by metal gantries.

Before the war, people said that you could hear the groaning of the prisoners of Loos from the centre of Lille, if the wind was in the right direction. But today, inside, all I can hear is the sound of muffled typing and, from time to time, boots clanging on the staircases. I am still clinging to the hope that our presence here is a clerical error. So it comes as a blow, when we are ushered through one of the grey doorways, to discover that an officer and his two armed flunkies have been expecting us.

'Grady, S?'

'*Oui.*'

'Lombard, M?'

'*Oui.*'

'I need to see your identity cards. You will empty your pockets and stand on the red line.' The man's voice hacks into the silence like a stone-chisel. 'Noses against the wall.'

I stand outside my body; watch myself placing my cigarette machine and tobacco on a scrubbed wooden table, along with my creased identity card. I see myself press my nose against the wall and the dream darkens. There is too much detail. A tiny spider, as small as a pinhead, abseils down a silken thread. I peer at the greasy smudges on the whitewash behind it. Other noses, I can see, have been squashed here before mine.

Now the officer is unfolding our cards. I swallow. Hold my breath. Pray. There is a long silence before he speaks.

'*Kourk, bitte.*'

A guard stomps up and frisks me from behind. He growls as he does so, mouthing German in an excited whisper. Even through the prison stench, I can smell garlic sausage on his breath as he forces his hands into my pockets and inside my clothing, seeking out secrets. I grit my teeth. Thank God I lost that RAF leaflet. Laughter from the other side of the room and a sharp command in German suddenly bring Kourk up short.

'I do believe our Kourk likes you, Grady,' hacks the stone-chisel, in French. And then it barks something in German and Kourk growls a monosyllabic response. '*Ja, ja,*' he cackles. 'Now, what Corporal Kourk wants to know is, do you have a sister?'

My blood is ice in my veins. To lie or tell the truth? Whatever I say may put Rosemary and Elizabeth at risk.

'I had a sister once,' I say at last, as coldly as I can muster. I picture my family sitting down for lunch in the rue du Sac, and an empty place at the table. I imagine helmeted soldiers, hammering on the front door. I see my sisters being dragged away.

Deep in the fuse box of my brain, I feel a switch flick. My thirst evaporates; my hunger melts. And for the first time, I feel not fear or self-pity at my own fate, but a white-hot wave of searing indignation, a fury of furies, that anyone, that any blasted Boche or Schleu or Fritz or Kraut, with their smirks and their eagle and their rifles, should think they have a right to affront my family.

'*Eine Schwester?*' grunts Kourk, peering hopefully at his superior.

'*Nein,*' comes the staccato reply. '*Keine Schwester.*'

Out of the corner of my eye I can see Marcel, leaning his nose against the wall. Another guard grabs him by the collar, giving the fabric a fierce twist as he forces his face into the wall. Marcel gasps and his ears turn as red as stop signs.

'*Was ist das?*' shouts the guard, waving a tiny book in front of him. Incensed, he holds it between finger and thumb as if he has pulled it, dripping, from a latrine. My heart sinks. I recognise the little green French–English dictionary with which Marcel likes to settle our frequent arguments over vocab.

My friend shuts his eyes.

'What you are wanting with this?' chips the stone-chisel, leaping in. 'Why you are needing to know Englisch?' For a moment the typewriters stop, and the guard eases his grip on Marcel's collar as we all wait to hear what he will say.

'It is for my English lessons at school,' he replies, in a clear voice.

'English is only used by spies and terrorists. Which are you, boy?'

'I am nothing,' says Marcel, more quietly now. At this, the stone-chisel mutters something and the guard gives Marcel a clout on the side of the head. Behind us, the tall black type-writers resume their rattled attack.

I must not be separated from Marcel. He is my ally, my sanity, my hope. He is also my only point of contact with the life I have left behind; the only one who knows I am here at all. But I am told to pick up one of the beaten-up mess tins stacked in the corner, and the two guards begin to march me towards the door.

The treads of the iron staircase resound like bells as we march up. I am about to ask about using a lavatory, but think better of it. At the top, Kourk jangles a bunch of keys; rattles metal in the lock of a door marked 54. His shaved head is covered in scabs and I can see the blue-black inking of a tattoo on the back of his beefy neck. Then he swings open the heavy metal door. A fug of fetid air envelops me, and he gestures with his boot for me to go in.

I hesitate, for the starkly lit box is already full. A cell that must be meant for just one prisoner, with a single bed folded against the wall, has three scarecrows slouched on its stone floor. Pale and gaunt, they do not look overjoyed to see me. But Kourk jabs me in the back and I am in.

There is a bang; a rattle; white silence. I wait, gazing at the lavatory at the far end of the cell. The scarecrows wait, too. I can feel them staring up at me, mouths open, as if I belong to some exotic species they have never seen before.

'*Bonjour, messieurs,*' I say at last. '*Je m'appelle Grady. Stéphane Grady.*'

Another silence.

'*Bienvenu, Grady,*' says one of the shrivelled bodies at last, leaning forward to shake my hand with his bony fingers. 'Welcome, on behalf of the Green Vermin, to Club 54. You're the last one in, so you'll sleep on the floor. And you'll be the last to put your mess tin on the trap.'

'*Merci bien, monsieur,*' I reply, confused. '*Et vous êtes . . .*'

The man's brief speech must have exhausted him, for it is a while before he speaks again. 'I'm Steen. Or at least I was once. And we all call each other *tu* around here, even if we are twice your age. How old are you, anyway? You don't look much more than twenty-one.'

'I just turned sixteen.' I am still standing; still dying to relieve my aching bladder.

'Christ,' he says, in a whisper. 'My son is your age. And I wouldn't want to see him in here. What did you do, kill someone?'

'They caught me nicking some souvenirs from a crashed fighter.'

The other two men nod. I wait until Steen speaks again. He is Belgian, he says, arrested for trafficking with German soldiers. He introduces me to Ragondin, a twitchy lizard of a man, who is supposed to have tried to bribe an SS officer with black market cognac. This is what defines us now: not the family to which we once belonged, or the street where we used to live, but what we have or have not done to the Boche. I am tempted to mention the slogan I scrawled, but something holds me back.

Ragondin never looks me in the eye. Instead, he sits with his arms folded, tilting his head from side to side. Blonduc, a factory worker who has been caught siphoning diesel out of an army truck, seems friendly enough. Yet he has a heaviness about him that soon becomes tiresome. When he speaks, I notice that the others mostly ignore him. After a few minutes of listening to his maunderings about how cruelly the world has treated him, I too find myself longing for him to shut up.

My first impression is that they are all old friends, that I am a child intruding upon their grown-up clique. And so, making myself as small and invisible as I can, I tuck myself into the far corner of the cell, beside the lavatory, and pretend that I am not here at all. If I concentrate hard enough, I find that I can make some of the smells and the fear go away.

And then I open my eyes again, and the cell and its occupants are all still here, only a little less welcoming than before. I peer at the stark walls, at the small window far above me, through which filters a shaft of watery daylight from which all goodness and hope have been squeezed, at the folding bed which, Steen warns, belongs to him. To my right is a chipped washbasin and, at the other end, the door, with its spyhole and trap. This trap door must be where our food will appear. Food: I have had no scrap to eat for two whole days and I am shivering in the humid cell. Yet, judging from the sunken cheeks and soap-like pallor of my cell mates, I cannot expect a banquet any time soon.

I need to pee right now. Yet there is no way I am going to with all these strangers scrutinising me. Lining up in front of a hedge or a steel *pissoir* with a bunch of friends is one thing. A solo performance before a silent audience is something else. I don't want them appraising the length of my tackle, the colour of my urine and the drumming it makes in the jakes. No, I will hang on somehow until they are asleep. As for doing that other bodily function in public, it is quite impossible to contemplate.

I wonder what time it is. And then, as if in answer to my question, a distant church clock strikes four.

'Three o'clock,' mutters Ragondin, eyes closed, head still tick-tocking from side to side.

'It's four o'clock,' corrects Steen.

'I swear to you, I heard three chimes.'

'You can swear all you like. It's still four o'clock.'

'I heard the clock strike four, too,' I say, quietly.

'Shut your trap, pipsqueak,' snarls Ragondin. 'Nobody asked you.'

'What the hell does it matter what time it is, anyway?' drones Blonduc. 'We have nothing to live for. And each hour that passes only brings us another hour closer to our deaths.'

'Thank you, Captain Philosophe,' retorts Ragondin. 'Give the man a medal for insight. Anyway, I need a slash. Look away now, pipsqueak. I don't want to splash your ugly mug.'

Ragondin stands for what seems like an hour, waiting for something to come out.

'Has it got stuck?' asks Steen.

'*Ta gueule*,' replies Ragondin. And then he lets out a sigh and I try not to listen to the torrent thundering into the bowl. 'That's better,' he says at last, buttoning his fly. 'I didn't get you, did I, pipsqueak?'

I shake my head.

'That's a pity,' he shrugs.

Rising to my feet, I take a deep breath. It is now or never; do or die. 'Do you mind if I use the lavatory now, please?'

All three men stare back at me, mouths agape. And then, one by one, their surprised faces crease into grins. Then the grins become giggles, and soon they are slapping each other on the back and cackling and hooting as if they have just heard the funniest joke in France. A sharp clang on the door silences them.

'Why was that funny?' I murmur, when the danger has passed.

'I'm sorry, Grady, it wasn't,' replies Steen, wiping his eyes with the back of his hand. 'It's just that, in this shithole, the silliest things can set you off. Now go on, do use the jakes.'

'I don't need to any more.'

'Oh, go on,' he urges. 'We won't watch.'

'Or listen,' adds Ragondin.

'I'm going to hold my nose,' says Blonduc, sounding almost cheerful. 'Just in case.'

With teeth clenched and one hand over my eyes, I unbutton, aim and let out a silent groan of relief. The steaming stream is almost orange in colour. I think it goes on for several minutes. My jaw falls slack. My shoulders drop. My life may be over, but at least I can breathe again.

'Ah, bravo,' says Steen, from the other end of the cell.

'The boy has a bladder of steel,' declares Ragondin.

'God knows what's going to happen when it's *caca* time,' adds Blonduc.

A volley of gunshots, far away, makes us all glance up at the window.

'Firing squad,' says Ragondin, turning to me. He narrows his eyes and grins. 'They've just turned some poor bastard into a sieve.'

Steen shakes his head. 'No, that'll be the four o'clock exercise detail in the quad. The guards fire their pop-guns in the air to make the prisoners dance. It makes them feel big and strong.'

'Firing squad?' I repeat, feeling my scalp prickle. 'So some prisoners are shot?'

'Only aircraft saboteurs,' replies Blonduc.

'*Tais-toi*,' growls Steen.

'Especially if they're too young to be sent to Germany for decapitation.'

'I *said* shut up.' Steen's voice hardens and he glares at Blonduc.

A rattle in the corridor makes us all sit up.

'Is he coming?' whispers Blonduc, to nobody in particular.

'Is who coming?' I croak.

'The *Kalfaktor*.'

'The feeding monkey who brings the slop,' translates Steen.

'Is he coming?' I ask.

'Is he coming?' echoes Ragondin, and I can't tell if he is asking or mocking.

We all listen; hear footsteps dying away.

Once more, I tuck myself into my corner and shut my eyes.

All that is precious to me, I consciously call to mind. And then I lock it away, like valuables in a safe. Nut by nut and bolt by bolt, with gritted teeth and cold resolve, I begin to turn over my memories and lock up my heart.

My father's smile, the first and only time he lit me a cigarette.

My mother's fingers trembling as she touches my cheek.

The soft and steady breathing of my brother Kléber in the night.

Rosemary at the piano, singing my name like a song.

My little sister Elizabeth, on tiptoes to be kissed.

I sit there, grimly packaging up my past, for what must be several hours. Days may pass; months, even. It is difficult to have any sense of time in the death-in-life limbo of Loos. And then I hear the church clock strike five. So only a single hour has gone by, and already I feel as if I have been in prison for half my life.

I open my eyes. The three ghost-men are still staring at me. I stare back. I must be the most interesting thing they have seen in weeks.

Suddenly there comes a loud clanging from outside the cell and the three of them dive for their mess tins.

'*Vite, Stéphane*,' hisses Steen. 'It's the *Kalfaktor*. Fetch your bowl.'

One by one, we push our mess tins on to the ledge of the open trap, each man snatching his away before the next shoves his in place. As the newcomer, I go last. I wait for the splosh and rattle of the ladle, then yank my mess tin back into the cell. It has been half-filled with a liquid that looks like dirty bathwater and smells quite a lot worse. Five haricot beans float on the greasy surface.

'Twelve beans for me today,' announces Steen solemnly. 'They have served me a feast.'

'It's not fair,' whines Blonduc. 'Share them out.'

'They're trying to fatten you up,' says Ragondin, between slurps. 'They're going to cook you next.'

Steen shakes his head. 'No meat on this carcase,' he sighs, patting his belly. 'Even the worms are going to be disappointed.'

'Why don't you both shut up,' snaps Blonduc. 'Some of us just want to eat our soup.'

After retreating to my corner by the lavatory, I put the five haricot beans into my mouth, one by one. Then I raise my mess tin to my lips and take a gulp. The rancid liquid tastes even more deadly than it smells.

'You'll get used it,' says Steen, watching me with a down-turned smile.

The second gulp is worse than the first. 'What do they put in it?' I ask, peering at what is left of the liquid in my bowl.

'Salt, soap and horse piss,' mutters Ragondin. 'And some bromide to cure your longings.'

'My longings?'

'It's whatever's left in the sink after they've done the washing up,' explains Steen, glaring at Ragondin.

'Shut it, all of you,' growls Blonduc, slamming his empty bowl down on the floor. Everyone falls silent. Even Blonduc himself looks shocked.

'Now you've done it,' whispers Ragondin.

'Done what?' I ask.

'Shh!' they gesture, fingers on lips. We listen, holding our breath. I wonder if anyone else has noticed that Blonduc has the shakes. Booted footsteps approach; stop outside the spyhole for a few seconds; retreat.

After finishing the liquid in my mess tin, I feel hungrier than before. I'm not sure how I am going to get through the next five minutes of Loos, let alone the next five years.

Steen breaks the silence.

'Here,' he says, leaning towards me and opening his bony fingers. 'You have these.'

I stare at the two haricot beans on his filthy palm.

'I couldn't possibly . . .'

'It's all right,' he replies. 'I'm already full.'

'I'll have them if he doesn't want them,' says Ragondin. He leans across to grab the beans. But Blonduc pulls him back.

'If you're sure?' I whisper, gazing at the beans. I take them, one after the other, and carefully put them into my mouth. 'Thank you so much.' I wonder what I have done to deserve such largesse.

Steen reads my thoughts. He shakes his head, pressing the bridge of his nose between finger and thumb. 'You'll understand one day,' he says, in a voice that is little more than a croak, 'if you're lucky enough ever to have a child yourself.'

I nod, pretending to know what he is talking about. In the far corner, Blonduc blows his nose.

Perhaps an hour later, the trap door flies open once more and Steen is already standing there with his mess tin.

'What's the next punishment?' I do my best to joke, as I take my place at the back of the line. If I can hide my fear from the others, perhaps I can hide it from myself.

'They call it coffee and bread,' snorts Ragondin, wincing as he sniffs the contents of his mess tin. 'But that's the German sense of humour for you. We call it piss and a brick.'

'That's your daily bread ration, so make the most of it,' Steen tells me.

'And don't drop it, whatever you do,' adds Ragondin. 'We all have to pay if you damage the floor.'

I peer at the stove-black rock in my hand and attempt to take a bite. Then I look at it again, more closely. Is it definitely bread?

'I can't do anything with mine,' shrugs Steen, putting his hand to his mouth as if in pain. 'It's even harder than yesterday's. Here, you've got young teeth, Grady. Can you help?'

I hesitate, thinking he is giving me his lump of bread.

'I mean, can you bite it for me?' he adds.

It is no good. Much as the thought of being helpful cheers me, I might as well be attempting to split a headstone with a twig.

'What we need here,' I say at last, 'are some explosives.' One or two of them laugh. Even Ragondin allows himself a cackle.

'I'm soaking mine,' declares Blonduc. He stares into his mess tin like a cat beside a fish pond. 'I know it'll taste even worse, but at least I should be able to break into it.'

I hand Steen's bread back to him, along with the gravel chips I have been able to bite off it, and start work on my own. My jaw aches, but it isn't my teeth. It is my saliva glands that have gone into spasm. Mémère is always telling me I eat too fast. Yet here I am, hungrier than ever before, and I must do battle with my bread, crumb by crumb.

So begins my journey into the darkness of Loos Prison, where I will soon learn that Steen's humane gesture is an eccentric aberration in a world where I must tussle like a beast, day after day, for scraps and floor space and my place in the brutal pecking order of the cell. I will learn, too, that boredom – that interminable lassitude which I always dreaded as a child – is a sign of privilege. For when I discover what lies in store for me at Loos, I soon become too panicked by every approaching footstep ever to sink into the convenient refuge of mindless lethargy.

Steen says that any one of us may be dragged out at any moment for interrogation, or *l'instruction,* as Ragondin calls it, since the Germans are in the habit of telling people, rather than asking them, how much they know. Such interrogations last until they consider that the prisoner has nothing left to hide. Ragondin tells lurid tales of people coming back to their cells with fingernails extracted, testicles crushed, eyeballs hanging out of their sockets. The sweat sticks my shirt to my back as he speaks.

The more I learn on this first day, the more I long for the

night. My body aches, nauseous with fear and fatigue. My mind feels crushed. And sleep, I keep telling myself, sleep will release me from my chains. Sleep will stop this frantic pounding in my brain. Because of course I don't yet know what the nights are like in Loos.

Perhaps half an hour later, there is another commotion outside our cell. Fierce shouts. The sound of someone clanging on the door of one of the cells far down the corridor. And then more banging, a little closer. And then closer. Someone must have tried to escape. Steen and the others begin to undress with some urgency. Perplexed, I copy them, ripping one of the buttons off my shirt in my confusion. Has the time for my first interrogation come so soon?

'Quick,' says Steen. 'Not much time.'

He unbuckles the leather straps that hold the folding bed against the wall. By now the guards are banging on the next-door cell. There is a rattling of keys in the lock and the door of our cell swings open. I watch as first Ragondin and then Blonduc race out of the door, exchanging their bundles of clothes for thin palliasses with which they hurry back in. Their waxy white skin and countable ribs come as a shock. Then Steen picks his way out and comes back empty-handed. He has the bed, after all. He gives me a shove and I dash out in my underwear, so fast that I almost tumble down the iron staircase just beyond the door. Steadying myself, I am stunned by the sense of release and the blast of cold air that comes whistling along the corridor.

'*Schnell! Schnell!*' roars a garlicky voice in my ear. I grab the last palliasse and jump back inside, a split second before the door clangs shut.

Steen is already perched on the edge of the folding bed, while the other two struggle to smooth the lumps and bumps out of their thin sacks.

'They're half-filled with straw, and half with fleas,' says Ragondin, glancing over his bony shoulder at me. 'So you won't be lonely tonight.'

I lower myself on to my bag of straw dust on the granite floor beside the jakes. One by one, the men stand up to relieve themselves. I turn my face to the wall, and try to block out the sounds and the smells. I'm not ready to go again myself; not until the light is switched off.

Perhaps I sleep for a while, because at one point Steen shakes me and tells me to stop shouting. I don't know where I am when I hear the banging on the cell door. And then I feel a splash on my neck as Ragondin stands swaying at the jakes, attempting to pee.

'*Achtung, réveille! Achtung, réveille!*' bawls a voice outside in the corridor. And the sickening, impossible truth thumps me in the ribs once more: I am now awake, yet the nightmare has not ceased.

Glancing up at the window, I can see that it is still dark outside.

The cell door swings open just long enough for us to exchange our warm flea-sacks for our clothing, by now cold and damp and stinking of disinfectant. Queuing blearily behind the others, I splash some water on my face at the washbasin. And then I sit back down in my corner and ask myself how I am going to stop myself going crazy, locked in a box with three strange men while my family are in grave danger outside.

I think of my brother Kléber, who will still be asleep in the bed that we share in my parents' room in the rue du Sac. I imagine my sisters, Rosemary and Elizabeth, sleeping peacefully with Auntie Val and Mémère next door. Rosemary will probably say I have got what I deserved. But little Elizabeth will be missing me. She calls me her Big Brave Brother, and somehow always manages to adore me, no matter how horrid to her I am. Once I tricked her into sitting on an ants' nest, because I was fed up with her following me around. Yet what wouldn't I give to see her now.

14 June 1941

In the distance, a volley of rifle fire.

'More exercise in the yard?' I ask.

'Yes,' says Steen firmly. Ragondin and Blonduc exchange glances.

'Poor bastard,' murmurs Ragondin. Blonduc crosses himself.

'When is it our turn?' I can already feel my limbs stiffening up. I am desperate for some exercise; to run and jump and escape the sticky confines of our cell.

'You'll get your turn in the yard soon enough, pipsqueak,' says Ragondin, exposing a row of blackened teeth as he smirks at Steen.

Suddenly Blonduc comes out with something that takes me by surprise.

'Mostly it's the English who get shot,' he announces, to nobody in particular.

Everybody ignores him, as usual.

'What makes you say that?' I ask, as casually as I can. 'Do you mean outside, in the war? Or here, in the prison?'

'What's the difference? We're all going to wind up speaking German in the end.'

'Don't even bother listening to him, Grady,' advises Steen. 'He's not right in the head.'

'I mean out there in the yard.' Blonduc jabs his thumb over his shoulder. 'The French and the Belgians get hard labour. *Les Anglais* get a bullet.'

'It's not true,' counters Ragondin. 'They shoot the French, too, the ones they call *résistants*. They do it at the citadel in Lille, so the public get to hear about it.'

We sit in silence. I feel all churned up inside. But Blonduc has not finished with me yet.

'It's an unusual name you've got, Grady,' he continues. Slowly he raises his eyes to mine. 'Where's it from?'

'From the south. From Lyon, I believe.'

And then he wants to know where exactly my family is from, and what my father does. My toes curl in my shoes.

'He's a gardener,' I say.

'And you, do you work?'

'Sometimes I work with him,' I reply. 'But I'm training to be a butcher.'

'So many questions, it's an interrogation,' says Steen, quietly. 'Just ignore him, Stéphane.'

Blonduc smiles to himself. 'When the world is entirely German, being a butcher should come in very useful.'

'Yes, the Schleus love a bit of butchery,' says Ragondin. 'And you'll be able to start with Steen, after they've turned him into a sieve.'

'I only know how to do pigs, so far,' I reply.

'In that case you'll know what to do with him.'

'They won't shoot me,' says Steen. 'I'll be out of here soon, you'll see. I've got a friend who works on one of the big engineering projects up on the coast. Says he's going to get me a job.'

'Then you're another Boche in the making,' hisses Blonduc. 'Working up there is as good as joining the German army. Funny you never told us this before, Boche-lover.'

'Do you kill the animals yourself, pipsqueak, before you cut them up?' asks Ragondin, ignoring him.

'Sometimes I do.'

'And what's it like, killing a living creature like that. Isn't it hard? Pigs squeal, don't they?'

'I don't enjoy doing it, but if someone asks me to, then I will.'

Suddenly Blonduc leaps to his feet in the middle of the cell. 'Yes, and I'll bet that's what the Boche squaddies thought, too, when they murdered all those women and children in Arras. Or when they lined up sixty people in a quarry in Aubigny, where my parents live, and mowed them down with their machine guns. Or when they executed all the English soldiers in Paradis-Lestrem, after they surrendered.'

'Take it easy, man,' says Steen. 'The boy's just talking about sticking a pig.'

'Forty-one civilians murdered in Beuvry. Fifty-four in Courrières. Eighteen in Carvin. Do I need to go on?'

'What's your point, Blonduc?'

Blonduc shakes his head, staring at the floor.

'We know they're bastards,' shrugs Ragondin. 'That's all there is to it.'

Now Blonduc seems to stagger, and from his chest there comes an eerie groaning sound. Heavy-legged, he drags himself to the wall of the cell and slides down on to his knees, covering his face with one arm.

'Are you all right, my friend?' whispers Steen, glancing at me and Ragondin. There is a long silence.

'It's my boy,' says Blonduc at last.

'You have a son?' Steen asks, surprised.

Blonduc nods, face to the wall. The rest of us just sit there on the floor, electrified. Blonduc is human, after all. He sniffs and wipes his nose on his sleeve.

'He would have been five years old, this Christmas Day.'

'He's dead?'

'They murdered him. Those Boche bastards murdered my boy.'

In the silence, I can hear someone clanking a pail of water along the corridor outside.

'And when I asked one of the soldiers why they did that to me, he said it was because they had to follow their orders.'

The rest of us look at each other, uneasy in the silence.

'I never knew you had a son,' murmurs Ragondin, raising his eyebrows. He scratches his head.

'We're sorry for your loss, Blonduc,' adds Steen.

'Yes, sorry, Blonduc,' I say.

'It's so ridiculous,' he adds, after a pause. With his back to us, he scratches at the wall with one black fingernail. 'But if at any point they had said that to me – if they'd once had the decency to say they had made a mistake and that they were sorry – I really think that might have made a difference. Instead, they've left me with this lump of iron in my chest, where my heart ought to be. And you keep saying that I'm not right in the head, as if it's a joke. But it's not a joke. Because too bloody right, I'm not right in the head. All I want to do is get out of this shithole so I can go and kill some bloody Schleus, the minute I have a chance.'

'Careful, Blonduc,' murmurs Steen, glancing at the door.

Too late. A few minutes later, we all freeze at the sound of a heavy key being scrabbled in the lock. Two guards with rifles slung over their shoulders barge into the cell. I recognise one of them: Kourk. The other utters a few words in German. But it is not Blonduc they want. Steen's name is mentioned. And I can hardly believe it when he stands up and replies to them in German himself: confident, assured, matter-of-fact. I gulp. Who is this man I thought I was getting to know?

Steen follows the soldiers to the door and turns to face us.

'Don't worry,' he whispers, smiling at me. 'I am not a spy. Yes, I am a Belgian who can speak German. But here, where it matters,' – he points to his heart – 'I am as French as you are.' And then, as Kourk bellows something, grabbing at Steen's arm to drag him out, he glances at Blonduc and Ragondin. 'Look after the boy,' he mouths. '*Bon courage.*'

The door slams shut, and I sit on the floor. Blonduc has his head in his hands.

'Right, I get the bed now,' says Ragondin, rubbing his hands together.

20 June 1941

At last it is our turn for an exercise session in the prison yard. About fifty of us are led out there one morning and told to jog round the outer courtyard, while a couple of fat sentries stand in the middle, firing their rifles into the air to remind us how god-like they are. Every shot makes me jump these days; my shredded nerves are worse than Mémère's.

I like seeing the sky, and it is a relief to move my limbs. But I hoped I might spot Marcel, and it is a blow to find he isn't here. It stings, too, to see all these grown men looking so scrawny and demoralised: to watch soldiers, bakers and teachers, farmers, gardeners and engineers limping round and round in a dismal circle, like some warped parody of a children's party game, and greeting each volley of rifle shots with a desperate little hop. In the end, I am relieved to return to our cell. I feel safer, locked in here.

Another day, we are told to strip and are paraded naked to the washroom, shielding our privates with both hands like a guilty secret. The showers are cold, of course, and the soap feels like gritty lard. I even try eating it, and immediately wish that I hadn't, scraping at my tongue with my fingers to get it off. But what bliss it is, to be able to feel almost clean for a moment, after the itchy-scratchiness of the preceding weeks.

Before he left, Steen told me that most people only remain in a cell at Loos for a couple of weeks, during which time they are treated to one or more sessions of interrogation by the German police. It depends how quickly they reveal all they know. And then, after sentencing, they are returned to the prison, where the cells on the ground floor are reserved for those who are awaiting deportation to Germany or the firing squad.

Those death-row cells hold a grim fascination for me. I have only been down there once, when I was ordered to clean up after a prisoner returning from *l'instruction* had bled and vomited all over the corridor. How dark and silent it is on that level, where the light from the roof barely penetrates and the mildewy damp wafts up from the flagstones as if from an open grave.

They say that even the luckiest prisoners on the ground floor can expect five years of forced labour in Germany. For the not-so-lucky, death is the reward, even for petty offences. I pray that improving the instrument panel of a crashed Messerschmitt with a tuppenny hammer does not qualify. Yet the hungrier and weaker I become, the harder it is to cling to the frayed threads of my own optimism.

Some days, we hear Allied bombers droning overhead, and I find myself wishing they would target the prison itself. Blow us up cleanly, bury us in stone; anything would be better than this constant fear of what the next hour holds. But at least the throb of those engines gives me a grain of hope to which I can cling. For that sound is a sign that someone, somewhere is continuing the fight. And what I discover is that, when you are in a very dark place, and you are frightened for your life, then the knowledge that someone is putting up a fight on your behalf, in however small a way, can make all the difference. For it gives you hope. And hope is the difference between giving up and going on.

Maubeuge has the opposite effect on morale. A wiry stoat of a man in his late thirties, Maubeuge is sent into cell 54 as a replacement for Steen although, as swaps go, this doesn't strike me as a particularly fair one. It is like replacing a healthy shrub with a withered clump of nettles. Maubeuge works for the French railways and is accused of having nicked some bits and pieces from a truck containing German army supplies.

'They can't do much to me, can they?' he declares, standing in the centre of the cell to make it impossible for the rest of us to distance ourselves from him. 'I mean, they only caught me with a dozen army towels. Twelve little towels. And you really can't – even *they* can't – shoot a man for having nicked a dozen towels, can you?'

It doesn't matter whether we reply to Maubeuge or not. He just ploughs on. One of his favourite ways of winding us up is having imaginary conversations with the drinking pals he has left behind.

'*Salut, Pierre. Ça va?*' he mutters, under his breath, to the washbasin, before turning to the lavatory and continuing: 'Come and have a drink with me. What about a good old Pernod? Oh, and can you spare me a fag?'

At first, the three of us laugh at his craziness, until it begins to disturb us. Hands fluttering, he begins to include the folding bed as another character in his warped little scenes. 'Good, yes, you know Pernod is awfully good for you,' he says, kicking the bed to get its undivided attention. 'The aniseed helps the digestion.' And then back to the basin again: 'Good health, Pierre. And how is the lovely Françoise?'

Ragondin is convinced that Maubeuge is a secret weapon developed by the Germans; a sort of nerve gas in human form. Ragondin has a point, too. Maubeuge is deadly. And as if his endless conjecture about what kind of sentence he is going to receive isn't bad enough, he enjoys speculating about ours, too.

'As for you, young Grady,' he says, picking on me for being a poor listener, 'I think you are in for the high jump. Sabotage of a shiny new Messerschmitt 109? *Oh, là là là là là*. That, my boy, automatically invites the death penalty. And don't think they will make any allowances for your age, either. No, they even shoot babies.'

'*Ta gueule, Maubeuge*,' spits Ragondin, with a cautious glance at Blonduc. 'We've had enough of your pig shit.'

Of course I pretend not to listen. And of course Maubeuge's words hit home.

'Mind you, even a death sentence has got to be better than twenty years' hard labour,' he continues, when he can see that I have my fingers in my ears and poor Blonduc is beginning to bang his head against the wall. 'Imagine: you'll be thirty-six, as old as I am, and a physical wreck by the time they've finished with you. Whereas the firing squad is so quick. They blindfold you, you know, and then – *bang bang* – they turn you into a colander. Unless they post you to Germany for decapitation instead.'

After a few days of Maubeuge's maunderings, I am almost beginning to think that an appearance before a well-run firing squad might not be such a bad future after all. Solace comes, however, when Blonduc is led away for sentencing and his place in our cell is taken by a boy of about my age, a scrawny fellow with dark eyes and a shock of black hair, called Dorion. I have a potential ally at last. Steen was kind to me, but he was as old as my father. Dorion is different, because he is even younger than I am. So I am not the baby any more, even though, in all sorts of ways, Dorion seems far more grown-up than me. Until a week ago, he was employed in an engineering works in Lille, making vehicle parts for the German war machine. And then one day he was caught sawing through a transmission belt he was supposed to be checking for faults. And his life, like mine, veered off the rails into a ditch.

Dorion is called often for interrogation, and sometimes comes back in a bad way. Limping and whimpering, he collapses on to his palliasse facing the wall, and sobs himself to sleep.

'There is no one else,' he mumbles, time after time, into the darkness. 'So how can I give you any names?'

Once, in the silence that follows, I hear Ragondin's voice respond from the fold-up bed.

'Why don't you just make up a name?' he says, quietly.

'*Oui, oui,*' agrees Maubeuge, almost making me jump. 'A name like Ragondin, say, or Grady.'

'*Putain de merde,*' hisses Ragondin in response. 'I swear if the Germans don't kill you one of these days, Maubeuge, then I will.'

'Keep your hair on, weasel. It was just a joke.'

Dorion says nothing. A few feet away, I lie staring up at the ceiling, trying to blot out the thought of the things they have done to him. I feel guilty that it is always him; never me. And I almost catch myself wishing that I could take his place.

20 July 1941

One stifling morning, out of the blue, I walk over to the regulations, which are pinned to a board on the wall, and I take out the pins.

'Hey, what are you doing, Grady?' whispers Ragondin.

'I thought we could play a game of draughts. I'll sketch a board on the back of this. We'll use scraps of paper as pieces. Who wants to play?'

'You're on, Stéphane,' says Dorion. 'Count me in.'

'They'll kill you if they catch you defacing that notice,' mutters Maubeuge. 'And then we'll all be for the chop.'

'Are you going to denounce him then?'

'I'm just trying to teach the boy how to survive.'

'Oh, is that what you're doing? Or is it the other way round?'

'I'll play, Grady,' says Ragondin, peering at the lines I am drawing on the cardboard. I managed to save a pencil stub from last week's letter-writing, not that I wrote a letter. I used the paper to begin a pencil drawing of the rue du Sac, making it as accurate as my memory will allow. With next week's writing paper, I shall do one of the Lombard farm. But for now I simply take the pencil and, using the metal frame of the folding bed as a straight edge, mark out a chessboard on the back of the notice. 'I used to be quite good at draughts,' adds Ragondin, rubbing the side of his nose.

No sooner have I begun to shade in the squares than there is a sudden commotion outside on the landing. Guards are shouting; boots ring on metal. They are about to turn over someone's cell. I slip the notice behind my back and we all sit there on the floor, paralysed with panic, not even breathing.

'I did warn you,' whispers Maubeuge. 'Besides, draughts is a stupid game.'

But the danger passes. Ragondin rubs his hands as he gazes at my makeshift board. 'I'm quite looking forward to this,' he says, cheerily.

He and Dorion play the first game, and it is agreed that I will play the winner, Ragondin. He beats me soundly, too. Dorion and I are rearranging the little squares of paper for a losers' match, when a small voice pipes up from the other end of the cell. It is Maubeuge.

'Do you mind if I have a turn next?' he asks, sheepishly.

3 August 1941

Ragondin is next to leave the cell. I am not sad to see him go. The weasel has a slimy malice about him that always made my skin crawl, even when it wasn't already crawling with the grime and the lice. And besides, now that I am the longest-serving resident of cell 54, the fold-up bed is mine. Maubeuge hates this – he says the rule shouldn't apply to minors – and so does Ragondin's replacement, a taciturn tax officer from Ypres who is adamant that he hasn't done anything wrong, and that it is outrageous to be banged up in Loos at all. So I suggest we put it to a vote and they are foolish enough to agree. Dorion votes for me, and that is that.

That evening, remembering the impact of Steen's generosity to me on my first night in Loos, I give my young ally two of my beans. The next day, he is called to the military tribunal in Lille and given a sentence of five years' hard labour. He is so frail by now that I doubt he will survive for even one. But at least the interrogations will stop.

I actually envy his sentence, knowing that the Boche may be about to hit me with something very much worse. And I miss Dorion. Even though we spoke very little, his presence in the cell made me feel less frightened and alone: a country boy adrift in a world of hardened, jaded men. Day after day, I work on my drawings of the Lombard farm and the rue du Sac. Using my mess-tin as a ruler, I make them as detailed as I possibly can. At least if my memory goes, I will having something to which I can cling.

I will never miss Maubeuge. It is bad enough having to

listen to all his ridiculous prattling conversations with the basin and the jakes. But one night, my irritation with him metamorphoses into pure, white hatred.

It is an evening just like any other inside our cell. Everyone is at their most irritable, and the minutes are passing as slowly as if they were boulders chained to our ankles. I sit leaning against the wall, gazing in a daze at my drawing of the rue du Sac. And then the trap opens for us to receive our splash of fetid soup. Taking my place in front of the tax officer and our newest recruit, a welder called Riffaud, whose shiny bald head reminds me of an egg, I set my mess tin on the ledge and am just about to retrieve it when Maubeuge shoves his own mess tin on to the trap.

I blink, and our eyes meet, in the split second of silence before metal crashes on to stone. I stare at the wall in disbelief as my mess tin bounces once on the stone floor outside, and then goes bash-clang-banging down the iron staircase in front of our cell, hurtling in leaps and bounds all the way to the ground floor.

In the stillness that follows, I hear a muffled cheer from the other cells.

The door of cell 54 opens more slowly than it has ever opened before. And there, covered in bromide-laced soup, soap and horse piss, is Kourk. His face looks roughly the same colour as the furnace of a smelting works.

'*Vier und Funfzig*,' he mouths. And then, in a coarse whisper: 'Whose mess tin this is?'

'*C'est la mienne*,' I reply. What I am not expecting is for Maubeuge suddenly to step forward and tell Kourk that it is all his fault. Sure enough, he doesn't.

Kourk draws back his fat hand until his arm is almost straight. Then he whacks me across the face so hard that I see the white flash of a phosphorus flare and my teeth rattle in my jaw.

'Fetch!' he cries.

Off I go, scrambling groggily down the iron staircase before he can kick me down there. Down past the first-floor gantry where Marcel is being held, down on to the ground floor where the rats and the slime are at their worst. The corridor of the condemned lies just behind me. My legs stiffen at the thought. Is this my future? As I bend down to pick up my dented tin, I cannot help but turn and glance over my shoulder. A guard is unlocking the door of one of the cells.

I know I should be racing aloft, but what I see inside glues me to the spot. The occupant of the cell is a stricken-looking boy, no older than Marcel and me. And he is half-praying, half-sobbing, on his knees.

For a moment, I simply stand and stare, like a child seeing himself in a mirror for the first time. But the boy must be able to sense me standing there, for now he raises his eyes and looks straight at me. I hold my breath. Our stares meet: my eyes, darting with questions, his, bloodshot with despair. I try to look away, but something in his gaze holds me there. And in that moment, another switch is flicked in the fuse box of my mind.

Grabbing the tin, I race back up the two flights of stairs, only for Kourk to hit me again – *too slow!* – when I reach the top. I duck and twist away, doing my best to protect my face. And then he kicks me so hard from behind that I am catapulted back into the cell and smack my head against the jakes.

There is no soup for me tonight. So I am touched when the tax officer and Riffaud each gave me a sip of theirs, and one precious bean apiece. Maubeuge, meanwhile, sits in the corner and solemnly slurps every last drop of his own soup. For once, he has not a word to say.

In the distance, the church clock in Lille chimes the hours. But I cannot sleep. My mind has come back to life. Bruised as I am, I roll off the fold-out bed and kneel on the cold granite floor. I press my cracked palms together. I screw my eyes tight shut. And I pray for the boy downstairs.

5 September 1941

At half past four on 5 September 1941, the door of cell 54 opens and a guard who is not Kourk says: '*Grady, Stefan, komm.*'

It is time. In rudimentary French, he tells me to bring my possessions; he says I won't be coming back. For a moment, I turn to look at my three cell mates. Their faces are blank.

I follow the helmeted guard down the metal staircase and along the corridor to the prison office. And there, looking pale and wretched as he stands in front of the desk of a German staff sergeant, is Marcel. I am so relieved to see him alive. I am appalled to see him half-dead. My old friend looks shockingly thin. His hair appears to be falling out. And, judging from the way he is staring at me, I must look just as bad.

The staff sergeant clears his throat.

'*Doch*,' he says, and something about that word makes my heart sink. I can read it in his cold eyes, in his slicked-back hair, in the way he is smirking at me, arms folded. He knows a terrible secret about me and wants me to know that he knows. I almost retch at the thought: we are condemned.

And then his smile fades. He leans back in his chair, suddenly serious.

'*Doch* . . .' he says again, pursing his lips. In one sudden movement, he lurches forward and plucks from his desk two manila envelopes, whose contents he examines with one eye before handing them to us. I don't understand. My envelope contains all the things that were taken from me on arrival at Loos: my identity card, my tobacco pouch and my cigarette machine. Marcel's even contains his little green French–English dictionary.

'*Doch*,' he says once more, handing us each a small piece of paper, on which are typed a few lines of German in purple ink. 'Sign this document, please.'

I peer at the document, which means nothing to me. Are we reassigned to the firing squad? Marcel is doing his best to decipher an identical one beside me. I watch his hands trembling as he holds it. Then his chin drops and, with one hand on the desk to steady his buckling limbs, he begins silently to sob.

'*C'est quoi?*' I ask the officer, shaking the paper at him. 'What does this mean, exactly?'

He raises his eyebrows.

'It wants to say,' he replies, with excruciating slowness, 'that you are free.'

'*Nous sommes libres?*'

'Go from here,' he says, sotto voce. 'And please do not come back and see us some time.'

Tongue-tied, we tiptoe out into the prison yard.

And nobody stops us.

I must not shout. *I must not shout*. But there, in the yard, is another surprise. Our bicycles. Disbelieving, we wheel them towards the great gate.

And the gate opens.

Ahead of us, on the far side of the gate, I can see a scrub-lined lane which looks strangely familiar. The sight of it sends a tremor up my weary spine. For I know that half-forgotten pathway. It is the road that leads to where the green grass grows, and there is mist at dawn in the rue du Sac. It is the road back to where my childhood used to be.

Side by side, aware that we are still being watched, Marcel Lombard and I stumble out through the gate of Loos Prison. With our puny arms, we pump up our flat tyres. With our chicken legs, we start pedalling for all we are worth.

And now, at last, we are free.

I can see grass and hawthorn, and cattle grazing in the fields. The air is fragrant with summer. The brilliance of the light makes me screw up my eyes. And now I dare to shout; I dare to sing. For the sense of space is terrifying. The sky seems so huge, the clouds so high. And I can't believe how beautiful the world looks and smells and sounds, as we whirr along with the sun warm on our backs and the birds chirping fanfares in the trees. Everything is a miracle: freshly tossed haystacks, standing in a field, a river with ducks bobbing in a line, vapour trails in the vast sky.

I am free. We are free. And here is an old man, sitting on a step, and he is free, too. We wave and yell, '*Bonjour, monsieur!*'

Tipping my head back to feel the wind on my face, I take great lungfuls of country air. How sweet and soft everything smells. Wild garlic and fresh-cut grass. It must be potato harvest time, because now I can even smell the warm, earthy fragrance of the potato plants in the fields.

I don't want to blink in case I miss something. Poppies are so red; grass is so green. I had almost forgotten. And look, Marcel: just look at the blue of the sky. I blow a kiss at the clouds.

Around the next corner comes a jolting surprise: an army truck full of helmeted German soldiers rumbles towards us. So our sudden release must have been a trick, after all. But the truck flashes by. We are still free, and our euphoria wafts us along: two grinning Lazaruses amazed to be alive again. Just wait till we get home, Marcel. Just wait.

Elizabeth is the first to spot me.

'Lou, it's Lou!' she screams, burying her head in my chest, pretending not to notice the stink.

'Is Dad safe?' I whisper.

'Yes, yes, he's fine, in Bailleul,' she nods. 'And you're home. And you're so bony!'

The door of our house is ajar, and I can see someone peeking out before it is flung wide. Auntie Val and Mémère come tumbling out like a pair of schoolgirls, with Rosemary and Kléber not far behind them. My little brother flings himself at me so hard that he almost knocks me over, and Rosemary slips her hand into mine. She doesn't need to speak; I can see all the words in her eyes. My mother is next to appear from the shadows, her white stick in one hand, crossing herself repeatedly with the other. Standing in front of me, touching the outline of my face with her trembling fingers, she looks dismayed at first. And then she announces that my deliverance is the miracle for which she has lit twenty-one candles to Saint Rita and prayed to the Virgin Mother.

'Thank you, Mummy,' I whisper, giving Rosemary's hand a squeeze.

'Perhaps next time, Mummy,' says Rosemary, 'if you light a few more candles, Lou might get out a bit sooner.'

'There won't be a next time, will there, Lou?' pleads my mother, holding my hand to her cheek.

'No, Mummy.' I shake my head. 'Never again.'

And then we are all hugging and crying, right there in the street, until Auntie Val shushes us and tells us that we must come inside, because we are making a scene.

I must look like a stick man, because the first thing they do is to sit me at the kitchen table with a knife and fork. And while Auntie Val bustles around, fetching anything edible she can find, and my mother sits sobbing in the corner, everyone else crowds around my chair, touching and stroking me as if I were a waxwork, which is almost what I am. But now it is my turn. I want to know everything that has been happening. Did the Boche come to the house? Is Dad all right? Is the war almost won?

I can't decide what to eat first, because I want to eat everything at once. Bread, fresh bread, as soft as clouds, I shove into my mouth, with a lump of chocolate stuffed inside it. For a moment my tastebuds are dancing the Charleston; a second later, I wince from the excruciating pain in my jaw, just below the ears, as my saliva glands go into spasm.

'Slow down,' warns Mémère. 'You'll do yourself an injury.'

'Did they torture you?' asks Kléber.

'What was it like in prison, Lou?' adds Elizabeth.

'It was very . . . slimming,' I mumble, between mouthfuls.

'Shh,' laughs Auntie Val. 'Let the boy eat.'

She wants to skin me a rabbit and cook potatoes in the fat, but I say I'd rather eat it raw than wait. So instead she fetches a precious baked ham from the cellar, and digs out a hidden tin of Heinz beans that my mother has been saving as a birthday present for my father. I eat the beans cold, struck by how extraordinarily sweet and salty they are, interspersing each mouthful with a handful of ripped ham, a bite from a hunk of Dutch cheese, a couple of quick spoonfuls of strawberry jam and some more of that miracle bread, please, which is probably meant to last a week, but I'm afraid is disappearing fast. Though my shrivelled stomach is already full to bursting, I just don't seem to be able to stop myself.

A second later, I lurch up from the table and dive out into the back garden, as everything I have just eaten reappears.

'Better?' asks Auntie Val, beaming, when I return.

'Sorry, yes, such a waste,' I reply, with one hand on my aching belly.

'We're just so happy you're back,' she says, her voice cracking.

This is the cue for another general outpouring of happiness, although I do point out that it looks as if everyone is most upset that I have survived. Why are they all crying? My family is not known for showing emotion. I suppose that's the British in us. But today, just for once, we allow ourselves to be a little bit French. So there is a lot of holding of hands, and wiping of eyes, and hugging of each other. I think I even hug Kléber, which is a first. And as I stuff another morsel of heaven into my mouth, I tell myself that I shall never, ever do anything to endanger the lives or the happiness of these people again.

Next day, after I have slept for sixteen hours solid, Marcel and I meet up in the pasture beside Pont d'Achelles. Neither of us is ready to talk about what we have just been through. Perhaps we never will. But we can at least discuss the miracle of our release.

'My mother is convinced it was Saint Rita,' I say.

'Mine is convinced it was because she caught a mole and, instead of giving it to Mirza, she buried it in a pot of basil in the garden.'

'Either way, it could be a trap.'

'You don't think they're spying on us now, do you?' asks Marcel.

We glance around us, scanning the flat landscape for the tell-tale glint of a pair of binoculars trained upon us. But all we can see is a scarecrow in the distance and a couple of bony cows, munching grass.

'That must be what we look like,' I remark.

'What, a scarecrow in a dress?'

I laugh. I hadn't noticed the skirt.

'I think my father must have decided that women are much scarier than men,' says Marcel, squinting at the scarecrow. 'And, on the whole, I'm inclined to agree with him.'

'Does he honestly believe that crows can tell the difference?'

We both consider this for a while. And then Marcel tells me about a man called Derisbourg, a prisoner who was brought into his cell shortly before his release.

'This Derisbourg claimed he hated the Germans and was going to be shot. Every day he would be called for interrogation, and he'd come back with not a mark on him, weeping and wailing about all the terrible things they'd done to him.

And here's the strange thing: he kept wanting to know why I'd been arrested and exactly what I'd done, down to the last detail. He even assured me that he could get a letter delivered to my parents without it being censored by the prison, if there was anything I wanted to let them know.'

'Very odd.'

'Something about the man didn't smell right,' continues Marcel. 'So I told him I had nothing to say to my parents, and just kept repeating the story we agreed on.'

'Good stuff. Was he wearing a dress, by any chance?'

'No, but listen to this: two days later, Derisbourg is moved to another cell. Another day after that and we're both released. Coincidence? I think not.'

'Sounds like our Monsieur Derisbourg met his match in special agent Lombard. Well played, Marcel.'

'Thanks.'

'But how about this? Do you remember Monsieur Faure, that cantankerous old buffer whose shutters I used to pelt with mud balls?'

'I remember you wished the mud balls were incendiary grenades.'

'Well, it turns out he spotted us in the recovery lorry in the town square after we'd been arrested. And he managed to warn our parents and Mayor Houcke that we'd been taken.'

'Why does that matter?'

'Apart from the fact that it gave my father time to hide elsewhere, it sounds as if good old Houcke pulled quite a few strings to spring us out of Loos.'

Marcel folds his arms. 'I still think Derisbourg was the key.'

'Maybe he was, Marcel. But we owe Houcke as well.'

'And your friend, the cantankerous Monsieur Faure.'

'All right,' I grin. 'Let's not go overboard, shall we?'

14 September 1941

A week or so later, a letter arrives in a brown envelope with a swastika on the back. Postmarked from the German *Kommandantur* in Lille, it is addressed to Stefan Grady. Everyone but Mémère gathers around me. And, in as steady a voice as I can manage, I read it aloud.

I am commanded to report to the *Kommandantur* at 11 a.m. on 18 September. The letter says that my father is to accompany me.

At first, there is absolute silence. My father looks almost as white as one of his own gravestones.

'It's impossible,' he says at last. 'It's quite impossible.'

Auntie Val wags her finger at my mother. 'It is you now, Berthe. You absolutely must.'

Mémère is talking to herself by the fireplace. 'I told you so,' she says. 'The boy has done for us all. I said it would come to this. And now of course it has.'

Elizabeth is tugging at my sleeve. 'What does it mean, Lou? What does it mean?'

On the other side of me, Kléber taps me on the arm. 'Are you going to be shot?'

Eventually it is agreed that my mother will accompany me to Lille. She is to explain that my father is bedridden and unable to travel. I dare to glance at her out of the corner of my eye. She looks stricken at the thought.

All I can think is: have I not paid enough? Has my family not paid enough? In Loos, the Boche stole three months of my youth. Already they owe me for that. When will the consequences of my actions, still rippling outwards from one stupid, tiny error, finally come to rest?

Clutching a rosary in each hand, my mother shakes her head, her lips a grim semicircle of despair.

'But I can't, I can't,' she moans. 'I am a weak and feeble woman.'

'You're made of steel, Berthe,' says Auntie Val, quietly.

'Val's right,' adds my father. 'We all know you're tough as old boots, love. You've just forgotten it along the way.'

'But I haven't been further than the end of the village in years,' she wails. 'How can I go all the way to Lille? I shall be run over by a tank.' Hands clasped, she begs them to relent. It twists a knife in my guts, to see my mother like this.

'You'll have Lou with you,' says Auntie Val, putting her arm around her sister's shoulders.

'And the baby Jesus,' mutters my father, under his breath.

'And Saint Rita,' says Elizabeth brightly.

'Lou will look after you,' insists Auntie Val, with a sidelong glare at them both.

'Yes, yes,' says Mémère, 'just like he looked after that German aeroplane and got us all into this pickle in the first place.'

'Mother, please,' snaps Auntie Val. 'This is not helping us.'

'And he's not helping us either, with his tricks.'

'The tricks are in the past now, aren't they, Lou?'

I nod.

'Well, then.' Auntie Val smooths her apron with her hands. 'You've convinced us. Now you just have to convince the Germans, too.'

The next few days crawl by. I feel weak and listless. There are borders to be cut in the cemeteries but I don't have the energy to face them. My fear is that the Boche have changed their minds, that on Thursday I am to be sent back to Loos, or even to Germany. I sip my coffee and puff on a cigarette.

'You're amazing, Lou,' says Kléber, watching me. 'You look like you don't have a care in the world.'

* * *

Thursday morning comes, and my mother and I take the bus to Lille in the rain. We travel in silence, for what is there to say? I could tell her what I can see outside, but mostly it is just German soldiers and greyness and empty shops, and a skinny carthorse delivering coal. Arriving at the boulevard de la Liberté in plenty of time, we are told to wait in a dimly lit corridor. We sit in silence for an hour. I try not to think about Kourk.

Beside me, my mother is a pathetic sight. I gaze at her in her ill-matched, threadbare clothes, and my heart goes out to her. Even that scarecrow we saw in the field looked smarter than she does. I can only imagine that Auntie Val must be trying to get back at her for something, to make her go out dressed like this. Perhaps Auntie imagines that, being blind, her older sister doesn't care. But I know *I* care, to see my own mother in such a state, with her hair plastered to her forehead and the buttons of her coat in all the wrong holes.

'Do you mind?' I begin to sort out the buttons for her and she smiles.

'You're good to me, Lou,' she says.

'No, I'm not.'

'Yes, you are. I'm lucky to have you.'

There is a long pause before my mother speaks again.

'Do you remember Monsieur le Curé's homily at Easter? The one where he talked about substituted love?'

'No, I don't,' I reply, as flatly as I can. And then, feeling guilty, I relent. 'Why?'

'It doesn't matter,' she says, quietly. 'I've just been thinking about it.'

'Ah,' I nod, surprised at the idea of my mother thinking about anything at all, besides her aches and pains and her rosary.

At last we are ushered into a very large and gilded office, with tall windows and a vast picture of Hitler above the empty desk at one end. My mother grips my arm. Seconds later, a tall German officer marches into the room and installs himself behind the desk. He arranges his files. He sharpens a pencil. And then arranges his files again.

'Approach, please, the boy Grady,' he says. I shuffle my mother into a metal chair just inside the door, before going to stand in front of him.

The man is in no hurry to tell me why I am here. He looks almost familiar and, with a shiver, it suddenly comes to me: he is the one who almost broke my shin with a mule kick back in June.

'You want to smoke?' He gestures to a packet on the table.

'Thank you, yes,' I lean forward to take a cigarette, but he snatches the packet away.

'It was a joke,' he says, unsmiling. 'My son is your age. If I caught him smoking, I would have him flogged. When he grows up, he will be a soldier in the German army. And you? What will you do?'

'I don't know,' I lie.

'Precisely,' he nods. 'It says here that you work. What work? You clean lavatories, perhaps?'

'I look after the cemeteries from the last war.'

'Ah, this is almost the same thing. We kill them, you bury them, *ja?*' He chuckles at the thought.

'Some of the graves I tend are German,' I reply, coldly.

The man frowns to himself. Then, with quick movements, he lights himself a cigarette, opens a manila file, leans back in his chair and puts his boots on the table.

'You are a very lucky boy,' he drawls, glancing up from the file. 'It says here that the Mayor of Nieppe interceded on your behalf after your arrest. He describes you as a child of good character from a law-abiding, respectable family. Ah, yes: the great Herr Houcke. He seems a most interesting man.' He pauses to peer over his file at my mother, raises his eyebrows, and shakes his head in a way that makes me want to punch him on his fat nose. I am waiting for him to ask for my father, but he does not. 'After considering your case, the German authorities have decided, quite exceptionally, not to press official charges.'

I raise my eyes to the ceiling, but he is only just warming up. 'You will be watched,' he barks. 'From this moment on, we have you in our sights. You understand?'

By now, I am not really listening. I don't know why it is, but as soon as I sense that someone is giving me a lecture, whether it's Auntie Val or Mémère or some jackbooted Schleu behind a desk, I just switch off. I know I shouldn't, but I just find my mind wandering. Because the thing about lectures is that you always know exactly what someone is going to say before they say it. Whereas the people who make me listen are the ones who talk quietly and don't say too much. Not Schleus, in other words.

So here I am, thinking about Marie-Louise Boulet's breasts and how long it is since I fished out a packet of tobacco from between them, and this German is still yelling at me.

'We know where you live, Grady. And if you take one step out of line, ever again – if you should so much as blink at a member of the German army, or touch any article of the German Reich – then that will be it. The consequences for you, and for your family, will be *catastrophic*. Do I make myself clear?'

'Yes, thank you,' I reply, cheerfully. 'Very clear indeed.'

'It's a pity for you that you are so young. If not, we could send you to work in Germany. You look strong enough. The idea you like?'

I shake my head.

'Well, before long you won't have a choice.' He looks at his watch. 'Now, I have wasted enough time on you. Get out of my sight. And take this rubbish with you.'

At first I think he is referring to my mother. But he hands me a bulky manila envelope, which I open as soon as we are outside. When I see what it contains, I shake my head. Here are my father's old pliers and screwdriver. And – is this a trick? – the two instruments we lifted from the Messerschmitt.

Almost in a dream, we hurry away down the boulevard de la Liberté before the German officer can change his mind. My mother's walking has improved since this morning, and I could swear that she looks taller and better dressed than she was when we arrived.

On the corner, she turns to me and puts her hand on my cheek.

'You're so brave, Lou,' she whispers.

'Not really brave, Mummy. Just stupid, probably.'

'No, you're brave.' She pulls a sad smile. 'It is a mother's worst nightmare. And how I wish that you were not.'

I must have been recuperating at home for about a fortnight when the first boils appear on my hands and feet. Each is a vivid red volcano, with a white crust of pus at its peak. I do my best to keep them secret, but Auntie Val is soon coming at me with one of her machining needles to lance them. She thinks I don't wash enough. I tell her it's the change of diet; I'm simply not used to eating food fit for human consumption. Then a boil appears on my shoulder blade; then another, and another. Before long I am covered from head to foot in the wretched things, and the ones on my rear hurt so much that I can hardly bring myself to ride my bike.

'You look like a monster,' says Elizabeth, encouragingly.

'Yes, really hideous,' agrees Kléber, peering up at me from his copy of *The Tailor of Gloucester*. 'It looks as if you've been machine-gunned.'

'Actually, they hurt quite a lot worse than that,' I tell him.

'Do you want me to put some of Auntie Val's special ointment on them for you?' asks Elizabeth. 'She had the lead powder and the olive oil out last night, and I saw her cooking up a batch.'

'Would you really do that for me?' I reply, taken aback. 'Some of them are pretty disgusting. And if they're not better by the weekend, she's threatening to lance them all again.'

'I don't mind,' she says. Kléber pretends to throw up, tucks his Beatrix Potter under his arm and hastily leaves the room.

Elizabeth turns up the lamp and, in the shadows of the warm kitchen, I take off my shirt and sit with my head bowed while she treats my sores.

'It was terrible when you were away in prison, Lou,' she says, behind me. 'Mummy and Dad both changed. I thought she was going mad. She insisted on laying a place for you at dinner every night, and would keep going to the door every five minutes, to see if anyone was there. And Dad, whenever he came back to the house for his laundry, barely even smiled. He kept saying that no one cared about him, that he was a prisoner himself, and why didn't we lay a place for him every night, too?'

'I didn't think anyone would even notice I wasn't here,' I shrug. 'I mean, I knew *you* would, Elizabeth. Ouch.'

'Sorry. Was that too hard?'

I shake my head.

'Oh, they noticed all right,' continues Elizabeth, quietly. 'There were a lot of tears. Dad blamed Mummy, saying all this would never have happened if we had moved to England long ago. And she blamed him, saying that it was because he wasn't a proper Catholic and wouldn't learn French that you didn't have anyone you could look up to, to teach you how to be a man.'

'Mummy said that?'

Elizabeth nods.

'And what did Dad say?'

'He didn't say anything. He just stormed out of the house, and slammed the back door so hard that the coffee mill fell off the shelf in the kitchen.'

I shut my eyes and wish I were three years old once more. Back in the days when I used to be brave, before the nightmares began.

'Now that you're back, Lou, please don't get sent to prison

again. Because I don't think I could stand it.' Elizabeth kneels and begins to dab cream on to the sores on my ankles. I don't like to tell her that those aren't boils, they're infected flea bites. There is a long silence, before she speaks again. 'I saw you and Marcel, one day, carrying a gun.'

I sit very still.

'Maybe it was a toy,' she adds. I force my ankles to relax, keep my breathing steady.

'You haven't still got it, have you?' she continues. 'That gun, I mean.'

'Of course not. There's nothing here.'

'Dad is worried you've still got a catapult hidden somewhere in the house. He says that if the Germans find that, we could all be shot. He looked for it every . . .'

'And what did he find?' The words come out more sharply than I intend. So I add, in a softer voice: 'There was nothing, was there?'

'No, nothing at all. But, Lou, will you promise me?'

'Promise what?'

'Promise you'll be good. Or at least careful. Oh, I don't know. Just no guns, all right? And no prison. Please.'

'I couldn't stand prison again, either.' I put my shirt back on. 'Although at least I'd be safe from Auntie Val and her needles.'

'So you won't play any more of your tricks? You won't take any more silly risks with the Germans? You promise me that?'

Elizabeth and I look into each other's eyes. She's beautiful, my sister. I don't just mean she's pretty, although she is. I mean there's something more in her, something deep down, that I see when she looks at me like this. I suppose it's a sort of lovingness. A way she has of making you know that she cares about you more than you have ever cared for anybody yourself. I've no idea what she can see in me. All I know is that whatever it is makes her sad.

Shoulders slumped, I lower my head and wish with all my

heart I could make the promise that she wants to hear. How I would love to empty out our cache and hurl all our weapons into the river Lys. Shadows have been coming at me in my sleep. I have not forgotten the boy in the cell downstairs. But the words will not come.

Seeing this, Elizabeth puts her arms around me, as Mummy used to do with Dad in the old days. I rest my chin on her head while she gently picks at a hole in my jumper, as if she were mending it. We remain like this for a while, saying nothing, lost in our separate worlds. Outside, dusk is falling but I can hear birds singing in the apple tree behind the house. And for a moment the gnawing, clutching fear that accompanies me everywhere ebbs from my tense limbs, and I feel safe. I dream I am a child again, and the world is simple and peaceful and whole once more. And then we hear the drone of bombers in the distance and the dream is gone.

2 December 1941

The house grows darker and more silent than ever. One day, even the clattering of Auntie Val's machines suddenly comes to a halt. She has run out of wool, and there are no more bobbins to be had.

'No more twist!' pipes Kléber, crawling around on all fours; 'no more twist!' I have no idea what this means, but he seems to think it's hilarious.

Auntie Val locks the door of her machine room, puts on her best coat, such as it is, and walks out of the house. Mémère says she will have gone in search of work, even though everyone knows that there isn't any, except in Germany.

By nightfall, my aunt has found a position as a waitress in a café run by her cousin. She says it's better than nothing. But the place must be filled with Germans snapping their fingers for coffee and potatoes. I can't imagine how she does it.

With Auntie Val out at work, Mémère now takes over the duties of cooking, assisted by her blind sous chef. So we eat a lot of mush, a lot of slush and, on feast days, a little piece of burnt shoe leather which they call rabbit. There is no coffee to be had, so we substitute a witch's brew of grilled barley instead. There are no matches, no soap. This does wonders for my boils. Short on tobacco, my father tries smoking the leaves of Jerusalem artichokes. A British soldier can survive any hardship, he says, just as long as he has his cup of tea. And then the tea runs out, and things become a little tense for a few days. But my father switches to strawberry leaves, and no more is said.

One morning, when out on an errand for Mémère, I spot a poster roughly pasted on to the wall of the Château de Nieppe. It depicts a fat German officer boarding a train marked 'Berlin', his suitcases overflowing with plundered goods. I stare at it, in awe of the nerve of whoever dared to stick it here. And I can feel the rage mounting in my chest, not so much at the message contained in the poster as at my own inability to do anything about it. I remember the words of Francis André, my friend in the bicycle shop, who said he would fight the Germans at the drop of a hat, if someone would just tell him how. Even after Loos, I know I would, too. But where to start?

At home, my father walks out of the front room looking even more sombre than usual. He says that the Japanese have sunk most of the American fleet in a surprise attack.

'What has this got to do with us?' demands Auntie Val.

'Who are the Japanese?' asks Kléber.

'And what's an American fleet?' pipes Elizabeth.

'Sometimes I despair,' groans my father, pressing the sides of his head with his hands.

'Oh, just tell us,' says my mother, silencing us all with the clarity of her voice. 'Tell us what it means.'

He hesitates. 'The signal's weaker than ever tonight. But I'd say it's bad news,' he shrugs.

And then, a day or two later, he emerges from his listening room and announces that Germany has declared war on America.

'So that must be very bad news,' declares my mother, confidently.

'No, no, it's good news.'

'But why?'

'Because America has declared war on Germany, too. The big boys have thrown their hat into the ring. Britain is no longer alone.'

'Yes, but who is America, Daddy?' demands Elizabeth.

'America?' He smiles and rubs his chin. 'America is Joe

Louis and Buster Keaton and Judy Garland,' he says. 'It is skyscrapers and chewing gum.'

'And George Gershwin,' chips in Rosemary.

'And James Cagney,' adds my mother. 'I met an American once.' She really is full of surprises these days.

'So will Judy Garland help us win the war?' asks Elizabeth, doubtfully.

'I should think so,' says my father, ruffling her hair. 'She and the Tin Man.'

A few days before Christmas, word reaches me that two sisters from my old school, the Eton Memorial School in Ypres, are in trouble. And one of them just happens to be Lilian Wilkins, the little girl with blonde hair who, whenever she was around, made me want to be there, too. I make an instant decision: I shall go to her and see if there's anything I can do. I'm not sweet on Lilian or anything like that. I just need to check that she is all right.

Like my father, Lilian's father used to work as a gardener for the Imperial War Graves Commission. Harry Wilkins managed to escape to England in 1940, a few days before my disastrous attempt to do the same thing with the Riouals. Yet his wife, Lilian's mother, was arrested and deported to Germany, leaving the sisters to fend for themselves in Belgium, where there are even more Krauts than there are in France.

God knows, I do not have a death wish. But I cannot abandon Lilian and her sister like that. I am thinking of asking Mayor Houcke to help me shelter the pair of them in Nieppe.

It is a grey afternoon, with low-lying mist and patches of rain. This suits me, because crossing the border into Belgium without the right paperwork carries a stiff sentence. Fortunately, the Krauts hate to get their precious uniforms damp, so there should be fewer roadblocks than usual today.

Ypres has changed since I was last here. Many of the houses are ruined, and all the road signs are now in meaningless

Gothic script. But after losing my way in the unfamiliar streets, I find the address at last and softly knock on the door.

Lilian looks shocked to find me on her doorstep. She stares at my bicycle as if she has never seen one before, and then just stands there, looking at my shoes.

'You cycled all the way here, just to see me?' she asks, in an incredulous whisper. She looks much thinner than before; her cheeks are hollow and sallow.

'I was just passing,' I shrug. 'You know, sightseeing.'

She allows herself the hint of a smile.

'Everyone always said you were different, Stephen Grady,' she says.

'Is that a good thing or a bad thing?'

'Oh, I think it's definitely good.'

'Well, aren't you going to invite me in?'

Lilian's face falls. 'I'm sorry. I mustn't. I can't.'

'Just for a cup of tea, I mean,' I add, embarrassed. 'I've come to help you. I was planning to rescue you and your sister.'

Lilian Wilkins begs me to leave at once. She says that there are German soldiers billeted in the houses on either side and that she is worried they are watching her.

I am about to leave, to cycle the twenty kilometres home through the rain, when she takes a step forward. And we just stand there, gazing at each other for a moment. Her eyes are brimming, and she is shaking her head as if she doesn't know what to say or do. So that makes two of us.

'Sorry,' she mouths, her eyes glittering. 'And thank you.'

I clamber back on to my bicycle and begin to pedal away. When I look back, she is still standing there, silhouetted in the doorway. The sky has cleared, and the ride home is across flat country. But it feels as if it is uphill all the way.

'Thank God,' says Auntie Val, when I walk back in through the door, much later than I would usually get home from the cemeteries. Taking me to one side, she explains that twenty-four young men have been shot at the citadel in Arras over the past few days. All were accused of participating in anti-German activities. And she says she had a horrible feeling that I might be one of them.

'I'm not as old and foolish as I look, Lou,' she whispers. 'I know you and Marcel are up to no good.'

'What do you mean?'

'I mean I wish you'd stay out of trouble, for all our sakes.'

'You flatter me, Auntie,' I reply. 'What's for supper?'

'Probably best not to ask,' she sighs, glancing at Mémère stirring a pot on the stove.

Marcel comes to me in a panic. A German patrol is rumoured to be heading our way, looking for concealed weapons. He says we have to shift the last pair of rifles from his father's barn at once. My father moves out of our house again, too, and goes to lodge with friends in Bailleul, or Balloo, as he calls it. Even after living a short cycle ride from Bailleul for a quarter of a century, he still cannot pronounce the name. Marcel's plan is that we should transfer the rifles into our cache at Pont d'Achelles. In my heart, I don't want to go anywhere near that cache, if Krauts are on the way. But in my head, I know this is the right thing to do. As it is, I feel as if I am being followed all the time. It must be even worse for Marcel, sitting on those weapons at home.

We carry out the operation after curfew, picking our way over the walls and hedges by moonlight and tucking the heavy rifles underground as quietly as we can. Afterwards, we do our best to cover up the access hatch of the cache with leaves and twigs and stones.

'What do you think?' I whisper.

Marcel shakes his head. 'Impossible to say in the dark. We need to come back in daylight, to see how it looks.'

In the milky sunlight the following morning, I glance out of the corner of my eye at the access hatch. Has someone disturbed it, or did we really leave it like that last night? All that is certain is that the damned thing is about as well hidden as the main gate of Loos Prison. Even my mother could spot it.

'Why don't we just go the whole hog and put a searchlight on top?' whispers Marcel.

'Yes, or a signboard: "Here Be Guns".'

I am doing my best to be cheerful, but my mouth is like sandpaper. What the hell were we thinking, to hide all these weapons right beside the Lombard farm, and only 200 yards from my parents' house? Hands in our pockets, pretending to loaf around, we begin to kick pebbles and earth and leaves over the access hatch.

'It still looks obvious,' whispers Marcel out of the side of his mouth, as we wander back towards the cemetery's stone gateway as casually as we can.

'Only because you're looking for it.'

'What if someone steps on the hatch?'

'They won't,' I reply, firmly. For this is the fear that has always dogged me, too, every second of every day. What if. What if. 'Nobody ever comes here these days. The French are too frightened, and the Boche couldn't care less about a bunch of Tommies their fathers shot.'

After passing through the little gatehouse, we turn to lean, side by side, on the boundary wall. I begin to roll a cigarette making a big show of being thoroughly at ease. The Cross of Sacrifice looks dazzlingly white in the morning sun.

Marcel lets out a great sigh. I know that he is playing the same game. 'This place would almost be beautiful,' he drawls, 'if I didn't know what it was.'

'It still is beautiful to me,' I reply. 'It has always been our garden. A rest camp, my dad calls it. He says all the men are landowners now. I used to come here to play.' The birds are singing in the trees around us; I can hear the buzz of a distant motorcycle.

My friend smiles. He is glancing around him at the neat lines of white headstones. 'How do you know which are the officers and which are the regular ranks?' he asks.

'You don't. The graves are identical, apart from the inscriptions.'

'Very democratic.'

'I think the idea is that we are all equal in death.'

'Except the Boche,' he reminds me. 'A dead German is a good German.'

'No, even the Boche.'

I can see Marcel's brain going tick, tick, tick. 'It was always such a waste, wasn't it?' he says, shaking his head. 'But now, the fact that we've started all over again. It somehow makes it so much worse.'

The distant buzzing becomes a full-blown roar, as two German motorcyclists in leather overcoats and dusty boots glide past us on their way up to the main road. Alarmed, I light my cigarette. Neither of us looks up. I can feel one of them giving us a long stare as he passes.

'*Merde alors,* that was close,' murmurs Marcel, when the sound of their engines has died away. 'You're sure the Boche won't actually stop here?'

'Quite sure,' I reply, taking a long drag on my cigarette.

'Because, if they do, you know we're *foutus*? They'll bring in a dog, and they'll find our stuff, just like that.'

'I know,' I shrug. 'But they won't stop here.'

The weather turns windy and, for the next two days, I check the access hatch of the cache twice daily, in case the leaves and earth have been blown aside. There has been no sign of the German patrol. Even so, I am finding it harder and harder to sleep. Kléber complains that I wake him with my kicking and shouting in the early hours.

On the third day, the wind is gusting more strongly than ever. Picking leeks in the vegetable patch behind the house, I am about to head over to the cemetery to check the access hatch yet again, when – from the direction of Pont d'Achelles – something glinting catches my attention. I stare at the glint, striving to focus with the wind blowing dust into my face.

A motorcycle is parked in front of the cemetery gate, in

the spot where Marcel and I stood leaning on the wall, three days ago. Its handlebars gleam in the sunlight. A few yards away, a man in grey-green uniform is picking his way along the outside of the cemetery's boundary wall.

Merde.

Crouching behind a row of withered tomato plants which still cling to their canes, I watch him carefully, holding my breath.

I glance across at the Lombard farm. It looks so peaceful, so unwitting.

Galloping footsteps, behind me, make me jump. Elizabeth is running down through the vegetable patch.

'Have you seen him, Lou?' she hisses. 'There's a German in the . . .'

She pulls up short and tiptoes the last few steps. 'Lou,' she whispers, 'why are you hiding?'

'I'm not hiding.' I duck a little lower behind what is left of the tattered tomato plants.

The soldier advances along the edge of the cemetery. I cannot see a dog. But I recognise that Schmeisser slung casually around his neck.

Just five more steps and I am dead; we are all dead.

'Are you sure you're all right, Lou? You're sweating.'

'Just shut up, OK?' I mouth.

No more than twelve feet short of the cache, the Kraut stops.

He glances around him. He looks straight at us.

As I watch, he takes another pace.

This wind.

I swallow, but there is no saliva in my mouth.

Please, Saint Rita.

I screw up my face. For a moment, the tall soldier turns towards the Cross of Sacrifice. And then, tipping back his head and dropping his shoulders, he unbuttons and relieves himself against the low wall.

22 October 1942

Months pass. Our clothes become a little more thread-bare, our stomachs a little more shrivelled, our backs a little more bowed. My work in the cemeteries, and my nightmares, settle into an uneasy rhythm. Asleep or awake, my mind teems with things buried beneath the surface: with soldiers, secrets, weapons, and with the mute sadness of defeated aspiration. I only wish I could do something to make myself feel alive in the midst of this war, rather than being tied to the dead of the last one.

I am upstairs, lying on my bed, when I hear a knock at the front door. Auntie Val pads down the corridor to answer it and, at the sound of a male voice, I peek through the banisters.

Mayor Houcke is standing there in his black hat and black overcoat. My secret saviour. And, according to Elizabeth, who comes rushing upstairs, he wants to see me.

My mother is already in the front room when I hurtle down there, taking the stairs two at a time. My father comes in from the vegetable garden a few moments later, wiping his muddy hands. He often works outside at dusk, when there is least risk of the house being searched.

'*Pardon moi*,' he tells Monsieur Houcke, offering the mayor his wrist to shake. '*Le jarding . . .*'

'*Il faut cultiver notre jardin*,' smiles Houcke, nodding. And then he shakes my hand and adds: 'I'm sorry I don't speak any English. But that's really why I've come. I wonder if you'd be willing to translate for me, Stéphane?'

'*Bien sûr*,' I reply.

'I'll just get Mémère to put the kettle on,' says my father.

'*Non, merci*,' replies Houcke, raising his hands and directing an anxious glance at me. He allows my mother to take his coat and my father urges him to take a chair, which creaks beneath his weight. Houcke offers round a packet of Gauloises. 'I'm sorry it has been a long time since my last visit,' he continues, running a hand through his hair. 'Have you noticed how long it takes to do nothing?'

'I'm afraid there's quite a lot of that at this time of year in the cemeteries, sir,' I reply.

'What's that?' asks my father, cupping his hand to his ear. With the other, he helps himself to a cigarette and waits for Houcke to light it.

'I said I've been working hard in the cemeteries.'

My father takes a long drag on his cigarette and thumps his chest to stifle a cough. 'That's my boy.'

'It's this wretched stasis that does a man in,' says Houcke. He leans forward in his chair, watching our faces carefully. 'For a man to be rendered powerless to act – for a Frenchman, above all, although I don't doubt that you English are the same – it's like, pardon me, Madame Grady, but it's like snipping off his balls.'

'Translation, please, Lou,' says my father.

'On second thoughts, Stéphane,' mutters Houcke, 'perhaps it is best if I speak with your parents alone. Your mother can translate. We will call you in when we need you.'

'Bring a cup of national coffee for the mayor here, Lou,' says my father. 'And sugar, too, if Mémère's not in one of her moods.'

I spend the next few minutes on the floor of the bedroom, with my ear to the boards. The voices are muffled, but I catch snippets of the conversation, especially when my father raises his voice. And then Elizabeth comes stomping up the stairs to fetch me.

My father looks alarmed, which is unusual. My mother has been weeping, which is normal. I want to thank Mayor

Houcke for springing me out of prison, but already it feels as if I have missed the moment.

'Say yes, Lou,' whispers my father. 'Remember that we owe the man everything.'

'Correct me if I'm wrong, Stéphane' says Houcke, pretending not to have heard him, 'but for us men, for human beings, to be able to look ourselves in the eye, we need to make a contribution to our world. And I don't know about you, but working to fill the bloated bellies of the German people somehow doesn't quite count, in my book. Are you with me?'

'*Oui, monsieur*,' I say, firmly. 'I most certainly am.'

'Good, because there is something I would like you to do for me, something I have already, in the most general terms, asked your parents.' Houcke hesitates, removes his spectacles, polishes them, and carefully places them back on his nose again. And then he asks the same question again: 'Are you with me?'

'Of course,' I reply. 'To the very end.' My shoulders tingle with a mixture of excitement and dread. Is it time for me to fetch the rifles from our cache? *À chacun son Boche*, people have started to say: if each of us takes down just one Boche, then we can obliterate our invader, just like that.

'Good, good.' Houcke looks relieved. 'And I have two witnesses here to prove that I didn't twist your arm.'

Rising to his feet, he flings open the door, to reveal Elizabeth kneeling there, her ear to the keyhole. Houcke chuckles. 'Make that *three* witnesses,' he says, patting Elizabeth on the head before she can flee. Finally, after ushering my parents out of their own front room, Houcke outlines what he wants from me.

In a hushed whisper, Houcke explains that more and more Allied airmen are being shot down in our region. And the dangerous business of helping them to escape back to Britain via Spain and Switzerland has just become a whole lot harder. It is rumoured that the Germans are starting to parachute-drop their own agents, disguised as Allied aircrew, to infiltrate the escape chains.

'Swift identification of these impostors is vital,' murmurs Houcke, locking his eyes on to mine. He says he is looking for a native English speaker to quiz any airmen who bail out in our zone, to test whether they are telling the truth.

'Perhaps my father . . .' I suggest.

Houcke smiles, nodding to himself. He walks over to the window, where he fiddles with the latch, to make sure it is shut fast. Then he returns slowly to his chair, stroking his chin.

'Your father is already in enough danger. Besides, you also speak French, Stéphane. And we're the same, you and I. I spotted it the moment I first met you. We are different from other people.'

'What do you mean, different?' I ask, my mind suddenly filled with thoughts of Lilian Wilkins.

Houcke rubs the side of his nose with his finger, brushing my question aside. In a low voice, he tells me that I will need to prepare three separate interview forms: one for Americans, one for Canadians and one for British aircrew. My job will be to ask them searching questions, which only a true native of their country should be able to answer. 'In other words, they need to go further than the sort of basic facts that a German agent might have picked up from his *Baedeker*.

'Right.'

'You don't know what a *Baedeker* is, do you?' he smiles. 'It is a guidebook for people who travel abroad, published in Germany. And I want you to ask the sort of questions that wouldn't even be in there.'

I ask him for an example, and he seems suddenly uncomfortable, tucking his shirt more tightly into the high waistband of his trousers.

'Well, supposing it's a British airman, you could ask him why *les Anglais* killed Joan of Arc.'

'Er . . .'

'It's a joke,' he smiles. And then he leans forward, his face close to mine. 'But here's the thing. If a single German agent, a single one, manages to infiltrate the escape chain, they won't give us a nice neat grave in one of your father's cemeteries, I can tell you that.'

'So it's up to me to decide if these airmen are telling the truth?'

Houcke nods.

'And if they're not?'

'Then you will let us know.' He pauses. 'And we will do what is necessary.'

'You mean —?'

'*Oui*.'

We both consider this for a while.

'Look, don't you think I should have someone else alongside me, just to make sure?' I ask. 'Marcel, perhaps?'

'My brother, Marcel?' Houcke appears surprised.

'No, you know, Marcel Lombard, who was with me in Loos Prison.'

'But he's just a boy.'

'He's the same age as me.' Houcke doesn't need to know that Marcel's English is even worse than my father's French.

For a moment, the mayor is silent. I can see his mind working.

'No, I'm sorry, Stéphane,' he says at last. 'I want you to do this alone.'

I nod.

'And you know that you and I, Stéphane, we never had this conversation.'

'What conversation?'

'*Bon*.' He gives his hat a firm tap and reaches out to shake my hand. With that, Monsieur Houcke swings open the door and strides out into the cold night.

26 November 1942

Though I am itching to start unmasking enemy agents, it is weeks before Mayor Houcke contacts me again. When he does, it is to invite me to a secret meeting at the École Laïque, which is to be chaired by Monsieur Cornette, the headmaster.

Before entering the room, I listen for a few moments at the door.

'Are we all here?'

'There's still Stéphane to come,' says a rich, gravelly voice I recognise at once as Mayor Houcke's.

'Stéphane?' asks another man. 'Surely you don't mean the Grady boy?'

Houcke pauses. 'Why? Is there a problem, Cornette?'

'Only that he's just a boy,' replies the headmaster.

'He's seventeen years old.'

'Exactly.'

'Oh, come, Cornette. Age is not biological. Look at me, I'm only forty-five, yet I can pass for sixty. And you, how old are you really? Sixty-five?'

'I'm forty-eight.'

'Which proves my point. The world can be unkind. But we manage. And Stéphane Grady has done good work in the cemeteries. I have begun to rely on him. More to the point, he is utterly fearless.'

'Oh, great. So he'll get us all killed.'

'Isn't he *un Anglais,* too? Can he really be trusted?'

There is a pause. I know I must enter the classroom, but not while they are talking like this. And Cornette is only just warming up. 'The boy knows nothing about fighting,' he continues, 'unlike the rest of us.'

'Oh? I knew you were in the school platoon, Monsieur Cornette. I didn't know you had seen active service.'

'Well, I was in the reserves . . .'

Gritting my teeth, I knock twice on the door and bustle in.

People leap to their feet. Mayor Houcke makes a hushing gesture with both hands and, one by one, they sit back down. While he sits at the teacher's desk, the others perch stiffly on top of the children's forms. Houcke introduces me to everyone, and we shake hands in silence. Then, his voice a low growl, Houcke outlines why we are here.

We shabby band of five misfits, either too old or too young to be soldiers ourselves, are to be the secret weapon with which Nieppe will fight back against the Boche. There are already similar cells operating in Lille and Arras, he says. Our numbers must be limited, because collaborators and informers are everywhere.

'Pétainist scum,' mutters one of the men. 'They make me sick.'

'So only those whom we can trust implicitly will we ask to join us,' continues Houcke. 'The less each of us knows, the less we can give away under torture. On which note, I have these for you, messieurs: a code name for each of you.' The mayor hands each of us a small brown envelope, marked on the outside with a single initial.

I open my envelope. Inside, a single word is written on a slip of squared paper. IROQUOIS. I swallow my disappointment. I was hoping for Tommy Gun, or Broadsword, or Silver Ghost. What sort of a name is Iroquois?

'This cloak-and-dagger stuff is all very well, Jules,' says the mayor's brother, once the hubbub has died down. 'But what is our purpose? We can't exactly wander around, bumping off Schleus.'

'Our purpose, for the time being, is non-collaboration,' replies the mayor. 'Our purpose is to be the stone in the occupier's shoe, not the one that whacks him on the head. Our purpose, messieurs, is to resist.'

The mayor's brother begins to grumble to himself. 'That's the thing about these politicians,' he whispers, loud enough for everyone to hear. 'They always have to say everything in threes.'

'Yes, Marcel,' chuckles the mayor, without amusement. 'But you get my drift. The moment when we will launch our attack on the German army must wait. For now, our resistance is chiefly to involve the distribution of secret pamphlets, and helping Allied airmen to make their way back to the safety of Britain. Perhaps also a little sabotage, from time to time. But we certainly won't be shooting any Schleus, any time soon.'

'We must still have weapons,' hisses Cornette. 'If we are to be soldiers, we must be armed.'

'Agreed,' whispers Marcel Houcke. 'With the risks involved, we will need guns to protect ourselves.'

'Guns are good for morale,' adds one of the other men, a glum beanpole with a walrus moustache.

'Carrying weapons means carrying risk,' counters the mayor. 'And besides, every shotgun and pistol in Nieppe was handed in during the amnesty. There are no weapons to be had. For now, we must make do with our wits, our cunning and whatever we can find in our barns.'

'Oh, great.' Cornette throws up his hands in disgust. 'So you call us to a meeting about how we are going to resist the Boche, and it turns out that we have nothing to resist them with, except a rusty scythe and a couple of mattocks. It's a joke.'

Houcke gazes wearily at Cornette. I can see him filtering various thoughts. 'If you have any better ideas, Monsieur Cornette, I am sure we would all be very interested to hear them.'

There is a long silence.

'We all still have our pocketknives,' shrugs Marcel Houcke at last.

'Yes, and I've got a pop-gun that I confiscated from one of the boys in my class,' replies Cornette.

'Without any guns, we'll be a laughing stock,' adds the man with the walrus moustache.

Another long silence. I clear my throat.

'I have weapons,' I say, quietly. Four pairs of eyes swivel to stare at me. No one speaks.

'What did you say, Stéphane?' Mayor Houcke leans forward in his chair.

'I said I have weapons,' I repeat, wondering if I have already betrayed Marcel's trust. 'If you need them.'

'*You* have weapons,' retorts Cornette, too loudly for my liking. I glance at the door. 'Oh, yes, I believe Monsieur Ruckebusch told me: a little wooden sword, and a peashooter that you like to use in church.'

'I have guns.'

'Even better. The boy has guns! Do they fire lumps of potato, by any chance?'

'That's enough, Monsieur Cornette.' A trace of colour darkens Mayor Houcke's cheeks. 'Stéphane, please tell us about these guns.'

I take a deep breath. 'Well, I have a pair of Fusils Lebel. That's the standard rifle some of you may remember from the last war. I also have two Mousquetons – the short cavalry rifle – and two Fusils Gras, which are old but well-oiled. On top of that, I also have a number of pristine Modèles 36, which are the latest French model with incorporated bayonet. And ammunition, of course.'

'Of course,' replies Mayor Houcke, his eyes glinting. 'Nothing else?'

I bite my lip. I am not used to speaking in public. 'I also have a Browning pistol, and a light machine gun with tripod, which is brand new.'

Again no one speaks. And then Marcel Houcke bursts out laughing. 'Not bad, for *un Rosbif.*'

One of the other men lets out a low whistle. Cornette

stares at the floor, his face dark. I glance across at the mayor, to see if I am in trouble. Arms folded, he beams at me, and winks.

'And where are they, these guns, Stéphane?'

'I'd rather not say, sir. But if you wish, I can take you there.'

The mayor slowly turns to look at Cornette. 'I wonder if you still feel, Monsieur Cornette, that young Grady here is surplus to our requirements?'

Cornette says nothing.

'Now as far as further recruitment goes,' continues Houcke, 'secrecy is everything. By all means enlist those with whom you would entrust your life. But remember that if one goes down, we are all likely to go down with them.'

'In that case, may I please propose Marcel Lombard?' I ask. 'To be honest, the weapons are partly his.'

'Of course, Stéphane,' nods Houcke. 'Recruit anyone you trust. Just remember to say as little as possible to anyone, including your family.'

Suddenly the mayor's brother leaps to his feet.

'What was that?' he whispers. We all listen, holding our breath. But there is nothing. Everyone looks at Houcke.

'The meeting is adjourned,' he says, hastily. 'Home safe, messieurs, and look to yourselves. *Bonne nuit.*'

I cannot sleep. How could I have been so stupid, announcing that I have guns? It was our secret, mine and Marcel's. And now, thanks to my ridiculous boast, we may both have to pay the price. There aren't a lot of Stéphanes in Nieppe. If someone was listening at the door, it won't take much for the Boche to put two and two together. We should all have taken code names from the start.

I cycle off to the cemeteries as usual, but it is hard to work when you have to keep stopping to check whether a German patrol has come to arrest you yet. The unceasing rain doesn't help. Winter is drawing in.

At lunchtime, I pedal straight over to the Lombard farm,

to find Marcel and confess my stupidity. Perhaps we should just bury the weapons in the woods and go into hiding ourselves.

'I'm so sorry, Marcel,' I begin, as soon as we are in the safety of the hay barn, listening to the rain drumming on the tin roof. 'I think I've really blown it this time.' I begin to tell him about the meeting at the school.

'You told them about the weapons, didn't you?' he says, coldly. I have always known that my friend is bright, but sometimes his intuition is frightening. 'Why did you do that?'

'Search me,' I shrug, peering at my muddy shoes. 'I suppose I was showing off.'

'Just like when you scribbled that stupid slogan on our Messerschmitt.'

'As I said: I'm sorry.' And then something clicks in my mind. 'Has someone already been round to quiz you about the weapons, then? That was quick.'

Marcel shakes his head.

'Is there by any chance something you aren't telling me?' I demand. I listen to the rain, which is getting heavier. I know that Marcel is no eavesdropper. But I am glad to deflect the spotlight of blame. 'Don't you trust me?'

'Considering that you appear to have blurted our secret, you'd understand if I did not.'

'Fair enough. But even so.'

We both consider this for a while. At last, Marcel speaks. 'I envy you,' he says, almost in a whisper.

'What?'

'I envy you, Stéphane.'

'Envy me? But we're in this together, Marcel. You're my best friend, comrades to the end, remember?'

'Yes, and you're the one whom the Resistance has recruited, and I'm not. You're the one who is going to get to fire our guns at the Boche, and I'm not. You're the one who has a job, and gets paid for it, and I'm still sitting at a desk in school, swotting up on logarithms and Latin. It's just not fair, so of course I damn well envy you. You'll be a hero, and I'll be nothing.'

'Please don't envy me,' I tell him, placing my hand on his shoulder. 'I'm a peasant with no education, Marcel. I tend the graves of dead soldiers for a few francs. My family life is a mess. Whereas you have everything: a brain the size of Lille; an old-fashioned life on a farm; wonderful parents; and enough food to go round. You're going to be someone important one day, you'll see.'

'You'll be someone yourself, too, Stéphane. You're not like anyone else I've ever met. You're special. You'll probably get to shake hands with the King of England, and he'll thank you for winning the war.'

'Yes, and you'll receive a medal from whoever takes over from Pétain and his cronies, once the Boche have been driven out.'

'A medal for what? Heroic schoolwork?'

'No, for your bravery as an ace fighter pilot, shooting down Messerschmitts.'

'I wish,' he sighs. 'But you know, I do still envy you, being recruited and everything.'

'I assure you, Marcel, it means nothing. Besides, the mayor says I can recruit you, too.'

'It's not quite the same thing though, is it?' he says, with his back to me. And then he jumps down from the hay, and stomps out of the barn into the rain.

Over the next fortnight, the rain turns to sleet and then to snow. I develop a hacking cough which has Auntie Val muttering darkly about Thermogene wadding, so I do my best to suppress it. Sleeping is hard, and made all the harder by a new and recurring nightmare which has begun to invade my unconscious. I am walking round and round the exercise yard of Loos Prison, and the guards are letting off their guns. But instead of firing them into the air, they are picking off the prisoners one by one, laughing at us as we walk faster and faster around the yard.

When I ask them why they are doing this, a guard – who turns out to be a woman – says it is because they have found all the weapons buried under the floor of cell 54.

I recruit two other chaps of about my age into the Resistance. One is the sunny-natured and fearless Francis André, who used to repair my bicycle and who has just finished his first term at the University of Lille, where he is studying engineering. The other is my friend, Maurice Leblon, the strapping socialist from Pont de Nieppe, whose family bravely sheltered an English squaddie called Charlie for several weeks in 1940.

I'm a little nervous about how the pair of them may get on, since Francis lives in a large *maison de maître* with too many windows and doors to count, owns a tailored jacket and at least three pairs of shoes. Before the war, he liked nothing better than to go and hunt wild boar with some rich uncle in Sologne. Whereas Maurice is a softly spoken factory worker who lives in a shabby terraced house just opposite Mayor Houcke's place in Pont de Nieppe, and whose idea of fun is dreaming about the Revolution and discussing miners' rights. Luckily for me, Maurice has decided that he loves the British almost as much as he hates the Germans, especially since Hitler invaded the Soviet Union. Whether he can learn to love a privileged engineering student like Francis André remains to be seen.

For now, however, Marcel and I have a job to do. The headmaster, Cornette, has asked us to deliver our weapons to the school. Officially, this is because they will be more accessible there. Unofficially, it is because he thinks we're too young and foolish to be responsible for them. Mayor Houcke is most apologetic. He acknowledges how risky it is to move the guns, but says that it is because Monsieur Cornette is 'that sort of man'. Even Marcel doesn't know what this means.

12 December 1942

Marcel and I meet at midnight, in the darkness of the Lombard barn. After a silent handshake, we tiptoe out towards Pont d'Achelles. The slim crescent of the new moon casts just enough light to see the boundary wall. Together, we pick our way along it as far as the access hatch. And then I am squeezing my away down the tunnel on my belly, praying that the frozen earth above me does not collapse.

Cornette is to have six rifles, a pistol and our light machine gun. We do our best to hide these, in pairs, inside bundles of hazel stakes intended for next year's tomato plants. The guns are heavy, and – with frozen fingers – it takes forever to wire the bundles to our bicycles in the dark.

At last, Marcel is satisfied, and we each have two rifle barrels poking out beneath our handlebars, with ammunition stashed in satchels on our backs. The Browning pistol is tucked into my belt. The other two rifles and machine gun must wait for our second run.

We exchange glances and prepare to stand on our pedals. It's now or never.

Suddenly we freeze: something is moving in the hay. Is there someone there?

I fumble for the pistol. Marcel flicks the switch of my father's work lamp. Surprised, the rat scuttles back into the shadows.

We ride down the narrowest, bumpiest country lanes towards the École Laïque in the centre of town. The snow-dusted landscape looks ghostly by moonlight, and I am worried about the tyre tracks we are leaving on the roads.

Not a moth flutters, not a cat skulks as we approach the stopped heart of Nieppe. There are no street lamps. The place is silent as a tomb. I want to cough, but I picture traitors watching and listening in the darkness. No wonder Marcel insisted we oil our wheels and brakes with a few squirts of sump oil drained from my father's motorbike. In this stillness, the slightest squeak would give us away.

Our cargo stowed in silence, the journey home is a breeze. After sneaking in through the back door, I creep upstairs and crawl under the covers of the bed I share with Kléber. It is three o'clock in the morning, but I am shaking with cold and my mind is racing too much to sleep. A faint glow of warmth radiates from Kléber's side of the bed, but not enough to take the icy chill off my side. And I'm certainly not about to cuddle up to him. It's bad enough that we have to share at all.

On the other side of the room, I can hear my mother's soft wheezing and the comforting rasp of my father's snores. Mémère says his presence in the house puts us all at risk. But I like it. I like having four of us in this room. Tonight, even so, I feel desperately alone.

Over the next few nights, with the guns safely delivered to the school, I begin to sleep a little better. I have fewer of my old nightmares involving subterranean metal staircases and firing squads in the exercise yard. Gone are my regular trips to the bedroom window, to check that no German police are waiting for me out there. Gone the suffocating nausea every time I arrive in Pont d'Achelles. Yes, we still have rifles there, along with the smoke bombs and flares. But a weight has been lifted. Even my cough improves.

Another meeting with Mayor Houcke, his brother Marcel, Cornette, and the rest of our motley crew. We have begun to style ourselves as Resistants, setting us apart from the many locals who, if they are not actively collaborating in the German rape of France, seem happy enough to accept it. All of us are starving, while the Boche are getting fat. We have guns and we have men. What are we waiting for?

I know the answer to this, of course. We are waiting for the British to return. In the meantime, ours is to be a passive resistance: helping Allied airmen to escape back to Britain, providing false documents for those who need them, and doing whatever we can to make the occupiers' lives uncomfortable. Yet I still haven't been asked to interview a single airman.

Has Mayor Houcke lost faith in me? He says he has made contact with the publishers of a clandestine newssheet called *La Voix du Nord,* which we are to help distribute in the mining areas around Lens and Béthune, as well as Lille and its surrounding towns. We will also adopt Voix du Nord as the name of our own Resistance group. So we are now officially members of the VdN. I think the French love their abbreviations almost as much as they love their meetings.

Delivering newspapers does not make my pulse race. At least when my mother did it in the Great War, she was hammering around on a horse and cart, often beneath an artillery barrage, and the people she was helping were British Tommies in the trenches. Whereas we will be pedalling push-bikes in the rain, taking soggy newspapers to French civilians in terraced houses, some of them built right on top of where those same trenches were dug. Where is the thrill in that?

Lying awake in bed, I formulate a plan. After breakfasting upon grilled-barley coffee and a porridge of watery oats, I quietly reach into one of Mémère's storage jars. And then I drop round to see Marcel.

'Come on,' I tell him, when he comes, bleary-eyed, to the door.

'Where are we going?'

'You'll need some sugar.'

Marcel blinks. 'Sugar?'

'You'll see.'

'Don't be ridiculous. I can't ask my mum to give me any of her precious sugar ration.'

'Then don't ask her. Just pinch a few lumps when she's not looking.'

I wait on the doorstep, watching a snail on a dock leaf, while Marcel disappears back into the house. A few moments later, he returns.

'I still don't understand what all this sugar is for,' he whispers, crossly.

'Francis André says it gums up a carburettor something rotten. Get my drift?'

'*Nom de Dieu.*' Marcel rolls his eyes. 'You don't seriously mean you're planning to sabotage a German army motorbike, are you, Stéphane?'

'Of course not.'

'Thank God for that.'

'We're going for the lorries.'

Marcel buries his face in his hands. But I can see him smiling through his fingers.

'All right,' he says, shaking his head. 'But this time – *this time,* Stéphane – when I say it's time to scarper, we scarper. Is that a deal?'

'Deal,' I nod. 'Thanks, Marcel.'

The two German lorries are still parked where I saw them last night, side by side, in the square outside the church. There's just room for a malnourished teenager to slip between the two. We come across a shiny black staff car in the square, too: a huge Daimler, with chrome bumpers and red leather seats. But the petrol cap on the first lorry will not budge. We'll have to go for the second one, against the wall.

'You loosen the cap,' I tell Marcel. 'If it comes off, I'll wander past and drop the sugar in the tank.'

'This one's stuck as well.'

'Then try the car.'

'What if someone sees?'

'They won't.'

'There. It's done.'

Sauntering behind the gleaming motor, I drop a handful of sugar lumps into the tank and, a few seconds later, Marcel casually wanders past, replacing the petrol cap in one smooth movement.

'You've done this before,' I murmur, as we stride back to our bicycles, hands in our pockets. To our right, a side door at the back of the church swings open, and two German officers in peaked caps walk hurriedly down the steps, deep in conversation. They barely glance at us before turning the other way, towards the Daimler.

'What if the car doesn't start?' whispers Marcel.

'It will,' I reply. 'They'll be halfway to Paris by the time they have to get out and walk.'

Buzzing with adrenaline, I want to hop and skip at the thought of what we have done. It is nothing, I know. Just a few sugar lumps in a tank. But we got away with it. In broad daylight, too.

A minute later, we hear the grinding shudder of the two lorries starting up. Both loaded with soldiers, they hurtle past us in the wake of the black Daimler. All three vehicles are hurrying towards Pont de Nieppe.

'Probably the Doryphores are off to arrest some poor *réfractaire* who doesn't want to go and work in Germany,' says Marcel, coughing from the fumes of their exhausts.

'Whatever they're doing, they're up to no good,' I reply. Standing astride our bicycles, we watch the tail-lights of the convoy disappear. 'I wish we'd managed to sweeten all three vehicles.'

'Something tells me they'll be back.'

'Then we'll get them next time round,' I say, firmly.

Next day, I am tidying the borders in the French military plot in the Nieppe municipal cemetery when I am conscious of someone approaching. A young man in a long coat walks quickly up to the boundary chain and stops a few feet away from me.

'Got a light?' he asks. And then, before I can reply, he

moves closer and whispers: 'Stéphane, have you heard what happened to Maurice Leblon?'

'Don't tell me he got drunk and fell in a ditch,' I reply, feigning not to care about one of the newest recruits to my section.

'A truckload of Verdigris surrounded his house, and he . . .'

'What?' I retort, incredulous. 'They arrested him? When did this happen?'

'Yesterday afternoon.'

'About four o'clock?'

'Yes.' The man's eyes widen. 'But how did you know?'

'Just a wild guess.' My mind is already racing, stacking up possible causes and consequences. How much do the Germans know? And, more to the point, how much will they be able to extract from Maurice? I ask the man where they have taken him.

'Nobody is quite sure,' he says. 'I was hoping you might know.'

I shake my head and, without another word, the young man slips away. I pack up my tools and head for home, half-expecting to find our house surrounded by Germans too. But everything is just as dark and silent as usual. Elizabeth is playing with her friend Justine up at the café on the corner. My mother is doing her rosary in the front room. And Mémère's cooking smells worse than ever.

At the Lombard farm, Marcel is as shocked as I am. What happens if they torture Maurice, and he talks? Maurice is a tough character, and a fiercely loyal friend. But he knows the guns are up at the École Laïque, and if he breathes a word of this, then Cornette may spill the beans about us all. The only consolation we have is that nobody but us knows the whereabouts of our cache. Suddenly there is a hammering on the front door. Are the Germans here so soon?

Marcel flies to the window and peers down into the street. Then he turns to me with a quizzical frown.

It's Auntie Val. She is already in the Lombard kitchen by the time we get downstairs.

'Maurice Leblon is asking for you, Stéphane' she says, hands on hips.

'What? Where? Not . . .'

'He's waiting for you at our house. And he looks hopping mad.'

My mind in turmoil, I hurry home.

'You won't believe this, Stéphane,' he says, the moment I walk in, 'but I've just been released by the *Feldgendarmerie* in Lille.'

'Thank God.'

'It seems some *couillon* told the Boche that I killed a German soldier in Lens. Can you imagine that? These bloody collaborators and denouncers. They seriously piss me off. I could have been deported.'

'Or shot.'

'Well, quite,' he replies, tugging at his collar as if it is too tight.

'So how did you get out? Don't tell me you've escaped.'

'No, my alibi was so darn bulletproof that they even drove me home.'

'I like it.'

'Yes, but not before they'd sweated me for some info.'

'Did you —'

'Of course I told them nothing. But after twenty-four hours of that place, I can't imagine how you and Lombard survived three whole months in Loos Prison. And I can't wait to find out who denounced me. They showed me the anonymous letter this idiot had written. I already have my suspicions.'

'Who?'

'No one you know,' he replies. 'And when I take my secret revenge, you won't hear about that, either.'

6 January 1943

A note arrives from Cornette, summoning me to his office. I feel as if I must be in trouble as I walk through the icy schoolroom, my breath making clouds in the air.

The headmaster's large office feels extravagantly snug, thanks to the chestnut logs popping and crackling in the Godin in the corner. Cornette clears his throat and stares at a wooden blotter on his desk. Its handle is carved into the shape of a small mouse.

'I have been warned . . .' he says at last.

'*Oui?*'

'I have been told by a friend . . .'

'*Oui?*'

'I have reason to believe that the German police may suspect me of being up to something.'

'I understand.'

'Do you?' Cornette reaches for the blotter, and begins slowly to waggle its handle from side to side. He lowers his voice. 'You've no idea what it's like, Grady, for a man in my position to be responsible for all those . . . you know, those *things*. You never should have brought them to me. I can hardly sleep at night. I do have a family to consider, you know.'

'But you asked us to bring them here.'

'Did I?' He winces. 'Well, perhaps I did. And now I am asking you to take them away again.'

I blink, speechless.

'There's just one problem.' Cornette hesitates, his eyes darting from side to side. 'I have thrown all the . . . you know . . . for safety, I have thrown them into the school latrines.'

'What?'

'In schoolboy language, if that helps, I dumped the guns in the bogs.'

I stare back at him. To think of the risks we took in moving those weapons. And now they're in the shit.

'Why didn't you tell me? I could have come with my group . . .'

'I couldn't wait. And how could I get a message to you in time?'

'Great.' I grind my teeth. 'I'll take them back to our cache.'

'Suit yourself.'

We do not shake hands. I head straight out to the school lavatories, which are in a long, narrow building in the playground. Even in midwinter, the smell in here is worse than in the earth closet behind our house. Half a dozen wooden thrones surmount a common pit, perhaps six feet by four in size. And there, when I peer down into one of the grubby holes, I can just spot the gleam of a rifle barrel.

The following Saturday evening, Marcel and I carry out the salvage. Wearing a pair of old Wellington boots from the Lombard farm, I take a deep breath and lower myself down through the service hatch.

'How come I always have to do the dirtiest jobs?' I ask, just before I duck beneath the wooden floor. My eyes water with the fumes. Some of the rifles are visible in the lamplight, others I have to fish for in the sludge.

'Because you're so good at them,' chuckles Marcel, whispering down through one of the holes. I poke a broom handle up through the next-door hole, making him yelp with surprise.

Suddenly he gasps. 'Down, down,' he hisses. 'Get down.'

I fling myself flat in the latrine, half-burying myself in the choking slurry. A few moments later, from somewhere above me, I hear an unmistakable sound in the silence. Someone is giggling.

'*Punaise*,' I spit, staggering to my feet and shoving the last of the guns up to him. The pistol and most of the ammo are nowhere to be found. 'I'll get you for that, Lombard.'

Marcel is still wiping the tears from his eyes as I clamber out of the latrine and begin to walk stiffly towards him; nostrils smarting, arms outstretched, feet squelching in my piss-logged boots.

'Really, I've done you a favour, Stéphane,' he stammers. He takes a step backwards. 'No German is going to arrest you smelling like that.'

I lunge. I grab. And then I give him the biggest, stinkiest, soggiest bear hug I can.

'I'd hate the Germans to arrest you instead of me,' I growl, laughing.

Aghast, he manages to squirm free, and gazes down at his sewage-soaked smock. 'My mum is going to kill me,' he wails.

We do our best to rinse the guns beneath the pump in the corner of the schoolyard, wrap them in feed sacks and shuttle them away. In the early hours, we wash them again by moonlight in the Lombard pond, and rub them with some more sump oil, before heaving them over the fence and returning them to our cache in Pont d'Achelles.

With the guns back in our possession, my nightmares come back, too. Faceless, hooded men pursue me through my dreams.

Cornette vanishes. According to Mayor Houcke, who announces the news at our next meeting, the former headmaster has changed his name and taken shelter with relatives in another region of France. I am not dismayed to see him go.

18 February 1943

'Did you forget, Lou?' asks Elizabeth when I creep in through the back door, long after curfew. 'Where have you been?'

'Forget what?'

'Mum and Dad's silver wedding anniversary. They said I couldn't go over to Janine's house because I had to be here. Dad's come down from the attic, and we had cows' udders as a treat. What have you been doing?'

'Oh, you know.' I barge past her, making for the front room. 'This and that.'

'Look who's here,' announces my father, wrapped in a blanket. Auntie Val has lit the fire – another treat, no doubt – but the room still feels almost as cold and damp as it is outside. Everyone is sitting around in their overcoats. In the flickering light, my father looks pale, and his waxy skin reminds me of the prisoners in my cell at Loos.

'Is it Lou?' asks my mother, sitting huddled over her rosary in the corner. She reaches out for me with her hands. 'You're so tall, these days.'

'How many years is silver?' I ask, bending to give her a kiss on each cheek, and then moving round the room, greeting Mémère, Auntie Val and Rosemary in the same way.

'It's twenty-five years,' replies my father. 'But it feels more like fifty.' He glances at my mother, who makes no sign that she has heard. 'Mind you,' he adds, 'nothing has changed. We married in wartime, when we had nothing. And now, twenty-five years on, it's still wartime and we still have nothing. That's what I call progress.'

'Well, congratulations to you both,' I say, leaning on the piano with one elbow. I roll myself a cigarette, doing my best to look relaxed, pretending to be quite at home. I wish I was still at my meeting with Houcke and the others. At least with those men I hardly know, I feel I belong.

'Thanks, son,' replies my father. He raises an empty glass. 'And here's to the next twenty-five years, if we live that long.'

'I'm not sure I want to,' whispers my mother.

'Oh, come on, Berthe,' he cajoles. 'Don't be like that.'

'How much longer will the war go on, Dad?' asks Elizabeth, clambering on to his lap with her favourite toy, an articulated doll dressed all in blue, in one hand.

'How long until the Last Crump? I don't know, love.' He opens his blanket, to let her snuggle inside.

'I already feel as if it's been going on *forever*. Janine's mum says it's all the fault of the British that people are still being killed. You know, by the bombing and everything. They say they hit the railway station last night.'

'Well, there's a thing,' he says. 'As far as the Frogs are concerned, the war's already over. They've all put their hands up. Pétain has made his grubby little pact with Hitler and, while he and his cronies swan around in Vichy, they've abandoned us up here for the Fritz to do what they want with us. They say there are more Huns here than anywhere else in France. And I'll bet they'll make us part of Germany, if the British don't come and get us soon.'

'We're all going to be German?' Elizabeth stares down at her doll.

'No, love, no. I'd sooner die than see my graves out there become part of Germany. And they *are* still my graves.' My father gives me a long, hard glance, which breaks into a smile.

'Janine has a picture of Pétain on her bedroom wall,' says Elizabeth.

'Does she, indeed?'

'Yes, and she says that the reason there's nothing in the

shops is because the British blew up the French navy, so there aren't any boats. But we didn't blow up the French navy, did we? I mean, we never would have done that, would we?'

'I don't know, love,' replies my father, stroking her hair. 'There are some things in this war that I don't understand myself.'

'If you ask me,' says Auntie Val, exchanging glances with him, 'you want to be careful of your friend Janine, Elizabeth.'

'Perhaps it would be best if she didn't go round there any more,' says my father, quietly.

'But Dad, she's the only girl of my age in the whole street.' Elizabeth pulls away from him. 'Janine is my only friend. We're both going to be hairdressers like Cousin Denise when we grow up.'

'No, you're not,' says my mother from the corner, making us all jump. 'You'll catch fleas from the customers, and get varicose veins from all that standing up.'

'But Mummy . . .'

'All right, love,' murmurs my father, cutting her off. He flips open his cigarette case. Finding it empty, he snaps it shut again. 'But just you be careful what you say to this Janine. Everyone's a collaborator these days.'

We all stare at the pitiful fire for a while, trying to get warm just by looking at it. I offer the cigarette I've rolled to my father. He hesitates for a moment. Then he tucks it into his cigarette case for later.

'I read in the *Voix du Nord* that France will be liberated this year,' I murmur, returning to my place beside the piano. I reach down to stroke the keys with my fingertips.

'Yes, and I'll be the Commonwealth snooker champion,' replies my father. 'What do the lefty Frogs know?'

'And I'll be the pianist of Radio Lille,' adds Rosemary, frowning at my fingers touching her piano.

'And I'll be a hairdresser,' pipes Elizabeth.

'No you won't,' says my mother.

'What will I be?' asks Kléber, from under the table.

The others all smile at each other when he says this. But I just think it's sad. Far away, in the silence, there comes the crump of distant bombing. The RAF must be hitting Lille again.

19 March 1943

In the cellar of a house in Armentières, I am standing in front of a dim lightbulb that makes my shadow look ten feet tall. Beside me on the dusty floor are two other shadows: one, as long as mine, leaps from the booted feet of Marcel Houcke, the mayor's brother; the other, a little shorter, belongs to a man I have only just met. Together we are gazing in awe at a mountain of newspapers in bundles, each one tied up with green twine.

This is what 15,000 copies of the *Voix du Nord* looks like. Possession of just one copy could be grounds for imprisonment. And we are supposed to be delivering 1200 of them, first to Marcel Houcke's house in Pont de Nieppe and then to depots in Béthune and Lens. They say that deportation to Germany is the minimum sentence if we are stopped. But Loos Prison would be bad enough. I'm not sure I could survive another stint in there. This winter, for the first time in my life, I have really begun to feel the cold.

Around us, crucifixes hang on every cracked and white-washed wall. Beside me, Marcel Houcke frowns at the mound of papers. A big, beefy man with greying hair, he wears a brown corduroy suit, made by his family firm in the days before all the yarn was diverted to Germany. In this light, he makes me think of a more troubled version of his brother, the mayor. Turning his head first on one side, then the other, he might almost be measuring someone up for a suit.

'Well, Stéphane, what do you think?' he asks, under his breath.

I shake my head. Sometimes I wonder if my mind is warped. What I was thinking was what a lovely bonfire you could have with this much paper.

'Here's the question, Pauwels,' says Houcke, glancing at the other man. 'Do we take as many as we can in one go? Or do we spread the risk over more journeys?'

'You're worried about German roadblocks,' replies the man. 'It's so hard to know where they will appear next.'

Houcke shakes his head. 'It's not the Boche I'm worried about,' he says, sadly. 'It's my wife. She'll say I should be putting up shelves.'

We all laugh. It feels good to relieve the tension in my chest. I can see why the mayor asked his brother to take over as leader of our group.

'How many papers are there in each bundle?' I ask, peering down at the familiar masthead of the *Voix du Nord*: a line of factories, cranes, farm buildings and windmills silhouetted against billowing clouds of smoke, with the words 'LIBERTÉ, ÉGALITÉ, FRATERNITÉ' on the left-hand side.

'There are 200 in each,' whispers the man. Maurice Pauwels is quite the opposite of Marcel Houcke: dark-eyed, thin and shrewish, he seems to buzz with electrical energy, and his small, quick movements give him the air of a frightened vole. Houcke introduced him to me as a member of the *Voix du Nord*'s editorial team. So he must be the real deal. But it makes me nervous, just standing next to him.

'Then we'll take 200 in each trip,' declares the mayor's brother. He tosses one of the bundles to Pauwels, who winces. 'Are you all right, Pauwels?'

'They're not light, are they?' coughs the newspaperman.

'You should know, you help write the thing.'

'Yes, but I don't print it. That's Noutour and Dumez's bag. Or at least it was, until they were arrested by the Gestapo. Fortunately, your brother has kindly . . .'

'Enough said,' says Houcke, briefly raising his hand.

'What my brother does is his affair. What I do is mine.'

'Sorry, yes, of course. How many can you take with you today?'

Houcke and I exchange glances. This trip was meant to be just a recce. We weren't expecting to take any newspapers today.

'I'm happy to take one bundle now,' I say. 'I'll stuff it under my shirt.'

'You see, Pauwels?' says Houcke, beaming. 'Not bad for *un Anglais,* is he?'

I begin to unbutton my shirt.

'You'll look like a pregnant skeleton,' protests Houcke, eyeing my jutting ribs. 'Are you sure this is a good idea?'

'I'll take the back routes.'

'All right, then I shall take a bundle, too.' He peers down at his belly. 'But there's not as much room under my shirt as there is beneath yours.'

Smiling, Pauwels presses his fingertips together. 'Thank you, thank you, both of you.'

'So how many are *you* taking?' asks the mayor's brother, staring hard at the little journalist.

'Me? I . . . I wasn't—'

'It's only as far as Pont de Nieppe. And I'll protect you from my wife.'

Pauwels looks to me for support. I stare hard at the dead flies on the floor. 'Oh, go on then,' he tells Houcke at last. 'I'll take 200 also.'

'Good, that's half the work done already,' says Houcke. 'We're almost there.'

He and I agree to leave ten minutes ahead of Pauwels, who wants to say a few prayers before setting out. The poor man is shaking like a leaf. I try not to let his fear infect me.

'Say a few for us, too,' chuckles Houcke, as he unlocks the door and we climb stiffly up the stone steps to the hall. I am beginning to feel quite sick.

'When we're cycling, stay at least 200 metres behind me,

Stéphane,' says Houcke, suddenly serious, over his shoulder. 'That way, if I hit a roadblock they won't get us both. You'll know something's up, because I'll raise my hat, like this. Don't try anything heroic. Just vanish, say nothing to my wife, and get a message to my brother when you can.'

With one hand on the front door chain, he turns to me.

'Are you OK, *Rosbif*?'

'Yes, of course,' I reply.

'It's just that you look a bit pale.'

'I'm fine,' I say, firmly.

'Of course you are.'

Outside, in the street, we hear a lorry grumble past. Houcke peers through the spyhole in the door.

'Troop carrier, stuffed with Schleus,' he whispers.

'Excellent.'

The mayor's brother turns and smiles. He places his hand firmly on my shoulder. 'You know why we're doing this?' he asks.

'I think so.'

'It's about the truth.' He pats the bundle beneath his corduroy shirt. 'It's the truth about the evil that Hitler represents, and how your countrymen, Stéphane, are beginning to push him back. People need to know this stuff. It gives them hope. Hope is so powerful. But it's fragile, too.'

'*D'accord*,' I reply. A sudden vision of my mother flashes into my mind. Not the blind and broken woman hunched over her rosary in the corner, but the young daredevil shaking the reins of a horse and cart, galloping up to the trenches under fire, advancing upon the Tommies with a cargo of truth.

'What was it that Jesus said?' continues Houcke. '*The Truth will set you free*. Well, that freedom has got to be worth dying for, hasn't it?'

I blink, and nod. 'I'm ready now,' I tell him. 'Let's go.'

Giving my shoulder a final squeeze, he unchains the front door. We glance up and down the street. There is nobody in sight; nobody to notice one grey-haired man in a corduroy suit and one seventeen-year-old boy in blue-dyed battle dress, hiding the truth beneath their shirts, as they stride out into the rain.

24 July 1943

On one of my missions into Lille, after dropping off my copies of the *Voix du Nord*, I head towards the little motorcycle garage where Francis André sometimes works. It is a summer afternoon, but the grey city seems as drab as if it were midwinter. Grey pigeons peck at grey crumbs beneath the tables of a grey pavement café, at which everyone appears to be wearing grey-green uniform. Only Schleus, after all, can afford to drop their crumbs these days.

Francis has his head under the bonnet of an old Citroën when I approach. Glancing down at his oily hands, he offers me his wrist to shake.

'This is a nice surprise,' he grins. 'What brings you to Lille, Stéphane? Got any little jobs for me?'

'Oh, you know,' I reply, doing my best to hide my shock at his sallow appearance. 'Even we country bumpkins like to come and see the big smoke every now and then.'

'Meanwhile everyone around here is hankering for the countryside, because at least you bumpkins can still eat.'

'If I'd known, I'd have brought you a food parcel.'

'Maybe next time, eh?' And I can see from the look in his eyes that Francis is not joking. He lowers his voice. 'By the way, have you heard the news about the engine factory at Fives?'

'That huge place where they build the locomotives?' Please, not again. I have indeed heard about the three RAF bombing raids aimed at the factory in Lille, and how every single bomb has missed its target. The civilian casualties have been catastrophic, and my family knows all about it. Cousin Denise's son, Michel, the delicate seventeen-year-old who used to come and cut my father's hair, was killed in one of the raids. I never really knew how to talk to the young *zazou*, and used to find his handshake unnerving. But even I could tell that he was a very gentle and sensitive fellow, who did not deserve a violent end. So please don't tell me that *les Rosbifs* have killed another bunch of Frogs.

'It *was* the place where they built the trains. But not any more,' says Francis, his eyes shining.

'The RAF did the business at last?'

'That's the weird thing,' he whispers. 'Nobody heard any aircraft at all. Nothing else was hit. Much of the factory roof at Fives is still intact. But a friend who works there says that all the vast electrical transformers that used to power the place have been blown to smithereens, so they haven't even got enough juice for a toy train. None of the men on duty were harmed. Yet the place is utterly *foutu*.'

'So who did it?'

'I thought you might know, Stéphane.' Francis leans inside the Citroën and pulls a slip of paper out of the glove box. I can see at a glance that it is a piece of German propaganda.

'WHERE ARE THE ENGLISH?' it sneers, in an attempt to convince the French that they have been abandoned by their staunchest allies.

'The Boche have been spraying these around for weeks,' he says, smiling at my puzzlement. 'But this one, which I found in the street this morning, is different. It's almost like a calling card. You'll see what I mean when you turn it over.'

On the back of the propaganda leaflet are four words, crudely stencilled, which make the hairs on the back of my neck stand on end.

'WERE THEY AT FIVES?'

22 September 1943

Another long day. Hunger makes everything so hard just now. I know we are lucky to have a *potager* still studded with a few vegetables, but it doesn't seem to matter how many beans and carrots I eat: five minutes later, I am starving and tetchy again.

This evening, after working until five in the cemeteries, I have spent the hours until dusk delivering bundles of the *Voix du Nord* to Marcel Houcke's mining contacts in Lens and Béthune. My partner in crime is Maurice Pauwels who, as far as I can tell, is constantly scared out of his wits. This makes cycling with him especially draining, as he insists on reciting prayers throughout the journey. *Sainte Marie, pleine de grâce* . . .

We no longer tuck the newssheets under our shirts, because it is too hard to lose them in a hurry that way. Instead, we stash them in a bag slung over our handlebars. If we spot a German roadblock, this makes it easier to toss the incriminating papers into a ditch. That's the idea, anyway. But the Germans are becoming ever more cunning. Often a couple of soldiers will sneakily tuck themselves behind a building or a hedge, well before the actual roadblock. So even if you spot the police barrier and turn back, you still get munched by the Doryphores. And, at this point, the Virgin Mother is unlikely to be able to help.

It is after eleven o'clock by the time I creep exhausted into the thick gloom of our house. I am surprised to see a light glimmering down the passage. Auntie Val and Mémère must still be up.

The moment I walk into the kitchen, Auntie Val shuts the door behind me and stands with her back to it. Mémère bars the other door. Their expressions remind me, absurdly, of Kourk. An empty place is laid at the kitchen table: an icy comment upon my absence, no doubt.

'What the hell is this?' I demand. 'An ambush?'

'We don't want to know where you've been,' says Auntie Val.

'Good, because I'm not about to tell you.'

'We just want you to know that we're worried about you, Lou.'

'Well, good. Because I'm worried about you both, too. It's way past your bedtime.'

'Seriously, Lou,' she continues, walking towards me. 'We're worried that you're doing too much. You're out half the night . . .'

'You never eat,' adds Mémère. 'You never sleep.'

'You break the curfew— . . .'

'So what?' I can feel the anger mounting within me. Or is it the hunger? I'm not sure I can tell the difference any more. 'There isn't anything to eat anyway. The Boche will be rationing fresh air before long. And what's it to you? What the *hell* does it matter if I go out when I choose to do so, and come back when I will?' I'm surprised to hear these words coming out of my mouth, when all three of us know that if I am stopped by the Germans after curfew the whole family will pay the price. But, right now, this is a mere detail. Visibly shocked, they just stand there, absorbing my rage.

When I have finished, Auntie Val takes a deep breath.

'And then there's this.' She draws a blue, unmarked envelope out of her apron and hands it to me. 'One of Marcel Houcke's boys dropped it off for you earlier today.' I glance at the envelope and tuck it into my back pocket. 'And it's just . . .' she continues, wringing her hands.

'*Yes?*' I glare at them both. Mémère is chewing her gums. I hate it when she does that.

'We just . . .'

'You just *what*?' It has been such a long day. All I want to do is go to bed. And now here I am, facing a stupid interrogation from a pair of old crones.

'We made you this.' Auntie Val holds out a small earthenware pot. 'We don't know what you're doing, Lou. But we do fear for you. And we wanted to say thank you. Whatever it is. Because we're sure that it matters. And it's good. And we're glad you're doing it.'

Flustered, she puts the pot on the table.

We all stare at it. Is it what I think it is? Is that real butter on top?

I narrow my eyes. I know that smell. The salty-sweet aroma transports me back to when I was a child and we were living in the shadow of an old war, not squinting in the glare of a new one. Back then, I didn't even know what rationing was. I can feel my jaw begin to ache and my empty stomach does a hollow flip. I know what they've gone and made me, the sly old birds.

It's only a whole pot of *pâté de lapin*. I know it is.

'That's real butter on top,' says Mémère.

'But don't ask us where it's from,' adds my aunt. 'Because we won't tell you.'

It must be smoky in the kitchen, because I can feel my eyes start to prickle. I clench my teeth and take a couple of deep breaths. And then I stop myself.

'Thank you,' I manage to say. 'I don't deserve this. But thank you both very much.'

'Aren't you going to eat it, then?'

'Sorry,' I whisper, shaking my head. 'I can't.'

Auntie Val's jaw hangs open. 'What's wrong with it? *Pâté de lapin* is your absolute favourite. You're a growing boy. Why can't you eat it?'

'Because of Dad.'

'What about him?'

'He's the one who deserves it, not me.'

'That *ingrat*?' snaps Mémère, crossly. 'He puts us all in danger. And you're the one who does all the work.'

'Please,' I beg. I try not to look at the dish of pâté, try to ignore its creamy butter crust. 'Let's share it tomorrow. All of us. Including Dad.'

There is a long silence, deep enough that I can hear the crickets whirring outside. And then Auntie Val, her cheeks bright red, solemnly removes the pot.

After the pair of them have marched up to bed, I extract the blue envelope from my pocket. There is nothing written on the outside. Inside, in the faintest pencil, is scrawled an address in Le Seau, the village from where I used to catch the tram when I was a schoolboy in Ypres. I'd like to believe that the handwriting belongs to some beautiful girl who is going to change my life. But it looks too jagged for that. Opening the fire door of the stove, I toss the envelope into the embers and watch it burst into pale yellow flames.

Next morning, everybody else is already up and about by the time I come down to shave at first light, and the rabbit paté is nowhere to seen. I don't like starting the day like this. Auntie Val, my mother and Mémère are already ticking off Elizabeth and Kléber about their table manners, and there is a hostile bustle in the kitchen as I wander in. I would rather have the silent house to myself, even if it means shaving in the dark.

Standing in the corner of the kitchen with my back to the others, I pump a few glugs of water from the well into the tin bowl and shave without soap. Like everyone else, we haven't had soap for months, so my chin is dotted with nicks and scratches in the places where the razor has snagged. I smart as another streak of scarlet appears.

Back upstairs, I pull on my underwear and blue-dyed battle dress, before stomping down for breakfast in unlaced boots. Three small grey lumps of bread sit in the basket in the centre of the table. One of these I spread with a thin film of

Mémère's sour apple jelly, made with grape juice instead of sugar. From the kitchen, the tutting and muttering follows me down the passage as I hurry out of the house.

After a slow morning trimming the borders in Pont d'Achelles, I cycle to Le Seau. But when I arrive at the address I have memorised, it looks all wrong. This house is far too grand to be used by the Resistance. It's just the sort of place that the Krauts commandeer. With my face pressed against the gates, I peer up at the tall, net-curtained windows. And then jump back, as someone taps me on the shoulder from behind.

'Looking for someone?' drawls a tall, handsome man in a light-coloured suit. With his black hair slicked back, and a tortoiseshell cigarette holder tucked into the corner of his mouth, he looks like a film star, or a gangster, or both.

'I am Iroquois,' I say, lowering my voice.

'Are you, indeed?' he chuckles. 'Well, in that case, you'd better come in.'

I follow the man as he wanders up the neat garden path to the house and skips up the front steps. His shoes look expensive. But I notice a hole in the elbow of his jacket.

After he has shut the front door behind us, he twists keys in three different locks, making me flinch. The man turns to me, extending his hand with a broad grin on his face. Clear skin; good teeth. He must be about thirty-five.

'It's Stéphane, isn't it?' he announces. 'I am Jean Sonneville. Thank you for coming.' His skin smells of cologne. His breath smells of liquorice. He does not appear ever to have cut himself shaving.

'*Bonjour*,' I reply. '*Mais . . .*'

'The Houcke brothers have told me all about you,' he says, putting his arm around my shoulders. 'The mayor says you are an exceptional young man, and Marcel Houcke assures me that if I am able to overlook your Britishness, then you and I will get on like a house on fire. Well, I don't know about that, but we can do our best, can't we?'

The mention of the mayor and his brother reassures me. Even so, it is strange that neither of them has ever told me about this man, Sonneville. The name seems familiar.

'Your house is . . . unbelievable,' I reply.

'Oh, just a few trinkets, picked up here and there,' drawls Sonneville, with a wave of his wrist.

We are standing in a marble-floored hall, which opens into a vast salon with tapestries and paintings on every wall, the polished windows hung with embroidered curtains that stretch from the ceiling to the floor. Chinese lamps glow on side tables that look as if they are veneered with tortoiseshell, and the mantelpiece glitters with trinket boxes of porcelain, enamel and gilt. I feel as if I have wandered into a movie.

'Beer or Pernod?' asks Sonneville, opening an octagonal drinks cabinet which is painted silver inside.

I hesitate.

'Or perhaps you'd prefer gin? I can only offer you Loos, I'm afraid. We haven't been able to get any Gordon's for months.'

'Loos is fine, thank you.'

Sonneville half-fills a crystal tumbler with gin, and then – with a surreptitious glance in my direction – drips a few drops of brown liquid into it from a black bottle.

'Are you . . .?' I croak. I glance through the archway to the front door. I can feel my pulse begin to race.

'You didn't want bitters?' He puts down the bottle with a clink.

'Sorry, I thought . . .'

'You thought I was trying to poison you?'

I hesitate. 'Well, I suppose I did wonder . . .'

Sonneville throws back his head and roars with laughter. It is the kind of full-throated belly laugh I have not heard since before the war began. I let out a muted chuckle.

'À *la tienne, Iroquois*.' He raises his glass of neat Pernod to me. 'You don't mind if we call each other *tu*, do you, since we're going to be working together?'

'Not at all,' I reply, wondering what on earth I am doing here. I stare at Sonneville. He stares back at me, swirling the amber liquid in his glass.

'You're wondering what on earth you're doing here, aren't you? Well, come with me. I have a surprise for you.'

Relieved to be able to put down my glass, I follow Sonneville through the salon and out into a large ornamental garden behind the house. Beyond this is a field, with a small green tool shed in the far corner.

'Go ahead,' he says. 'Open the door.'

Before I can ask him to open it himself, the door of the shed flies open. I jump backwards as two figures emerge, blinking, from the darkness. And then we all shake hands, as if this sort of thing happens all the time, and the two strangers introduce themselves.

Squadron Leader Clarence Motherall and his navigator, Bill Dumsday, say they were flying a Mitchell bomber when it was shot down by German flak over Saint-Omer. I cannot help gawping at them, because these are the first Allied airmen I have ever met. The first Canadians to boot. The three of us have a stilted conversation in English, most of which consists of them being amused (Motherall) and amazed (Dumsday) at how little I know about French women. Sonneville looks on, arms folded, uncomprehending, visibly delighted.

'So what do you think?' he whispers, as we walk away, leaving Motherall and Dumsday in their shed. 'You're the expert. Are they German agents, or the real deal?'

My mind races. 'I didn't bring my Canadian questionnaire with me, I'm afraid. But I'm pretty sure they're genuine.'

'*Bon*,' he says, smiling up at the trees. 'Me, too.'

Back in the salon, Sonneville offers me a cigarette from a teak-lined silver box. He explains that he is in a Resistance organisation called the War Office, or WO, and that sheltering Allied airmen is really just a sideline for him. And then he tells me something that makes my eyes widen. The group is run by a young British officer, parachuted into France. A real officer of the British army, right here in our midst.

I try, and fail, to look unimpressed. He lights my cigarette.

'You haven't heard of your fellow countryman, Captain Michael – or Capitaine Michel, as we call him?'

Sonneville studies my face with a disappointed frown. 'In a way, it's good you didn't know, of course. But Capitaine Michel really is someone exceptional. So you will. Before long, everyone will.'

Intrigued as I am to hear more, I tell Sonneville about my own work with Marcel Houcke's Voix du Nord Resistance group and happen to mention that I am in charge of a section of four men myself.

'Ah, yes: the Four Musketeers. I've heard all about your section from the Houckes.'

Leaning on the marble mantelpiece, Sonneville becomes expansive. He says he would prefer his own section to hand over certain elements of resistance activity – sheltering Allied airmen, distributing newssheets and helping forced-labour evaders – to our group. This would leave the WO free to take more direct action against the Germans, such as the sabotaging of military targets.

'All the fun stuff, in other words,' I say.

Sonneville winks at me. 'We do what we can.'

'What have you blown up so far?'

'Oh, loads of stuff.'

'Such as what, exactly?'

Sonneville turns away, rubbing his hands. 'It's funny,' he says, turning to face me at last. 'But you're one of the few people I've ever met, Stéphane, to whom I find it very hard to lie.'

'Me?'

He shifts from foot to foot; looks slightly annoyed. 'Look, we haven't actually blown up anything yet,' he says, thrusting both hands into his trouser pockets. 'We're still waiting for the explosives. But I've had the training. I know what to do.'

'Ah.'

'And we did manage to derail a train a few weeks ago, when we undid all the bolts on one of the rails.'

'Really?'

'Yes, *really*,' he laughs. 'God's honest truth. Actually it was bloody hard work, I can tell you, which doesn't really suit my *modus operandi*. There we were, wrestling for hours with all that rusty metal. And, forty-eight hours later, the Schleus had the line repaired and the train was back in steam again. Life will be a whole lot better all round once Capitaine Michel gives us some high explosives to play with.'

'Unless you happen to be a Schleu.'

At this, Sonneville emits such an explosive guffaw that he has to pull out his handkerchief and wipe his nose.

'It's all right for some,' I add. 'Meanwhile I'm still cycling for miles, doing my blasted paper round.'

'Delivering propaganda is dangerous work,' he replies, emphasising the point with his cigarette holder. 'And far more valuable than making a few trains late.'

'Even so.' We both take a long drag on our cigarettes.

'Well, look, Stéphane,' he says at last, exhaling the smoke through both nostrils, 'how would you feel about your little section accepting the occasional WO mission ordered by Capitaine Michel?'

'VdN or WO, it's all the same to me,' I lie. Sparks shoot up my spine. A real officer of the British army. 'But yes, we shall be more than happy to follow your Capitaine Michel, if Mayor Houcke agrees.'

'Leave Houcke to me,' says Sonneville. 'The man's a politician, not a soldier. He'll do what's expedient; that's his job. Besides, now that the Germans are on to him, it's his brother Marcel who is in the hot seat. And what neither of them seems to understand is that some of us need a little excitement in our lives – to play a few tricks, blow up a few trains – just to keep things interesting. Isn't that right?'

'Yes,' I reply, a big smile creeping across my face. 'I think that's absolutely right.'

2 October 1943

The Allied bombing raids are beginning to intensify, especially around Saint-Omer and Hazebrouck, where the workers of the Todt Organisation are labouring on huge engineering projects. The German air defences are improving, too. And as more and more aircraft are shot down, so more and more airmen are floating to earth beneath silk umbrellas. Brave local peasants race to find them before the Germans do. Fortunately, Pierre Glorian, the son of the pharmacist in Cassel, is rather good at this. The local farmers trust him; their wives give him tip-offs when they go in to pick up their suppositories.

But locating the fallen airmen is only the start. Next they must be moved, sheltered, fed and helped to escape back to Britain via Spain or Switzerland. Everyone involved in this shadowy operation is putting their life on the line.

At last, I receive a message from the mayor's brother at Pont d'Achelles. I am to meet up with another contact, a woman in Méteren, who will lead me to a secret address. He says she will be well-dressed and carrying a straw basket.

I roll a celebratory fag, scraped from the little pot of dust that is all the tobacco I have left in the world. And then I rush home to tell Marcel. As usual, Lombard is still at school. So I smoke the cigarette alone, on the front step. All I can think about is my impending adventure. Houcke says there is a British airman they want me to check out.

Mademoiselle Plouvier is waiting for me when I cycle into the town square of Méteren, almost an hour's ride from

Nieppe. At least, I hope it is Mlle Plouvier. Why else would a well-dressed lady be sitting in this drab little square, when some of the puddles have ice on them? Houcke told me she is in her fifties, but this pert and pretty woman looks younger than that to me. I glance at the straw basket beside her, its contents covered with a cloth. A jar or two of apple compote, perhaps? Or a Luger with the safety catch released?

'Bonjour, Mademoiselle Plouvier?' My breath makes clouds in the early morning air.

She turns her head towards me and frowns, before breaking into a smile.

'Bonjour, and how good it is to see you,' she replies, kissing me on both cheeks as if we are old friends.

'I hope I'm not late . . .' I begin. And then the church clock strikes nine above our heads, and we both smile.

'Right on time,' she says. 'So let's be off, shall we, lest we be late for our meeting?' I notice that she uses the subjunctive, her speech a cut above the colloquial French we rabbit in Nieppe. 'Our friend is staying in a farmhouse just outside Eecke. Do you know the village? The farmer and his wife are delightful people.'

Suddenly a black German staff car and a truck full of soldiers swerve into the square. They spill out their contents in front of the *mairie*. I try not to look. That's a lot of Germans, for such a small village. Has somebody tipped them off?

'Come on,' says my new old friend. She sounds calmer than I feel. 'It's time we went.'

Soon we are cycling side by side through the open countryside, with the winter sunshine just beginning to warm our backs.

'This is nice, isn't it?' she calls, from just behind me.

'Are we going too fast?' I can't help thinking about all those Doryphores outside the *mairie*.

'Actually, I think you're keeping up rather well.'

I laugh, grateful for her lightness. My father always says

that French women have no sense of humour, but I like Mlle Plouvier. An elegant nettle-stalk of a woman, with glossy brown hair pinned up at the back, she has an electrical charge about her which almost makes her light up and crackle when she speaks. I wonder why she has never married, for she is pretty and so full of life. Reassuring, too. Wouldn't it be a good idea for her to come and interview the Allied airman with me, to make sure I don't make a mistake? The question keeps bouncing around my head. But so, too, do Houcke's words: I want you to do this alone.

At last we come to an isolated farmstead, where we lean our bicycles up against a block of empty rabbit hutches.

The front door opens. In place of a blood-stained airman in RAF uniform, we are confronted by a rubicund farmer in faded blue overalls and rubber boots. A white cat streaks through his legs and out of the house.

Mlle Plouvier says a few words and introduces me to the farmer without naming him. She sounds urgent now, with none of her former chirpiness.

'*Bonjour, monsieur*,' I say, before uttering the line I have silently rehearsed: 'My name is Iroquois. I have come to collect your guest.'

'*C'est bien*,' he whispers, glancing over my shoulder. 'Perhaps you would both like to come in?'

Mlle Plouvier makes her excuses and turns to go. This time we shake hands, rather than kissing. I tell her I hope we meet again. Smiling, she holds my gaze with her kind eyes and then leans forward to give me a peck on each cheek. I notice how clean and fresh she smells.

'*Bon courage, Iroquois*,' she says. 'I will think of you.'

In the kitchen, the farmer is agitated. He explains how he found their British airman, Malcolm Whiting, stuck in a tree almost a fortnight ago. He is supposedly the navigator of a Halifax bomber, and claims to have been shot down on the way to Germany during a night raid.

'He's quite the talker,' says the farmer, picking at his black fingernails. 'But it's all in a foreign language, so my wife and I haven't a clue what he's on about. Could be English or German or Chinese, for all we know.' He peers anxiously at me. 'But you'll know whether he's telling the truth, won't you, Iroquois?'

I nod, glancing at a half-eaten mouse in the middle of the stone floor. Then I sit at the kitchen table with my sheet of questions, while the farmer goes off to fetch Whiting and his wife makes coffee on the wood-burning stove.

'Are you all right?' she asks.

'It's just that my hands are cold,' I explain, pretending to warm them under my arms.

A moment later, the door opens and the farmer returns with a tall young man in tattered blue uniform. With his dark hair and pencil moustache, he reminds me of Clark Gable. And he might as well be Clark Gable, for – even after meeting Motherall and Dumsday – I feel utterly in awe of this airborne warrior, who has jumped out of a burning aircraft on his way to destroy Germany in the dark.

'Hello,' I say to him in English. 'I'm Iroquois.'

Without a word, the farmer and his wife slip out of the kitchen, and we are alone.

'Funny name,' replies the airman, in a refined English accent. 'Where did you learn to speak English?'

Aren't I supposed to be the one asking the questions? 'I went to an English school in Belgium for a while,' I reply, coldly. 'Now, I need to ask you some questions to verify your nationality, if you don't mind.'

'Not a bit. Let's get cracking.'

My mind begins to whirr. He seems almost too English, almost too convincing. 'Shall we sit down?' I offer.

'Sorry, I should have offered you a chair. Here, let's sit by the window.'

'No, no, please,' I say hurriedly. 'In the corner, I prefer.'

I can feel my heart beating fast. It's not just that I may be about to unmask Whiting as a German agent. It's also that I may be about to unmask myself as an idiot. My English has deserted me. My coolness, too. I glance down at my list of questions and cringe at the thought of asking any of them.

We sit facing each other on wicker chairs beneath the staircase. Biting my pencil, I leap into the void.

'Where is the statue of Eros?' I ask, looking Whiting straight in the eye. Veins bulge at his temples.

'Outside Lillywhites, just along from the Criterion.'

'Pardon?'

'Except that it isn't, just now, because they've packed it away.'

'I simply want to know where it is.'

'Right now, I'd say it's probably under Mr Churchill's desk.'

'Mr Whiting . . .'

'Do you want me to say Piccadilly Circus?' He smiles. But I can see his irises flickering, the hint of a twitch at the corner of his eyelid. There is something else going on, behind that suave performance.

'I want you to cooperate.' We stare at each other.

'It's *Flight Sergeant* Whiting, if you must know.' He crosses his legs. 'But chiefy will do.'

'Flight Sergeant Whiting, I have to explain to you that if you want us to help you to get back to Britain, you need to help me. I mean, you need to *cooperate* with me.'

'All right, old boy.' He uncrosses his legs. 'Sorry, go ahead.'

'What product beginning with W gives you vim and vigour?'

'Oh, cripes, don't tell me . . .'

'I'm not going to tell you.' Nor am I about to tell him how much my questions owe to a single postcard of the advertisements at Piccadilly Circus, postmarked in Ramsgate.

'Whisky? Wright's coal tar soap?'

'And what G is good for you?'

'Apart from girls, you mean?' Whiting grins. But our eyes meet and his smile freezes on his lips. 'Sorry. It's Guinness, isn't it?'

'Next question: what are Bile Beans for?'

'Bile Beans!' Whiting snorts. 'You've got me again. Is it gippy tummy? You know, the trots in the extremis?'

I make a note on my piece of paper. I have already heard enough to make my mind up about Whiting. But he is becoming agitated.

'Look, Iroquois, have you got any proper questions? You know, what date was the Battle of Hastings, that sort of thing? I don't mean to bind, but I don't seem to be doing too well here. And I need you to help me out. Please.'

Once again, our eyes meet. And this time I see something different in Whiting's eyes.

'All right, who beat Wolverhampton Wanderers in the last FA Cup final, in 1939?'

'Is it Portsmouth?'

'And whose works are performed by the D'Oyly Carte Opera Company?'

'Was Portsmouth right then?'

'I'm afraid I can't say. Now, the D'Oyly Carte . . .'

'Gilbert and Sullivan. I saw their *Yeomen of the Guard* at the King's in Hammersmith last year. Can I have an extra point for that?'

'Which railway would you use to travel from London to Ramsgate?'

'The Southern Railway?'

'How many balls are there in an over?'

'Six. Unless there are any no-balls or wides.'

'Please just wait now, Flight Sergeant, while I review your score.'

'You really are taking this seriously, aren't you, Iroquois?'

Without looking at the questionnaire, I walk over to the fireplace, pull out my cigarette lighter and set fire to the sheet of paper.

'I've brought you a set of overalls to wear over your uniform,' I announce as we watch the edges of the paper curl and blacken. 'It's not much of a disguise, but it's something. I assume you can ride a bicycle?'

'Yes, but I . . . look . . . I didn't realise . . .' Again, Whiting is running his hands through his hair.

'Please, we haven't much time before curfew.'

'Are we going far?'

'Far enough. Be sure to stay at least 200 yards behind me, but keep me in sight at all times. The Germans often set up roadblocks on the outskirts of towns. I'll pull a white handkerchief from my pocket if I see one up ahead.'

'And what do I do then?'

'You disappear, if it's not too late. *Parlez-vous français?*'

'Afraid not, old chap. Unless you count *deux bières, s'il vous plaît* and *où est le Moulin Rouge?*'

'All right, so we'll just have to keep our fingers crossed and hope for the best.'

'Which happens to be precisely what I was doing just the other day.'

'Oh?'

'Yes. Shortly afterwards, my aircraft caught fire. I was lucky enough to bail out and survive. But all my crew mates are dead.'

'You seem quite cheerful, considering.'

Whiting stares at me for a long time. It is a stare that emphasises the vast gulf in our life experiences and the yawning distance between us, though we are standing just a few feet apart. When he finally speaks, his tone has changed.

'Please do not mistake my levity for cheerfulness, Iroquois. When you fly an aircraft as part of Bomber Command, lift is what keeps you in the air, until the flak blows you to bits. But it's levity that keeps a man from spiralling in. Do you see?'

'I think so.'

'No, I don't suppose you do. You're too young to have learned anything yet, and you French peasants are completely insulated from the war. You haven't a clue what it's like to lose your closest chums, just like that.' He clicks his fingers. 'Six friends dead, and you want me to tell you how many balls there are in an over. You haven't been bombed, as London has been bombed. No, you just sit here, filing your nails and sipping your wine, waiting for us to win the war for you.'

Confused, I look into Whiting's eyes, and wonder why he is saying these things to me. I did my best with the interrogation. I am about to risk my life for this man whom I do not know. Whereas the worst that will happen to Whiting, if the Germans catch up with him, is that he will be sent to a military camp to sit out the war.

'I'm sorry,' I say quietly, 'but now we really do have to go.'

It begins to rain as we pull away from the farm, and I keep glancing over my shoulder to see how Whiting is doing. He looks wobbly on the bicycle, but he hasn't fallen off. And then a thought strikes me, and I have to pedal all the way back to warn him.

'Wilco,' he says. 'So on the right is in the right, just like in flying. Although why you chaps can't just drive on the left is beyond me.'

I settle to a comfortable pace, and try not to think about German patrols. We keep to country lanes and farm tracks where we can, but there is still the main road to cross about three kilometres from Méteren. With the rain becoming heavier, I look over my shoulder to check on Whiting.

He has vanished.

Panicking, I pull up at the side of the track, in a place where I can see at least half a mile behind me. Still no sign of him.

Where the hell is he? We haven't crossed any difficult terrain, and we certainly haven't seen any Germans. There is no reason for him to have stopped. The thought that I have just lost my first Allied airman a few minutes into my very first mission, throbs in my head. I have no choice but to turn back.

More than a kilometre up the road, I find him kneeling on the ground over his bicycle. His hands are covered in grease and his overalls are soaked.

'Bally chain's come off,' he says. 'I thought I'd lost you.'

'Here, let me fix it,' I reply. 'My chain has a habit of coming off, too.'

I feel relieved and exhausted by the time I get back, soaked to the skin, to the rue du Sac. My debut mission is complete. Papa Lombard comes hurrying out of his house at the sound of my squeaky old bike. I am about to collapse into his arms, when he shrugs.

'Oh, it's you, Stéphane,' he says, making no effort to hide his disappointment. 'I was hoping you might be Marcel. The poor chap had a tough exam at school this morning, and he was so nervous about it. I'm dying to hear how he got on.'

Waving my weary apologies to Papa Lombard, I let myself into our house.

Still dripping, I wander through the veranda and out into the *potager*. I can see my father down at the far end, stooped over his Brussels sprouts. The rain-splashed plants glisten on either side of me as I trudge noisily down the muddy path. I don't want to surprise him. He stands up stiffly at the sound of my approach, with one hand on his lower back.

For a second, we make eye contact. I wonder if he can tell, just by looking at me. I would love to tell him. Not just about Whiting, but about all of it. I wish I could just give him a hint of where I've been. I want him to know what I've done. And even though I know I can't tell him, what wouldn't I give for him, just this once, to ask?

'Hello, Lightning, it's you,' he says, under his breath. He eyes me quizzically, with just a hint of the old glint I remember from before the war. 'I wanted to ask you . . .'

'Yes, Dad.' I hold my breath.

'I've been wondering . . .'

'Ask anything you like.' I grin. If he asks, I'm going to tell him. Because who is he going to tell, and what's he going to do: denounce his own first-born son to the Boche?

'I was just wondering if you still have any of that tobacco left. I'm dying for a fag. Would you mind if I . . . ?'

'Of course, Dad. Of course.'

8 October 1943

Jean Sonneville is a very interesting man. Everyone says he comes from a family of notorious smugglers, but I'm not sure about that. All I know is that much of his work appears to take place at night, and he is always full of new ideas for how we can make life difficult for the Germans. He is itching for something he calls a Spectacular,

After I have made a couple more visits to his house, during which I chat again with Motherall and Dumsday in their shed, he asks if I am ready to join him on a nocturnal mission. My heart lifts. I picture us unbolting railway tracks and blowing up bridges. So it comes as a surprise when he tells me that our first operation is to catch a number of sheep from outlying pastures, drag them back to his wood by their hooves, and slaughter them by moonlight. On other nights, we raid chicken houses. We even steal a pig. Sonneville has me stun it with a sledge hammer, stick it with a knife, and cut it up into large chunks, all in the dark. He assures me that what we are doing is all right, because it is a German pig. We rob potatoes from silos, too, and rabbits from their hutches, all in the name of the Resistance.

The idea, as I understand it, is that our commando raids are to teach a lesson to farmers who have been collaborating with the Boche or dealing on the black market and attempting to charge exorbitant prices for their wares. I can't help thinking that what we are doing is illegal, that it amounts to petty theft. Won't what we are doing make people hate the Resistance almost as much as they hate the Germans?

Sonneville is having none of this. With a world-weary

sigh, he points out that our nocturnal activities are a necessary sacrifice to sharpen us up for the exciting sabotage missions – perhaps even the Spectaculars – which lie ahead.

'Nothing is ever black and white in wartime, Stéphane,' he reminds me, laying a hand on my shoulder.

'I know, but it's just . . .'

'Look, when the poor are going hungry, someone has to take a stand. Someone has to provide food for the airmen in hiding and for the *réfractaires* who don't want to make bombs for the Boche.' Sonneville says we are like Robin Hood. I certainly cannot accuse the man of favouritism, for even his own relatives are not exempt from our raids, if they have not behaved to his satisfaction in the past. I just hope that at least some of our loot finds its way to people who deserve it.

He gives me some daylight duties, too. Mostly these involve keeping guard outside a shabby café in the hamlet of La Crèche, where he goes for top-secret meetings to discuss important War Office business. The café is a good cover because, according to Sonneville, it is the sort of place the Germans despise.

'Did you happen to see Capitaine Michel?' I ask, after an unusually long meeting one afternoon. Sonneville has invited me back to his house for a drink. We sit in his big, dark kitchen, sipping Belgian beer.

'Not Capitaine Michel, no,' he replies, grinning at my boyish fascination with his British chief. 'I saw someone else, someone with some very sensitive and valuable secrets.'

'*D'accord*,' I reply, knowing better than to ask any more.

In the midst of all this, my work in the cemeteries continues. There is little to do at this time of year, but I follow my father's practice of scrubbing the headstones with water and a brush. I clip the grassy edges of the borders with my long-handled shears, too, before straightening the turf with a cutter shaped like a half-moon. I appreciate my simple routines among the graves more and more, now that the rest of my life has become so complicated. It isn't just the guard duties and the nocturnal sheep-rustling for Sonneville. It is the constant unease about the weapons hidden in our cache. It is Elizabeth watching me at the kitchen table with her big, tear-filled eyes. It is the niggling twitch I feel whenever I see Marcel Houcke walking towards me.

I am not bad at coping with surprises. Even so, I do feel my mouth go dry when I receive word from him about the next airman I am to interview. This one claims to be an American, which is fine. I have already put my questions to several of his countrymen, and I know roughly what to expect: the gum-chewing swagger; the easy kinship; the ignorance about anything east of New York. But this particular American is being sheltered in a farmhouse just outside Calais, and this is less fine.

Not only is Calais almost a hundred kilometres from Nieppe, but Houcke wants me to cycle all the way there with an extra bicycle for the airman. Allowing five hours to get there, an hour at the farmhouse, and then a quicker journey home with my charge, it means a ten-hour round trip. It helps that Pierre Glorian, the pharmacist's son, will be accompanying me for part of the journey. But on the whole, I would rather kill a pig in the dark.

I leave the house at daybreak, with my two bikes and a stomach fluttering with foreboding. It feels good to be riding beneath a clear sky for once, but exhausting to be juddering along the bumpy *pavé* with one hand clutching the handlebars of an extra pair of wheels. Though I am not yet breaking any laws, my eyes are out on stalks for the first sign of any Germans.

I have been pedalling for about a month and a half when, just up ahead, on the outskirts of Arques, a bespectacled figure in a black overcoat several sizes too big for him holds up his arm, gesturing for me to stop. I am relieved to see Glorian, especially when he offers me a thin grey *tartine* which I scoff in one mouthful. He also offers to push the spare bicycle for a while, and I am not about to refuse. But there's a trick to the technique and somehow he can't quite get the knack. So I go back to my hunched position over the handlebars, with one arm outstretched. And on, on we go, line astern, carving a path across the flat landscape.

By the time we are ushered into the farmhouse, just outside Calais, all I want to do is eat and lie down. Yet our mission has only just begun. Glorian has a hushed conversation with the farmer, a bearded pipe-cleaner of a man, who fetches a ladder and indicates a trap door into the hayloft.

'*Là-haut,*' he murmurs. 'I shan't be sorry to see him go.'

'You and your wife have taken a considerable risk in sheltering him,' says Glorian.

'*Bof,*' shrugs the farmer, pouting, 'it's not the risk we mind. It's what he eats. Every time he comes down, he expects more. I tell you, he's cleared out our store cupboard. I've had to hide my last few Gauloises or he'd have smoked those, too.'

Glorian winces. 'I'm so sorry, monsieur. He must be traumatised, after bailing out from his aircraft and losing all his friends.'

'Well, what about me? I'm traumatised, too, after losing all my smokes.'

'They *are* a bit different, the American airmen,' replies Glorian, with the hint of a smile. 'It's not that they are greedy. Most of them simply have no idea of how the Occupation has traumatised France or of how little food we have, especially here in the forbidden zone. And I'm afraid that some of them may think, because they have done us a favour in helping to bash the Boche, that it is only right that we should do them a favour in return.'

'Oh, do they really?' asks the farmer, glaring up at the trap door. But Glorian raises his hands.

'Leave this to my friend, monsieur,' he says. 'He is an expert in these matters. And please remember that you have been sheltering a very brave man, who has flown across an ocean to fight alongside us. In helping him, you do a good deed for France.'

The farmer harrumphs and nods. And, having established that the airman is not armed, I quickly climb the ladder into the dark space above.

'Who goes there?' comes a low voice from the shadows.

'A friend, come to talk to you.'

'Holy shit, a Brit.' There is a rustle, a clunk and a sharp cry of pain as the man stands up too fast and whacks his head on a roof beam. 'It's good to make your acquaintance, Limey.'

'My name is Iroquois,' I reply, without warmth. 'How are you feeling?'

'Like I just went twelve rounds with Jack Johnson, if you must know, Iroquois. And hungry as hell. These Frenchies have been trying to starve me ever since I arrived.' He reaches out a hand. 'John McGuire. Or Airman McGuire, if you prefer. But they probably already told you that. Hey, I don't suppose you've got any smokes, have you?'

I shake my head and explain why I have come. I don't want this tough-looking fellow seizing the initiative. So, before he can protest, I launch into my first question.

'Who gave the Statue of Liberty to America?' I ask. I watch him closely as he screws up his face and strokes his chin with one finger and thumb. Tanned and stocky, John McGuire certainly doesn't look like your average Aryan Nazi. His black hair is cropped short, and his heavy-lidded eyes are so dark that I cannot see the pupils.

'Search me,' he answers at last, gazing down out of the dormer window into the courtyard. 'Was it Abraham Lincoln?'

'Question two. Where do US naval pilots do their basic training?'

'That's classified, sir.' He looks into my eyes. 'All right, so it's Pensacola. But don't tell anyone I told you, Iroquois.'

'Three: who wrote *Rhapsody in Blue*?'

'Seriously? This is the $64 question, right?'

'Airman McGuire . . .' Expressionless, I study the way his eyes move. I have already made up my mind about him.

'Was it Picasso?'

'Four: what was the squadron insignia of the Lafayette Escadrille?'

'Hey, I know this one.' McGuire jumps up.

'Sit down, please.'

'It was an Indian chief in a headdress, wasn't it?'

'And how many states are there in the United States of America?'

'There are forty-eight, so help me God.'

The answer should be forty-seven, according to the encyclopedia Houcke lent me. But since this was published in 1899, I give McGuire the benefit of the doubt.

'So how did I do?' he asks, seeing me gazing down at my sheet. 'Am I top of the class?'

The man still thinks this whole thing is a joke. Unsmiling, I hand McGuire a set of overalls and tell him to put them on. Then I break the news to him about the sixty-mile cycle ride that lies ahead of us.

'Whoa, now just a minute, Iroquois.' He scratches his head and pulls a pained expression. 'You have *got* to be joking. I mean, I ain't ridden one of them damn-fool bikes since I was a kid. And sixty miles? No way, Limey. You'll just have to find me an automobile. You copy?'

I can feel the blood begin to throb in my temples. I clench my fists. I want to grab McGuire by the collar and shake him. 'Look, you can't stay here,' I hiss, my face so close to his that he flinches. 'German patrols are everywhere, and it's only a matter of time before they find you. When they do, that good man downstairs, that kindly farmer, whose meagre rations you have been scoffing, will be shot.'

McGuire's mouth hangs open. 'But I, I just . . .'

'And his wife: she will be shot, too. Because of you. Do you understand? We have to go. We have to go *right* now. It's too far to walk, and I'm sorry I don't have a luxury

Rolls-Royce for you, with a nice soft blanket to put over your knees. So you'd better give the damn-fool bike a try – the one I just hauled sixty miles across country for you – because it's your best, no, it's your *only* hope of avoiding a German prison camp. And if you can't ride the damn-fool bike, then all of us are very likely going to end up dead. Do you copy that, Mr McGuire?'

Glorian's head appears in the opening of the trap door. 'Everything all right up there? We should be making a move.'

'Almost done,' I tell him. 'We'll be down soon.'

'All right, Iroquois,' says McGuire quietly, swinging his head from side to side. 'You've made your point. You show me this bicycle. If the damn-fool thing can be ridden, I'll ride it. Now, can we please get out of this dive?'

'After you,' I murmur, with a nod towards the trap door.

I watch Sergeant McGuire attempting to master the bicycle in a series of wobbly circuits around the farmyard. It is a terrifying sight. Glorian has his head in his hands. The farmer politely looks away.

'What do we do?' whispers Glorian. 'This monkey's going to get us all killed.'

'It's going to be all right,' I lie. 'He'll get it, you'll see.'

Glorian looks at me. 'I wish I had your nerve, Stéphane. I honestly don't know how you manage to stay so calm.'

'It's an act,' I reply, grinning as if this is a fib. McGuire topples off his bike yet again. I swallow, hard.

'OK, OK, I think I've got it now,' he calls, a minute or so later. 'As long as I don't have to slow down or go around any sharp corners, I'll be fine. I'm ready for takeoff, Limey.'

Glorian and I exchange glances. Even now, the American clearly has no inkling of the danger we are in. And perhaps this is a good thing. The Germans won't believe that anyone having so much fun on a bicycle could possibly be an Allied airman on the run.

'Remember, McGuire,' I tell him. 'Stay well behind me, but don't ever let me out of your sight. If you see me pull this white handkerchief out of my pocket, then disappear. Do whatever you can to vanish. Because it means there's a German roadblock up ahead.'

'What happens if you get a nosebleed?'

'Not funny, McGuire. Let's go.'

The hours of daylight, and the time left before curfew, are running out. The sky is still clear, but a wind is beginning to pick up out of nowhere, and I can see dark clouds starting to bubble up on the horizon. We have just under five hours to get back to Nieppe. As we set off down the dirt track from the farm, I keep looking back over my shoulder, waiting for McGuire to start. At last, I see him give his bicycle a mighty shove, and wobble left, right, left, straight into a ditch. Undaunted, he picks himself up, dusts himself off, and repeats the manoeuvre, with remarkable precision, all over again.

'This is not a problem,' the American mutters to himself. 'I can do this.'

'Just a minute, McGuire,' I call. 'I've had an idea.'

Standing astride his front wheel, I shut one eye and study the alignment. I give the handlebars a sharp twist, then another. 'There, that should do it,' I tell him. 'You'll find it easier now.'

And off we go, with me in front, McGuire in the middle, and Glorian almost out of sight to the rear. I can just see his overcoat flapping in the breeze. The American looks more confident now, and might even pass for a local, with his swarthy skin and his ill-fitting blue overalls. This is just as well, for we are now approaching Bergues, a small town outside Calais. And the outskirts of a place like Bergues are classic roadblock territory for the Boche, especially on a sunny afternoon like today.

Act naturally, I tell myself. Be ready for a roadblock, if one should lie around the next corner. But nothing can prepare me for what is about to happen. As I pull out wide on a sharp right-hand bend, I glimpse a flash of grey-green just around the corner. Seconds later, I plunge straight into the midst of a squad of German soldiers, who are chanting a song as they march in the middle of the road. There must be about forty of them.

Braking hard, I swerve. I can feel my rear wheel slipping away from me. But I manage to hold the turn and somehow avoid hitting any of them. One of the Germans, a stout fellow with a shiny red face, glares at me as I pass in a blur of adrenaline and disbelief. In less than half a minute, McGuire will be upon them. Too late to wave my handkerchief. I race through our options. But we don't have any. If I stop and attempt to create a diversion, McGuire will ride straight into a baited trap. I press on at half speed, on jellied legs.

After a minute or so of this, I risk a glance over my shoulder. And there, waving and grinning, is an exultant Airman McGuire, who has just seen his very first Germans of the war. As I breathe a silent thank you into the sky, all I can hope is that they may be his very last ones, too.

At our house, Elizabeth is in tears again. There has been a lot of this recently and I can't help feeling it is my fault, that somehow she knows more about my other life than she is letting on. Auntie Val is standing behind her now as she sits at the kitchen table, her head buried in her arms.

'Losing one little doll is hardly cause for all this crying, day after day,' says Auntie Val, laying her hands on Elizabeth's shoulders. She glances at my mother, sitting across the table from my sister. From either end, having finished our dinner of mashed swede and carrot, Kléber and I look on in silence. 'Are you sure there isn't something else, Elizabeth?'

'What if it was your favourite doll in the whole wide world?' sobs my sister.

'Did she lose the blue doll?' asks Kléber, beaming. 'Well, I didn't take it.'

'Nobody is saying you did,' says Auntie Val. 'But it can't just have vanished into thin air.'

'Oh, I don't know,' replies Mémère, standing with her back

to us at the stove. 'People vanish all the time these days.'

'Yes, but that doll didn't have a yellow star on it,' says Kléber. We all stare at our empty plates. There is a long silence.

'My doll hasn't vanished,' Elizabeth says quietly. 'I know exactly where she is. Janine has her.'

'So *she* took it!' Kléber sounds jubilant. 'You see?'

Elizabeth shakes her head. 'She didn't take it. I gave it to her.' And then her shoulders begin to shake. 'Janine said that if I didn't give her my blue doll, she'd tell the Germans.'

I sit very still.

'She'd tell them what?' demands Auntie Val. 'That you wouldn't give her your favourite doll?'

'No,' sobs Elizabeth. 'She said . . . she said she'd tell them that Dad is English.'

At this, even my mother gasps. I think we are shocked as much by the sound of a word that has not been spoken in the house for so long, as by the use to which Elizabeth's so-called friend is threatening to put it.

'I was so frightened, I didn't know what else to do,' continues Elizabeth.

Auntie Val is already buttoning up her coat.

'I'll come with you,' I tell her.

'No, Lou. You wait here, with the others,' she commands. 'I don't need the cavalry. Elizabeth Grady, you are coming with me.'

That night, Elizabeth marches up the stairs to bed with her blue doll safely tucked under her arm. Auntie Val is still in the kitchen when I creep back in from my latest mission with Sonneville.

'*Sacre bleu*,' she exclaims, her face a picture of horror. I look down at my overalls, spattered with blood. 'Please tell me you haven't . . .' But the words die in her throat, and she shakes her head. She hands me a folded piece of paper and begins to hurry out of the kitchen.

'Wait, please,' I say.

She stops in the doorway, still with her back to me. I know she cannot bear to look at me.

'I haven't killed anyone, Auntie, if that's what you're thinking.'

'Please, Lou, I don't want to know.'

'It's sheep's blood. I promise.' I tuck the piece of paper into my pocket. She nods, still with her back to me. I wait until her shoulders drop before I go on. 'Now, please: what did you say to the grandmother, to get Elizabeth's doll back from the awful Janine?'

Slowly, she turns to face me, with a solemn look in her eyes. 'I told her that if we are denounced, then when France is liberated, I will personally ensure that she and her family are the first to be shot by the patriots of the Resistance.' She glances down at the bloodstains on my overalls. 'I think that was fair enough. Don't you?'

13 October 1943

Next morning, I cycle out into a light drizzle and head straight for the pharmacy in Cassel. To my relief, Pierre Glorian is on duty and there are no other customers when I walk in.

'You got Houcke's message, Stéphane,' he says. 'I'm sorry to drag you away from your work at short notice. And in this weather, too.'

'*Pas de problème*. The men I look after are not in a great hurry.'

He smiles, and begins to polish his spectacles. 'Well, look: another of our friends from high places is in town, and we'd like you to take care of him. Routine stuff, you know. Can you come and see him now?'

'But what about the pharmacy?'

'Oh, don't worry about that,' replies Glorian, swapping his white shop overalls for his huge overcoat. 'The customers are used to it. Besides, there's hardly any medicine left to sell these days.' He gestures over his shoulder at the empty bottles of salts and tinctures on the wooden shelves, before turning the sign on the door from *Ouvert* to *Fermé*.

On our way to the village of Oxelaere, riding carefully over the greasy cobbles, Glorian explains that the airman is a Canadian pilot who doesn't speak any French, and whose plane must have broken up in midair because no wreckage has been found. 'So go easy on him, Stéphane. The poor chap has had a rough time. He can't even remember where he left his parachute.'

Half an hour later, we arrive at a farmhouse just outside

Oxelaere, and Glorian introduces me to the cheery farmer and his wife.

'Iroquois is much older than he looks,' he assures them, before making his apologies and hurrying back to his shop.

'Follow me,' whispers the farmer, Monsieur Bourlioux. Ducking his head to avoid the rain cascading off the gutterless roofs, he leads me to an outbuilding with a heavy wooden door. A grizzled, powerfully built man, Bourlioux has one of those faces in which all the lines are smile lines. I don't suppose he has ever frowned in his life. Someone has chalked a rough target on the door of the outbuilding, like a dartboard. After knocking three times, Bourlioux presses down the latch with his thumb and I creep in.

It is so dark inside that at first I can't see a thing. All I can hear is the steady drip-drip-drip of the rain coming through the roof. Gradually, however, I begin to pick out the contours of heaps of paint pots and piles of feed sacks, an array of dusty chains hanging from nails on the walls and, at the back, the shadowy outline of a man.

'*Bonjour*,' growls the figure, in a bad French accent. As he comes into the light nearer the door, he fixes me with his clear blue eyes.

'You can speak English now,' I tell him. 'If you wish.'

'It's good. Then I am Lieutenant Eastwood of the RCAF. At your service, sir.'

'And I'm Iroquois,' I reply, cautiously. Tall and handsome, the man looks like the hero of a cowboy film: the one who saves the town from the marauding Indians, and then rides off into the sunset with the sheriff's daughter. Definitely not a German agent. 'I am here to ask you a few questions, just as a formality. After that, I'll escort you to your next address. Do you understand, Lieutenant Eastwood?'

'Perfectly, thank you. Although you seem young for the job. Who do you work for?'

'I work alone.'

'Well, so, it is kind of you to come, eh?'

'Not at all,' I reply, touched by his civility, but surprised by his turn of speech. Apart from Motherall and Dumsday, Eastwood is the first Canadian airman I have been asked to escort. We sit down on two dusty old wine casks near the door. 'Now let's see. Can you please tell me the motto of the Royal Canadian Air Force?'

'Of course. It is *Per ardua ad astra,* just like the RAF.'

'And in what year did your air force become Royal?'

'Nineteen twenty-four.'

'Who's in charge?'

'Er, I think this is classified? I am not sure I should reveal . . .'

'I assure you, Lieutenant Eastwood, that I already know the answer. It begins with a C, if that helps.'

'Good, then I think it will not do any harm. It is Air Vice-Marshal Croil.'

Though struck by something odd in his diction, I am happy that Eastwood is a bona fide Canadian airman. He knows his stuff. I begin to fold up my list of questions. But then, in the half-light of the storeroom, I notice that his right knee is jiggling up and down. Now I look more closely, he is gripping his thighs so tightly that his knuckles are white.

'Just a few more questions now,' I tell him, holding the page as steady as I can. 'What's an acey-deucey?'

'Er, is it not something in poker? A pair of aces?'

'Good,' I reply. Perhaps, as a lieutenant, he wouldn't know the nicknames of the lowlier ranks in the RCAF. 'And what's the difference between a Yale and a Harvard?'

'That is a trick question, is it not? Hahaha.' Eastwood has the hollowest laugh I have ever heard. 'They are both universities of America. Very good universities, too.'

'Excellent.' In Sonneville's shed, Dumsday assured me that any pilot in the RCAF would know the standard training aircraft, and the subtle differences between them. But perhaps Eastwood has forgotten these details, in the chaos of being shot down.

'What is a yellow doughnut?' I ask him, praying that he will tell me that it is an airman's dinghy. Both his legs are now jiggling. He keeps swallowing, too. And the sweat is beginning to gleam on his brow.

'Is it a lemon cake?'

'It certainly is,' I reply, feeling slightly sick.

'And what about a yellow peril?' I give Eastwood one last chance to show that he knows what a Harvard is. But his face looks blank.

'I cannot be sure. I am saying it is the wasp or the hornet.'

'Not bad,' I say, forcing a smile. Even his perfect grammar is beginning to crumble, now that he is scared. 'It certainly flies.'

'Haha,' he replies, forcing a chuckle.

'And, finally, talking of flying, how do you become a member of the Caterpillar Club?' Both Motherall and Dumsday thought this question was too obvious, that every Allied airman knows that you join the club by bailing out of an aircraft. And this is what makes it a good question.

'Ah. Oh. Now, do not tell me. I am sure I know that.' Eastwood glances at the door. He clutches his head. He strokes his chin. He tears at his hair. He crosses and uncrosses his legs. He glances at the door again. 'Well, perhaps, is it a type of club for the people who are still learners to fly, and have not yet got their wings?'

'Absolutely it is,' I reply. 'Very good, Lieutenant Eastwood.'

He pulls a thin smile and nods. I can feel him studying my face intently.

'We'll soon have you on your way back west,' I tell him.

'Thank you,' he says. 'I am pleased to be speaking English again, I am telling you.'

'I'm sure. Now, the only problem we have is the weather, because it's tipping down outside. So I'm just going to have a word with the farmer about transport. Wait here, please, and I'll be back for you a little later. All right?'

Slowly, I rise to my feet and wander out of the storeroom

as if I had all the time in the world. The rain has almost stopped. I walk along the front of the farmhouse. And then, the moment I have rounded the corner, I explode into a hell-for-leather sprint. Two cows, chewing the cud, gaze at me as I pass. Old Bourlioux is sawing logs in one of the barns.

'Look,' I blurt, in a hoarse whisper, 'I am pretty certain that that man in there is not a Canadian airman. He is a German agent.'

'*C'est pas vrai.*' Bourlioux pulls a scarlet rag from his pocket and mops his brow.

'I'm afraid it is, Monsieur Bourlioux. So, please, you must keep him here a little while longer. I will bring help by tomorrow morning, I promise. But in the meantime, you must continue as though nothing has changed.'

'That's easy to say,' growls the old man. 'But how?'

'I don't know. Give him something to eat.'

'You want us to feed a German agent?'

'His orders will be to uncover the entire escape chain. So he will remain undercover for as long as he can, until he twigs that we are on to him.'

Bourlioux looks blank. 'I still don't understand why we have to feed him.'

'If you don't, he will kill you.'

'Ah. Well, now that you put it like that . . .'

'Do you think you will be able to convince him that you know nothing?'

Bourlioux beams at the thought. 'Look at me,' he says, gazing down at his threadbare overalls and bashed-up clogs. 'I've been doing it all my life, haven't I? But perhaps we'd best not tell my wife. She's a bit sharper than me, and she's not going to want to cook for a Schleu.'

I pedal like mad through the drizzle back to Nieppe. Marcel Houcke will not be at home, so my best chance is to try his brother.

Jules Houcke, who looks older and thinner than when we last met, looks up from his desk in surprise.

'Stéphane? Are you all right, my boy?'

I do not sit. I tell him about Eastwood, as quickly as I can. 'Please, Monsieur Houcke, please. You told me once that, if I identified a German agent, then you would do what is necessary. And I really think it is necessary now.'

'I see.' Mayor Houcke strokes his beard. His eyes dart from side to side. 'Are you quite sure about this, Stéphane?'

'As sure as I can be.'

'Very well. I shall go and see my brother myself. You have played your part; now you must leave things to us.'

'You will go right now?'

'Right now,' he replies.

My mind is full of images of Eastwood as I work in the Nieppe cemetery that afternoon, tidying the borders of the War Graves plot beneath a lowering sky. Perhaps the mysterious German is already dead by now. Yet this man will have no white headstone in a military cemetery, no gracious resting place for his mother to visit. No, Eastwood, if that is his name, will simply be made to disappear.

In the early evening, as I cycle back past the *mairie*, I notice that yet another yellow poster has appeared on the notice board outside, denouncing and demanding information about the whereabouts of yet another patriot.

FAHNDUNG
OPSPORING
RECHERCHE

The poster offers a reward of 500,000 Belgian francs for information leading to the arrest of two men, called Woussen and Volkaert. The names and the faces in the photographs mean nothing to me. But the reward is a huge one, and I find myself wondering what they have done. A light rain begins to fall, spattering the yellow paper. It will soon be getting dark.

The sound of footsteps, approaching from the square

behind me, makes me walk on. Glancing over my shoulder, I notice that the footsteps belong to a young woman: Mayor Houcke's stolid daughter, Andrée.

Silent and aloof, Andrée has always unnerved me, on the few occasions when I have met her with her father. I can never think of anything to say to her. In my scrubby clothes and wooden-soled shoes, I feel like a peasant urchin, tumbling through life, whereas she is an urbane adult, who already has it all worked out.

'*Bonsoir, mademoiselle.* I am surprised to see you out alone,' I say, reaching out to shake her hand. Her skin feels as cold as stone. 'Are you looking for your father?'

She nods, glancing up and down the street.

'I believe Mayor Houcke has been called to an urgent meeting. Would you like me to walk you home?'

'Oh, but would you really?' Mademoiselle Houcke smiles down at the wet cobbles. 'I feel so embarrassed to put you to the trouble. But I was hoping to meet Papa at his office. He is always so busy, helping people. And Maman will not be free for another half-hour.'

'Won't she be worried, if she comes and you are not here.'

'Not if I'm with *you*, Stéphane Grady,' sighs the mayor's daughter. And with that, putting her arm firmly through mine, she begins to lead me up the road towards her house.

31 October 1943

'Who was that?' hisses my father from the top of the stairs, after Sonneville has left.

I was expecting my family to be impressed with my new friend, for Jean Sonneville is a tall, powerfully built chap who cuts quite a dash in his well-cut jacket and slacks. His shoes look almost new, while everyone else in Nieppe is making do with wooden soles. And his slicked-back hair gleams with real brillantine.

Yet for all Sonneville's efforts at charming my family, there was no disguising the sniffiness with which Mémère shook his hand, or the way Auntie Val left him standing in the corridor rather than inviting him into the front room. My mother has annoyed my father by lighting several candles for the souls of the departed in there, and the air is heavy with the scent of chrysanthemums. Things didn't improve when Sonneville presented them with gifts from an inside pocket of his jacket: a bag of coffee and a small jar of olive oil from Provence. If anything, this only made things worse.

Waving away my apologies, he slipped out into the night almost at once, asking me to report to his house with the rest of my section on the day after tomorrow, at first light. He said it would be worth our while, and winked. I explained that Marcel would be at school, and Francis André off at college in Lille. So he wants me just to bring Maurice Leblon, and not to breathe a word to the others.

Two days later, an ancient Citroën lorry is parked in front of Sonneville's house. A smoky black stove – a *gazogène* – is bolted to one side. This primitive power unit is supposed to drive the lorry's cylinders using the gases produced by burning charcoal. Dirty, smelly and unreliable, the gas makes the engine pop and backfire like a platoon running on *haricots blancs*.

'Don't blame me,' mutters Sonneville. 'It was the mayor who rented this damn thing from some bloke in Merville. I'm just the poor stooge who has to stoke it.'

Maurice Leblon and I sit in the back, wondering where we are heading. I have been on enough missions with Sonneville to know better than to get too excited. Sure enough, we have only been clattering along for a few minutes before he halts the *gazogène* beside a turnip field, and orders us to start loading up.

'I suppose these things are the new armour-piercing shells,' chunters Maurice, as we dig the turnips out of the grey earth and lob them into the back of the lorry. Next, we stop off at a neighbouring farm and balance a couple of bales of straw on top of our pile of turnips.

'There, that should do it,' says Sonneville, gazing at our cargo. 'Soon, boys, soon we will be ready to take on the Boche.'

'See?' whispers Maurice, jabbing me in the ribs. 'I told you the turnips were ammunition. Your big friend has really lost it this time.' And then, with a sour expression, he turns to Sonneville. 'Where are we off to this time, Jean? Feeding the elephants at the zoo? Don't tell me this is another of your stupid games. Are you having us on?'

'Would I really do that to two of my most trusted friends?'

'Yes,' we reply, as one.

Only somewhat crestfallen, Sonneville grins at Maurice. 'As it happens, my boy, we are going to Ransart, south of Arras. And we're off to meet someone rather special.'

Anticipation fizzes up my spine. Could this be who I think it might be? And, if so, what does he want with turnips and straw?

Maurice sounds less enraptured. He grimly points out that

Ransart is almost seventy kilometres away, which will take us three hours at our current rate of progress. And Arras is crawling with Verdigris.

The trees are beginning to shed their golden leaves as we thunder along. I haven't noticed this until now, but everything is dying again. Autumn was once my favourite season, but not any more. No, I am already looking forward to spring.

On the outskirts of Nieppe, we meet up with the Houcke brothers and a man called Michel Pladys, who runs the Resistance group in nearby Erquinghem. Mayor Houcke is driving a second *gazogène*, which seems quite a lot quieter and a whole lot less stinky than ours.

'Do take special care around Arras,' Houcke warns. 'And be aware that, if we are unlucky enough to be stopped, we must either bluff or fight our way out of trouble. Neither of these trucks has a permit to be on the road.'

'Oh, great,' mutters Maurice.

'I shall fight, because I am armed,' replies Houcke's brother, solemnly. He produces a tiny 6.35mm calibre revolver with four rounds in it, which might just about stun a rabbit at point-blank range.

'Yes, and I have this turnip,' adds Maurice. Nobody laughs, except me.

Keeping to the humblest country lanes, our convoy crawls south-west towards Arras, and then along a road which feels as if it is lined with cemeteries. I wonder if the others see these as I see them. Not just as stiff's paddocks, as the Tommies call them, but as magical gardens where mothers' sons may sleep, and where once I used to play. Inside my head, the rocking of the *gazogène* lulls me into a kind of deafened reverie as I watch the ranks of headstones pass us by. Death unites us, and the wars of the past are no longer separate events. They are all one to me now. We live for a moment in the air, live forever in the earth.

With so much tension in the air, there is little conversation until, having bypassed Arras, we finally arrive in the main square of the little village of Ransart and pull up just behind Mayor Houcke's lorry.

'*Merde*,' whispers Maurice. We watch in disbelief as a uniformed figure marches towards the first lorry. 'What the hell do we do now?' Maurice is already reaching for a turnip. I peer through my fingers at the man advancing upon us. He is even more dangerous than a German: his dark blue uniform marks him out as a member of the Vichy Security Police, a slimy organisation rumoured to commit by stealth many of the same crimes against France which the Germans commit quite openly.

But the policeman climbs up into the first lorry, and Mayor Houcke drives away.

'*Putain de merde*,' exclaims Maurice, with a gulp. But now we begin to pull forward, too, as Sonneville follows the first lorry, looking alarmingly unperturbed in the cab in front of us. Marcel Houcke, too. His decision to climb in with us, armed with that menacing little revolver, now takes on a sinister aspect. Beside me, I can see Maurice's brain going tick, tick, tick. Like me, he must be wondering if we have walked into a trap. The four older men, with their tame police collaborator, are going to stand us up against the hay bales to shoot us, and then spirit our bodies away beneath the turnips.

Both lorries drive down a track into an isolated field. We park next to a silo full of mangelwurzels, from behind which another two men appear. More assassins. The doors of the first lorry open. Maurice and I jump down from the back of ours, ready to run. The ground underfoot is still soft with dew. We watch from a little way off as the other men shake hands. Mayor Houcke points in my direction and the Vichy policeman strides purposefully towards me in his navy blue uniform. He is wearing a holstered side arm and a thin smile. I watch his hands very carefully and glance back up the farm track to see how far I have to sprint and jink. A few feet from me, he holds out his hand.

'Hello, Iroquois,' he says, in English. 'Thank you for coming.' His accent is as finely clipped as his slim moustache. 'I expect the chaps will have warned you about me. My British code name is Sylvestre. But most people call me Capitaine Michel.'

I cannot speak. I have been looking forward to this moment for so long, and now it has caught me by surprise. I just stand there, feeling stupid, while Capitaine Michel waits, his blue eyes twinkling. I can feel everyone else waiting, too – hanging on his every word, wondering what he is saying to me.

'An honour to meet you, sir,' I reply at last, in English. 'God save the King.' And then I cringe, because I have no idea why I said that.

'God save the King.' He smiles, extends his arms, and turns a full circle to include everyone present. '*Vive la France. Vive de Gaulle. Vive les Forces Françaises Libres.*'

We set about removing the mangelwurzels from the silo. Suddenly Maurice and I stare at each other. For beneath the heavy vegetables, solid metal gleams up at us. We work faster now, until we have exposed three large capsules, each one made up of five aluminium drums.

'Christmas has come early this year,' Sonneville tells me, with relish. 'These were dropped by the RAF during the October moon.'

While Capitaine Michel busies himself over one of the drums, the rest of us stack the remainder in the lorries. We do what we can to cover them with turnips and straw. This done, the Captain calls us over. His brow shiny with sweat, he appears to be shivering.

'Right, gather round,' he says, in French. 'You're about to learn how to assemble and dismantle a Sten gun.'

'A *what*?' asks Marcel Houcke.

'One of these fire-spitters.' Capitaine Michel holds up a small machine gun with a hollow metal stock and a narrow magazine projecting from its left-hand side. The thing looks as if it is made out of Meccano. 'Small, light and easy to hide, the Sten is your friend to the end, or at least until the bloody thing jams. There are a couple of magazines for each gun, but you can use Luger rounds if you're stuck. Different colour, same size, same effect.'

After a swift demonstration of how the gun works, he distributes two of them to the occupants of each lorry, with a pair of magazines apiece. Although Capitaine Michel does everything at pace, his manner is so fluid and unflustered that you'd think he has all the time in the world.

'Any questions? Right, let's get this first lorry going,' he announces. Jules Houcke takes the wheel, with Michel Pladys and Marcel Houcke sitting on the turnips in the back with a Sten gun each. They leave a few minutes before us, doubling the chances of at least one of us making it back to Nieppe. Capitaine Michel joins Sonneville in the cab of our lorry, while Maurice and I renew our friendship with the turnips in the back, our brand-new Sten guns tucked out of sight beneath the straw.

By now it is late afternoon, and the golden sunlight is beginning to fade. Time before curfew is running out. We are struggling up the Côte St Catherine, a hill just outside Arras, when disaster strikes. The *gazogène* begins to make a violent banging noise, far worse than its usual clatter. Then it is spurting white clouds of noxious vapour. A few seconds later and the wretched thing clatters to a halt. Maurice and I sit very still, listening to the inert *gazogène* hissing and ticking in the silence.

'*Quelle surprise*,' he mutters.

Emerging glumly from the front of the lorry, Sonneville starts tinkering with the *gazogène*. While he lambasts it in patois, Capitaine Michel leaps down from the cab. With his hands he apologises, explains that he must leave us here, and slips away into the gathering darkness.

Maurice and I look at each other, and he presents me with something that I think at first is a skull.

'Fancy a turnip?' he asks.

Suddenly there is a shout from Sonneville, and the *gazogène* coughs and splutters back into life. It doesn't sound pretty, but at least we're moving. There is still a glimmer of mauve daylight as we grind past Lens and La Bassée, but by the time we reach the long stretch to Estaires the stars are beginning to appear. Now there is just the bridge over the river to Lys to negotiate, and then we will be home and dry. But everything is so quiet after curfew. And Sonneville's blessed *gazogène* must be audible from Paris.

It is pitch dark when we reach the environs of Nieppe. With blackout filters on the headlights, the road ahead is no more than a brown smudge. Yet somehow Sonneville, with his nose pressed to the windscreen, manages to find his way to the barn at l'Épinette. The occupants of the other lorry are waiting for us, wide-eyed with worry. Together we unload the drums, and I am introduced to someone who looks more nervous than anyone: Monsieur Cuvelier, the owner of the barn.

Sonneville's house becomes a haven for me, now that I feel a stranger in the rue du Sac. It helps that he has an inexhaustible supply of firewood and keeps the place ten degrees warmer than ours. Often I drop round for a drink with him after work, and we sit in the warm glow of his kitchen, sipping cider or weak gin, and smoking Belgian cigarettes.

We talk about how the war is going, and whether or not the British really will return to liberate France before the end of 1944, as the *Voix du Nord* has been promising. We talk about Sir Francis Drake, and how he defeated the Spanish Armada, and Napoleon, and how he was defeated by snow. We talk about the Spectacular we could create with the explosives and Sten guns stashed in the Cuvelier barn, about how much it might hurt to be shot and about the meaning of the English phrase 'Their name liveth for ever more'. We talk about women. Or rather, Sonneville talks about women and

I listen. But, most of all, we talk about our favourite subject, the one to which we return, time and again. We talk about Capitaine Michel.

It emerges that Sonneville and the British officer have spent a good deal of time together. Not just on the drive back from Ransart before the *gazogène* broke down, but on other occasions, too. They appear to like each other.

I ask Sonneville if he isn't worried about Capitaine Michel's health, but he simply shrugs and says that our man is made of steel. The captain was once a brilliant boxer and rugby player, he says, and is rumoured to be a bit of a ladies' man. He has been strafed at Dunkirk, imprisoned in a concentration camp in the Dordogne and led an escape party across the Pyrenees on foot into Spain. And now he is back in France, where he runs the Sylvestre-Farmer network of the SOE in the uniform of the French police. Apparently he has a very beautiful accomplice, who may or may not be his lover, called Denise. And a black cat, which has become his symbol.

Moving gracefully around the room, Sonneville refills our glasses and brings a silver dish of almonds to the table. 'The thing about Capitaine Michel,' he says, returning to his seat, 'is that he makes everything seem possible. He's just so bloody intelligent, and so damn brave. Single-handedly, he is the fellow who has stopped your chaps and the Americans from dropping all those bombs on the factory workers in Lille.'

My mouth full of almonds, I gesture to Sonneville that I want to know more.

'The story is that he sent a coded message to the bigwigs in London, asking them to stop the air raids. Naturally they wanted to know why. So he told them he was going to do the job himself.'

'Yes, but how?'

'In one engineering works, he marched in and ordered the guards to search the place, because he said that terrorists were planning to blow up the factory. And while the guards were running around like blue-arsed flies, he and his men, disguised as German soldiers and French police, did exactly what he warned them was going to happen: they blew up the place.'

'The locomotive factory at Fives,' I murmur to myself.

'You've heard about Fives, then? I tell you what, that was a Spectacular, all right. You'd think London would have been satisfied, but not a bit of it. They simply didn't believe that one man could have done what an entire squadron of Wellington bombers had failed to do. So they demanded photographic evidence. And Capitaine Michel, being Capitaine Michel, returns to the wrecked factory and walks straight past the guards, disguised as a journalist. He photographs everything, and sends the films back to London by Lysander. I almost wish he'd climbed into that plane himself, to save his skin, because the Boche want him so badly now. But we cannot do without him. Without Capitaine Michel, our entire organisation would crumble to dust. I tell you, Stéphane, that man is a miracle. If you ever wonder why we French like you *Anglais* so much, look no further. So amusing. So *sympathique*. And utterly, utterly without fear.'

A few days later, Sonneville summons me to a meeting at the Cuvelier barn. He says Capitaine Michel may be there. There is to be a distribution of early Christmas presents.

When I tiptoe into the barn with him, Marcel Houcke and Michel Pladys, the place is in darkness. Just a single shaft of sunlight streams in through a high window, making the dust dance in its beam and casting a dazzling parallelogram on the earthen floor. Clutching the collars of our overcoats tightly around our necks, we sit, hunched and weaponless, on a pile of hay bales at the back of the barn, waiting for someone to appear.

'That's the thing about *les Anglais*,' growls Marcel Houcke, giving me a nudge. 'They're always late.'

'How late is he?' asks Sonneville.

'About three years,' replies Houcke, drawing a tense guffaw from Pladys. 'We could have used him in 1940.'

Suddenly there is a groan of old hinges above us, and the barn door slams shut. The four of us hold our breath. I wait to hear the thud of a grenade or the click of a safety catch being released. We must have walked into a trap.

A second later, from the hay bales just to our left, there comes the rasp of a match and a sudden flare in the darkness. A man's face glows briefly and, a second later, the glowing tip of a cigarette begins to advance towards us.

'*Bonjour, messieurs.*' The voice is warm and familiar. 'Cigarette, anyone?'

Capitaine Michel must have been here all the time. But when the barn door and shuttered window are reopened, I can see he is not laughing.

'You see how easy it is?' he says. I feel as if his cool blue eyes can see right through me, that he knows, at a glance, who I am. I wish I knew this myself. 'Always visualise your escape route. Like that window, for example.' I turn to look at the blank wall he is indicating. When I turn back, Capitaine Michel has vanished.

A moment later, he reappears on the opposite side of the barn. 'All right, that's the end of the cabaret.' His face breaks into a weary smile, and he hands round a packet of cigarettes. 'At ease. Help yourself to a smoke.'

Capitaine Michel looks different today, but I can't put my finger on how he has changed. He introduces us to two of his men from Lille, then opens the metal containers from the Ransart drop and divides up the contents. Our share, to be split equally between Houcke's VdN and Sonneville's WO, amounts to twenty-five Sten guns with magazines and ammunition, five pistols, a dozen Mills bombs and incendiary grenades, and perhaps seventy kilos of explosives and accessories.

With a Mills bomb in each hand, Sonneville is in clover. 'So, when do we commence the liberation of Nieppe?'

Capitaine Michel smiles. He strokes his upper lip with his fingertips, as if expecting to find a moustache there. He must have shaved it off. 'Let's just start by liberating this barn of fireworks, shall we?'

Kneeling beside the open canisters, we wrap the equipment in straw, ready for its onward journey. Each time I glance across at Capitaine Michel, he seems to be watching me. At last, with a nod, he waves me over. Sitting in a pool of sunlight, he has made a table from a couple of hay bales and is examining the explosives equipment upon it. We sit opposite each other, with the table between us.

'Remember, remember, the fifth of November,' he says, in English. Though his eyes twinkle, I am struck by the dark circles beneath them.

'Gunpower, treason and plot.'

'It seems that you and I have quite a lot in common, young Grady,' he replies, sotto voce. 'You have Anglo-French parentage, do you not?'

I nod, unsure if I should be resisting his interrogation.

'And are you English or French?' he asks.

'English,' I reply, without hesitation.

'Excellent,' he says. 'So we are both Englishmen in France, although my mother is technically Irish. You are a gardener, are you not?'

'I look after the war cemeteries. It was my father's job. I inherited it.'

'He died?'

'You could say that. But he still lives with us.'

Capitaine Michel glances up at the open window, high above our heads, through which the sun is streaming in. I have never seen anyone look so pale and sombre. 'So even now, in the midst of all this, someone is looking after the fallen? For a gardener, there can be no higher calling.'

'It is my life,' I reply.

We sit in silence for a few moments. Though I am somewhat in awe of Capitaine Michel, I feel at ease with him, too.

'I have heard good things about you from Sonneville,' he says, at last.

'Oh, lord,' I reply. 'You mustn't believe everything Jean says, sir.'

'I don't, and I won't,' he chuckles. 'But I hear that you supplied your group with arms and that you have interviewed and escorted several Allied airmen, and distributed several hundred copies of the *Voix du Nord*, among other exploits. Is it true you also spent a few months in Loos Prison?'

When I tell him what I wrote on the Messerschmitt, he bursts out laughing. This sets off his cough, and he winces as he clutches his chest. 'No wonder they were cheesed off. All in all, old chap, I'd say you have a very bright future ahead of you.'

I shrug, doing my best to feign indifference. And then I confess my ambition to be a soldier in the British army, and Capitaine Michel turns suddenly serious.

'What is the most dangerous mission you have carried out so far?'

'I don't really think about the danger,' I reply. 'I suppose I'm a bit stupid like that.'

Once again, he looks into my eyes. Reaching down beside him, he hauls an aluminium drum on to his lap and extracts from it two Luger pistols, one of which he hands to me.

'Have you ever shot anyone?'

I shake my head.

'Right, here's the drill. Two shots, no more, no less. One to the stomach and one to the heart. Even if you miss with the second, the first will kill him in the end. And don't look at his face.'

I nod, pretending that I have conversations like this every day.

'If they capture us, they will torture us.' He watches me carefully. 'And, unfortunately, one of the few things Jerry is good at is torturing people. So it is quite possible that, in the end, we may talk. And then they will feel obliged to kill us anyway.'

Open-mouthed, I nod.

I love the feeling of this cold, heavy pistol in my hand.

'Now, I don't know about you, Stephen. But, on balance, I should rather die in battle, taking a bunch of Jerries with me, than in some windowless room, having the life slowly squeezed out of me by a couple of spineless bastards wielding nutcrackers. Do you get my drift?'

'I think so.'

'Better to die in silence, than to live and talk. That's what I tell myself, as I lie awake at night. And I pray that, when the moment comes, I have the balls to carry it off.'

'Whereas I pray that the moment never comes.'

'Very good,' he whispers, brightening. 'You stick with that, for now.'

Another open drum beside him is filled with NAAFI supplies. He rummages in it and presents me with some plain white packets of Gold Flake cigarettes, some bars of chocolate in foil, and a couple of boxes of tea.

'Give these to your father.'

'My father?'

'You have no idea what he goes through, every time you creep out of your house.'

'Have you spoken to my father, then?' I ask, wide-eyed.

'No. It's just that I happen to have one myself.' Capitaine Michel narrows his eyes, and I can see the muscles in his jaw clench and unclench. 'I don't suppose I shall see him for a while.'

Next he teaches me how to use the explosives arranged on the straw bales in front of him. There are several fat sausages of Nobel's 808 plastic, which look like yellow plasticine and smell of almonds.

I ask him why it is called 808, and he seems amused by the question.

'The boffins at Nobel's must have named it after my cat. She's called 808, too.' He shrugs and gazes into my eyes. 'Funny coincidence.'

The sausages are to be kneaded by hand to soften them up. They may then be combined or divided, depending on the size of explosion required. Apparently the plastic can cause a violent headache when handled, so tubes of Vaseline are included in the kit, as protection for the hands.

Capitaine Michel introduces me to the small white cones which comprise the primary charge, and to the slim metal detonators. These I am to handle with great care and to pack, one by one, inside a glass drum.

Next we move on to the L-delay units. These delay pencils come in three colours: red for a half-hour delay; white for two hours; green for six hours. The top of each pencil is moulded from soft copper, beneath which are a thin wire and a phial of acid. By pressing the copper and breaking the phial, the acid is released and gradually melts the wire. This, in turn, drops a plunger which strikes the detonator. The thicker the wire, the longer the delay. But if a delay pencil happens to be damaged, the detonator will explode in your face the moment you stick it in the primary charge.

'How come you are not afraid?' I ask, watching his steady hands as he demonstrates how to set a detonator. 'Is it because you are English?'

'Of course I am afraid,' he chuckles, glancing around him. 'Like you, I am just better at hiding it than the others.' There is a pause. 'I've never told that to anyone before, Stephen. I'd appreciate it if you kept it under your hat.'

I nod, even more in awe of Capitaine Michel than before.

He gives me a crash course in the use of Bickford fuse for causing a rapid explosion when fitted to a detonator, and explains how an explosive white cable, Cordtex, may be used for joining explosive charges. 'Some people like to darken the wire with earth or boot polish, because it catches the light at night like the interesting bits at the Moulin Rouge.' He demonstrates how to attach the charges I have created to railway lines and other targets, for maximum impact. And he gives me a number of plastic boxes of RDX explosive, fitted with magnets, for more hurried applications.

Finally, rising to his feet, he asks me to give the second Luger to Sonneville, who is still wrapping Sten guns in straw, and entrusts me with an American Colt revolver for Maurice Leblon. My mind reeling with so much new information, I tell Capitaine Michel that I am worried I may not have learned all that I need to know about the explosives. I am wondering if we couldn't perhaps meet again for a refresher course.

'You know,' he says, 'the fact is that I should like that very much. I have enjoyed our little chat. I should like to meet your father, too. But I cannot imagine that I will. Not until after this is all over, anyhow.' He waves his arm in the air, as if he is referring not just to the war but to every molecule of air in the atmosphere, to the whole of human existence. 'And I have a strong suspicion that I am to be posted elsewhere, very soon. That is why it is so important that you remember what I have taught you. And, if you can, that you carry on the work that we have begun together here. You don't need any refresher course, Stephen. Spread the word. Continue to be brave, so that you inspire bravery in others. And be ready to sacrifice yourself, in the name of the King.'

'I am ready for that sacrifice,' I nod. 'And God save the King.'

He smiles. 'I know you are, Stephen. I know you are. By the way, I almost forgot. You roll your own, don't you?' He tosses me a cellophane packet. 'This is for you.'

As he turns away, I watch Capitaine Michel pull a handkerchief from his pocket. I am half-expecting him to produce a live dove from it, or to descend into another fit of coughing. But he appears to have something in his eye.

With Monsieur Cuvelier anxious to have everything out of his barn as soon as possible, we transport our share of the weaponry using handcarts, and Marcel Houcke hides the whole lot behind the rabbit hutches in his garden the next day. There are still the aluminium drums to deal with. But Houcke is already cheesed off about having so much equipment stored so close to home.

'That oaf Delbecque, who thinks he runs the Resistance in Steenwerck, was meant to take half of what's left,' he tells me, when I arrive at his house to collect another stack of copies of the *Voix du Nord*. 'But the bastard's chickened out. Says he's worried he's being watched.'

'Aren't we all,' I reply, attempting to make it sound like a joke.

'Actually, it's not the Germans I'm worried about.' Houcke pulls a pained expression. 'It's my wife.'

'She's getting twitchy? Then let me take the weapons.' My firmness surprises both of us.

'But there's almost 250 kilos of kit. Are you sure?'

'If you and your men can get everything to the war cemetery at Pont d'Achelles, I'll do the rest.'

'*Formidable, Stéphane,*' says Houcke. 'And I'll invite you to my golden wedding in thirty years' time.'

I decide not to tell Marcel Lombard how much extra equipment I am about to load into our cache. There's no point in both of us having sleepless nights. Sonneville, too, I keep in the dark. All he knows is that I have access to the explosives from the Ransart drop, as and when required.

'You and the capitaine were thick as thieves at the Cuvelier barn,' he says, as we sip Pastis at his kitchen table. 'I can't believe he's put you in charge of all the plastic for our group. He knows I love explosions.'

'That may be why he didn't put you in charge,' I reply. 'We're not supposed to let it all off at once.'

'Just *imagine*.' Sonneville shivers with pleasure. 'But suppose you brought just a *little* of your plastic round here one night? We could have a controlled explosion in the garden, as an experiment.'

'I think that is one of your worst ideas ever.'

'All right,' he shrugs. 'So I'll come up with something else for us to blow up.'

My father is often absent in Bailleul, and with Auntie Val, Mémère and my mother floating around our house like a trio of wraiths, it is not easy to catch him alone. He almost shrinks from the sight of me. In fact, everyone in my family has begun to avoid me of late. I'll walk into the kitchen or the front room and they'll pretend they were on their way out. Even Mémère, who claims to be chained to the stove.

This evening, however, when I walk into the front room my father is sitting there with his ear pressed to the radio, just like the old days. He jumps to his feet when he sees me.

'I'm sorry to disturb you, Dad,' I whisper. I reach inside the piano for the things I have stashed there. In the vaguest terms, I tell him about Capitaine Michel, and how he wanted my father to have these English gifts.

'A British officer in our midst, taking the war to the Boche?' he says in awe. 'What regiment?'

'I don't know. Sorry.'

My father's hands tremble over a bar of chocolate. He holds it so delicately that you would think it was a detonator. Next, he lifts one of the boxes of Gold Flake cigarettes to his nose and inhales deeply. Then, almost swooning, he does the same with the tea. I thought he would be happy to have these things. But he looks as if a friend has died.

'I don't believe it,' he groans, shaking his head. 'It's too much. How much did you have to pay him for this?'

'I didn't pay him anything, Dad. He wanted you to have the things. And he wants to meet you, too.'

'*He* wants to meet *me*?' My father collapses into his chair and shuts his eyes. Then he rises to his feet again and walks to the window. He stands there, a shambolic figure, knees slightly bent, peering at the blackout blinds as if he can see through them, as if he is gazing out at the forbidden world, as if he can actually see his own village street, the one down which he may no longer walk.

'But I am nothing, Lou. I am a Cuthbert, a complete C3. What the hell will I say to him?'

Behind me, this is what I hear him say. But, unable to listen, I am already on my way out of the room.

Even now, the operation at the Cuvelier barn is not over. The weapons have been brought and stowed in my cache. But the empty drums, all fifteen of them, have yet to be made to disappear. Someone has the idea of melting them down; another man suggests burying them. The most bird-brained scheme of all is to transport them in handcarts to the river Lys, a good kilometre away, and attempt to submerge them there. Unfortunately, Marcel Houcke thinks this is a good idea.

By moonlight, Maurice Leblon and I help two of Houcke's men – Paul Saint Maxent, who runs the café in front of Francis André's bicycle shop, and a fellow called Montagne – to push the heavy old handcarts to the river. But when we get there, the banks are a tangle of weeds, reeds and rushes. The water is too shallow to submerge a teacup, let alone a hefty metal drum.

'I thought you two were supposed to know the river like the back of your hand,' I mutter, forgetting that Saint Maxent is deaf as a post.

'We did,' replies Montagne. 'But it's changed.'

Saint Maxent gives a helpless shrug.

'So who's going to jump in then?' I ask.

'You're the youngest, Stéphane.' Montagne winks at Saint Maxent. 'You do it.'

We all peer down at the oily black water, glinting in the moonlight.

To my shame, Saint Maxent beats me to it. Mumbling curses in patois to himself, he goes sliding down the riverbank and into the water with one of the drums clutched to his chest. Montagne guiltily decides to follow.

'*Merde,* it's cold,' gasps Saint Maxent. 'I'm too old for this.' When he has waded through the reeds and reaches the clearer stream, he presses down hard on the drum, so that it begins to fill with water.

'Help, it's gone,' he whispers, as the drum begins to float away. 'Someone give me a hand before we lose it.'

'Idiot,' hisses Montagne, a few yards further out. Then he loses grip of his drum, too.

'Keep a lookout,' I blurt at Maurice. Leaving my clogs on the riverbank, I leap into the icy blackness, a little further downstream. I have to stifle a yelp, my breath coming in hurried snatches as I wade out to the containers. *Merde.* They both float past me, too, just out of reach of my fingertips.

A loud splash, just to my right. And then another, even closer. What the . . .?

Maurice is lobbing rocks like howitzer shells. He misses both drums, but almost manages to hit me.

'*Attends!*' I bark in outrage.

Undaunted, the bombardment continues.

'I think I hit one!'

'Fat lot of good it's done.'

'*Merde.*'

Subtle as lighthouses, the half-submerged drums float on.

The next evening, something extraordinary happens in the street where nothing ever happens. Capitaine Michel visits our house. I can't quite believe it. He has come.

Auntie Val almost faints at the sight of a uniformed Vichy policeman on our doorstep, but Sonneville's presence alongside him acts like smelling salts upon her; I have never seen such concentrated vitriol in her eyes.

The captain requests a private word with my father. Awed, I head out on to the veranda to smoke a chilly cigarette with Sonneville as the two Englishmen disappear into the front room. Except that Sonneville doesn't want to smoke because he is trying to cut down, so we tiptoe back into the kitchen instead. We have only just sat down when my father pops his head round the door. His eyes are shining. He is looking for Rosemary, but she is already in bed.

'That's a pity,' he says. 'I'd have liked her to have met the captain.'

'Which reminds me, Lou,' remarks Auntie Val, standing with her back to Sonneville, as if to blot him out. 'I think Rosemary wanted to have a chat with you.'

'Oh, yes?'

'She said it was something about drums.'

Beside me, Sonneville stiffens. 'Perhaps I will take you up on that offer of a cigarette, after all, Stéphane,' he says.

A few minutes later, he and the captain slip out into the night. My father closes the back door softly behind them. He looks taller and straighter than he did yesterday. And, for the first time since the Middle Ages, he smiles at me.

23 November 1943

Marcel Lombard brings the message, skidding his bicycle to a halt at the gateway of the Pont de Nieppe cemetery. Sonneville wants to see me urgently.

When I arrive at the house, there is a coded message pinned to the door. I am to come to his wood. Sonneville is hiding in the densest part, a copse of young oaks. He is deathly pale and chain-smoking.

'We're fucked,' he says. One of Capitaine Michel's key contacts, André Martel, has been arrested and tortured. He must have spilled the beans a while ago, but nobody knew. Many members of the WO have already been rounded up. Sonneville is convinced that it is only a matter of time before the Germans come for him.

'Look at this,' he says gruffly, unfolding a dog-eared piece of yellow paper from his pocket.

I gaze at the wording, which looks dimly familiar.

FAHNDUNG
OPSPORING
RECHERCHE

It is the same poster I saw on the wall outside the *mairie* in Nieppe, offering 500,000 Belgian francs for any information leading to the arrest of two men I have never met. Judging from their photographs, one of them is very young and one very old.

'The boy Woussen looks like a baby, doesn't he?' says Sonneville.

'It says he's eighteen. That's my age.'

'Too young, in other words.'

'Jean-Edouard-Gaston Woussen and Alberic Volkaert,' I murmur, reading the names aloud. 'Do you know them? I don't.'

'No, but the Boche clearly do. Half a million Belgian francs is a hell of a lot of money for a man's head. People will talk for a lot less than that.'

According to Sonneville, the net must have been closing in for months. And Capitaine Michel has kept it to himself.

'Living with the secret every day, he chose not to pass it on.' He lights yet another cigarette from the stub of the one he has just finished. 'I cannot imagine the pressure that man is under.'

The first blow was struck as long ago as August, when Martel was arrested carrying a false identity card by the *Geheime Feldpolizei* in Brussels. Within a week, under severe interrogation, he must have told them all he knew.

'Fifty people have since been arrested, including all those involved in the recent parachute drops.'

'You and I were at Ransart, Jean. Are they coming for us? I need to warn my father . . .'

'No, wait.' He grabs my arm, pulling me back. 'We brought our own transport. So, for once, Woussen did not act as driver.'

'That wretched *gazogène* saved our lives?'

'For now.'

Thanks to our code names and information cut-offs, the sections around Lille have largely been spared. But it is only a matter of time before the trail of torture and denunciation leads the Germans to us.

I can feel the familiar nausea rising in my chest. My throat tightens and demons gnaw at my guts.

'So what do we do now?' I fumble for my tobacco.

'That's the worst of it,' he says. 'You and I, Stéphane, we are men of action. But all we can do now is wait.'

'Wait to be arrested? Superb. I've always wanted to see the inside of Loos Prison again.'

Sonneville runs a hand through his hair. 'We can't disappear, because that would only arouse suspicion. And we don't want to spook the others. Fear can make men do foolish things. No, we must do as Capitaine Michel does. We must carry on as if nothing has happened.'

'But the weapons . . . Shouldn't we move them?'

'No, don't touch them. Stay as far away from them as you can.'

'Jean, that cache is where I work. I keep my tools a few centimetres from where all our explosives and Sten guns are buried.'

'Well, that's good.' Sonneville smiles. 'The Germans will never think you'd be that stupid.'

I smile back at him. It's all so crazy.

'You don't mind my having shared this bad news with you?' asks Sonneville.

'It's better that I know to lie low. Forewarned is forearmed.'

'Sometimes ignorance is bliss.'

'Then why did you tell me?'

'I'm not as brave as Capitaine Michel, Stéphane. I'm afraid it was selfish of me to tell you. But I just felt that I must.'

'I'm glad you did,' I reply. Although, as I say the words, I realise that I have now grown so used to lying that I can no longer be sure if I am telling the truth.

28 November 1943

Bad days. I jump at every sound and twitch at every unexpected movement.

The only time I feel safe is at Mass. I sit hunched in the very heart of the congregation, rather than in my usual place near the door. But today, when we all emerge into the watery sunshine, a tap on the shoulder almost gives me a heart attack.

It is Madame Houcke, the mayor's wife. She wants to know if I might start giving them a hand in the vegetable garden beside their house.

Composing myself, I explain that there is little that needs doing at this time of year and, besides, the soil is too hard to dig. But she insists. The mayor is a busy man, she says, and gardening is not his forte. The place is such a mess. I reply that the whole country is a mess – does she want me to fix that, too? She gives me a funny look, and I feel bad about this. Sometimes I say things, and they just come out the wrong way.

On Friday lunchtime, we are sitting around the kitchen table when there there is loud pounding on the front door.

'I'll get it,' says Elizabeth.

I dash out on to the veranda, scanning the fields for grey-green uniforms. But the only figure I can see is Papa Lombard, ploughing behind Paul, his skinny old horse. Mirza the dog is limping along at his heels.

A moment later, Elizabeth joins me on the veranda, with one of Sonneville's men in her wake. He is out of breath.

'*Bonjour, Stéphane*,' he pants. 'I'm very sorry to disturb you, but I've got a message for you from Jean.'

'Yes?' I whisper.

'He says the message is about a black cat.'

'I see.'

'I'm to tell you that the cat has been taken, and that you'll understand.'

Suddenly dizzy, I lean against the veranda's rotting wooden frame.

'He says the black cat has been taken? Are you sure about that?'

'He said you'd understand.'

'Yes.'

After he has gone, I climb the stairs, unlace my boots, lie down on my bed and gaze up at the ceiling. So it's over. The Krauts have captured Capitaine Michel. I think of the Luger hidden in the eaves, just a few feet from where I am lying. And I utter a silent prayer that, when the moment comes, I have the balls to use it.

Later that day, there is another, quieter knock at the door. This time it is Sonneville himself.

'I'm sorry to come here,' he whispers, bending towards me. Auntie Val takes his coat and, holding it between finger and thumb, passes it to my mother to hang on one of the green-painted hooks in the corridor. 'Did you get my message?'

'It has been burning inside my mind all day. And there is one thing I must know straight away: the cat, did they take him alive?'

Sonneville straightens his tie, and waits until my mother and aunt have retreated into the kitchen.

'Capitaine Michel is dead,' he says, quietly.

'Thank God.' I sink into a chair.

'I beg your pardon?'

'It's what he wanted.'

'I'm not sure . . .'

'Better to die in silence, he once told me, than to live and talk.'

Sonneville hesitates. 'Look, is there somewhere we can have

a word? I think you should hear this, Stéphane, because you're the one with the brains. Maybe you'll be able to tell me what the hell we do now.'

We sit amid the silent machines and the cobwebs in Auntie Val's old workroom and – with that hushed urgency which comes naturally when a conversation may be one's last – Sonneville tells me the story of the last days of Capitaine Michel, and with what shining courage he met his end.

'It turns out that they caught young Woussen a while ago. They must have been torturing him in Paris for weeks. But, unlike Martel, he refused to talk. So then the bastards take what is left of him to Loos Prison, your favourite place, and show him his mother. She has been beaten up, too, and begs her son to cough. Which, finally, after a lot of whipping and hot pokers, he does.'

I shut my eyes, trying not to look at the pictures that are flashing in my mind. These are images from some other eighteen-year-old's life, I tell myself. This is Woussen's story, not mine.

'Next, on the evening of 26 November, Leutnant Lynen takes three police cars and a coach full of policemen and soldiers from Lille and sets about fingering the ringleaders named by Woussen. Woussen is seen handcuffed in the back seat of the first car. The traitor Martel has been brought along for the ride, too. They head for Arras. And one of the men they arrest, an English SOE agent known as Olivier, gives them Capitaine Michel's address in Lille. So Olivier can burn in hell, as far as I am concerned.'

Another man whose story is not mine, I tell myself. I am not Olivier. I am just the boy who looks after the graves. I don't know anything. You don't need to torture me.

'So now, as far as we can tell, Leutnant Lynen rushes to Lille with Olivier and Woussen. At 6.45 a.m., the Germans seal off both ends of the boulevard de Belfort with about 150 soldiers, and Inspector Gottwald of the GFP knocks on the door of Capitaine Michel's apartment.'

My mouth is dry. I can hardly listen to what comes next. For this, this is my story. I am in this one. I am in it with the captain, to the end.

'Open! German police!'

Sonneville knows this story in such bewildering detail that, for one flicker of a moment, I almost begin to wonder if there is more to him than meets the eye. But no, I remind myself. Sonneville is just that sort of man. With what he knows, if he is ever caught, the whole world will hang.

'Witnesses say that Capitaine Michel, armed with two pistols, shot through the door, killing Gottwald with two bullets and wounding a German soldier. Firing from the hip, he then charged out of the back door on to the street, into a storm of gunfire. He collapsed on the pavement with a bullet in his chest and another in his stomach. His beloved Denise, caught in a hail of machine-gun bullets upstairs, died thirty minutes later.'

We both sit like statues.

'I know it seems impossible,' says Sonneville, after a time. 'Even the Germans can't quite believe that the man they have killed is Capitaine Michel. The pictures they have of him were taken when he was still blond and sporting a moustache. But Olivier identified him to them as our chief.'

Another long silence. I only met Capitaine Michel three times, in all. Yet I feel as if I have just lost the most important person in my life.

'So it is finished,' murmurs Sonneville. 'They buried him in an unmarked grave.'

And this does it for me.

'No, Jean,' I tell him, through clenched teeth. 'It has only just begun.'

On 22 December, a poster appears on the walls of Arras and the surrounding villages, including Nieppe, announcing the executions of eight local men. Sonneville and I are not on the list. But all were members of the WO.

2 January 1944

At the pumps in the kitchen, I gaze into the shard of mirror above the wash-bowl. Not so long ago, I had to stand on tiptoes to see myself here. These days, I have to crouch. And when I look into my eyes, I barely recognise myself. Whatever happened to that fun-loving boy, who had a trick up his sleeve for every occasion? Are those his heartless eyes? Is this his dead-man's skin? I do my best to smile at the expressionless face in the mirror. But it only makes things worse.

The long-awaited invasion, the one we were promised before the end of 1943, has not come. The WO in Arras has been wiped out. Capitaine Michel is dead. Yet our four-strong section of the Voix du Nord – Marcel Lombard, Maurice Leblon, Francis André and me – is still gunning for action. Sonneville still wants his Spectacular. And the Houcke brothers, Jules and Marcel, remain central to our efforts to claw back our freedom, our future, our stolen lives.

At home, Elizabeth still wants to be a hairdresser, Rosemary still wants to be the pianist for Radio Lille, and my mother is still having none of it. I am lucky to have a family, I remind myself. Even a family of strangers, like mine. Sometimes I wish I could swap them for Marcel's family, or Sonneville's, because at least I can talk to them. Whereas at home, we are united in silence. It is safer this way. Some days, we say nothing at all.

I splash water on to my face, pull on my overcoat and cycle over to Mayor Houcke's house with the theadbare sleeves of my jumper pulled over my fingers, to stop them freezing to the handlebars.

Madame Houcke's daughter, Andrée, opens the door. I

have not seen her since that time I walked her home from the centre of Nieppe.

'It's you,' she says. '*Bonne année.*'

'Yes, it's me. *Bonne année* to you, too.' She proffers her cheek. But we hardly know each other, so I shake hands.

'Is your mother in?'

Before she can reply, the burly figure of Mayor Houcke appears in the doorway behind her.

'Ah, Stéphane,' he growls. '*Bonne année.* I've got something for you. It just came, hot off the press.'

He ushers me into the house, and Andrée insists on taking my coat. While she has her head in the cupboard under the stairs, her father hands me a sealed cream envelope, with the letter 'I' scrawled in the top left-hand corner.

'You're a soldier now, Iroquois. A commander in the Secret Army.'

'Ah.' I hold the envelope in both hands.

'My sentiments entirely. If you're arrested, you're supposed to show this to the Gestapo, to encourage them to treat you as a POW, not a terrorist. Personally, I think it's a damn fool idea. We might just as well carry around cards with "Please Shoot Me" on them. But make of it what you will. Nice photo by the way.'

'Thank you, sir.' I tuck the envelope into my pocket.

'Oh, and my brother wants to see you, if you don't mind popping over there before you head home.'

Marcel Houcke crushes my hand with his usual cheery greeting.

'*Bonne année, Stéphane,*' he exclaims. And then, in a low voice, he gives me my next mission. I am to escort five members of a Flying Fortress crew from Boeschepe, on the Belgian frontier, to La Bassée, thirty kilometres along a difficult road. Maurice Bouchery, a popular and prominent figure in La Bassée, has agreed to shelter the men at his house in the rue des Héronvals until they can be moved along the escape chain towards Paris.

Each day, I escort another member of the crew. Each day, I feel older by another year. Though we are welcomed warmly every morning by brave Monsieur Bouchery, whose eyes twinkle behind his owlish specs, the journey itself is terrifying. The bitter cold only makes things worse. I begin to dread the T-junction outside Estaires and the bridge over the Lys at La Bassée, where the Doryphores like to park their motorcycles when they are off duty. Even more excruciating is the twelve-kilometre stretch between the two. The straightness of Roman roads may have helped Julius Caesar to avoid being ambushed by Gauls, but it does nothing to help me avoid German road-blocks. I become very grateful for drainage ditches.

Arriving at Bouchery's on the third morning, I am stunned to find the two Americans I have already moved to La Bassée sitting outside the house in broad daylight. Bouchery's wife, a statuesque woman with eyes that sparkle with kindness, wrings her hands; they have even persuaded her husband to let them out in the evenings.

I can't believe it. Do the airmen not realise that the penalty for sheltering Allied personnel is deportation to a concentration camp for the whole family, if they are lucky? The men roll their eyes when I force them back inside.

'Keep your hair on, Iroquois,' one of them tells me. 'We're going crazy with boredom here. And it's far too cold for there to be any Krauts about.'

It doesn't seem to have occurred to them that collaborators and informers may lurk behind the net curtains of every other house in the village and that they are endangering Bouchery and his family's lives. I didn't want to say it before, because it felt unpatriotic. But I say it now. 'It's not just the Krauts that you people have to worry about. I'm afraid it is the French, too.'

They nod their apologies, hanging their heads like guilty schoolboys caught with catapults in their pockets.

Saturday turns out to be a grim, blustery day, with steel-grey clouds scudding across a low, flat sky. I make yet another round trip to La Bassée, and then head over to Jules Houcke's house, to set about clearing the garden. Madame Houcke seems to like me; sometimes she even asks me to stay for meals. This is a treat, as the mayor is well known to the farming community in Nieppe. So the stove is always lit and the food is of pre-war standard.

'Eat up, Stéphane,' orders Madame Houcke, who has more than a hint of the *Kalfaktor* about her. 'A big, strapping boy like you can't just live on fresh air. Can he, Andrée?'

Beside me, Andrée's three brothers giggle. I stare at the chicken bones on my plate and wonder if I can sneak them home for Mémère. They would make a wonderful soup.

'You, too, urchins: eat your meat. Otherwise you'll never grow up to be as tall and handsome as Stéphane here.'

Embarrassed, I glance across at Andrée. But she does not look up. I suppose I am a bit of a joke to the Houckes: the peasant gardener; the boy who tends the graves. Mayor Houcke himself says little to me at mealtimes. With him, I feel much as I do with my own family: there is so much that we must not say, it is almost easier not to speak at all.

At last my fifth airman is safely hidden. Our luck has held. Another group will be tasked with the next leg of the escape route, moving the airmen to a safe house near Arras or Lille. And good Monsieur Bouchery and his family will be able to breathe again.

The following Friday, I report back to Marcel Houcke, to announce the success of my mission.

'Then you haven't heard,' he says, as we stand amid the rabbit hutches behind his house. 'I'm so sorry, Stéphane.'

'Sorry about what?'

'The Gestapo have already arrested your airmen at the railway station in Lille.'

'Not . . .'

'Every single one. You'd think they were expecting them.'

'We have to warn Bouchery.'

'The Germans surrounded Bouchery's house at dawn, yesterday morning. There were a GFP car and two truckloads of soldiers, searchlights, the works. They took the whole family.'

'They won't find any evidence. Bouchery's place is clean. He's just a sweet, simple man.'

'The Boche also removed a radio transmitter, weapons and explosives.'

My mouth opens and shuts. 'Maurice Bouchery?'

'Probably being tortured, as we speak.'

Houcke and I look into each other's eyes. I have no words.

'You stuck to your code name?'

I nod.

'You're sure nobody followed you back to Nieppe?'

Another nod. 'But how on earth . . . ?' I begin.

'Someone must have heard the airmen in the local *estaminet* and told the GFP, because the Boche knew exactly how many aircrew Bouchery had been sheltering and where to find them.'

My head lolls. My body weighs a thousand tons. I have worked so hard. I have taken such risks, to do something I believed was good. And in so doing, I have merely condemned the men I sought to help, and the brave and innocent souls who dared to hide them, to death.

Houcke puts his arm around my shoulders. He slowly shakes his head. And, together, we watch the rabbits eating their wretched weeds.

A few days later, Sonneville begins to outline his plan for a mission – an experiment, really, to try out our explosives. He tells me about a man called Daumier, who runs a small factory in Nieppe producing bed sheets and pillowcases. According to Sonneville, Germans have been seen coming and going from this place.

'The man is a collaborator,' he says, with a shrug. 'And it is up to us to teach him a lesson.'

'We're going to blow up his house?'

'Oh, nothing too grand. I thought we might just drop a little something down the chimney, to give him a bit of a fright.'

'You know we're not just talking about fireworks here, Jean. But if he's working for the Boche . . .'

So while Sonneville goes off to do a final recce of Daumier's house, I stand shivering in front of a rickety table in his yard, gazing down at the bomb-making equipment I have extracted from our cache. A quantity of yellow 808 plastic, wrapped in brown paper. A white conical primary charge. A small tube of Vaseline. And a white-tipped L-delay pencil, made of dull copper. It all looks so harmless, laid out like this.

My breath makes clouds in the air as I slather my hands with Vaseline and unwrap the 808. A smell of almonds wafts up from the packets. Working as fast as I can, I attempt to knead half a dozen yellow sausages into a fist-sized lump of plastic explosive. But it's so cold that the material remains brittle in my hands, and my frozen fingers ache with the effort. As I press the white cone of the primary charge into the plastic, I try to picture Capitaine Michel standing beside me. He made it all look so easy. Steady hands. What I need are steady hands. More Vaseline next time, too. My temples are already beginning to throb. Within seconds, a blinding headache has sneaked inside my skull.

Here goes nothing. Squinting through a cloud of pain, I begin to insert the white L-delay pencil into the hole in the cone. I pray that the glass phial inside the detonator is still intact, and try not to touch the detonator's soft copper top. *Come on.* I hadn't expected the thing to be such a tight fit. *There.* Leaving the bomb on the table outside, I stagger back into the house and scrub my hands until they are raw. Then I lie down under a table and fall asleep.

Long after curfew, Sonneville and I cycle into Nieppe and place our bomb on the windowsill of Daumier's house. There are no street lamps. Every house in town is observing the blackout. Yet here we are on the main road, with a terrace of brick houses directly in front of us, and I imagine a thousand eyes upon me. I grasp the slim shaft of the L-delay pencil between my fingers and glance up at Sonneville.

'Are you absolutely sure you want me to do this?'

'*Mais . . . oui.*'

'Why the hesitation?'

'Just do it. How long do we have, anyway, to run away?'

'Two hours.'

'Two *hours?*'

I press down hard on the pencil's copper top. A soft click and the acid is doing its work. I force myself to walk, not run, away. Sonneville lopes along beside me.

'Two hours is a long time,' he sighs, before disappearing off into the night.

'Is that Lou?' asks my mother from the front room, as I creep back into the house.

I shut my eyes. I am waiting for a bomb to go off. I have no desire for a long lecture about Saint Rita and the Virgin Mother.

'Madame Houcke paid me a visit, Lou.'

'Did she.' Sliding my hand up the banister, I climb another two stairs.

'Yes, she did.' She pauses. 'She asked me something. Something about you.'

'Can it wait until tomorrow?'

At dawn, Auntie Val shakes me awake.

'Come on, Casanova,' she says. 'There's someone for you at the door.'

Why Casanova? My dread mounts as I hurry downstairs. In the corridor, I recognise Paul Saint Maxent, one of the brave old boys who made such a mess of sinking the drums.

'Some silly buggers have blown up one of the houses on the main road, up near Houcke's place,' he shouts. I suppose he's too deaf to whisper. 'It was rented out to that bloke Daumier, the *couillon* who makes bed linen for the Schleus.

There are Germans with dogs everywhere, looking for clues. So Marcel says to tell you that tonight's furniture removal is off.'

I had almost forgotten that Marcel Houcke's men were due to collect a load of Sten guns from our cache tonight. Mumbling my thanks, I hurry Saint Maxent towards the door, praying that nobody saw him come.

I am still shaving when the tap-tap-tap of my mother's white stick precedes her into the kitchen. Before I can speak, she reveals the purpose of Madame Houcke's visit yesterday.

'It was quite extraordinary,' she says, easing herself into one of the chairs at the table. 'She said she had come on behalf of her daughter, Andrée. Would you believe it?'

'Believe what?'

'Madame Houcke asked me for your hand in marriage.'

Razor in hand, I stare at my reflection in the shard of mirror.

'Did you hear what I said, Lou?'

'She asked you if I would marry her daughter?'

'Yes, isn't it wonderful? What a family! And what an honour for us! Did you know that they own several houses in the centre of town?'

I peer down at the grey blade of my razor, flecked with rust.

'So naturally I told Madame Houcke that you would say yes, because of course we are sensible of what an opportunity it is for you.'

'An opportunity? Mummy, I'm only eighteen. I want to be a soldier in the British army.'

'This is not just about you, Lou,' says my mother, beginning to sob. 'It's about all of us.'

I walk over to her and place my hand gently on her shoulder, struck by how scrawny she has become. 'I'm sorry, Mummy,' I murmur, as I slip out of the room.

When I cycle past Daumier's house in the afternoon, the Boche have already left. I am shocked at the state of the place. All the windows have been blown out. A chandelier lies tangled on the floor, amid the wreckage of a piano that has been blasted into about a thousand pieces. The windows of some of the houses on the other side of the street have been blown out, too. One of them is Mayor Houcke's.

Sonneville is delighted that our bomb worked. Leaning on the mantelpiece in his salon, waving his beer glass at me, he sweeps aside my doubts about whether this was the sort of action for which Capitaine Michel sacrificed his life.

'The end justifies the means,' he declares. 'The main thing is that we have given a stark warning to any potential collaborators.'

In the chilly gloom of our dining room in the rue du Sac, the dinner to celebrate my engagement to Andrée Houcke is in full swing. Candles have been lit, and a single rabbit has been divided between the twelve of us, along with a handful of potatoes and some green beans from a jar that Auntie Val has been hiding in the cellar. I am sitting next to Andrée, although I haven't yet been able to think of anything to say to her. Mayor Houcke, who brought a jar of honey as an engagement present, makes an apologetic little speech, in which he explains that he was as surprised as anyone when our engagement was announced.

There is fruit for pudding and, while everyone eats their apple slices, Mayor Houcke gestures for me to join him in the corridor. We shut the dining-room door behind us.

'I hope you know what you're doing, Stéphane,' he whispers. 'My daughter is not the sort of woman to set the world on fire. But she will keep your house cleaner that you could possibly imagine.'

'Yes, sir. And my family owes you so much.'

'I hope that's not the only reason we're here. I know my wife can be very forceful.'

'No, there are several reasons.'

'Good, good,' says Houcke, without conviction. 'And

there's something else.' Glancing towards the dining room, he lowers his voice. He tells me about two American airmen who have been arrested and taken to Loos Prison. Houcke is worried because both airmen are carrying the same false identity papers, signed by him. He quizzes me about the German section of the prison, and how the place is run. Marcel and I only saw each other once in our time at Loos, I tell him, but our files appeared to be kept side by side. Houcke nods, with a pained expression, and mutters something about staying as far away from Loos as he can.

By the time we return to the table, our green apple slices are already going brown.

19 February 1944

A freezing night. Lying in bed beside my brother, I hear the shriek of a train whistle and the thunder of a heavy locomotive hauling wagons across the flat landscape. I shiver beneath the bag of feathers that is supposed to keep us warm. If this snow settles, the mission is off.

I have made another bomb. It is out there now, in Sonneville's yard. Out there, too, in the darkness, is a French guard, stomping back and forth along his section of railway line, keeping an eye out for any trouble. If we play our cards right, he will not see the trouble until it is too late.

At a meeting yesterday, Sonneville earmarked a stretch of the main Lille–Calais–Dunkirk line, on the banked-up section between Nieppe and Steenwerck. I asked him about the risk of reprisals, this being so close to home. But he didn't want to hear. 'Nothing blunts a weapon so much as conscience,' he declared.

I nodded, but Marcel Lombard and Maurice Leblon exchanged glances in a way that made me wonder if I was missing something.

'Lose our conscience and we lose ourselves,' Maurice said. 'It's all we have left, now that the Boche have taken everything else.'

'In Lille, Stülpnagel has been shooting ten hostages – ten innocent patriots – for every German killed,' added Marcel. 'Surely we can't take that risk.'

'Look, we're not going to kill any bloody Boche,' retorted Sonneville, looking to me for support. 'Not yet, anyway. In the meantime, yes, our actions may have consequences for others beside ourselves. That is the burden we must carry. But I am rather hoping that the Germans will not believe that any patriots would be so bloody stupid as to piss on their own doorstep.'

'And if they do?'

'If they do, then it's the people of Steenwerck who really need to watch out, because that short-arsed viper Delbecque is bound to start shouting his mouth off about how he's the one who's blown up the rails with his magnificent numbskulls.'

It is 2 a.m. As I tiptoe out of the sleeping house and cycle along the frosty lanes, I picture the smoke and the sparks, the shiny face of the fireman glowing orange as he shovels coal into the firebox and the rails, straight as blades, juddering on their sleepers. Within those sinister brown trucks, each marked CHEVAUX 8, HOMMES 40, there could be men or horses, leather or linen, machine guns or gold. All I know is that every train is strengthening the people who slaughtered Capitaine Michel and that the railway lines themselves are the veins and arteries that allow the heart of Germany to pump with French blood.

I hide my bicycle in a field and make for the level crossing on foot.

'Have you got it?' A voice hisses from the shadow of the banking.

'Of course I've got it,' I reply, cradling my father's old work satchel like a rugby ball as I slither down the slope to join Sonneville, Lombard and Leblon.

From the satchel, I pull out two large mustard-yellow lumps of softened and sculpted 808. I have attached a primary charge and Bickford tape to the first, and now connect them with a metre of knotted Cordtex detonating cable. According to Capitaine Michel, the knots should help make the cable explode.

'*Vite, vite,*' urges Sonneville. 'We haven't much time.'

As our eyes grow accustomed to the dark, we see the glow of a cigarette tip in the distance. A lone figure is walking towards us, his boots crunching on the ballast between the rails. We hold our breath as the guard passes above our heads and trudges on down the line.

'When he comes back, we take him,' whispers Sonneville. 'Leblon, it's you and me.'

'*D'accord.*'

'Cross over the track now, and wait. You grab him from behind when I surprise him.'

'Understood.' Maurice scrambles up the banking.

'When we've got him tied up, Lombard here will guard him, right?'

'Right,' says Marcel, uncertainly.

'What's the matter?' asks Sonneville.

'I'm dying for a piss.'

'*Nom d'jou!* Couldn't you have thought of that?'

'Shh,' I remind him. 'That guard will be back any minute.'

We wait. I hear an owl shriek and, further away, the yowling of a fox. Then, suddenly, the low grumble of a vehicle approaching from Maurice's side of the level crossing.

We throw ourselves flat. I shut my eyes as the car slows. But it rattles on past us, bouncing over the level crossing and off down the road towards Nieppe.

A few minutes later, the crunching footsteps return.

A dark blur of movement. A muffled yelp. And with the guard trussed and gagged, everything speeds up.

Sonneville and I hurry down the line into the darkness. I press my twin charges into the hollow on either side of one of the rails, a metre apart, and give the knotted Cordtex that links them a tug to be sure it is firmly seated.

Then I pass the Bickford fuse through the gap beneath the rail and stretch it out as best I can. It looks awfully short.

'Come on,' growls Sonneville. 'The war will be over by the time you've finished.'

'A few more seconds,' I reply. I don't want to get this wrong. 'Right, that's done. Now all we need is a match. You got one, Jean?'

'You don't mean . . .'

'Only joking.'

'*Putain de merde.*'

'Here goes.'

The first match goes out. And the second. Sonneville cups his hands around mine. The third light, I think to myself. The sniper has had time to line up and aim.

But this time, when the match flares, the Bickford tape begins to splutter and sparkle. We tear off down the line, gather up Marcel and Maurice, and hurry back to our bicycles.

Moments later, there is a white flash and we are all thrown to the ground. Gravel rains down around us.

Dazed and exhilarated, we vanish into the darkness. The French guard, still blindfolded, will be obliged to tell the tale of what he did not see.

'Maybe make the fuse a little longer next time,' suggests Sonneville as we split up.

'Oh, really? Two hours is a long time,' I remind him, and he grins.

I spend the next day at work in the cemeteries, pruning the climbing roses and shrubs in the borders. Symphoricarpos, fuchsia and philadelphus; buddleia, heuchera and tamarix. My father has taught me all the names. Yet the plants look different to me today. For now, at last, I feel as if I can look myself in the eye. It will be weeks before the line is repaired.

Twenty-four hours after our triumph, the four of us meet for a celebratory beer and a well-deserved smoke at Sonneville's place. Marcel says he has heard that the rail we attacked is as twisted as a piece of cooked spaghetti. What a lesson we have taught the Krauts.

The following morning, less than forty-eight hours after our mission, I awake to a bad sound, worse even than my father's snoring. I can hear an express thundering along the very stretch of line we took such pains to destroy.

Shaken, I make another bomb. And then another. Four times, over the next few weeks, we blow up the track. Each time, the Germans manage to repair it, almost before we have had time to celebrate. So we venture closer to the railway stations, and blow up the points where two lines join. There are more guards to neutralise, but these complex junction plates take a whole lot longer to repair.

Patrols force their way into various addresses in the rue du Sac. I hear the clumping of their boots from my vantage point in Pont d'Achelles and watch them hammering on the door of Rioual's house, and the Lombard farm. But our house is spared, and no arrests are made.

Francis André joins us for the next meeting at Sonneville's house. With his studies in Lille finished for the time being, he has come home to help in his father's bike shop. I am pleased to see my old friend, and not only on behalf of my bicycle. Francis has a lightness about him which makes me realise how morose the rest of us have become.

'I can't believe I've been missing out on all this action,' he says, rubbing his hands together in front of the roaring fire. 'When do we get to blow up some more trains?'

'If only,' replies Maurice. 'We are risking our necks for nothing.'

We nod gloomily into our coffee. One of these days, we will strike lucky and send a goods train plunging off the tracks. But with most of them heading east to Germany, laden with French plunder, the traffic is light to the west of Lille and impossible to predict.

'At least you have been taking the fight to the Boche,' says Francis. 'Which is more than can be said for most of the French.'

'Bloody traitors and collaborators, denouncing each other for a handful of rice,' scowls Sonneville. 'I'd like to blow up the lot of them.'

'Jean, I . . .' I mumble. But he is already in full flow.

'No, slowly squeezing the juice out of them in a cider press would be more like it,' he decides. 'I'd cut off their dicks, too, because that's what they've done to us.'

'Steady on, Jean,' says Francis, who has only just met our chief. 'It's the Boche we have to fight.'

'*Bof!*' Sonneville flings his glass into the fire before storming out of the room.

The four of us stand there in silence.

'He's quite something, isn't he?' says Maurice, helping himself to another splash of beer.

'Yes, he's a real man, our chief.' Marcel holds out his glass. 'Brave as a lion, but a bit bloody scary with it.'

'Is he Belgian?' asks Francis André.

'He's as French as they come,' I tell him. 'So, naturally, although he loves France more than life itself, he really can't stand the French.'

'Ah.' Raising his eyebrows, Francis purses his lips and peers into his empty glass. 'You're *anglais,* Stéphane, so you're all right. But where does that leave the rest of us?'

Before I can answer, Sonneville marches back into the room. He is holding a small photograph of a young woman. He holds it up now as if it were a piece of evidence in a courtroom.

'They killed her,' he says, flatly.

'Is it your wife?' asks Francis, before I can stop him.

'Not my wife, no. But someone rare.' Sonneville holds the photograph at arm's length and stares at it in silence.

'Beautiful,' says Francis, in a low voice. 'She was beautiful.'

'She was too beautiful,' nods Sonneville, with feeling. 'So some jealous bitch writes an anonymous letter to the *Kommandantur,* accusing her of making jokes about the Germans and of having a Jewish mother. And, a few days later, they come and take her away.'

'Bastard Gestapo,' mutters Francis. 'Bastards. Utter bastards.'

Sonneville shakes his head. Carefully setting down the photograph, he begins to tap a cigarette on his silver cigarette case. 'No, my friend,' he says, turning his face away from us. 'It wasn't the Gestapo. It was the French police.'

15 March 1944

As winter slowly turns to spring, there is more work to do in the cemeteries. 'Weeds are like people,' my father always says. 'It's the ones you wish wouldn't grow that multiply the fastest.'

Madame Houcke is insistent that I come to her house, too: her potatoes need planting. But when I knock on their door, nobody comes to answer it. The shutters are closed. The place looks as dead as the rest of Nieppe. At last, I hear the clunk of brass bolts being slid back.

'*C'est toi*,' says Andrée, staring at my feet. She looks a state; her eyes are red-rimmed, her skin blotchy, her hair unkempt.

'Yes, it's me.' I stare at my shoes, too; I notice that my bare toes are now sticking out of the worn leather.

'You must go.'

'Oh, really?' I reply, with some enthusiasm. 'What have I done?'

She shakes her head. 'It's Daddy. They came in the night. He is gone.'

'Mayor Houcke? Is he all right? I mean, is he injured?'

She holds a handkerchief to her mouth; she says nothing.

'Did they say where they were taking him?' I ask, taking a step backwards.

'I don't know,' she sobs. 'Uncle Marcel is trying to find out. I heard him mention Loos.'

I am doing my best to act as if nothing has happened when Marcel Houcke comes to find me at Pont d'Achelles. He confirms that his brother has been arrested by the Vichy police for issuing false identity cards to STO *réfractaires*, to the many young men who, summoned for compulsory labour in Germany under Laval's *Service du Travail Obligatoire* scheme, have preferred to go into hiding. The only good news is that Mayor Houcke is currently being held in the French section at Loos, where the prisoners sleep in dormitories rather than cells and are allowed out on fatigues from time to time. The two US airmen who were issued with false identity papers are still in the German section where Marcel Lombard and I were held.

I do not tell the rest of my section about Mayor Houcke's arrest. The less any of us knows about anything, the better.

This morning, when Rosemary came and asked me if I'd play the drums for her band in a few weeks, I almost bit her head off. Every train that passes, billowing smoke and steam, annoys the hell out of me. And I don't even know how to play the drums.

'Have you noticed, Lou,' asks my mother, 'that the wax above the front door is working?'

'What do you mean, it's *working*?' I can feel the heat rising in me again.

'Saint Rita is keeping the Germans out. Every other house in the street has been searched. But she is protecting us.'

'That's marvellous, Mummy, absolutely marvellous,' I reply. 'Now, do you think you could ask Saint Rita if she could protect us from Rosemary, and derail some trains for us, too?'

'What do you mean?'

'Sorry, Mummy. Stupid joke.' I hang my head. 'I'm just so tired. I'll be better in the morning.'

When the four of us meet in the shadows of the Lombard barn to discuss our next mission, Maurice Leblon wants us to change our tactics. He says we should be setting off our charges with a petard on the rail, activated by the locomotive itself. But Marcel Lombard is having none of it. As soon as we start killing Germans, he reminds us, the danger of reprisals is multiplied.

'Besides,' says Francis André, 'the Boche are attaching a wagon of French hostages to the front of every train.'

'How do we know that?' Maurice's eyes narrow.

'I've seen them in the main station at Lille.'

We all nod, impressed. Francis is such an urbane fellow, compared with us country bumpkins.

'That's sick, even by German standards,' says Maurice.

'It's sick, but it's effective.'

'I doubt it would stop Sonneville,' mutters Marcel, drily.

'I've already spoken to Sonneville.' Everyone turns to stare at me. 'I told him how frustrated we are. I told him we want to hit some other targets.'

'And?' Maurice slips down off his hay bale and takes a step towards me.

'He says we can do nothing until we receive orders from the new head of the WO in Lille.'

Francis stays behind after the meeting and asks me for a couple of magnet bombs. We look into each other's eyes. I do not ask him what he is planning to do with them.

The escape plan for the mayor is beautifully simple. And it has to work, because trying and failing to escape, even from the French side of Loos Prison, will be swiftly rewarded with a volley of bullets in the prison yard at dawn.

According to Marcel Houcke, his brother has managed to get himself on the milk fatigue, which means traipsing out to a local farm every morning under a French police escort. A brick wall runs for fifty metres or so along the track from the farm, ending at a sharp bend. Marcel Houcke, Maurice Leblon and I will be waiting here with an extra bicycle.

'No breakfast, yet again?' frowns Auntie Val, as I sit at the kitchen table, nursing my cup of barley coffee, unable to eat.

'I ate a lot last night.'

'No, you didn't,' retorts Kléber. 'You ate almost nothing. None of us did. Don't you remember, we had Mémère's Special Surprise?'

'How could I forget?' I reply, barely listening.

Rosemary wanders into the kitchen. Seeing me, she grimaces and looks as if she may be about to walk out again.

'I'm sorry I shouted at you the other night,' I tell her quietly. 'Of course I'll play the drums for your concert.'

She blinks with surprise. 'Thank you,' she says, planting a kiss on my cheek.

'And Kléber, you know I said you couldn't borrow my bicycle after school? Well, you can now.'

My brother gazes at me, stunned. 'Seriously?'

By the time I arrive with the extra bicycle, my Luger in my pocket, Sonneville is already in position at the edge of the wood in his black Citroën sedan. At least, I hope that's Sonneville. It's typical of the man to drive around in an unlicensed car, identical to the ones favoured by the Gestapo. The other two blokes are waiting for me at the wall, smoking cigarettes.

We shake hands in silence. In the distance, I can see the dark, helmet-shaped stub of the main tower at Loos.

'Almost time,' says Marcel Houcke at last, consulting his watch. He throws his butt-end into the grass. 'Let's go.'

While I head behind the wall with the spare bicycle and make for the bend, Maurice and the mayor's brother pretend to tinker with their bike chains.

In my hiding place, I stand on hollow legs and wait. Breathe, just breathe.

I stare at the brickwork a few inches from my face, trace the mortar with my finger and comfort myself with the thought of the men who built the wall standing here, years ago, whistling while they worked. And then my fingers find a bullet hole, a limpet-shaped recess, gouged in the red stonework.

All too soon, I hear the bell-like din of a full milk churn being dragged down the road towards us. Then the scraping of a weary man's boots. It sounds as if he is limping.

A small rock clatters over the wall: my signal from Maurice to stand to.

I am just wondering how on earth the mayor will detach himself from the procession when I recognise his voice.

'I've got the trots. I need a shit, right now.'

'You what?' The French guard emits a torrent of guttural expletives.

'I've got *la chiasse*. And I need to have a shit *right now*.'

'A shit?'

'Right now, I tell you.'

'You'll have to wait until we get back.'

'It's coming! It's coming!'

'All right,' blurts the guard. 'But make it quick, understood?'

'You won't even know I've gone,' says the mayor, darting around the corner of the wall so fast that I jump.

I almost retch at the familiar stench of Loos. The mayor looks astonished to see me. I notice he has grown a beard.

Without a word, I show him the spare bicycle.

He climbs on to the saddle, but can't get himself going on the soft earth. One of his legs is all but useless.

In a flash, I dismount and give him a push, running on my toes as best I can over the grassy soil.

And then the mayor is away, pedalling for the woods with his head down, as if he is leading the Tour de France. *Allez, allez!*

A few seconds later, and all four of us are cycling like mad across the field. The guard must have sat down to enjoy the rest of his precious fag. I can hear the mayor puffing and blowing behind me. He is making alarming wheezing noises by the time we reach Sonneville's car.

'*Vite, vite.*' Sonneville bundles the mayor into the back of the vehicle. The engine coughs and roars, and off they speed. Their destination is a lonely farmhouse close to the river Lys, where the mayor must now lie low. The rest of us split up and ride, helter-skelter, back to Nieppe.

'I can't believe we got away with it,' declares Sonneville, eyebrows raised. He clinks his coffee cup against mine.

The two of us are sitting at his kitchen table, enjoying the warmth of the stove and the companionship of outlaws. A green-eyed cat watches us from the dresser. Jean Sonneville is old enough to be my father. But we seem to understand each other, he and I. Neither of us is much of a talker. And it's good to be able to speak almost openly with a kindred spirit every once in a while.

'It was too easy,' I reply. 'I feel sorry for the French guard. God knows what they'll do to him now.'

He shakes his head. 'Pity is for fools. Always remember that. People make their own destinies, Stéphane, and he has made his.'

Sonneville hesitates. He raises a hand and turns his head to one side. Did we hear something? Eyes locked, we hold our breath. There is nothing – only the sound of the wind whistling in the leafless trees outside.

And then another urgent, muffled knock at the front door.

Again, we stare at each other. Almost in a single movement, Sonneville tips the contents of our coffee cups down the sink and hurries me through a doorway hidden behind a tapestry. 'Stay here.' I find myself at the top of a steep stone slope.

A few minutes later and the door reopens.

'Come and see who's here,' says Sonneville, calmly. Installed at the kitchen table, Maurice Leblon grips his cup of coffee in both hands, as if he is worried we might pinch it. Pleased as I am to see him, I can tell from his handshake that this is not a social call. It is long after curfew.

'There is a bar in Steenwerck,' he begins, 'where the lady owner's daughter is having it away with a German soldier. He works on one of the big engineering projects on the coast, and comes down at weekends to spend time with his mistress.'

'Collaborationist whore,' growls Sonneville. 'I can guess the bar you're talking about. *Au Pigeon Voyageur* is run by a right old cow. I hadn't heard that her daughter was knocking off a Schleu, but it doesn't surprise me. We should teach her a lesson.'

Captured German soldiers in the schoolyard at Pont de Nieppe. The more prisoners we captured, the more we despaired of what to do with them all. Many seemed relieved that their war was over – until the German SS came and released them, and shot any who refused to continue the fight.

The bullet-scarred road sign in Pont de Nieppe. During the fierce fighting to stop the Germans blowing up the bridge, I was stationed on a balcony of the house on the right. There is now a memorial here to those who died resisting the Nazis.

We captured three of these 88mm anti-tank guns, and did our best to put them out of action. The Germans made a better job of destroying them when they blew up the bridge.

The remains of the bridge over the Lys, after the German retreat. So many of my friends died attempting to protect that bridge. Yet it was all for nothing in the end.

The funeral of the brave people of Nieppe who died at the hands of the German SS. I was part of the escort (front right-hand side) carrying the coffins.

Liberation at last: my dad (trilby hat, top left) went crazy when the first Tommies arrived in Nieppe, ending the virtual imprisonment he had endured for the past four years.

Conquering heroes: it was extraordinary to drive our captured *Kübelwagen* through the liberated streets. Sonneville is the one leaning on the bonnet holding some German binoculars; Mayor Houcke, with beard, is in the centre. I'm the one in the tin hat behind him. On my right is Colonel Cargill and on my left is Dad.

Rosemary, Kléber, me, my 'fiancée' Andrée Houcke and Elizabeth.

Members of my Resistance group a few days after Liberation, in La Crèche. Conrad, Sonneville and I are in the centre of the back row, in tin hat, armband and battledress respectively. Beside Conrad, Jacques Flahou poses with his Sten. The small fellow two to my left is Roger Rioual; the tall man beside him is Abel Rotsaert. Front row, from left: Chaban, my brother Kléber, Lutun, Marcel Lombard, Francis André.

A British soldier at last: on embarkation leave in the garden
of 6, rue du Sac, alongside Kléber (left) and Dad in his
War Graves Commission uniform.

With my lifelong friend
Marcel Lombard.

With US airman Conrad
Kersch right, and Dad's
Royal Enfield motorbike,
September 1944.

November 2012: with my friends on the terrace of the house I built
in a lonely corner of Greece, overlooking the sea.

'But here's the thing,' replies Maurice, setting his jaw. 'This German, Hans somebody-or-other, claims to know that several men in the village are active members of the Resistance. And now he has started boasting that, if he talks, a number of them will be for the chop.'

'It's good of you to come and warn me,' says Sonneville, in a low voice. 'But I can look after myself.'

'*C'est bien.*' Maurice sighs. He looks as if a weight has been lifted off his chest.

'Leaving aside the WO, the Steenwerck group are mostly a bunch of charlies,' adds Sonneville. 'Active members? *Bof.* The worst they've done is put itching powder in an officer's cap. Yet the great Pierre Delbecque is convinced that he is beating the Boche single-handed. Probably he'll be flattered that someone is threatening to denounce him. Now, Maurice, haven't you got any good news for us, for a change?'

Maurice shrugs. He says that Francis André claims to have stuck a pair of magnet bombs on to two heavily laden goods trains in Lille station, with the fuses set for six hours.

'Six *hours?*' exclaims Sonneville.

'How do we know they actually went off?' I ask Maurice.

'We don't,' he says, with a sour expression.

'Not seeing the bloody thing go off is as bad as cooking a meal and not tasting it,' mutters Sonneville. 'It's like undressing a woman with the lights off. Unless the woman is your wife, obviously.'

A week later, a message comes through from Fertein, one of Capitaine Michel's former deputies in the WO. My entreaties to Sonneville have borne fruit. We are to attempt a large-scale sabotage operation, in a mission shared between Sonneville's section of the WO and Marcel Houcke's Voix du Nord.

After Saint-Omer, the river Lys becomes navigable by barge, flowing through Belgium and Holland and out into the North Sea. Huge sluice gates for regulating the water level are installed at Bac Saint-Maur, an enclosed basin a few kilometres from Nieppe. And, since the Germans are thought to be using this route to transport raw materials to their V-weapon sites around Calais, we are to put the gates out of action.

Long after curfew, I creep over to our cache and root out several packets of 808 in the darkness, along with a primary charge and a length of Bickford fuse. I move them to Sonneville's house in the morning.

With his jacket collar turned up, Sonneville comes out to watch me work. It is a bitterly cold day, and I can see my breath in the air. Having gone off to fetch me a cup of coffee, he returns instead with a small wood-burning stove which, with typical generosity, he sets up and lights in the corner of the courtyard. On top of it, he places an old iron pot.

'Your method takes forever, doesn't it?' he says, arms folded, fingers twitching with impatience. It's true that I can only knead a couple of sausages at a time, to warm and soften the 808. And I will need perhaps five kilos of plastic for this bomb.

'What's the pot for?' I ask, beginning to spread Vaseline over my hands.

'This,' he replies. He has an alarming glint in his eyes. Before I can stop him, Sonneville has grabbed two of the 808 sausages and popped them into his pot.

'Jean! Wait . . .' I exclaim. But it is too late.

'What are you supposed to do with sausages,' he yells, 'if not cook them?' He gives the pot a little shake.

'Are you mad?' I crouch down, eyelids scrunched, waiting for the pot to explode.

'Madness and genius are but two sides of the same coin, are they not?' he declares. 'I have just invented the modern way to warm 808.' He taps the side of the pot with a wooden spoon.

There is a hissing, spluttering noise, and Sonneville jumps backwards. I put my fingers in my ears. A sulphurous yellow flame erupts ten feet into the air, accompanied by a sickening whiff of cordite.

In the silence that follows, I feel almost sorry for Sonneville, as I picture his embarrassment, his shame at having put both our lives in danger and his contrition at having wasted our precious 808.

'*Nom d'jou,*' he exclaims at last. 'That was fun. Shall we try it again?'

The following evening, Sonneville, Maurice Leblon and I cycle with our Sten guns and my bomb – made traditionally, by hand – to the river basin at Bac Saint-Maur. Here, we are joined by Marcel Houcke and two of his men.

It is another shrivellingly crisp night, and the brick-built lock-keeper's cottage is clearly visible on a boat-shaped island in the middle of the river. From one side of the island, a reinforced concrete barrier runs to the shore and the village of Bac Saint-Maur. On the other side, two huge lock gates connect the island to the fields beyond.

I wince as Maurice and one of Houcke's boys draw the short straw and are deputed to break into the cottage. Their job is to neutralise whoever is inside. The place could be crawling with Boche, for all we know.

Maurice's pale features do not flinch. He shrugs, mouths something to himself and allows himself the hint of a smile. Then he turns towards the man he is to accompany and, shaking hands, they share something terse with their eyes.

The seven minutes that Maurice spends inside the cottage are seven of the longest minutes of my life.

From over here, the house looks so still. I try not to imagine the ferocious struggle within. I recruited Leblon. I feel responsible for him. I want to smoke about a hundred cigarettes.

And then the door of the cottage flies open. We hold our breath. And our comrades are racing back to us, almost laughing at how easy it was.

'There was just this old boy and his wife,' says Maurice, the whispered words tumbling out. 'They begged us to tie them up. They even provided the rope.'

'Are you sure they couldn't have got a message to anyone when they heard you breaking in?' asks Marcel Houcke.

His man, a stout little rugby player with a bushy moustache, shakes his head. 'They were asleep in bed, poor dears. But Maurice here pulled the phone off the wall, just to make sure.'

I slap my hand to my forehead. We forgot to cut the telephone wires before they went in. Sometimes our naivety terrifies me.

Now it is my turn. We creep out across the barrier to the island. I lower my bomb, stuffed into the inner tube of a car tyre, from the centre of one of the lock gates, with a length of Bickford tape attached.

'Does it really work underwater?' asks Sonneville.

'Ready?' I blurt, ignoring him. This is the bit I hate: the seconds ticking away when you could still change your mind.

They nod, their eyes wild with excitement.

I light the fuse and we scatter.

A few minutes later, there is a dull crump and a jet of water leaps up from the basin, so high in the air that it blots out some of the stars. Euphoric, we cycle home.

The following day, Marcel Houcke brings news to the cemetery in Pont d'Achelles.

'Word has it that some *couillon* tried to blow the sluices at Bac Saint-Maur last night,' he says, grinning.

'Oh, yes?'

'Yes, and they totally ballsed it up. The gates are operating as normal today.'

'*Merde.*'

'Quite so.' He glances around us, and lowers his voice. 'Any idea why it didn't work?'

'I suppose they didn't get the bomb in the right place. But perhaps they'll have another try in a fortnight's time, when things have quietened down.'

'Perhaps they will.' He looks pleased at the thought.

Two weeks later, we return to Bac Saint-Maur, conscious

that it may be more heavily guarded after our botched first attempt. But, once again, the place is eerily peaceful. This time, we cut the telephone wires and Maurice orders the lock-keeper to open the gates, as if a boat were coming through, before tying him up. While the huge timber boom is drawing an arc across the water, I lower the bomb – another five kilos of our precious plastic – against the wall, and allow the gate to open against it. Then I say a few words to myself and light the blue touch paper of my firework.

The following day, Marcel Houcke is back in the cemetery.

'Bull's-eye,' he whispers. 'One of the gates has been blown clean off its hinges.'

'Ah,' I reply, continuing to work on the piece of turf that I am in the middle of cutting.

'In fact,' he adds, 'the operation was such a professional job that people are saying it must have been the work of a British agent.'

We stare at one another. Leaning on my edge-trimmer, I smile up at the sun glowing on the trees.

31 March 1944

In Steenwerck, Delbecque is beginning to panic about the German soldier who has threatened to squawk. He shares his fears with Marcel Fertein, the new head of the WO in Lille. And Fertein, after taking soundings, orders that Hans be assassinated. Delbecque knows a lot of people in the network, after all. If denounced and interrogated, nobody expects him to follow Capitaine Michel's example of selfless heroism. So who does Fertein select to carry out the assassination? Delbecque himself, naturally.

According to Sonneville, Delbecque is not enthralled by this news. For the first time ever, he will have to prove himself to the rest of the group. And he faces not just a very dangerous mission but, after it, the prospect of being a fugitive until Doomsday. His plan is to dig a hole in a field near the station, abduct Hans when he arrives on the train to see his floozy, kill him, transport his body by handcart to the field and drop him in the hole.

The day allotted for the operation arrives. Everyone is in their places at the station. But at the very moment when Hans's train pulls in, Delbecque gets cold feet.

News of the aborted mission reaches Fertein in Lille. Furious, he summons Sonneville.

In the late afternoon sun, Sonneville and I wander into the deserted municipal cemetery. We sit on a large family tomb from where we can keep an eye on the gates and not be overheard. Having outlined the Delbecque debacle, Sonneville says he wants to discuss a mission of our own at the railway station in Steenwerck. A goods train is being loaded with hay for the German army. It could, he says, make a Spectacular.'

'A hay train? Sounds like a waste of explosives to me.'

'I know. That's why I'm proposing that we do it with incendiary grenades.' He smiles innocently. 'We've got some of those ones that look like small brown bananas, haven't we? Good, then we'll do it tonight.'

'Are you sure we want to be going to Steenwerck just now?' I ask, tracing my finger along a fissure in the marble of the tomb. 'And you haven't yet told me what Fertein said when he summoned you.'

'Oh, well, he . . .'

'Yes?'

'He wants me to organise the killing of the German myself.'

'*Merde.* Bad luck.'

'Yes, I can think of nicer ways of spending an evening, but it's what we've all been dreaming of, isn't it, Stéphane? The chance to kill some Boche.'

'I suppose so.'

'Good. I'm glad you feel that way, because unfortunately I'm a bit of a celebrity in Steenwerck. You know, I'm a face there.'

I sit very still. I can feel my pulse beating in my temples.

'I even know the old bitch who runs the bar,' he continues. 'So it's not *prudent*, as Capitaine Michel might put it, for me to undertake the mission myself; I'd put too many others at risk. So I . . . I was wondering . . . I had this idea . . .'

'You want me to do it for you.'

'Well, I thought perhaps you and your team could take it on. Obviously I'd come with you, for moral support. But I'd stay outside the bar, so as not to jeopardise the mission.'

'Good thinking.'

The old nausea begins to wrap itself around my guts. Tomorrow I have to deliver another pile of *Voix du Nord*s with Maurice Pauwels, on my ropey old bicycle. The sprockets are so worn that the chain keeps slipping off, and even Francis André has given up attempting to fix it. The day after

tomorrow, Houcke has an American airman for me to interview and move to his next address. Then there is the mission
with incendiary grenades at Steenwerck station tonight. This
is all fine. Or at least it was fine, until a second ago. Because
now we have to kill a man in cold blood. 'So what do you
think?' asks Sonneville.

'Is it an order from Fertein?'

'Yes.'

'And are you ordering us to do it?'

Sonneville winces. 'No, Stéphane. I'm asking you, as a
friend, to help me out.'

'It's just that I think I'd find it easier if it was an order.'

There is a long silence.

'All right,' he says, quietly. 'If it helps, it's an order.'

Another silence.

'I'll have a word with my section,' I say. 'Let you know
tomorrow?'

'Of course.' He jumps down from the tomb; he pats it as
if it were an old friend.

'Do you know them?' I point at the names inscribed in the
stone.

'No,' he smiles. 'I'm just trying to get used to the idea of
being dead. We'll all be in here, one day, won't we?'

'Yes,' I say, although I am thinking: no. Not because I am
not ready to die, but because the cemetery I have always
pictured for myself will have symmetrical white headstones
and English shrubs and perfect grass.

'Well, stay alive.' Sonneville shakes my hand and walks off,
whistling a jaunty tune.

The following day, after cycling to Lens with Maurice Pauwels
and another stack of the *Voix du Nord,* I convene a meeting
of my section in the Lombard barn.

'*Putain,* the sky was lit up all red over Steenwerck last
night,' exclaims Marcel, when we are gathered. 'Did you see
it?'

Maurice nods. 'The flames were fifty feet high. I could see them from my bedroom window.'

'Everyone was talking about it in town,' says Francis. 'Apparently someone set fire to a hay train. The local *pompiers* couldn't control it. And now the station guard, who was half-cut at the time, is up before the tribunal in Lille. They say he'll be deported unless he can name the culprits.'

'Was anyone seen?' I ask, casually.

Francis shakes his head. 'Looks like the Steenwerck group aren't quite as hopeless as Sonneville seems to think.'

It is time to tell them about Delbecque, and what we have been ordered to do. When I have finished, there is a deep silence.

'How many of us do you need?' asks Marcel, quietly.

'I was thinking three: myself, Maurice and Francis.' I pause, waiting for the protest. 'I don't mean to exclude you, Marcel, but there's no point implicating us all, and your school obligations make it hard to know when you will be free.'

'That's OK,' he says, with a sigh. 'What will you do: simply carry out the Steenwerck plan?'

I shake my head. 'The station will be more heavily guarded, following last night's . . . Spectacular.' I grin at them, trying to break the tension. 'So I think we should do it in the café. Choose a moment when it's empty, and shoot him there.'

'You make it sound so easy,' says Maurice. 'What if the girlfriend's there as well?'

'What's difficult about it?' I shrug. But the truth is that it is only now, when I have spelled it out aloud, that I realise the enormity of what we have been asked to do. I have always imagined spraying the Krauts with bullets in an almighty gunfight. I never pictured myself being asked to shoot an unarmed man in cold blood.

Maurice pretends to yawn. 'You can count me in,' he says. 'I don't like it. But it's about time I put that Colt to good use.'

'What about you, Francis? If three of us fire at the same time, there'll be no way of knowing who's killed him.'

'Like a firing squad,' adds Marcel, with a shrug.

'And that makes it better, does it?' Francis jumps to his feet. 'I just don't see why it's up to us to do someone else's dirty work.'

I run my hands roughly through my hair and tug at the roots with my fists. 'Look, I don't like it any more than you do. But we have been given an order, and if this man squawks before we can stop him, many brave men will die.'

'And some not so brave men, too,' says Maurice.

'All right, count me in,' says Francis, gruffly. 'I don't have a gun, but I suppose you'll lend me one.'

'Of course,' I reply. 'We'll do the thing at dusk. As long as we're not seen, we're in the clear.'

When I walk back into the house, I can hear Rosemary at the piano. I tiptoe past the doorway of the front room, hoping not to be heard.

'Lou?' she calls. 'Is that you?'

'Hello,' I say, putting my head round the door.

'Gosh, you look terrible.'

'Thanks.'

'Do you want to practise for the concert? It's only three weeks away.'

'I'm a bit tired. Do you mind? I think I'll just go to bed.'

'How's Andrée, by the way?'

'Francis André?' I reply, holding my breath. 'Why, do you know him?'

'No, Andrée Houcke.'

'I have absolutely no idea.'

'Are you all right, Lou?'

'Never better,' I reply, as I begin to climb the scaffold of the stairs.

All I can think of now is Steenwerck. On Saturday 8 April, I have arranged to meet Sonneville, Maurice Leblon and Francis André in an alley just off the square.

When the day comes round at last, I head over to Steenwerck

just before dusk. I have loaded my Luger with copper-coloured Sten ammunition, because I can't find any of the proper, dark stuff in our cache.

Sonneville, Maurice Leblon and Francis André are already waiting in the alley, 200 yards or so from *Au Pigeon Voyageur*. There is a fourth man with them, a wiry figure, dressed all in black. At a signal from Sonneville, he slips away.

'He has just gone to see if our friend is at home.' Sonneville looks as relaxed as I have ever seen him. 'And, if so, how many friends he has in tow.'

'*Très bien*,' I reply as cheerfully as I can.

Maurice mutters something about the cold. Francis doesn't say a word.

After a while, Sonneville's man wanders up the alley with his hands in his pockets. My calves stiffen. I wipe my hands on my trousers. This is it.

'Our friend couldn't make it this weekend,' he whispers. 'It's a pity, no?'

A wave of elation and relief sweeps through me. Sonneville leans back against the wall. Maurice exhales sharply. Francis flexes his legs, one after the other.

'I thought he came every weekend for a bit of the local *pâtisserie*?' I say to Sonneville.

'Perhaps he's getting it elsewhere,' mutters Maurice.

'His loss, not ours,' replies Sonneville. 'We'll give him his present next week.'

'*Entendu*,' says the man in black. 'I'll see you then.'

As the days pass, my misgivings multiply, and with them my hatred of Delbecque. I keep trying to work out how I have got myself into this mess. I can't help thinking that our German may just have been shooting a line when he threatened to tell tales about the local boys. If Delbecque hadn't got windy and whimpered to Fertein, no one would be any the wiser. And if he had only carried out his orders, the matter would have been closed. Instead, we are the ones who must carry the can.

The following Saturday, 15 April, I meet up with Maurice and Francis on the corner of the rue des Meuniers, just opposite the rue du Sac, and we cycle to Steenwerck together. We all lean against the same wall in the same shadowy alley as last week. I can feel my left knee joggling just a little more than it did before. I know I can pull the trigger. I'm not scared of being shot. But there's something else, and I can't put my finger on it.

'I knew it,' growls Maurice. Sonneville's man has just come back down the lane and shaken his head at us. Again, our man hasn't showed up.

Francis and Sonneville do not attempt to hide their relief, but I just feel annoyed. I want to get this thing finished. I'm not sure I can stand another week of waiting. And what if our German talks in the meantime? If Delbecque is interrogated under torture, then one name on his lips will be Sonneville's.

On the third Saturday, 22 April, the usual problems with my bicycle chain mean that I arrive a few minutes late at our meeting place on the corner of the rue des Meuniers. Maurice and Francis must have gone on ahead, so I cycle to Steenwerck alone. I have only been riding for a minute or two when I feel a prickling on the back of my neck. I pull in and pretend to check my bike chain while scanning the road behind me. But there is nobody on my tail.

Soon I am passing the white steeple of the church in Steenwerck. Sonneville is leaning against a lamppost, a little further on.

'What about it?' he asks, folding his newspaper. 'Shall we do it?'

'Is he here?'

'He's here.'

'*Merde.*'

'Exactly.'

'Sorry. I just wasn't expecting him to turn up.' My legs tingle; my head feels light. 'Are the others with you?'

'I thought they were with you.'

I can feel Sonneville watching me, weighing up whether I am ready or not.

'Right, we'll give them half an hour,' he says, quietly.

I lean against the wall and roll myself a cigarette. Sonneville pretends to read his newspaper, even though it is almost too dark to see.

'Are you quite sure our man is there?' I rub my palms on my thighs.

He nods. 'Our scout has already been and gone.'

I put the cigarette between my lips and draw on it as Sonneville thumbs the flint of his brass lighter. We both watch the tip glow for a moment. Then he flicks shut the lighter, and the flame is snuffed out.

'The last cigarette,' I murmur.

'Oh, are you giving up?' he asks.

'It's just an expression.'

While Sonneville goes back to his paper, I trace the outline of the Luger in my pocket and think of all the things I would rather be doing right now, all the places I would rather be than here.

Three-quarters of an hour later, there is still no sign of the others. The sky is almost black.

'What about it?' says Sonneville again. 'Shall we do it?'

'Just you and me? *Nous deux?*'

'Yes. I'll be keeping watch outside.'

'So it's just me, then.'

'Yes, it's just you.'

This is a new development. But I am the leader of my section. I am the only British member of the group. I need to set an example. If only Maurice and Francis were here. If only I could have another cigarette.

Sonneville bends down and picks a couple of spent matches out of the gutter. Both have been broken in half, to make the shape of a V for victory. With a quick glance up and down the street, he holds them up to me. 'You see?

We are not alone. Everyone finds their own way to resist.'

'*D'accord.*' Is that the extent of the Steenwerck group's resistance, then: breaking matchsticks in half?

'Know that I'll be right there with you, in spirit. Oh, and Stéphane . . .'

Our eyes meet, and I can see that Sonneville is going to say something important, that he is finally going to acknowledge the work I have done. I know he is a hard man, and it isn't like him to pay compliments. But I can feel one coming now, because perhaps this will be our last conversation and there won't be another chance. I shall be glad of it, too, because, God knows, I need something to ease the rictus of tension that is crisping my muscles, and to remind me that I do actually have it in me to be brave, even when my legs are leaden with panic and I can taste fear like metal in my mouth.

'If you can manage it,' he whispers, 'would you mind putting a bullet in the old girl's backside while you're at it? She's a nasty bitch, I can tell you.'

The wind slaps me in the face when I turn out of the alley. I do my best to walk my bicycle across the square and down the passage which leads to *Au Pigeon Voyageur,* but my legs keep wanting to run.

There's the sign now: a pigeon with a message tied to its claw.

Does the man inside know how little time is left?

Slinking into the shadows, I lean my bicycle against a wall. I pull out the Luger, release the safety catch, pocket it again. One last time, I wipe my hands on my trousers. Then I push open the café door.

The place is dimly lit. Sawdust on the floor. A smell of stale beer and tobacco in the air. My wooden soles resound on the boards. Nobody here.

On the wall to my right is a small painting of a horse, and an advertisement for Leffe beer. The zinc bar is straight ahead of me, topped with a white ceramic pump and a small bronze statuette of a racing cyclist. The kitchen must be behind that wall. Another door at the back of the room probably leads to the *pissoir.*

Sounds of movement from behind the wall. My heart races. A doughy old woman in a hairnet comes waddling out of the kitchen. This must be the old bat. She looks all right to me.

'*Qu'est-ce que vous désirez, monsieur?*' she asks.

A question heard long ago. Sandpaper in my mouth.

'*Un demi, s'il vous plaît, madame.*'

She points to a table and leans on the pump handle to draw me a beer.

I sit with my head down, doing my best not to fidget. I don't want her to look at me. But there's too much froth. The beer is taking forever to come out. Five more seconds, and I shall make a dash for the door.

'*Voilà, monsieur,*' she declares, bringing the drink to my table. Sonneville will be having kittens outside.

I take a sip of the beer, and then another, glad to relieve my dry mouth and throat. Behind the bar, Madame polishes a glass, pretending not to be watching me.

'The German officer, is he here?' I ask, with all the casualness I can muster.

'Why? What do you want with him?'

'I'm looking for work,' I shrug. 'I thought he might be able to find me something on the coast.'

'How old are you? Twenty-five? At your age, you should be on the STO in Germany.'

'I'm eighteen.'

The old woman narrows her eyes and sucks air through her teeth. Finally she turns and calls out: 'Hans, there's a young man here. Says he's looking for work.'

He is right there, just behind that wall. A man called Hans.

My mouth goes dry again, and my stomach lurches. Capitaine Michel, help me to be brave.

A moment later, a tall, fair-haired man in his early

thirties appears from the kitchen, wiping his hands on a cloth.

I do my best to swallow. I was expecting him to be in the khaki uniform of the Todt Organisation, with a scarlet swastika armband stretched around his bicep. Instead, he is in shirtsleeves and a pair of pleated corduroy trousers, thoroughly off duty. Perhaps he was doing the washing-up.

He is a German officer, I remind myself. He has threatened to talk.

In no great hurry, Hans sits on one of the bar stools opposite me. He folds his arms.

I reach for my glass then think better of it. My hands would give me away.

He looks me up and down.

'What is it you want?' he asks, in perfect French. No accent. He even smiles.

Madame retires to the kitchen.

I put my hand in my pocket.

Now. It's now.

I leap to my feet. The Luger jumps wildly in my hand as I pull the trigger, once, twice, at point-blank range. First at his chest and then just above the waist.

Hans screams in a far-off voice and glares at me, his eyes full of shock and rage.

So loud. I didn't expect the gun to be so loud.

His shirt is all messed up.

I am just standing there, holding the gun.

And then his eyes disappear into his head, and he goes straight down.

The old woman explodes out of the kitchen. She stares at the gun in my hand. Her mouth gapes into a horrible 'O'.

She tries to turn away, but her arse is so bloody enormous that I can't miss.

I shut my eyes and pull the trigger for Sonneville.

Merde.

The Luger has jammed. I stuff it back into my pocket,

vault over an upturned bar stool. Then I hurl myself at the door of the café and out into the night.

Where the hell is Sonneville?

Bastard.

And where is my bike? Where the hell did I park my bloody bike?

Spinning on my heels, I glimpse somebody running away towards the square.

Sonneville?

At last I spot my bike, right where I left it. But I have only just started to pedal when the old bag comes flying out of the café, screaming for her life.

'Murderer! Murderer!' she shrieks. 'Someone stop him! Murderer!'

I am accelerating now, but still the old bitch is screaming behind me – *L'assassin! L'assassin!* – and now people begin to appear from the streets and alleyways: shadowy figures, running and shouting, grabbing at bicycles, chasing down the murderer, shouting for me to stop. As if I would stop now, even if I could.

On I pedal, faster and faster, only I seem to be going nowhere, however hard I work. I know I can beat most people in a straight race. But I need to go faster.

Beneath me, with sickening lurches, my chain begins to slip.

Now there are trees on either side, but the mob is gaining on me. I can hear them at my back. And then I see a familiar figure cycling just up ahead. Jean Sonneville, pedalling for France. He has not abandoned me.

Elated, I am racing on fresh legs. Even my chain seems to be working better now. For I do have an ally after all.

Sonneville knows the countryside around Steenwerck far better than I do. If anyone can get us out of this fix, he can.

My friend glances over his shoulder as I pull alongside him; gives me a desperate nod. I draw ahead, urging him onwards, away from the furies at our back. Sonneville puts his head down and I can see him digging in.

And then my chain clatters right off the chainring, and I am pedalling in thin air.

'Come on,' he barks. 'Off your bike and follow me.'

Picking up our bikes, we hurdle a ditch and force our way through a thorny hedgerow. And now we are slogging across what feels like a ploughed field, with me following Sonneville as best I can.

My legs are lead. My lungs are shot. My heart is about to explode.

And still he pushes on, into the darkness.

At last we arrive at a cart track running parallel to the road and, grateful for the solidity of the ground beneath my feet, I work the chain back on to my bicycle in the moonlight.

'*Merde*,' I exclaim, still panting.

'What?'

'The licence plate of my bicycle.'

'What about it?'

'It must have fallen off, somewhere back there. With my name on it.'

'Too late to worry about that now.'

And on we go, bumping along the cart track through the woods, through a gateway, and into Sonneville's lair, past the shed where I met the two Canadian airmen, Motherall and Dumsday, in the days before I became a murderer.

I sit in silence at the kitchen table, while Sonneville pads around in his socks, finding all the things he needs to make coffee. He winds his Peugeot grinder with intense concentration, while a saucepan of water heats on the stove. At last when it is done, and the smoking black liquid has been poured into two porcelain cups, he sinks into his chair, lights two cigarettes, and passes one of them to me. He can see I'm in no fit state to roll my own.

'So what happened?' He takes a long drag on his cigarette, holding the smoke in his lungs before blowing it out of his nostrils.

'What *didn't* happen? He looked all right. That was the worst part of it. You know, just an ordinary bloke. I put two shots into him. And he went straight down, staring back at me. Good God, but the gun sounded loud in that place. And the old bag . . .'

'What about the old bag? Did you get her? Did you give the old witch an extra hole?'

I shake my head. 'My Luger just went click. I put Sten ammo in it. Think it's too powerful for the gun. She was screaming like a bloody Stuka. Anyway, where were you? You were meant to be waiting outside.'

'To be honest, you were in there so long that I thought something had gone wrong. And then I heard the shots, and I had to scarper, because there were people around, people who could have recognised me.'

'But what if I'd been stopped? You were supposed to be watching my back.'

'Well, you weren't stopped, were you? And of course I was watching your back. I helped you escape the mob, didn't I?'

I pull on my cigarette, every nerve ending still electric with adrenaline. Sonneville leans forward in his chair and we shake hands.

'You did it, Stéphane. I didn't think you'd go through with it.' He pauses. 'You'd better stay here tonight, just in case the Boche send out patrols.'

'Thanks.' I am surprised to find that I feel no elation, no warmth in my belly at the thought of having killed a Kraut. I just feel numb and hollow inside.

'Isn't it lucky that you managed to get those two shots off before your gun jammed?' Sonneville waves his cigarette at me.

'Yes,' I say, almost inaudibly. 'Yes, I suppose it is.'

The following day is Sunday, and I hurry out from Sonneville's house to the church in Nieppe. Too late for the early Mass, too early for the later one, I creep around the deserted building, looking for Monsieur le Curé. Relieved to have the place to myself, I gaze up at one of the carved Stations of the Cross on the wall of a side aisle. Carrying his cross, Jesus has stumbled.

'Are you looking for me?' Monsieur le Curé appears from behind a pillar. He must have been watching me for a while.

'Yes and no . . .' I can hear the wobble in my voice. 'I mean, I *was* looking for you. I wanted to make my confession. But now I've changed my mind.'

'I can wait.' He smiles. 'But God will not.'

'What do you mean?'

'Remember, my son, that God knows everything already.'

'In that case, why do we need to confess?' I am beginning to wish I had never come.

'Because Jesus says that the truth will set you free.'

His words – this half-forgotten mantra from my childhood – stop me in my tracks. I glance at the priest's face and duck into the nearest confessional, pulling the red velvet curtain shut behind me.

'Perhaps it is a little while since your last confession?'

'Perhaps,' I reply, firmly.

There is no preamble. I do not discuss the lambs I have rustled with Sonneville, or the lustful thoughts I have had about Marie-Louise Boulet. I do not say who I have killed, or when or why or how. I simply tell the priest that I have killed a man. And then I ask him if I can ever be forgiven.

'Jesus says that all who truly believe him, and who repent of their sins, will be forgiven,' he says.

'And what if I do not truly believe?'

'Then, my son,' says Monsieur le Curé with a heavy sigh, his tone changing, 'then be warned that this crime you have committed will pursue you down all the days of your life. And after you are dead and buried, it will pursue you beyond the grave, into the shades of purgatory and the fires of hell, until the last days, when your unforgiven soul will be tormented by the furies of holy vengeance. Is that quite clear, my son?'

I do not wait for Monsieur le Curé's absolution. Head spinning, I stumble out of the church, tugging at the collar of my shirt, craving fresh air in my lungs which are suddenly filled with smoke and fire and dust and moths and darkness.

I run all the way home to the rue du Sac, arriving breathless at the front door. Everyone else must be out, because my mother comes hobbling out of the kitchen to check who it is.

'Lou?' she asks, doubtfully. 'Is it you?'

On any other day, I would grunt and give her a dutiful kiss on each cheek. But not today.

'Mummy,' I sigh, wrapping my arms around her and feeling the sparrow-like scrawniness of this frail, blind woman. And then I say it again, in French: '*Maman.*'

At first my mother keeps her arms outstretched. She must be shocked to receive an embrace from her wayward son, after all these years. And then her white stick clatters to the floor, and I close my eyes. I do not know how long we stand there. But after a while, my mother begins to sob.

'*Maman,*' I repeat. And I feel her gently patting my back, because I suppose she doesn't know what else to do, and perhaps she is embarrassed. But she isn't embarrassed. It's just that I'm hugging her so tightly that she can't breathe.

'Lou,' she sighs, when I release her. She wipes her eyes. 'Lou, is everything all right?'

'Not really,' I whisper.

'Please don't tell me what you've done.'

I shake my head again.

'Whatever it is,' she says, 'I'm sure it can't be too bad.'

There is a long pause before she speaks again.

'Is there anything I can do?'

Her question hangs between us in the silence. For my whole family knows that she is incapable of anything. I stand very still. And my mother, for the first time since I was a small child, begins to stroke my hair.

Sonneville wants me to vanish. I am desperate to disappear, too. But just as I am stuffing a few bits and pieces into a bag, ready to flee the rue du Sac, Rosemary comes up behind me. She hopes I haven't forgotten her concert, because she thinks the man from Radio Lille may be there. So just when I want to bury myself underground, I must play the drums in the schoolroom at Pont de Nieppe, to raise funds for the church organ.

Rosemary leads from an upright piano with the front taken off, looking poised and polished in a navy blue dress. I have heard her play this music so often at home – Mozart, Strauss, Tchaikovsky, Khachaturian – that it is as familiar to me as weeding or wallpaper. Yet the music-starved audience applauds every piece as if it were a miracle.

I establish two possible escape routes during 'Für Elise'. For the rest, I sit in the dusty corner of the schoolroom, crouched behind a cymbal I have set at head height, trying to make myself invisible.

Last time I played for Rosemary, I bashed and crashed away like a toddler with my sticks. She had to keep glaring at me to shut me up. Today I patter away with a pair of brushes on the snare, and softly pedal the downbeats on the bass drum. Every so often she glances across at me, her eyes full of questions and a smile on her lips.

And then they are taking their bows, and my sister is pointing at me, encouraging me to come out from behind the drums.

I shake my head. No, I mouth. Please don't make me. Please.

And of course Rosemary, being Rosemary, insists.

A few rows back, I catch sight of Monsieur le Curé. As I do so, he points directly at me and mouths to an old man in a tailored overcoat, who is sitting next to him: 'That's him.'

I sit straight back down. But it is already too late.

Behind the cymbal, I glance at my two escape routes. One is blocked by a pair of volunteers already attempting to manhandle the upright piano on to a trolley, the other by most of the audience, still milling around as they enjoy the free warmth of the people-heated hall. My pulse hammers in my temples. I am cornered.

Now the old man in the tailored overcoat begins to make his way towards the stage.

I stand my ground. Too late now to flee. And with no gun in my pocket, am I about to be taken alive?

The man stands straight in front of me and rasps somthing in an accent I do not recognise. 'Uh?'

'Are you quite all right? You are the young man who looks after the war graves, are you not?' He pulls a gap-toothed smile, and it dawns on me that he has not come to arrest me, after all.

'Yes. I'm sorry. Better now. What did you say, please?'

'Good drumming,' he repeats. 'You like to hear compliments over and over again?'

'No, no, I just didn't quite hear what you said. It comes of playing the drums. So loud, you know.'

'Yes, of course,' he says, smiling. 'Bang bang.'

'That's it,' I reply, backing away from him. He says he's come over from Lille especially for the concert, but I can't find the words to reply.

I am standing, barefoot, in the early morning mist at Pont d'Achelles. The grass feels cool beneath my feet, and the silence soothes my jittery brain. I wander over to the line of German graves at the side of the cemetery, each identical headstone inscribed with a Maltese cross, and I wonder where Hans will be buried. In the municipal cemetery at Steenwerck, no doubt. For he died, not in battle, but in cold blood.

'I'm amazed how well you keep the graves of our enemies,' says a familiar voice behind me.

'Thanks for creeping up on me,' I mutter, spinning round to find Sonneville standing there.

'They said I'd find you here.' He sounds almost cheerful. But his smile fades. He says that the Germans are turning Steenwerck inside out. Nieppe will be next.

'Some members of the Steenwerck WO have visited the café. It seems your German died almost at once, so he wasn't able to pass on any information. But the police came in, looking for fingerprints. They were desperate to get their hands on the beer glass you were holding.'

'*Merde.* How could I have been so stupid?'

'It's all right,' chuckles Sonneville. 'The old bag had already washed it up. But I still think it's time for you to disappear. And I have the perfect place for you.'

Hemmed in with brambles, nettles and bracken, I crouch in a chicken house in the middle of Sonneville's wood, listening to the rain drip through the roof. My clothes are sodden; my boots squelch. The only good thing about this icy hovel is that nobody will ever find me here. I didn't even spot it until Sonneville pushed back the nettles to reveal the loose-fitting door. There are no windows. The only light, filtered by the overhanging trees, arrives via the gaps between the roof tiles, shrouded in moss. The olive-green darkness is oppressive, but it suits my mood.

In the corner stands a tiny rusted bedstead covered in cobwebs. It is a bed for a child. I sit slouched on the bare iron frame, wondering whatever happened to my life.

Sonneville has equipped me with a Sten gun, two magazines of ammo, a small hunk of bread, and a bashed-up saucepan for fetching water from the stream a quarter of a mile away. I also have a damp red blanket and, for a pillow, a feed sack filled with straw. It's quite comfortable, really, if you have spent any time in Loos Prison.

I can deal with the teeth-chattering cold, the rustling of rodents and the overwhelming sense that I am marooned at the very end of the world. But night, when it comes, is worse than day. For I have killed a man, and the nights are when he visits me. He always wears a crisp white shirt and pleated corduroy trousers. Sometimes he comes alone. Sometimes he is accompanied by my former cell mates from Loos. They torture me with questions. Others visit, too: Kourk wants to be my friend; a woman in a floral print dress tries to kiss me; another woman, in black rags, arrives with blood spewing out of her mouth.

I have ended a man's life. I think of the way he smiled at me, moments before I shot him. Who will tend his grave?

Sonneville visits me every once in a while, to bring me a small pot of food and a twist of tobacco, as well as information about the investigation in Steenwerck. And, finally, after three weeks, he announces that he has some good news for me.

'The *Sicherheits*-whatshisface have arrested a Pole,' he says. 'This bloke was seen hanging around near the café on the night of the killing, and had a heated argument with Hans a few weeks ago. How about that for a result? He's already been deported on a one-way ticket. Chances are, he'll be beheaded. Which means that you, Stéphane, are in the clear.'

'That's excellent news.'

I hang my head. So now I have sent not one, but two men to their deaths.

15 May 1944

At last, after three weeks in the chicken house, I am allowed to venture back to the rue du Sac. Seeing my family again is bittersweet. My mother's health has declined, and the chasm between us all is wider than ever. I am an outsider, even in my own home. The Four Musketeers are my family now. The aching loneliness I felt in Sonneville's wood has been replaced by an icy solitude. I feel more alone than ever. And this suits me. The further I can keep people from me, the less likely they are to get hurt.

Sonneville himself isn't quite so sure. He thinks I am too quiet; he is worried that I have had too much time to think. He says that whenever Capitaine Michel used to suffer one of his inconsolable spells of what he called *le chien noir,* his answer was to go out and do something dangerous. He would walk openly in the streets, singing patriotic British songs at the top of his voice, and then go and sabotage something, under the very noses of the Boche.

'So that's what *we're* going to do,' he tells me, slapping me on the back.

'What do you have in mind?' I manage a smile at Sonneville's appetite for destruction.

'You remember what you told me about Sir Francis Drake?' he replies. 'We're going to play fire ships. Only with a train.'

A hay train is going to be passing via Steenwerck tonight, on its way to Lille. Sonneville wants me to bring Marcel and a handful of incendiary grenades to hit it on the hoof.

'Haven't we done this already?' I am not thrilled at the

thought of going back to Steenwerck. 'You know we can't afford to waste grenades.'

'This isn't just about burning a heap of hay,' he responds, with a wounded expression. 'It's propaganda, too. You'll see.'

Marcel leaps at the opportunity with such enthusiasm that I feel guilty for not having included him more often. Especially now that Maurice and Francis have let me down so badly, without explanation, on the most terrible night of my life.

A few hours later, when Kléber and I are getting ready for bed and we have the room to ourselves, my brother suddenly turns to me. 'I know your secret, Lou.'

'What secret?' I turn away so that he cannot see my face.

'You're in the Resistance, aren't you?'

'What makes you think that?'

'It's obvious. You keep going out at night.'

'Maybe I'm going to see a girl.'

'A *girl*? Don't be silly.'

'Look, I'm just doing my own thing. Always remember that, Kléber. If anyone ever asks you, I'm always alone. You have never seen me talking to anyone else.'

'What about Marcel?'

'Especially Marcel.'

'But he's your best friend. You're always together.'

'That's why. Please.'

Kléber considers this for a moment.

'Take me with you,' he says. 'I want to do it, too. Whatever you're doing.'

'No, you don't.'

'Yes, I do.'

'Trust me, Kléber, you don't.'

'I never trust people who say "trust me",' he declares.

I can't help laughing, because my little brother has a point. Is he really fifteen already? He must have been growing up on the sly, while my back was turned.

'Look, I'll think about it,' I lie. 'But don't hold your breath.'

At midnight, I push back my side of the feather sack and

creep out of bed, stepping only on the floorboards that do not creak. I am turning the handle of the bedroom door when a sound comes from behind me. Kléber shines a torch in my face.

'Off to see another girl?' he whispers.

'Go to sleep,' I hiss, flicking him a V-sign.

Half an hour later, Sonneville, Marcel Lombard and I are huddled a few hundred metres outside Steenwerck station, at a place where the railway line bridges a small stream. We sit for hours, peering into the darkness, saying little. Though there is no moon, it is a sparklingly clear night. I can see about a billion stars twinkling in the sky above my head and, in the distance, the flickers and flashes of yet another bombing raid on Lille.

We wait. Someone comes walking up the line towards us, swinging a torch. Marcel wants us to scatter, but the torch beam soon retreats.

A passenger express rattles down the line the other way, heading for Calais, and we crouch down low as the glimmer of its coaches thunders past.

At last, we hear the low rumble of our target in the distance. I can see red sparks flying up into the night as it comes clanking into view.

Now I can smell the stink of the coal smoke. Marcel and I wait for Sonneville's signal before flinging our incendiary into the trucks.

'You see? You see?' sighs Sonneville, as the monstrous, fire-spewing dragon clatters away towards Lille, lighting up the landscape as it goes. Even when the travelling inferno itself is out of sight, we can still see its orange glow in the night sky. 'We are showing people all over northern France that we are here.'

'Jean, it's the middle of the night,' I remind him. 'Everyone's asleep.'

I slip back to the rue du Sac, and tiptoe up to bed. Kléber does not stir.

Burning hay trains is all very well. Yet as I point out
to Sonneville next time I see him, at the end of another
session of guard duty outside one of his secret meetings in
La Crèche, we are wasting our weaponry. We should be
doing more to help the British put the Germans on the back
foot.

The wily smuggler looks hurt. But he promises to have a
word with Fertein, to see if he can come up with an objective
more in keeping with my lofty ambitions.

'It just touches a nerve when you call me a wastrel,' he
says.

'Because I'm right?'

'No. Because you sound exactly like my dad.'

Next day, the house feels more sombre than usual when I
arrive home for lunch.

'Look, I brought this.' I pull a small paper bag out of my
jacket. 'Real coffee beans.'

The silence in the kitchen deepens to a cathedral awe.
Open-mouthed, Auntie Val takes the package from me. I can
see her fingers trembling as she reverently unwraps it. She
lowers her nose to it and takes a sniff.

'Oh,' she moans, with a sort of religious ecstasy. 'Oh,
Berthe . . . smell this.' She passes the bag to my mother, who
looks as if she may burst into tears. Mémère, too.

'It is too beautiful,' she says, shaking her head.

'It's a gift from Monsieur Sonneville,' I announce,
casually.

'So that's it.' Auntie Val snatches the bag from Mémère's
grasp, and tucks it without ceremony behind the wooden
grinder on the shelf.

'But . . .' protests Mémère, her voice wobbling.

'Something has happened, Lou,' begins Auntie Val. 'You're
our tin soldier. I think you should know.' And then she
explains why the house is bathed in today's unusual gloom.
The Germans have committed a massacre in the village of

Ascq, just outside Lille. She says they killed eighty-six civilians in a single night.

My aunt doesn't even look at me as she divides a withered brown carrot between six of us. The massacre was, it seems, a reprisal for something the local Resistance did to a train. I listen, shell-shocked. And then she adds that one of Marcel Houcke's men dropped round this morning. The mayor's brother wants to see me.

I eat my carrot, doing my best not to look as if I am in a hurry. All I can hear is the soft clinking of forks on earthenware. It is as if everyone is trying to hide from each other, as if none of us wants to be here.

At last, I excuse myself from the bleak house and escape into the open air. My thoughts are jumbled as I cycle over to Marcel Houcke's fabric works on the edge of town.

'Hello, Stéphane.' He ushers me on to a fire escape and offers me a cigarette from a plain white packet. A distant drone makes us both crane our necks. Another huge wave of Allied bombers dots the sky, heading for Germany.

'No, thank you,' I reply, with difficulty. Tobacco is gold dust these days.

'Long time no see.' He lights his cigarette, and I inhale deeply, attempting to share the smoke.

'Yes, I've been . . . unwell. But I'm back now. I thought I'd go round to see Maurice Pauwels tomorrow and we can take the latest issue of the *VdN* to Lens and Arras.'

'That's just it,' sighs Houcke. 'Pauwels has been arrested.'

We both gaze down at the steel latticework on which we are standing. Through the holes, I can see a dead dog lying in the gutter beneath.

'Perhaps I will have that cigarette after all,' I say.

'He was arrested in Lens last week. Caught red-handed, distributing the *Voix du Nord*.'

'I should have been with him.'

'And got yourself arrested, too?' Houcke flicks his lighter.

'I could have protected him.'

'You were unwell. Besides, he always thought the Virgin Mother would protect him.'

We both take deep drags on our fags.

'But look,' he adds, 'there's no reason for the rest of us to panic yet. Pauwels is a cunning little devil. He'll think of something to throw the Boche off the scent if they interrogate him.'

'They seem to be growing more brutal by the day.'

'You've heard about Ascq, then?'

'And all because the Resistance put a petard on the track?'

Houcke nods, drops his cigarette on to the steel latticework and crushes it beneath his boot.

'Don't let it eat you up, Stéphane,' he tells me, studying my face carefully. 'With strong faith comes overwhelming doubt. Maurice Pauwels told me that.'

I drop my butt-end to crush it with my heel. But it falls through the grating, and lands on the dead dog.

26 May 1944

'Thank goodness you have come,' says Monsieur Genty, standing in the doorway of his farmhouse and crossing himself. 'We've got a right one here.'

'What's the problem?' I ask.

I have just cycled the forty-five kilometres from Nieppe to Lederzeele, a village close to the V2 rocket site at Éperlecques and the anti-aircraft batteries around Saint-Omer. The place is crawling with Germans. And the journey here has not been helped by the fact that I have had to bring along both a spare bicycle and Jean Houcke, Andrée's seventeen-year-old brother. I am grateful to Pierre Glorian for guiding us on the last part of our ride.

'When he arrived, the man was speaking German,' says Genty.

'I see.'

'And now he's speaking some other language.' The genial farmer removes his ill-fitting spectacles and rubs them on his jumper, which appears to be coated with tractor grease. 'I thought it might be English. But my wife is no fool, and she says it's not like any English she has ever heard before. According to her, he doesn't say *yes*, he says *ja*. So we're pretty sure he is a German spy.'

'*Pas de problème.*' I smile at Monsieur Genty, as if I deal with German spies every day. 'This is why we are here.'

'And he has a German name, too,' adds Genty, leading me out to a small animal shed. Inside my jacket pocket, I slip the safety catch off my Luger. The hinges groan as the farmer pushes open the door of the shed. 'Gentlemen, may I present Monsieur Conrad Kersch.'

The shed is empty. The four of us stand there in silence, gazing at straw. Monsieur Conrad Kersch has fled.

My mind races. Genty starts rabbiting away about how our German agent was here only five minutes ago, so he can't have gone far. And then a body drops from the rafters. I don't have time to go for my gun. Inches from my face, a tall, fine-looking man in a light-coloured flying suit, his face covered in tiny scratches, lands lightly on his feet, straightens and grins.

'*Guten Tag.*' He glances at Genty before reaching out to shake our hands.

'*C'est lui, l'Allemand,*' says Monsieur Genty.

'Hello, Mr Kersch,' I reply. 'My name is Iroquois, and these are two friends of mine.'

'Hey, you speak English! Thank Christ for that.' He steps forward, and the three of us instinctively step back.

'I have come to ask you a few questions,' I tell him. And after a brief exchange with Genty, who doesn't wish to have a German in his house, we decamp to a large hay barn where there is room to sit.

'I am *so* pleased to hear an English voice after all this time, let me tell you.' Kersch rubs his hands. 'I just can't figure out why my German is no good. I thought everyone spoke it in Belgium.'

'Perhaps because we're in France?'

'No kidding?' He roars with laughter. 'Anyway, thanks for coming to visit me, boys. When do the grown-ups arrive?'

I shift uneasily on my hay bale and pull my interview paper out of my pocket.

'You have a German name. You speak fluent German. How come?'

'My parents were German-born Rumanians who emigrated to the US a few years before I was born,' he says, glancing down at my paper. I pull it to my chest.

344

'How many states are there in the United States of America?'

'Whoa, whoa, whoa. Now wait just one minute. You're gonna give me the third degree, just because I can speak German? You really think I'm a Kraut? That's a bum rap, I tell you, Iroquois. Who exactly do you think I was in the middle of pounding with high explosives when I got shot down?'

'The French.'

'Fair point. But it was the German long-range rocket emplacements we were targeting. Unfortunately, the skies were so darn clear that we were sitting ducks for Fritz's flak.'

'What happened to your face?'

He grins. 'I guess I was born ugly.'

'I mean the scratches.'

'Oh, these,' he says, touching his cheek. He tips his head to reveal a red-brown dressing taped to his neck. 'That's what I'm telling you. It was such a perfect day. We all thought it was going to be a milk run until these evil black puffs starting walking through the sky towards us, in fours. We were right on our bomb run when the Tennessee Hillbilly took one, right in the kisser.'

'Who's that?'

'The Tennessee Hillbilly? That's our B-17. Or at least she was. I got hit in the chest. My flak jacket protected me from most of it, but I had all these evil little needles of shrapnel pinning my mask to my face. I got the bombs away, but the Hillbilly was toast. I remember sitting on the edge of that darn escape hatch, dangling my feet in the slipstream, and thinking: "Jeez, Conrad, you're about to jump out of a goddam aircraft." But I never even got the chance, because right then Mars, the pilot, pushed me out.'

'What's he saying? What's he saying?' asks Glorian.

I do not reply.

'Hell only knows what we hit.' Kersch slowly shakes his head. 'But I sure hope it was worth it.'

345

We look into each other's eyes. I do not need to ask him any more questions. Leaning forward, I reach out to shake his hand.

'Welcome to France, Mr Kersch.'

'It ain't exactly Gay Paree, is it?' He peers up at the cobwebs strung from the ancient timbers of the stone barn, and then at the three of us, in our ragged overalls and wooden shoes. 'But at least it's not Belgium, I guess.'

Ignoring Kersch's yelps of protest, we hack the tops off his flying boots with a knife, to make them look more like shoes, and then I present him with the overalls I have brought for him. The last time I wore them was when I was mucking out the earth closet at home.

'Jesus H Columbus,' he says, screwing up his face when he takes them from me.

'Sorry. Do you mind?'

'No, no, I like it, I like it,' he insists. 'Don't they say that's why dogs roll in shit: so that the wolves can't sniff 'em out? Well, let me tell you, I've had enough already of being chased by the Krauts. So I'd rather stink and be free, than smell like Deanna Durbin and end up in front of a firing squad.'

Satisfied that I am not about to be jumped by a German agent, Glorian and Andrée's brother head off on their bikes, while I brief Kersch about our imminent journey to Nieppe via Hazebrouck.

It is the usual set-up: he is to cycle 200 yards behind me, and do his best to disappear if I drop my handkerchief.

'You call that thing white?' He glances at the brown rag in my hand.

I laugh. 'Well, it's off-white.'

'It's diaper brown, Iroquois, that's what it is. You need to have a word with your local Laundromat.'

'Right,' I reply, blankly. 'Shall we go?'

As we head off along the cobbled road towards Hazebrouck in the afternoon sunshine, I glance back over my shoulder. Incredible. Some of the Americans I have escorted have terrified me with their obvious foreignness. But Conrad Kersch exudes a casual fearlessness which makes him seem invincible. Pedalling away in his stinky overalls, he doesn't look anything like a fugitive. You'd think he was enjoying the ride. My spirits lift and I begin to relax, too. For I feel as if I am doing something good for a change.

How soon confidence can tip over into complacency. We soon find ourselves cycling along a main road, on a long straight section which runs parallel to the railway for more than a kilometre. The moment I commit us to this, I know it is a mistake. We are too visible, too exposed.

The first warning is sounded by the shriek of a train whistle from behind us. There is nowhere to turn, and – a few seconds later – the air is rent not with the steam-driven thunder of its pistons, but by the clatter of bullets and exploding cannon shells all around us.

A roar from on high. I duck as a twin-engined Lockheed Lightning streaks overhead at no more than 200 feet and pulls up sharply to the right, its leading edges glinting in the sun.

With the train hissing and producing clouds of steam on our right, we need to take cover in the ditch on the left-hand side of the road. But when I glance across, I can see that a pair of grey-green lorries has pulled in over there. My skin prickles at the sight of the black crosses stencilled on the cabs.

Too late, already, to drop my diaper-brown rag.

Now men are shouting in German.

The engine note of the Lightning rises as it wheels in for a second pass. I scan the road for whoever is yelling at me.

'*Achtung! Achtung! Gabelschwanzteufel!*'

And there, waving at me from beneath one of the lorries, is a group of German soldiers, making frantic gestures for me to come and shelter with them beneath their truck.

Another barrage of gunfire from the Lightning's nose cone hammers the train. I glimpse a spattering of sparks and flames; ragged holes are stitched in the road surface ahead of me.

Still the Germans are yelling and waving at me to save myself. But no: I prefer to take my chances with American bullets than with German ones.

I can feel them gawping in awe as, head down, I stand on the pedals and accelerate. I even manage to pull ahead of the stricken train.

The Lightning is diving in again. A colossal explosion behind me, then another. The bullets are almost chasing me, and then the black fury climbs up and away.

I glance over my shoulder. Both German lorries have been blown to pieces. And there, cycling through the smoke and fire with a smile on his face, is Monsieur Conrad Kersch.

'Did you *see* that, Iroquois?' he says, when we finally stop outside Sonneville's house. 'Four 50-calibre machine guns. One 20mm cannon. Twin Allison engines, each capable of developing fourteen seventy-five horses for a max airspeed of four-fourteen mph. I tell you, Iroquois, we get enough of those babies over here and we'll soon have this war wrapped up.'

Marcel Houcke has arranged for Kersch to be billeted with Sonneville until a safer house can be found for him.

Unfortunately, this new billet is required rather sooner than anticipated. I am not sure what goes wrong between Sonneville and Kersch, but Marcel Houcke comes to me a few days later and asks if we could possibly house the American airman with us in the rue du Sac for a short while.

Around the kitchen table, Auntie Val, Mémère, Mummy, Kléber, Elizabeth and Rosemary sit, wide-eyed, as Conrad Kersch sips barley coffee from our best cup and tucks hungrily into a small bowl of boiled potatoes. We are all aware of the risk we are taking. What if the Germans should hammer on the front door right now? Yet, just for these few moments, we indulge ourselves, luxuriating in the arrival of this handsome alien who has brought a great whoosh of exotic flair into our half-starved and humdrum lives.

'Are you really from *America*?' asks Elizabeth, in a small voice.

'Yes, ma'am. From the United States.'

'And you're the *pilot* of an aeroplane?'

'Not quite, ma'am. I just decide when to drop the bombs.'

'So you dropped the bomb which killed my cousin Michel?'

'I'm sorry, ma'am?' Conrad looks to me for help. 'Might I please use your bathroom, *Stéphane*?'

I show Conrad into the earth closet and, holding his nose, he casts me a stricken grin as I shut the door on him. Then I return to the table.

'Conrad here was bombing the V2 bunkers at Wizernes, not Lille, when he was shot down,' I whisper. 'The rest of his crew have all been killed or disappeared. I was hoping he might stay here for a few days, until an onward address is found for him.' I glance at Auntie Val, who glances in turn at Mémère.

'We'd better ask your father,' says Auntie Val.

'Aren't we already enough at risk?' mutters my grandmother.

'Oh, please don't ask him yet, Auntie,' begs Rosemary. 'He'll only send me straight to bed.'

Conrad emerges a few moments later. He has a haunted look about him.

'I thought England was primitive,' he says, shaking his head. 'But France is really something, isn't it?'

There is a long silence. And then, at the insistence of Kléber, Conrad tells the story of how he jumped out of a shattered Flying Fortress at 22,000 feet on 26 March, parachuted down into a field about fifty yards from a truck stuffed with German soldiers, and has somehow ended up in our kitchen, eight weeks later.

When he has finished, I glance across at Rosemary and Elizabeth. Both of them are gazing starry-eyed at Conrad, as if he has them under a spell. Auntie Val is just as bad. She says she wants to have a proper look at Conrad's wounds, but I manage to dissuade her. Our American is clearly a brave fellow, but everyone has their breaking point. Even Mémère has an alarming glint in her eyes. Only my mother, reliable as a cold compress, remains unstirred. Lips pursed, eyes hooded, she clicks away on her rosary, waiting for the world to end.

Spring is warming towards summer. In the Crimea, German troops have surrendered. And, in the vegetable garden, the soil is beginning to teem and thrive with new life. The radishes are first. Then the cucumbers spread their tendrils and the tomatoes climb their canes. The dark green shoots of the potato plants explode into leafy crowns, marking secrets buried underground. I think their subtle fragrance has become my favourite smell in the world, ever since I was released from Loos.

Conrad can't believe it. 'I never grew anything before.' He scratches his head as he watches me work. His hair is so blond it is almost white. 'I guess in the States we don't really need to.'

'Here, look, you can help by removing any *doryphores* you find,' I tell him, in a low voice. 'These brown beetles, the ones with stripes.'

'*Doryphores*, huh? Ain't that what you call the Krauts?'

'Yes. Like the beetles, they eat all the potatoes. And, when they pass through, they leave nothing behind.'

Conrad squashes a fat beetle between his fingers and wipes the juice on the front of his overalls. 'Just like that, huh? It's easy when you know how.'

'Yes, now keep your voice down, will you?' I pull my hat down over my eyes and scan the horizon for the telltale glint of binoculars.

'Sorry, yes. You ever killed a Kraut, Stevie?' Conrad ventures deeper into the potato plants, looking for more beetles.

For an instant, I glimpse Hans's face. Sawdust at my feet. An acrid whiff of smoke. The sink-gurgle from his throat as he goes down. I stare hard at a potato leaf.

Conrad straightens and looks at me. 'It's OK,' he says. 'You don't have to answer. I shouldn't have asked.'

'It's all right. I don't mind.'

'So what about girls,' he says, changing the subject. Over his shoulder, I spot Auntie Val walking towards us from the veranda. 'I've heard those French girls are real lookers. Your sister Rosemary's not bad herself.'

Auntie Val stops, as if she has forgotten something, and goes back into the house.

'You got a popsy, Steve?' asks Conrad, unperturbed.

'I don't think so.'

'What do you mean, you don't *think* so? Jeez, man, either you do or you don't,' Conrad squidges another fat *doryphore* between his fingernails. 'So what's she like, this popsy?'

'To be honest, I can never think of anything to say to her. My mother made me say yes to her. Or perhaps it was her mother. I'm not too sure how it started. I just wish it would stop.'

'Promise me you'll introduce me to her?'

'I'm not promising anything,' I reply, squishing every last *doryphore* in sight.

Creeping out at night has become harder than ever, now that someone else always wants to come along. It's not Kléber badgering me to be included. It's Conrad, soon to be reborn with the false identity papers of a mute French farmer called Albert de Groote. With his shining blond hair and inability to speak a word of French, the American is not my ideal accomplice. But like Sonneville and Capitaine Michel, he just seems to have a natural affinity for risk. So when next I am called to blow up the railway line, Conrad tags along, too.

'You've no idea how I envy you, Steve,' he whispers, as he watches me pressing the 808 into the concave section of a junction plate near Bailleul. The night is absolutely still, with not a breath of wind in the trees. 'You get to place your bombs with your fingertips, just where you want them. Whereas I have to drop mine from four miles high in the sky. It doesn't make any sense, when you think about it.'

'I think my sister Elizabeth would agree with you. And Capitaine Michel, for that matter.'

I press the small white cone of the primary charge into the mustard-yellow plastic, and extend the knotted line of the Cordtex further down the rail.

'I wish I'd got to meet that guy.'

'So do I.'

'We could have done some serious damage together.'

'Just let me concentrate on this, will you?'

I gently slide a red L-delay pencil into the small metal tube of the detonator, and insert it in the hole in the primary charge. 'Ready? This'll give us thirty minutes.'

'Aw, as long as that? We won't even hear the bang.'

'Ready?'

'Do it, Steve.'

'Then here goes . . .' I grit my teeth. With my thumb, I press the soft copper top of the L-delay.

'Bombs gone,' he mouths.

Heads ducked, we make a dash for our bikes.

In the morning, Auntie Val ambushes me in the kitchen.

'When's he leaving?' she says, very quietly.

'When's who leaving?'

'You know. Our American friend.'

'Ah.'

'Your father and I are worried he's sweet on Rosemary.'

'You're joking.'

'I'm serious. Will you have a word with him?'

'About leaving, or about Rosemary?'

'Both.' She gives me a sour smile. 'That's if you're not too busy winning the war single-handed.'

'But where's he going to go?'

'Mémère wondered about her friend, Depreiter, on the ruelle du Coude.'

'Mémère offered to help?' I ask, incredulous.

'That's not what I said.'

Arms folded, Conrad looks quite wistful at the thought of having to leave the rue du Sac. I was expecting him to leap at the chance of being moved another step closer to Britain, and to the chance of going into action with his squadron again. But not a bit of it. I begin to have an uncomfortable feeling that Auntie Val may be right.

'Is it that you don't want to fly any more?' I ask him. 'I can imagine that your bail-out must have left you feeling a bit windy about getting up in the air again.'

'Windy, me? Not in the least,' he retorts. 'I could fly a daylight mission to Berlin tomorrow, no sweat. It's not that. It's more that my heart is . . . someplace else.'

'What do you mean?'

'I mean, what if I wanted to stay here?'

'But we have no soap or plumbing. It's a primitive country. You said so yourself.'

'Yes, but there are, shall we say, *other attractions*.'

'Not my sister Rosemary?'

'*Whaaat?*'

'Sorry. Pretend I didn't ask that question.'

'Now, come on, Steve. I mean, *really*. You think I go to sleep at night, dreaming of *her*?' Conrad leaps to his feet; marches over to the kitchen window and stands there for a few seconds, his shoulders rising and falling. He shakes his head, and begins to speak with his back to me. 'Here I am in occupied France of all places, and my crew mates are missing. Every last one of them may be dead or captured. Do you have any idea how that feels?'

'Conrad, I . . .'

'And yet your big worry is that I may be sweet on your sister.'

'No.'

'Well, you know what?' Conrad turns to face me. 'I had a pal I used to fly with in my previous crew, a real swell guy, who was scared of nothing. He was married to this girl, Doris, just before our tour began. I was his best man. I stood there at the church, and I held the rings for them and every-thing. And now he's dead, because we got jumped by 109s, only maybe she doesn't even know it yet. And that's what I think about, when I can't sleep at night.' He turns back to the window. 'She's who I think about. I need to find Doris.'

'I'm sorry, I . . .'

Conrad spins on his heels. 'And then there's Mars, our pilot for this op. The Bringer of War, we used to call him. If you could have seen how he kept us on that fucking bombing run, even though the Hillbilly was toast, even though the fucking navigator's got a lump of shrapnel for a tongue and he's spewing blood all over the place. Do you see? I told you, didn't I, how Mars pushed me out of the escape hatch himself, because I wouldn't jump? I just remember all these flakes of aluminium falling past me. I mean, how can an aircraft turn to confetti like that?'

We sit in silence for a while.

'I'm sorry,' I say at last. 'But say you find Doris, and you tell her how brave her husband was. That still won't bring him back.'

'Of course it won't.' Conrad fixes me with his cool blue eyes. 'But it might help her to let him go.'

I look at him, at this tall, fearless American who has fallen into our lives, and I can't quite believe he's here. We come from such different worlds. Yet I don't want him to leave any more than he does. I feel a strange kinship with this blond German-speaker from a far-off planet. There's just one thing that's still nagging me.

'You said there were other attractions about staying here in France. Do you mind telling me what they are?'

He smiles. 'I wish I could take you on a bombing raid one day, Steve.'

'Yes, I'd like that very much. Are you free tomorrow?'

'No, but seriously. You need to see what it's like up there. I tell you, it gets so cold that your tear ducts freeze up. For most of the time you're on the edge of space, miles from anywhere, and you and your crew feel completely alone. And then you're over the target, and if the Krauts don't manage to shoot you down, you fly home again. Do you see?'

'I think so.'

'Whereas here, with you . . . You know, until I parachuted down into that field, and all those Krauts started firing at me – or the other day, when that Lightning shot up that train – it was all so far away, this war. You can't see it, not really, until you're here on the ground, and you see their ugly faces and the colour of their uniforms. And now I'm here, and you're doing something that matters: you're taking the fight to the Krauts. May I ask how many of you there are in the Resistance, here in Nieppe?'

'I don't know,' I reply. 'Maybe fourteen.'

'*Fourteen?* Only fourteen miserable guys with guns, in a town of, what, four thousand people?'

'That's active Resistants. But there may be hundreds of patriots who are passively resisting the Germans in other ways. Why do you ask?'

'I want to join you. I want a piece of the action, Steve. Hell, it sounds like you *need* me.'

'I'm not sure . . .'

'Look, even if I make it to Britain, they won't put me back on a tour now, not with all that's brewing. At twenty-eight, I'm one of the old men of the group. I've done it all: turret specialist; flight engineer; bombardier.' Conrad holds out his arms. 'I'd end up flying a mahogany Spitfire, as you guys put it, and I don't want that. I want some action. I want to do something for my crew – pay back the Krauts. You know what I'm talking about? What you and I did last night was awesome. This is where the war is, Steve. I want to take on the bad guys. Here, with you. I don't want to escape. I want to stay and fight.'

I listen. I nod. And a great big smile creeps across my face. Because for the first time in as long as I can remember, I no longer feel alone.

30 May 1944

The aching sadness I felt after I shot Hans is giving way to anger: cold, hard rage at the life that is still being stolen from us. Everybody is saying that the tide is beginning to turn and the Allies are winning the war. Not in Nieppe, they're not.

Day and night, the convoys rumble through, making our front windows rattle as they pass the rue du Sac. Thousands upon thousands of bottles of wine and spirits, leather shoes and sacks of flour, household fabrics, antique furniture, engine spares, rifle ammunition, bobbins of wool and cotton, works of art. All of it passing under our windows and our noses, on its way to Germany. The other day, a Boche soldier even walked off with Auntie Val's bicycle, just like that, in broad daylight.

I would love to find some way of stopping the pillage of France – some way to hinder the German plunderers. Sonneville wants to blow up the bridge across the river Lys in the middle of Nieppe. But the Houcke brothers are firm: all the bridges must be protected, for it is not just the Germans who need them. The Allies will, too, if the long-awaited invasion ever comes.

I hear male voices in the kitchen as I walk down the corridor. Hurriedly folding up a piece of paper, Kléber turns and glances at me when I open the door.

'Lost something?' he asks.

'Why, what were you two talking about?'

'Oh, you know,' replies Conrad. 'This and that. Engineering talk. Resistance talk. Your brother here has some neat ideas. See you round, Kléber.'

'Bye,' says Kléber, tucking the piece of paper into his pocket before leaving the room.

'I hope you're not putting ideas into my brother's head,' I tell Conrad, sternly. 'He's only fifteen.'

'He was telling me about all the neat things he builds in that workshop in Nieppe.'

'He makes mattocks for peasants.'

'He's a budding engineer.'

'Look, I'm not taking him out on any operations with me, and I don't want you leading him astray, either.'

Conrad's eyes widen. 'Me?'

'I mean, I don't want you recruiting him,' I reply. 'He's too young to understand the rules. Or the consequences.'

'So what *are* the rules?'

'Whatever you're making in your workshop, never tell anyone about it.'

We gaze at each other.

'My family wouldn't believe this place, if they could see it,' says Conrad, changing the subject. He wanders over to the sink in the corner and begins to pump himself a cup of water from the cistern on the roof.

'You might want to boil that before drinking it,' I warn him. 'But I'm afraid the stove's not lit.'

'You see? You *see*? Steve, this place is incredible. It's like a museum. I mean, even the Romans knew something about plumbing, didn't they? And look at this coffee grinder with the cute little drawer in the front: it must date back to the last century.' He winds the crescent-shaped handle on the boxy Peugeot grinder, identical to Sonneville's. I happen to know that Auntie Val bought it new, just before the war. But I don't want to spoil Conrad's time-travel fantasy.

'And what about this table and these chairs?' he says, sitting at the table beside me. 'I mean, they look even older than my *house*. And then you've got your neighbour out there, still ploughing his fields with a cow.'

'Only because last week the Germans took his horse.'

Conrad considers this for a moment. 'Bastard Krauts. Now that I'm here, now that I can see it all, I hate them so much more than I did. Before, I guess I just hated an idea. Now I can see what they're doing with my own eyes – the way they're taking this lovely, soft old country apart, piece by piece – it just makes me really, *really* pissed. You know, I joined the air force for fun. I didn't join it because I wanted to bomb Germany. I just thought it would be cool to be up there in the sky with some good pals and a great big machine gun. And then we get into the war, and suddenly I'm in England. In RAF frigging Molesworth, of all places. You ever been to Molesworth, Steve?'

'No.'

'Well, don't. That's my advice to you. It's so darn flat it makes this place seem like the Rockies. And there's nothing there. I mean *nothing*.'

'Welcome to Nieppe. I like to think we take nothingness to new heights.'

Conrad chuckles. 'It ain't Vegas, I grant you that. But I'm liking your France.' He suddenly splutters and coughs. 'I just think it's going to take me a little while to get used to the water.'

'I did warn you.'

But Conrad doesn't laugh. He is standing very still, listening. He holds his finger in the air, and then dashes out on to the veranda. A second later, he is back.

'Come see this.'

As we watch, the sky far above us begins to fill with aircraft – with hundreds of aircraft.

Silver bombers, four engines apiece.

So many, they cover the sky, like a pattern on a tablecloth. But these aren't German bombers. No, they are American B-17 Flying Fortresses, as Conrad's dreamy grin attests.

'Look at those boys,' he says. 'I'll bet that's the 303rd from Molesworth. They're flying their pants off up there.'

'Aren't they a bit close together? Doesn't that make it easier to shoot them down?'

'For the ack-ack, yeah. But not for the fighters. They're tucked in, as we call it. With the firepower on each Fortress, you fly like that, and the Jerry fighters can't get close. But, heck, there's a lot of them today. Must be softening up the Krauts for the invasion.'

'What invasion?' I ask, studying his face carefully.

'Yeah, exactly. What invasion?' he grins. 'Your dad was asking the same thing, just the other day. I'd tell you if I knew, Steve. I really would. But up in Molesworth, nobody told us jackshit. We just knew that something was brewing.'

Nobody has told Nature that something is brewing. And as the weather turns warmer, the grass in the cemeteries mounts its spring offensive. My head is jangling with distractions. Yet still I must strap my push-mower to my bicycle every day and mow stripe after perfect stripe beneath the sun. Naturally, Conrad wants to help. It is all I can do to persuade him that Albert de Groote, the tight-lipped farmer, should really be ploughing behind cows, not mowing stripes in a military graveyard.

We have come to a compromise about where he stays. For part of the week he dosses down at Emil Depreiter's house in the ruelle du Coude. But when there's a mission in the offing, he comes and sleeps on the floor of the attic in the rue du Sac.

The mood on the streets of Nieppe is changing, too. The Germans, on the rare occasions when I see any, look a little more ragged in their uniforms, a little hotter under the collar, a little more lost in their eyes. And while the locals appear as wretched and destitute as ever as they queue outside the empty shops, people are at least daring to raise their heads again and to catch each other's eye. Yesterday, I even saw a couple of women talking in the street.

The old poison is still there, though, just beneath the surface – the familiar stench of suspicion and recrimination and doubt. It's just that the Pétainists and collaborators who were once so full of themselves and their German friends are now the ones scuttling, heads down, in the shadows. And it is the others who, at last, are daring almost to stand up straight.

In the Trois Arbres war cemetery, I lean back on the Stone of Remembrance. I am not officially responsible for this vast place, and it is a little too close to Steenwerck for comfort, but I come in occasionally to tidy it up, even so. I am casting an eye on the state of the borders when a boy on a bicycle draws up at the gate. I recognise that loping gait. It is my brother, Kléber.

'No work today?' I ask.

'The welding torch has packed up.' He pulls his old red India rubber ball from his pocket and starts bouncing it on the stone plinth of the cross. 'Someone used up all the gas. So by the time I'd swept the floor three times, the workshop owner sent me home. I thought I might find you here.'

'*Someone* used up all the gas,' I echo. I know my brother too well; I know when he is hiding something and when he has a secret he wants to share. And the way he is bouncing that ball definitely means something. I haven't seen him playing with it since he was about five. 'And who might that have been, I wonder?'

'Search me,' he says, concentrating on the ball. And then he reaches into his other pocket, draws out a handful of shiny objects and flings them on to the flat surface of the Stone of Remembrance. They jingle as they land.

'Jacks?'

'Not exactly,' he replies, with a half-smile.

I pick one up for a closer look.

'Nails?' And then I can't help smiling, too. 'Kléber, these things are works of art.'

'I thought you might like them. I made them for you.'

I gaze at my brother. 'Thank you,' I say, quietly. 'I love them. How many have you got?'

'Maybe a dozen. I'd have made more – the owner turned a blind eye – but I . . .'

'Someone used up all the gas.'

'Something like that,' he grins. 'I thought we could go on a mission together, Lou. You know, creep out at night. Lay a few nails on the main road. Just the two of us.'

I close my eyes and shake my head. 'No, Kléber. I'm sorry. You're too young, and it's too risky. If anything happened to you, I would never forgive myself. And nor would Mummy or Auntie Val or Mémère. But thank you. I'll see that these are put to good use. You know: by the Resistance.'

To my relief, he smiles and nods. He understands.

'Do you remember when we used to play here together, Kléber,' I ask him. 'When Dad was mowing the grass? Just you and me: Cowboys and Indians, Cops and Robbers, Tommies and Fritz?'

'I remember you always made me be the Fritz,' he says.

'Well, yes. Sorry about that. But we had fun, didn't we?'

Kléber turns and gazes at the lines of gravestones. He shields his eyes from the sun. 'It's strange,' he says. 'As a child, I never minded this place. It all seemed so far in the past, what they had done. But now, today, it haunts me a bit.'

'Why's that?' I smile. Trust my little brother, with his wild imagination, still to be afraid of ghosts.

'Because it's not just the past, is it, Lou? It's us, now. And it's the future, too.'

'Lou! Lou! Come quickly!' Auntie Val's voice sounds urgent and breathless, as if she has been stung.

'What is it?' I ask, rushing in through the veranda from the vegetable patch. And then I skid to a halt. My mother, Elizabeth and Mémère are all sobbing. Elizabeth has her face in her hands. Kléber is lying motionless on the kitchen floor. His face is purple and swollen. A clotted trickle of dried blood runs from his mouth to his ear. His matted hair looks like he picked up a wig far too small for his outsize head.

'Is he . . .?' I ask.

'Still breathing,' replies Auntie Val. 'But only just.'

'Where did you find him?'

'A retired couple, Monsieur and Madame Morice, brought him home. They found him in a ditch.'

I kneel beside Kléber. I touch his puffy forehead with the back of my fingers; I cannot believe that this purple, pummelled thing is the same little brother to whom I was chatting a few hours ago.

'They saw the whole thing,' continues Auntie Val behind me. She explains how a cargo lorry on its way to Germany was strafed and put out of action by a Spitfire on the rue des Trois Arbres. I nod; I think I saw it. And the soldiers inside it, rather than leave their rich haul of leather shoes and bottles of wine to be reclaimed by the French, set it on fire. Kléber must have arrived on the scene just after that. 'The poor child was so busy pulling things out of the flames, to bring home to us, that he didn't hear the motorcycle pull up behind him.' She gazes down at him. 'Two great big louts started on him with their fists. On a boy of fifteen. And then, when he was down, with their boots.'

That night, I cannot sleep. I lie very still in our bed, beside the bruised and broken body of my little brother.

Did I do this to you?

I can hear my mother's laboured breathing from the other side of the room, and my father snoring beside her. And with every hour that passes, another switch flicks in the smoking fuse box of my mind.

At last, I close my eyes and slip into a fitful doze.

I am unprepared for the sight that greets me when I wake. The bedroom on Kléber's side is piled high with bottles and boxes: with wine and champagne, and a heap of gleaming leather shoes.

There is a muffled groan from the bed – the first sound Kléber has made since his ordeal. His eyes are open. He swivels them towards me, then at the bottles and boxes, then at me again.

'Champagne? Is the war over?'

'Not exactly.'

'Did I bring all this stuff home with me?'

'Almost,' I reply. 'I think Conrad must have rescued it for you. To help celebrate your recovery.'

He smiles, and then sinks back into such a deep sleep that I have to check to make sure he is still breathing.

When Conrad joins me on the veranda after breakfast, I point up in the direction of our room.

'What the hell is all that stuff up there?' I demand.

He glances up at the beams. 'Spider webs?'

'You know exactly what I'm talking about. You must have made half a dozen trips to bring that stuff back here last night. You put us all at risk.'

'I'm sorry, Steve, I don't know what you're talking about,' he shrugs. He looks me straight in the eye. 'Now when are we going to go and stick some Krauts?'

'The most patriotic thing we can do right now is to sit tight and await further orders.'

'Patriot bullshit, no action,' he snorts.

Auntie Val bustles out on to the veranda. Her eyes glint at Conrad; her lips are pursed.

'Are you still here?'

'I'm afraid so, ma'am,' he replies, lowering his head.

'Good, I'm glad.'

Conrad and I both stare at her.

'I never thought I'd hear myself saying this,' she adds, 'but I almost think I feel safer with you around, young man.' And with that, she goes clomping back into the kitchen in her clogs.

'Did you hear that, Steve?' whispers Conrad, with a wink. 'She called me "young man".'

8 June 1944

My father is hopping up and down in the corridor, mouth open, arms in the air.

'Ohhhhhhhhh,' he exclaims. And then again: 'Ohhhhhhhhhhh.'

'Are you all right, Dad?' I ask, as I emerge from the kitchen with Kléber. Though he is still limping, my brother is on the mend.

'Is it your heart, Dad?' adds Kléber, alarmed.

My father shakes his head, his mouth opening and shutting, as he struggles to find the words to explain. By now, the others have come out into the corridor.

'It's happened,' he blurts. 'They're coming.'

'Who's coming?' demands Auntie Val. 'The Germans? The Italians? The little green men?'

'No, *us*. We're coming. The Brits. The Yanks. *Everyone*. It's the invasion. It's happening. It's happened.'

'Is it Calais and Dunkirk?' I ask.

He shakes his head. 'Normandy. They landed in bloody Normandy.'

'You're making it up, Dad. Why would they land in Normandy? It's miles from anywhere. There's nothing there.'

'Come and listen.' He beckons us into the front room and gestures for us to approach his wireless set. 'You'll see.'

My father is right. I hurtle upstairs to tell Conrad the news.

'I *knew* it.' He punches his palm with his fist. 'I could *smell* it was coming.'

Within a day or two, Sonneville declares mobilisation. The time has come for the Fighters in the Shadow, as he calls us, to tackle the Boche in their own nests. Some twenty of us gather at an isolated farm called Le Feutre, near Bailleul, which belongs to the father of Jacques Flahou, one of the smugglers in his section.

'I thought you said there were only fourteen of you,' whispers Conrad.

'That was *before* the invasion,' I reply, with a sarcastic grin.

Over the next two nights, a group of us move all the Sten guns from my cache at Pont d'Achelles to the Le Feutre farm. In the darkness, I can smell that the cemetery shrubs are in full flower. I picture the delicate blue flowers of arabis, the pink of heuchera, the tiny white spheres of symphoricarpos. Tamarix must be flowering, too, by now, along with the fuchsias, buddleia and philadelphus.

On the road, we keep as far as possible to the drainage ditches, crawling along through mud and brambles, for the Germans are still very much around, and jumpier than ever. But progress is so slow that we resort to hauling the weapons in heavy handcarts dragged by two men, with an armed escort in front and behind. I don't allow the carts into the cemetery itself, however.

'Good thinking, Steve,' nods Conrad. 'We don't want to leave any tracks.' He needn't know that I am just trying to protect the velvet smoothness of my turf.

Before long everyone has a weapon, and Sonneville wants us to practise using them.

'Come on,' he says, his eyes glittering with excitement. He whacks a clip of ammo into the breach of one of the Stens. 'Let's make music.'

'Jean, wait,' I call. Taking him aside, I whisper that we have only two or three magazines of ammo for each Sten.

'Ah.' Unfazed, he decides that we should do some physical training instead.

'Physical jerks?' Conrad looks stunned. 'Why?'

In my new role as his official translator, I pass Conrad's

question on to Sonneville, doing my best to make it sound more like idle curiosity than a challenge to his authority.

'To prepare us for hand-to-hand combat,' sniffs Sonneville, glancing at Conrad. 'In case we run out of bullets.' And then he turns to me. 'I think your American friend is worried about being shown up by the superior fitness of the French, no?'

I decide against translating this for my American friend.

'It's just to keep us sharp,' I tell Conrad. 'Although I think Sonneville here is a bit worried that we Frogs may not be able to keep up with the athletic Yank.'

Conrad bursts out laughing; he gives a big thumbs-up to Sonneville, to show how much he approves of his Gallic humility.

We do press-ups, with Conrad leading from the front. If we do twenty, he does thirty. If we do thirty, he does forty.

'You always have to win, don't you?' I goad, with a grin.

'Yes, luckily for the French, we do.' And, luckily for Conrad, none of the French have a clue what he has said.

We do star jumps. We do a great deal of running on the spot. And we spend days scanning the horizon, waiting for the Allied advance and the waves of terrified German soldiers who will be fleeing before them, just waiting for us to pick them off.

'I've never seen so many phoneys in my life,' Conrad mutters one evening, as we pick over the bones of a sheep we have rustled and roasted on a spit.

'Phoneys?'

'Fakes. You know, Steve, people shooting a line. Some of these guys have probably never shot anything bigger than a sparrow in their lives.'

'I'm sorry,' I reply. 'We're all doing our best, but . . .'

'And you know who's the biggest phoney of all?'

'Me?'

'No, no, you're different, Steve. You're all right.'

'I do wish people would stop telling me I'm different,' I

tell him. 'I find it unsettling. I'm not different at all. I can't see it myself.' Conrad thinks about this for a moment.

'And perhaps that's what makes you different.' He pauses. 'No, I was talking about *him*.'

I glance, stunned, at the man at whom Conrad has just jabbed his thumb: Sonneville.

'But Jean is the bravest of the brave,' I protest.

'Is that so?' Conrad casts his gaze around the room, and starts picking men off with his finger. 'He's all right, and *he's* all right.' He stops at Maurice Leblon and Francis André, who are bickering about something, their faces lit up by the flames. 'They're all right, those two. I'd have them in my crew.'

'Would you?' I gaze at my fellow musketeers, and wonder if I really know them as well as I thought I did.

After a week of training and talking and waiting, we grow restless. Conrad wants us to go out and find some Germans to attack; others are worried about the risk of reprisals against the local people if we attempt too much too soon. And so, after many cigarettes and late night discussions, Sonneville gives the order to disband. We all creep back home with our tails between our legs.

'Patriot bullshit, no action,' snorts Conrad in disgust.

A day later, however, and things are looking up. An order comes through from Fertein, instructing us to step up our sabotage activities. He wants us to cause maximum disruption to German military traffic.

This is more like it. But we have almost run out of 808. Too late, we regret wasting our limited stocks of plastic on blowing up railway lines, the ten kilos it took to destroy the sluice gates at Bac Saint-Maur, the incendiary grenades we squandered on hay trains heading east. Forced to go back to basics, we start unbolting and dragging away lengths of track from the railway by hand. This is a hard, sweaty business, and dangerous simply because it takes so long. Cutting telephone cables is quicker and simpler but, as Sonneville laments, a whole lot less satisfying, too. I think all of us, deep down, want a Spectacular.

Conrad is growing more impatient than most. If I don't find a decent mission for him soon, I'm worried he may take matters into his own hands. So when Kléber comes to me with a big box of his carefully welded four-point caltrops, I do not hesitate. I brief Conrad. We're on. Tonight.

Our first experiment with the nails is a disaster. Having mined a section of the rue du Sac with the precious objects, the one vehicle we manage to disable is a donkey cart belonging to a local farmer. Thankfully, the donkey's hooves are not injured. But the old boy's pneumatic tyres are shredded into spaghetti.

Once upon a time, I might have found this hilarious. Now I just feel ashamed.

Undaunted, we sneak out of the rue du Sac the following night and creep along the main road towards Nieppe. Halfway there, we decorate a twenty-yard strip of road with an intricate pattern of nails.

We must have scattered fifty or sixty of the things when a low rumble makes us both freeze.

Conrad stares at me in the darkness. It sounds like a lorry in the distance. Coming this way.

This is not what we planned. We weren't expecting any traffic until the morning. We need to be far away.

Conrad is still placing his nails on the rough stone surface.

The vehicle is closing fast. Now I can see the glimmer of its headlights through the slits of their blackout covers. And it's not just one lorry. It's a whole bloody convoy.

We begin to run back towards the rue du Sac. The nails glint on the road surface between us and the oncoming trucks. At the last moment, we fling ourselves down into the ditch.

This is it.

The roar of engines rips through the night. And then, suddenly, we hear a gunshot, or something like it. And another, and another.

A squeal of brakes; the grinding surge of engines being gunned to accelerate. That sound is not gunfire, I realise. It is the sound of balloons bursting on spikes. I experience a physical shudder of terrified ecstasy – euphoria mingled with dread. What have we done?

Beside me, Conrad is running through his entire lexicon of swear words.

On comes the crippled convoy. Do they think it's an ambush? Shoulder to shoulder, we peer out through the long grass on the lip of our trench; watch showers of sparks spraying from juddering wheels.

The first lorry swerves. It's heading straight for us. We will be crushed in the ditch.

A howling screech and a stink of sulphur. The vehicle pulls up short.

Infuriated, guttural shouts in the darkness.

Shaky with adrenaline, we crawl away along the ditch.

The convoy, its tyres turned to rags, remains stranded on the side of the main road for the whole of the following week. Conrad and I congratulate ourselves on a job well done. It is only later, when I meet up with Maurice Leblon, that I learn of the viciousness of the reprisal – the way the enemy soldiers used their rifle butts to shove everyone in the houses along the main road out of bed, how they made old men and women crawl along it in their nightshirts, their knees and hands raw and bleeding as they were forced to pick up our nails. By some miracle, no one was shot.

I do not pass this on to Conrad. Because the penny has finally dropped. I must not act without considering the conse-quences of my actions upon others; fair enough. But if I spend my life in fear of possible repercussions, then I will never be able to act at all. Yes, my actions may bring unin-tended suffering upon others. But that pain is, I now see, the price of courage. It is the officer who urges his troops over the top. It is the bill I must pay in the end.

15 July 1944

Over a month has passed since the D-Day landings. In Pont d'Achelles, the heather and the climbing roses are in flower. But there is still no sign of Allied forces anywhere near Nieppe. Mémère says this is hardly surprising, for how can the British and the Americans hope to succeed where the French have failed? While we wait for Kléber to machine us some more nails, Conrad and I are getting quite fed up.

'So do you want to hear about our next mission?' I ask him, as we stand out in the vegetable patch, squashing *doryphores*. It is a baking hot day, and I have had a struggle to dissuade him from taking off his shirt. I think this might push Auntie Val over the edge.

He almost knocks me over with the bear hug he gives me.

So I explain to him about the STO, and all the young men just older than me who have been forced to go into hiding to avoid being conscripted as unwilling labourers in Nazi Germany. Often living in ruined farms or hiding out in the woods, they need ration cards in order to eat. And it is up to us to steal these cards for them, from the *mairie*.

'The Mary?' Conrad narrows his eyes. 'Ain't that where Andrée's dad works?'

'Mayor Houcke hasn't been seen for months, and the German administration in Lille is watching the *mairie* like a hawk. That's why we can't just ask for the ration cards. We have to stage a hold-up.'

'A *hold-up*.' Conrad eyes me carefully, to see if this is another wind-up. 'You serious, Steve?'

'Deadly.'

A grin spreads across his face. 'Then now you're talking, partner. I've seen the movies. Edward G. Robinson holds up banks all the time. For you and me, it'll be a cinch.'

'Well, I hope so. Because you are going to have to speak some French.'

'*Ooh là là*,' murmurs Conrad, shimmying his shoulders amid the potato plants. And then '*Ooh là là*' again.

20 July 1944

'Sorry I'm late,' I pant, as I race into Sonneville's house through the back garden. 'Got held up in a bit of a sticky situation, but everything's all right now.'

'Boche?' asks Sonneville, amused. He is holding a cup of coffee with his little finger sticking out, looking every inch the aristocrat with his tailored suit and his swept-back hair.

I shake my head. 'Women.'

'*Nom d'jou,* that's much more dangerous.'

I recognise Jacques Flahou and Alfred Vankerkove, one of Marcel Houcke's men, who are to join us for the mission to the *mairie.* Conrad – or Albert de Groote, as we are supposed to call him – is annoyed that the mission has been taken out of our hands; he is convinced we could accomplish our hold-up more safely with just the two of us. But the mood in Sonneville's salon is buoyant as we run through the final details. The sun streams in through the high windows criss-crossed with masking tape, making all the polished objects in the room glitter and throwing fine points of reflected light on to the elegant mouldings of the ceiling.

'How come I'm the one who has to do the talking in the *Mary*, when I'm the only one who doesn't speak French?' whispers Conrad. He glares at Sonneville.

'Because that's just it,' I tell him. 'You're the only one whose voice can't be recognised.'

'Yeah, they'll never spot my American accent, will they?'

'Let's try it again,' I tell him. 'What is it that you're to shout when you rush in?'

'Holy man,' he says, pumping his fist.

'Yes, but what are you going to shout?'

'That's it: *Holy man*. What's wrong with that?'

Smiling to myself, I turn to Sonneville. 'Can you tell what he's saying?'

Sonneville looks blank.

'Holy man,' Conrad says again, pointing an imaginary pistol at us.

And now the penny drops, and we all burst out laughing. Sonneville holds his sides. I have to sit down. Flahou and Vankerkove shake their heads. Conrad pulls a face at me.

'*Nom d'jou*,' gasps Sonneville. 'We've got a right one here, haven't we?'

'Translation, Steve?' barks Conrad, narrowing his eyes at the Frenchman.

'He says you're incredible,' I manage to say.

'*Holy man*. What's wrong with that?'

'It's not "Holy man", Conrad. It's "*Haut les mains*". You know: hands up. Do you want to try it again?'

'*Olé man*,' he says, without enthusiasm. And then again: '*Olé man*.'

We give him a round of polite applause, and hope that the staff in the *mairie* will give him the benefit of the doubt.

A few minutes later, we are all squeezed into Sonneville's Gestapo wagon: he and Flahou in the front, Conrad, Vankerkove and I in the back. But the damn thing won't start.

'This crock of shit reminds me of the Tennessee Hillbilly,' mutters Conrad. 'Nightmare to start and full of holes. But at least the Hillbilly didn't smell of rotting jockstraps.'

'I think it's been kept in a damp barn,' I reply. 'Some of the leather's perished.'

'What are you two devils whispering about?' demands Sonneville, over his shoulder. 'Plotting against the French, as usual?'

'Albert here was just commenting on how fragrant your car smells,' I tell him.

'Yes, well, he can get out and walk if he doesn't like it.'

Sonneville looks daggers at Conrad in the rear-view mirror on top of the dashboard.

'What did he say?' asks Conrad.

'He wishes he had an American car instead.'

'Aw, really?' he laughs. 'He's all right, isn't he, your dodgy smuggler friend?' And he gives Sonneville a grudging thumbs-up in the rear-view mirror. Sonneville manages a thin smile, pushes the starter switch more fiercely and the engine finally splutters into life.

The centre of town is deserted, although we can see our two guards – Maurice Leblon and Jean Houcke, the mayor's son – already in position in the square. With pistols in their pockets, their job will be to intervene if any Germans emerge from their office at the back of the church.

Sonneville pulls up outside the red-brick *mairie*, with its arched windows and stone balcony above the main door. He is to wait here with the engine running while the rest of us launch our careers in armed robbery.

'Don't be long,' he hisses, as we clamber out. 'Running at idle like this really fouls up the plugs. If the engine stalls, you'll be pushing me home again.'

I pull my scarf up over my face and lead the others up the stone steps.

My job is to stand guard in the hallway and stop anyone who attempts to come in, with a bullet if necessary. Flahou, Vankerkove and Conrad, whose faces are not known in Nieppe, prepare to burst into the payments office. This contains the safe and at least four members of staff.

From my end of the hallway, I can see them standing outside it, guns at the ready, psyching themselves up for their attack. Suddenly Flahou kicks the door open and the other two spin into the room. There is a stunned silence and then, echoing down the corridor, comes Conrad's shouted command:

'*Nom d'jou!*'

My eyes widen. My jaw drops. And Conrad yells it again, even louder this time.

'*Nom d'jou!*'

He has forgotten his one line. Instead of saying 'hands up' in French, he is shouting Sonneville's favourite patois curse.

Call it nerves. Call it immaturity. But I just can't stop myself: I put my hand over my mouth and bend over, shaking with suppressed laughter.

Fortunately the Colt revolver being waved in their faces communicates Conrad's message to the *mairie* staff more powerfully than his pidgin French. Within a couple of minutes, he and the others are galloping down the marble corridor towards me, clutching a large canvas pouch stuffed with anything they could find in the safe.

As Sonneville roars away, I glance over my shoulder to see our victims on the steps of the *mairie*, shouting and waving their arms at us. I am pretty sure they are protesting for the benefit of any Germans who may be watching. But they look very much as if they are celebrating, too.

Back in the sunlit salon, we unwrap our loot.

'*Nom d'jou,*' breathes Sonneville as he opens the canvas pouch, from which bursts a heap of blue and brown banknotes.

'Funnily enough,' says Flahou, 'that's exactly what Albert here said to the staff in the *mairie*.' We all erupt into helpless laughter, watched by an aggrieved Conrad. Then Sonneville begins to count the money, and we fall silent.

'*Putain,*' says Flahou.

'Fuck me,' whistles Conrad.

I nod. 'Ditto.'

The pouch contains a total of 10,572.50 francs. Inside, too, is a coupon stating that the money, remitted by the German army, is for the compensation of local farmers who have provided wooden pickets for anti-glider defences on the coast.

'Collaborators, in other words,' snorts Sonneville. He brusquely tucks the money and the ration cards into his safe, hidden behind a painting of a horse. Conrad rolls his eyes and whistles to himself. I glance across at Sonneville, but he is too busy straightening his horse to notice.

And then Conrad and I are marching away together, enjoying the cool protection of the sun-dappled woods, and forgetting for a few blissful moments that constant grey-green threat – dark, evanescent, impalpable – which shadows our every step. For now, we are a couple of boys, playing games in the woods. We are cowboys. We are bank robbers. We are, both of us, Robin Hood.

As the battle rages on in Normandy and it becomes clear, even to Mémère, that sooner or later the Allied armies will overcome German resistance, recruitment into the ranks of the Resistance becomes an easy game. Suddenly everybody wants to line up for a bit of Boche-bashing. Ever the opportunist, Sonneville assembles a crack team of policemen and customs officials, his peace-time enemies.

'I have chosen all my most powerful and skilful adversaries,' he tells me, grinning, 'because I know they will be useful to us. It is pure coincidence that, after the war, these same people will be even more useful to me as friends.'

My own section is expanding, too. I have persuaded big Abel Rotsaert, a notorious smuggler who lives in Ploegsteert, to join me, along with my old friend Michel Roussel, with whom I flooded the *Petit Galopin* all those years ago. Roussel is now a strapping farm labourer, with a kindly, open face and the strength of a pair of oxen. There are ten of us in all: mostly boys I have known for a while, who are more than ready to become men.

It suits me to be spending less and less time at home, where the general mood has not been lifted by the better news coming over my father's wireless and I have too much time to think. My mother has finally quashed my sisters' dreams with the sheer weight of her negativity, persuading Rosemary that being a musician with Radio Lille would combine both harlotry and frippery, and Elizabeth that hairdressing is the

377

swiftest route to varicose veins and lice. When he is not staying in Bailleul, my father rarely emerges from upstairs, where he winds his little wheat-grinding machine and has begun to befriend the mice. I can see why Kléber spends most of his time at work.

One Tuesday afternoon, Sonneville asks me to come with him to the café in La Crèche. He is meeting one of his top-secret contacts, and needs me to stand guard for him.

La Crèche is such a sleepy little hamlet that I always feel I am wasting my time here. But not today. No, today I spot two German soldiers striding down a nearby street. One tall, one short; both ugly, and far too close for comfort. I can feel my scalp prickling at the sight of them. I wonder if Germans will always have this effect on me.

Heart thumping, I duck into the café. The place looks deserted. I push my way through a curtained archway and hear voices from behind a door at the end of a short passage. In a hurry now, I knock and enter.

Inside, it is suprisingly dark. The curtains are drawn. But there is enough light for me to see all that I need to see: a pair of shiny white buttocks squeezed beneath enveloping, doughy thighs; a woman's pained smile, red and sweaty beneath tumbling auburn locks; Sonneville, squirming, turning, frowning at me as I attempt to flee.

'Good meeting?' I ask, rubbing my chin as he emerges from the café.

'Very helpful, thank you.' He straightens his tie. 'And you: anything to report?'

'Only that I spotted a couple of German soldiers sniffing around, and thought I'd better come and warn you.'

'Quite so, quite so.'

'I'm sorry to have interrupted, Jean. But at least now I know I have been risking my life for a worthy cause.' Sonneville eyes me carefully. And then he breaks into a smile and whacks me on the back.

'You're not bad for *un Anglais,* Stéphane Grady,' he whispers.

On 3 August, I take Conrad and my Four Musketeers, as Houcke still calls us, to join a WO contingent in mounting a large sabotage operation. The overall aim is to cut off all rail traffic to and from Lille. My section's specific job is to arrest any French patrols we encounter on the section of line between Lille and Pérenchies.

By moonlight, the five of us cycle out with dismantled Sten guns and lengths of rope concealed in bags dangling from our handlebars. Tonight a mood of subdued excitement electrifies the air. We are becoming a team. The Germans are on the back foot. And from the smiles we exchange as we rattle over the cobbles, I know that I am not the only one who is having fun. Even Marcel gives me a wink.

There aren't many station guards on duty, and we take it in turns to capture the ones that are. To everyone's surprise, Marcel Lombard wins the prize for the most silent attack, whereas Francis André lets his one escape for a few paces, shrieking like a fox, before he brings him down with a flying rugby tackle from behind.

We soon have them all trussed like chickens, their eyes bulging with fear. And then we kick our heels. We take shelter in a chicken house near a level crossing, and wait for the main sabotage team to carry out their attack. The plan is for them to hitch an enormous plough to a pair of locomotives, and use this to tear up the sleepers along a huge length of track. They don't make it as far up the line as our position. Yet the fearsome din of ripping and grinding, carried on the night wind, fills me with such euphoria that I suddenly feel nostalgic for my childhood and the tricks I used to play. Life was so much simpler then.

Marcel Houcke comes to me, a few days later, with an uncomfortable look in his eye. He says that six chickens have gone missing from the chicken house where we sheltered.

I shake my head and insist that I know nothing about it.

'Probably whoever took them was paying back a collaborator,' I shrug. 'You know how it is, Marcel.' I am not about to tell him that I taught Conrad how to pluck the birds, before personally roasting them in Sonneville's yard.

'That's all very well,' replies Houcke. 'But the birds you stole belonged to the chief of the local Resistance.'

We have become bandits. We rustle chickens. We destroy threshing machines that have been turned to work for the Germans. We burn whatever we can of the summer's harvest, torching wheat stacks to stop the Boche from shipping the stuff back to Germany on the very trains we have been doing our best to derail. This is a strange time. It feels more like vandalism than war.

One train we are unable to stop affects me more than most. They are calling it the last train from Loos. The Resistance boys in Lille mount an ill-fated operation to storm the prison and liberate the patriots held there, many of them under sentence of death. In revenge, the Boche shoehorn 1250 prisoners into a single death train, bound for Germany on a one-way trip.

'If only we had known,' growls Conrad, on the day that news of the Last Train filters through. It is evening, and he and I are sitting at the far end of the vegetable garden, smoking cigarettes in the warm night air. The Allies are getting closer to Nieppe. There is a growing sense of confidence on the streets.

'All I know is that it won't be long now,' I reply.

Conrad stubs out the butt of his cigarette in the dry earth. 'And in the meantime, what are we going to do to avenge those prisoners? Some of them were probably Brits.'

'We must sit tight,' I insist. 'Wait for the right moment to strike.'

'Patriot bullshit, no action,' mutters Conrad, stalking back to the house.

27 August 1944

Soon after dawn, Kléber shakes me awake. His eyes are shining.

'You're wanted,' he says.

Downstairs in the kitchen, Conrad is already pacing like a caged tiger. I am surprised to see Marcel Lombard sitting at the table.

'There you are at last,' he says. 'Come on.'

British and American soldiers have finally broken through the German lines in Normandy. The Boche are in disarray. And a message has come through from the Houcke brothers: now is the time for us to use the weapons for which Capitaine Michel sacrificed his life.

Beyond the veranda, the brilliance of the sunshine takes me by surprise. My Luger is loaded and ready in my pocket. In the Lombard barn, Marcel hands us each a Sten gun, already assembled.

I raise my eyebrows. 'I didn't know you had these.'

'Strictly for emergencies,' he says.

'Is this an emergency?'

'You tell me, *Rosbif*,' he replies. 'You're in charge.'

'Let's roll, Limey,' says Conrad, grinning at me. 'It's time.'

In town, things begin to happen fast. Sonneville's Section 2, composed of policemen and customs officers, shoots up a German motorcycle. They kill one German and capture the other. After tying him up, they drag him down into the cellar of one of the gendarmes, a cheery beanpole called Depape.

The next day it is the turn of Maurice Leblon and Francis André, whom I have sent out on patrol together. They surprise two Germans in a *Kübelwagen*, which pulled up in front of Sonneville's house for the driver to get out and have a pee.

Brandishing his Colt, Maurice orders them to put their hands up. Panicked, the passenger does so. But the driver goes for his pistol. In a flash, Maurice shoots him, and the German tumbles into the roadside ditch. While Francis ties up the passenger, Maurice clambers down into the ditch to recover the dead man's pistol. When he returns with it, he has a strange look in his eyes. For the pistol wasn't even loaded.

While Sonneville drives the jeep off the main road and hides it in a pasture, the rest of us help to bury the dead man in the field beside his house. We hold the second prisoner in a cottage nearby.

'Wouldn't it be simpler just to shoot them all?' asks Daniel Rotsaert, one of the younger boys in my section and Abel's little brother. 'I mean, after what they've done to us.'

'We are men, not murderers,' I declare, firmly. Beside me, Maurice glumly nods. He and I now have a strange bond: we have both shot unarmed men.

The following day, Sonneville suggests that I move my section to a farmhouse on the rue des Meuniers, which runs between Pont d'Achelles and Steenwerck. And he wants to come, too.

'I thought you'd want to be with your section, Jean.'

'Sleep with policemen?' he retorts. 'No, Stéphane, I feel safer with you.'

We all sleep up in the hayloft: me, Marcel, Conrad, Maurice, Francis, Sonneville and half a dozen others, cheek by jowl on the straw, with our Sten guns at our feet. I feel happier and safer than I have felt for months. For I am part of something bigger than my family. I exult in the camaraderie of my men.

'You awake, Steve?' whispers Conrad in the middle of the night.

'Yes, why?'

'It's kinda exciting, isn't it?'

'You can say that again.'

'It's kinda exciting, isn't it?'

'Haha. Very funny.' I can see his eyes glinting at me. 'But yes; I feel as if I'm a soldier at last. You know, I feel I'm part of something.'

'You shoulda been born a Yank, Steve.'

'Why's that?'

'Because we get to feel that all the time. It's why we invented the United States. Whereas you're a mongrel, aren't you? I'm not surprised you don't feel you belong.'

Early on the morning of 30 August, word reaches us that there are some German soldiers hiding in a farmhouse about a mile outside town. Six of us – the Four Musketeers, plus Conrad and Sonneville – creep up there and surround the place. Anyone would think we do this sort of thing every day.

Crouched in a field of maize, I can see the Boche soldiers through the grubby kitchen window. Bare-headed, open-shirted, they are enjoying a peaceful breakfast of stolen bread and jam. There must be about a dozen of them in there. Some of them look as old as my father. I wish I'd had a pee before I came.

On tenterhooks, we wait for the signal to strike. Then Sonneville fires a shot through the glass and the window just explodes. Yelling like bells, we come crashing in through the front and back doors.

There are shouts of surprise; some of the Germans scream. It's pathetic, really. A pool of spilt coffee steams on the table. We bustle around the room, crunching on glass, looking for weapons. But none of them is armed. When they put their hands up, one of them wets himself. Others clutch above their heads the hunks of pilfered bread and jam they were about to shove into their mouths.

There are fourteen of the poor brutes, mostly men in their

forties. Hearts racing, we stare at them, feeling stupidly powerful, because we're the ones with the guns.

'What the hell do we do now?' I mutter, through my teeth, at Sonneville. I'm surprised to find that I am shaking, so I simply can't imagine how the Krauts must be feeling.

'I suppose we'd better take them prisoner,' he shrugs.

A stolen farm cart with two horses in harness is parked outside. This we commandeer, along with all the soldiers' weapons and stores. And then, at Maurice's suggestion, we lead the prisoners into a large barn littered with rusting agricultural machinery.

But who is going to guard our fourteen Boche prisoners, while we are busy helping the Allies win the war? Our orders are to attack small groups of retreating Krauts, not imprison the ones having breakfast.

Slipping back into my house, I surprise my father, who is shaving in the kitchen.

'Corporal Grady,' I say, addressing my father by his old military rank. I don't know why. It just comes out that way. How odd it feels to be standing in my own kitchen with a Sten gun under my arm.

The razor drops from his hand and clatters into the bowl. Standing there in front of me, so pale and frail, he looks like a lost boy.

'Lou,' he replies. You'd think he has seen a ghost. His eyes flicker towards the Sten gun, and for one awful moment I think he is going to surrender. But he does not flinch. Until now, I have not noticed how hunched my father has become – how the years of literally keeping his head down, while France collapses around his ears, have bowed him into a stoop. He looks so much smaller than the proud young man who marched home with a bicycle for me, all those years ago.

'Dad, we have taken some German prisoners,' I blurt, in much the same tone with which I might once have confessed that I have smashed a neighbour's window with a football.

'And we need someone to guard them. Someone reliable. Are you free?'

He stares at his feet; he looks as if he may be about to burst into tears.

'Am I free? Am I free?'

I wait.

'Well, you tell me, Lou: am I free? You know what's going on out there better than I do. Have you won the war yet, single-handed?'

'Dad, we need you. Will you help?'

Now he does not hesitate. He suddenly straightens up and grins, making creases in parts of his face that have not once been creased these past four years. And then, as stiffly as if he were on parade, he salutes.

'Just try and stop me,' he replies. 'Sir.'

'Dad,' I beg him, 'please don't call me Sir.

'In that case, sir,' he shoots back, 'please stop calling me Dad.'

Outside in the street, we bump into Roger Rioual, who begs to be allowed to come with us. But his mother says no.

'Come on, Roger,' I urge him. 'This is your chance. I'll give you a rifle.'

'I want to,' he says, taking a step towards us. But his mother pulls him back.

My father puts his arm around my shoulders as we hurry back across the dewy fields together, right-left, right-left, doing our best to keep in step. It is odd to feel him touch me. I don't think he has ever done so before.

'I shall need a gun, of course,' he announces, as we clamber over the first fence.

'Of course.'

'By the way, how many of these blighters are there?'

'Fourteen.'

He stops in his tracks. 'You want me to guard fourteen Huns?'

'You won't be alone, Dad. Henri Blanquart, one of your fellow veterans, has volunteered for guard duty as well.'

'And Blanquart will have a gun, too?'

'You both will.'

'Ones like yours?' He eyes my Sten gun again.

'Probably rifles.' I do not add that these will be German rifles, taken from our prisoners.

'Jolly good,' he says. His stride lengthens. 'It's a long time since I've had the chance to point a gun at a Hun. And I can see why you've asked proper soldiers like me and Blanquart to guard them. Anyone can run around the countryside with a machine gun, like you and your friends. But it takes the nerve of an old soldier to pull the trigger on a man at close range. No disrespect to you, Lou, but I really don't think you could do that.'

'No, Dad.' I bite my lip. 'I really don't think I could.'

A few hours later, Auntie Val bustles across the fields to find me at the farmhouse.

'Lou, they say you're needed,' she announces, breathless, from the doorway. 'And your section, too. Whatever that means.' She does her best to ignore all the young blades sitting bare-chested around the table, cleaning their guns.

Auntie Val wrings her hands. 'I'm sorry I ever doubted you, Lou,' she adds, as I hurry out of the door. 'And I'm afraid Paul Saint Maxent is dead. You know, the deaf chap who ran the pub. They shot him through the head. Will you tell his daughters?'

The words only half register; they merely add to the growing numbness in my heart.

Marcel Houcke wants me to bring my section to Pont de Nieppe, where he and his men are trying to defend the two bridges over the river Lys. I am not keen for us to move. This farmhouse feels safe, and our orders are to mop up retreating Germans not defend bridges. As much as anything, I want to keep an eye on my dad.

But off we all trundle in the captured horse-drawn cart, while Sonneville hurries off to fetch his Citroën.

A black-clad figure in a beret flags us down in Pont de Nieppe: Marcel Houcke, weighed down with weapons. He manages a weary smile. I jump down from the horse and cart, and we exchange a few terse words.

My section is to take up a position flanking the main road, on the Nieppe side of the bridge. The local Resistants here have already driven back one group of Boche who were trying to blow up the railway bridge, a kilometre upstream. That was where Saint Maxent, doing his best to be brave, took a bullet in the head. I shiver to think of his two daughters without a father. Yet, as Houcke exultantly explains, Saint Maxent has survived. The shot entered near his right eye, and ploughed a furrow up to his right ear. Yet somehow it missed his brain.

'Hardly surprising,' remarks Roussel, as he tucks himself down behind his Sten gun. 'In Saint Maxent's case, there's plenty of room in there.'

In the skirmish, Houcke's men have captured a few weapons, including a small anti-tank gun. René Martel, a bristly ferret of a man who looks about twenty-five but is probably closer to fifty, is trying to work out how to fire it.

'*Panzerschreck*,' nods Conrad, glancing at the weapon, which looks more like an oven chimney than a gun. 'I recognise it from the books.'

'Do you know how it works?' asks Martel.

Conrad shrugs. 'I know you mustn't stand behind it.'

More volunteers join us, including Maurice Leblon's father, who served with the French army in Macedonia in 1917. Like my father, he looks ecstatic at being handed a rifle. No, not just ecstatic: he looks twenty years younger than he did last time I saw him.

We all keep glancing up the road, wondering what is coming next.

Suddenly Maurice sprints over and flattens himself in the dirt beside me.

'This is all wrong,' he gasps. 'We shouldn't be here.'

'What do you mean?'

'Stéphane, we're not soldiers.'

'Aren't we?'

'Of course we're not. And here we are, setting ourselves up to fight a battle against an army of highly trained stormtroopers. We'll be crucified.'

'We're patriots, aren't we?' retorts Francis André, on the other side of me. 'If we believe we can win, we will win.'

'No, Francis,' I say quietly, 'Maurice is right. We are not soldiers. We are boys with guns. A bunch of peasants with pitchforks. We haven't a clue how to fight an army.'

'Too late,' says Francis, in a voice that scares me. 'Look what's coming now.'

Grinding and clanking, clinking and rumbling, a vast German half-track vehicle is lumbering down the road towards us, out of the darkness. It looks as big as a house.

'Hold . . . hold,' I call, under my breath. I glance left and right at the motley company I am attempting to command. And my heart goes out to them. This is what courage looks like, I think to myself. For I can see that they are utterly, utterly terrified.

The closer the monster comes, the more massive it seems. Looming over us, it looks as big as an airship, as impregnable as a Panzer. The panic is crackling all around me as, open-mouthed, we watch it approach.

'Hold . . . *hold* . . .'

With the beast almost upon us, everyone lets loose with their weapons at once.

The noise and smoke are incredible. My eyes are dazzled with tracer fire.

In the midst of all this, René Martel suddenly stands up and lets loose with his *Panzerschreck*.

And it's a hit. He's only gone and bloody hit the thing.

There is a brief cheer. And then, all around me, the boys and men sliced by the shrapnel are screaming for help.

Through the smoke, it appears that two men have been blown out of the half-track. I can see them lying sprawled in impossible positions on the road, toys flung from a pram. Someone yells that poor Martel has bought it, too. But what a way to go. He must have been standing in front of a wall when he fired the anti-tank gun, and the fiery blast backed up on him.

Old father Leblon has a grenade splinter in his guts, almost certainly caused by one of our men.

Meanwhile, the damaged half-track limps on towards Armentières. It is all I can do to persuade my men not to give chase. We are not soldiers, I remind myself, aloud.

Early in the morning, a small detachment of Germans arrive on foot, and we capture them without a fight. If anything, they look relieved.

I send two men to fetch the fourteen prisoners from the barn, and we incarcerate all the captives in the schoolyard at Pont de Nieppe. We now have roughly forty prisoners, several of them wounded. And the numbers keep growing, as more stragglers are rounded up. Our own ranks are being swollen with volunteers, too.

The trouble is that, as soon as the new recruits are handed a German rifle, they become deaf to any orders being given by Houcke or Sonneville. I never really realised, until now, how the possession of a gun can change a man.

On the foggy night of 2 September, I am on watch with Conrad and Maurice Leblon, just short of the bridge, when we hear an eerie, rhythmic sound coming towards us out of the gloom.

We can't see a thing. But I know that sound. It is the crunch of massed hobnail boots stamping on cobbles. We open our eyes as wide as they will go, staring out into the blackness, but there is no sign of anyone heading towards us. No lights, no glint of weaponry, nothing.

'Boche infantry,' whispers Maurice. 'How many of them are there?'

'Maybe thirty?' I reply.

'At least fifty,' signals Conrad. 'Fewer than a hundred.'

'Oh, great,' nods Maurice. He leans over to me. 'So do we keep our heads down and hope they march straight past, chief? Or do we heroically sacrifice ourselves in a firefight?'

'I think . . .' But now the sound suddenly changes. The boots are not crunching any more. They are hammering on the wooden boards of the bridge.

In less than a minute, the Boche will be upon us. I glance down at the Sten in my hands and release the safety catch.

Suddenly, there is a shout, in German, just a few paces in front of me, and I scramble to my feet. They have taken us by surprise. Jittery with fear, I peer blindly into the darkness and point my weapon in the direction of the voice.

But Maurice rips my hand off the trigger.

'No, you fool,' he hisses. 'That's *Conrad*.'

Creeping forwards, we take up positions on either side of Conrad, who is crouching behind a cart, right on the threshold of the bridge. He signals for us to spread out.

The Germans have stopped. They are standing, motionless, on the bridge.

Now, once again, Conrad calls something out in his best German. There are more words this time. It sounds like a series of commands.

I hold my breath. I shut my eyes. Alongside the bridge, I cock my Sten gun as noisily as I can. From the other side, I hear Maurice do the same.

And then in the silence, we hear an extraordinary sound: the thud and clatter of rifles being dropped to the ground.

A few moments later, seventy-five grim-faced Krauts emerge out of the darkness with their arms in the air.

Conrad marches forward to meet them, Sten gun poised, while Maurice and I hurry to join him on the bridge.

We have to call up reinforcements to collect all the weapons.

The Boche commanding officer, furious at having surrendered his entire platoon to a trio of amateurs, stands cursing and stamping in front of us. Conrad and I just laugh.

'What the hell did you say to them?' I ask him, out of the side of my mouth.

'I just said what the Germans always say in the films.'

'And what's that?'

'Drop your weapons and come forward with your hands up. We have you surrounded.'

'Seriously?' I gaze at him in awe.

'Works every time,' he grins.

Into the schoolyard at Pont de Nieppe go Conrad's seventy-five prisoners. We now have 150 prisoners all told, and guns to spare. Along with the warm Luger in my pocket and the Sten gun slung over my shoulder, I am now the proud owner of the latest German rifle, the automatic Karabiner 43. Even in the heat of battle, I cannot resist the lure of a gleaming new gun.

Everyone is running low on food and sleep, but the adrenaline of our success is keeping us going. This reaches a peak on the morning of 3 September, when a German convoy of four lorries appears, with three of them towing 88mm guns. Battle-hardened as we have become, the trucks and guns are still a daunting sight. I find myself wishing for some of Kléber's nails. Somehow I manage to keep everyone from firing until the lorries are fifty metres away. And then we all let fly.

I have yet to get used to the inaccuracy of a Sten. It doesn't have much of a kick, yet I still feel as if I'm spraying most of my bullets into the sky.

The convoy jerks to a halt. Helmeted Boche leap out, just when most of us are reloading. A number of them are killed or wounded, but the rest manage to take up defensive positions.

This is the moment when good old Roussel takes the defence of France into his own hands. Before I can stop him, he has leapt out from behind a bollard and is rushing at the survivors, yelling obscenities and firing from the hip as he goes. It is an incredible sight. Even when his ammunition runs out, Roussel still battles onwards. I swear he knocks down one of the Krauts with his fist. Awed by our secret weapon, the remaining Germans are quick to surrender. One or two look positively grateful to be taken prisoner.

Within a few minutes, three of the trucks are ablaze, and we are all so thrilled at the spectacle that we barely notice the fourth reverse and get away. I am dimly conscious that we have made a mistake, but it is hard to resist the triumphant mood that is sweeping through the ranks. So far, we have beaten all-comers.

Maurice wants us to use the 88mm guns against the next wave, but nobody knows how to load and fire them. And, after Martel's experience with the anti-tank gun, nobody very much wants to try. So we do our best to put the guns out of action. The sight of their half-charred hulks is a symbol of how powerful we have become.

We have done well so far. Our casualties are light, although Daniel Rotsaert is dead, shot through the neck at point-blank range. Another boy in my section has a bullet up his arse, but is not in danger. Yet things are quickly falling apart. Our volunteers are a rabble, coming and going as they please.

Suddenly a bicycle appears on the road. One of the men meant to be guarding the prisoners in the schoolyard at Pont de Nieppe comes pedalling, hell for leather, towards me.

'Stéphane! Stéphane!' he yells. I can see panic in his eyes.

'What the hell!' I shout back at him. 'You shouldn't be here. You should be at your post.'

'I had to warn you, Stéphane. The prisoners are escaping. We saw a lorry with Germans. They picked up a man from a ditch. They were shouting and angry . . .'

His words come tumbling out, and I cannot think what I am supposed to do about them. Why does it matter if the blasted prisoners escape? Any fool could see that none of them had any fight left in them. And if you keep prisoners, you have to feed them in the end.

With Jean Houcke, Andrée's little brother, I chase down two more Germans. They're running fast, and it takes a good shot to wound one of them in the leg. Then I take Jean to Maurice Leblon's house, 500 metres from the bridge on the Nieppe side. Neither of us has eaten for twenty-four hours. I am hoping we may be able to cadge some food, and we each have our own reasons for not wanting to go to his mother's house, just opposite.

I perch myself on a stool in Maurice's kitchen and tear ravenously at the hunk of bread that his kindly father has given Jean and me to share. Old man Leblon is lying down in the front room, nursing his shrapnel wound. He suddenly looks very old again. I tell him how bravely his son has been fighting. He shrugs, unsurprised.

In the kitchen, I am trying to figure out how to pump myself a cup of water when Maurice's father calls out to me with an alarming edge in his voice.

'Stéphane, come quickly.'

I dash in to him. His wound must have begun to haemorrhage.

'Look,' he mouths. With a tremulous, bony finger, he points at the window.

Movement in the street. I bend to look more closely.

'Jean,' I say slowly, under my breath. 'We have to go. Right now.'

A phalanx of Germans in camouflage is advancing up the rue d'Armentières towards the centre of town. Cold, hard faces, too many to count. Fingers twitching on the triggers of black machine guns. These Krauts don't look as if they want to be taken prisoner any time soon.

'*Putain*,' gasps Jean, standing beside me. The soldiers are driving a large group of townspeople in front of them – people we know: shopkeepers and school friends, their faces contorted with terror. A human barricade.

Jabbing at their backs with the muzzles of their Schmeissers, the Boche soldiers are heading, hatchet-faced, for the bridge.

There are men at the bridge, men who will fight. Marcel Houcke, Roussel and others. But no one can shoot a soldier who is using a woman for a shield.

Looking more closely, I recognise that insignia: the soldiers are SS. Hard-bitten, professional killers who will not drop their weapons without a fight. There must be a couple of hundred of them out there. And I know this is the beginning of the end. We don't have much time.

'Quick, Jean,' I tell young Houcke. 'We'll escape across the fields.'

But the Germans are one step ahead of us. When we glance out of the back window, more SS soldiers in camouflage gear are already setting up heavy machine guns on tripods out there. They look purposeful and unhurried as they prepare to mow down anyone attempting to flee their trap.

At the front of the house, the firing has already started. Firing, then screaming, then silence. A few moments later, the pattern is repeated: firing, then screaming, then silence.

We do what we can to make old Leblon as comfortable as possible. And then I make my decision: we will run the gauntlet of the machine guns out the back. The main road in front is hemmed in with houses on both sides. Whereas to the rear, at least we may be able to scramble away across the roofs.

By this time, the heavy machine guns are loaded and ready. Through the back window, I can see two gunners in forage caps sitting calmly behind their weapons, each with a loader lying prone in the grass beside him, poised to feed a ribbon of lead into the breach.

'Now,' I call to Jean. 'It's *now*.'

I keep one eye on the machine-gunners as we sprint across the scrubby grass, heading away from the centre of town. Suddenly one of them glances up.

Now dust and brick chips are flying everywhere, and the

sound of shooting is deafening in our ears as we clamber along the party walls at the back of the row of houses. We only make it as far as Monot's garage, a couple of doors down.

Monot is there, looking pale and ragged and petrified. He wants us to go away.

I point my gun at him. He jabs his finger at a vehicle inspection pit, covered with warped duckboards.

'In there! In there!' he yells.

Down we leap, into the murk, heedless of the stink. They will be here, any minute.

I have two grenades in my pouch and hand one to Jean. Panting, we exchange glances. I can see that he knows what he must do, if we are discovered.

I will not be taken alive.

Monot rearranges the duckboards over our heads, and the sky is blotted out. We are dead and buried. I shut my eyes, as the oily slurry soaks through to my skin.

The shooting continues throughout the night. From time to time there is an explosion. We feel the shock of it through the fetid sludge in which we are embalmed.

Next morning, half-dead with cold, we crawl out of our pit and find a new hiding place in the garage roof. Here we remain for another twenty-four hours. Sporadic gunfire crackles in the distance. And then silence.

I can hear birds singing.

The Germans have gone.

5 September 1944

A sombre morning. In the thin sunshine, columns of smoke waft up from the burnt-out vehicles in the rue d'Armentières. Amid the shattered debris, dark liquids seep from the mangled shapes strewn in the road. There is a charred and pungent smell in the air.

I have come to take away the bodies of the dead.

Among them lies what is left of my friend Michel Roussel, with whom I tipped over the *pissoir* at the *Petit Galopin*. He was a big bloke, Roussel. But not today. When I find him, his face looks perfect. But a machine gun has chopped his body almost clean in two. I hardly dare move the pieces, in case they come apart.

I move from corpse to familiar corpse, struggling to believe this is real.

The Boche have blown the bridge. It was all for nothing that our friends died.

A few minutes later, two young women push a handcart slowly towards me, their faces wet with tears. One of them is my sister, Rosemary, the other, Roger Rioual's sister, Olga.

'You're alive,' gasps Rosemary, putting her hands to her face. Olga steps away from us. She moves softly among the bodies, straightening contorted arms and twisted legs.

'Am I?'

I gaze down at my blackened skin, my ripped and stinking clothes, my broken wooden shoes. I don't even recognise myself any more.

But Rosemary does. She takes a step forward and puts her arms around me.

'Is it over?' she whispers.

I cannot speak, so I shake my head.

'Please don't fight any more, Lou,' she says.

Again, I shake my head.

'What are you going to do?'

'Dead soldiers. Bury.'

'We'll do it together.'

I nod.

'Dad's safe, by the way,' she says.

'Others?'

'Everyone's at home. They're praying for you. Especially Mummy, who's sick.'

Through an open front door, I hear music; beautiful music. A gramophone. How long is it since we heard music on this street?

'*Inneggiamo*,' says Rosemary, softly, but I don't know what she means. Lone figures pick their way amid the carnage, heads bowed, shoulders slumped, faces blank.

Marcel appears, limping on stiff limbs. He looks as creaky as an old man. Maurice and Francis are here, too, arms around each other's shoulders, with matching haunted stares. And now Conrad staggers out of the shadows, grim-faced as a gun-slinger after the final shoot-out in a film.

Maurice was right. We are not soldiers. It was all for nothing in the end.

When the SS advanced behind their barricade of human hostages, the rabble of men at the bridge abandoned their position. They rushed down to the river bank below. They did their best to hide among the reeds. But the SS set up a pair of heavy machine guns on the bridge.

They sprayed the banks with bullets. It was easy to pick off the patriots as they fled.

Marcel Houcke was lucky. He was shot, but only through the foot. He'll walk again one day. Submerged beneath the river waters, he used a reed as a breathing tube. And the hail of bullets almost passed him by.

Now the Germans blew up the bridge. But this wasn't enough for them. They rounded up all the men in the houses nearby. And, one by one, they shot them in the back.

Forty of our comrades – our neighbours, our friends – have been killed. All the German prisoners have escaped.

No, not all of them. One or two were shot on the spot by the SS, for refusing to join their ranks. And two of them sought revenge.

The prisoner held in the cellar of the gendarme, Depape, returned to the house with a squad of SS men. Being captured must have wounded his Boche pride. He made a big show of dragging Depape into the square in Nieppe. There, he tied the lanky policeman to a tree, spat on him, and drilled him full of bullet holes. Then he mutilated the bleeding corpse with his dagger, and left it there for the flies.

Later, one of the fourteen prisoners from the barn, who had been guarded by my father and old Henri Blanquart, must have spotted Blanquart going back to his house to fetch his camera. He knocked very politely on his door. And when the old soldier opened it, he shot him through the head.

6 September 1944

Three British soldiers appear on the far side of the river Lys, at the place where the bridge used to be. But the cavalry has arrived too late. Nieppe is already a place of mourning and vengeance – a smoking, blackened shell.

I can feel my grief giving way to rage again. So when Sonneville comes rattling up in our captured *Kübelwagen*, with Conrad, Marcel, Abel Rotsaert and Alfred Vankerkove looking grim-faced in the back, it doesn't take much to persuade me to jump in. Sonneville says we are going to chase down the Boche who have fled into Belgium. I have never seen him look so determined, or so tired. The lines on his face are white. Loaded up with Sten guns, Schmeissers, rifles and grenades, we are going to seek our revenge.

He has spread a large French flag on the vehicle's bonnet.

'I thought you hated the French, Jean,' I say, as we pull away.

'I hated what we had become, until these last few days,' he says, swerving to avoid a pothole. 'And this tricolour should avoid us being shot at by our own side.'

A mile or two up the road, we arrive at a British outpost, manned by a handful of Tommies who are guarding a group of German prisoners. A young lieutenant steps forward.

'*Français?*' he asks.

'Frogs, Yanks and Brits,' I tell him, in English. 'We have some urgent business to attend to, up ahead.'

'I'm afraid you can't go any further than this, sir,' he says. 'Beyond this point, the Jerries are still putting up considerable resistance. We can't guarantee your safety if you proceed.'

'Jolly good,' I reply, gesturing for Sonneville to put his foot down, 'because it's Jerries we're after.' With that, we roar away.

Big miskake. At a bend in the road towards Comines, just past a lone farmhouse, we come under fire. Gunshots explode in our ears, slam into the bonnet of our vehicle and make rags of Sonneville's flag.

We duck, but there is nowhere to hide. Hammering into the trunks of the trees on either side, the bullets gouge out great chunks of sappy wood.

Now we are piling, rolling, falling out of the *Kübelwagen*. Dust and smoke and confusion. Several pinging thuds as the vehicle is turned into a sieve.

There must be at least two machine guns, and rifle fire.

I am in a ditch with Vankerkove. He is shouting something at me, but I can't hear. The bullets are fizzing and thumping all around us.

Vankerkove screams. A bullet has drilled a hole in his jacket. His eyes open wide and he clutches at his chest with bony fingers.

I wait for him to drop. We stare at each other. But the bullet has been stopped by a Sten gun magazine in his pocket. And, after a second, Vankerkove's glassy stare becomes a grin.

Sonneville has made it to the farmhouse above us. I can just spot him crouching behind a wall, shooting when he can. The gunfire is still intense. He's signalling to me.

He wants me to get back to the British outpost to request reinforcements. This must be at least two kilometres behind us. I glance at Vankerkove.

'You ready?' I shout, over the clattering of the small-arms fire on either side of us.

We grit our teeth. And then we are clambering out of the ditch, zigzagging to avoid the bullets. We tear back up the road to the next farm.

'Come on,' I yell. Two bicycles are parked against the farmhouse wall. *Thank you, Capitaine Michel.*

'But . . .'

Pedalling like mad, we make it back to the British outpost. I blurt our emergency to the young lieutenant. Can't he understand? I have friends back there who are going to die.

He tuts and shakes his head. 'I'm sorry, sir. I'd very much like to come and help your friends. But I have twenty German prisoners under guard here.'

A few minutes later, Vankerkove and I are marching back to Nieppe, on either side of a column of twenty German POWs. The brave young lieutenant has headed off in the opposite direction, leading a small raiding party of two Bren-gun carriers. He assured us he would bring back Sonneville and the others, dead or alive.

It is a long, slow march. I cannot help thinking about Conrad and Sonneville, their backs to the wall, lashed with a hail of bullets and God knows what else.

And here am I, strolling back to Nieppe behind a bunch of dejected prisoners. Already some of the heat has gone out of my hatred of the Boche. When I see them like this, weaponless, pitiful, they begin to seem almost human.

Next day, a miracle. Conrad comes crashing in through the front door of the farmhouse in the rue des Meuniers. As he collapses into a chair, I can see that he is hurt. But he and the others are safely home.

The young English lieutenant has not been so lucky. He has paid for our hubris with his life. A rifle bullet went straight through his helmet, the moment his Bren-gun carrier reached the bend in the road.

Conrad says that 200 Germans were dug in along the canal bank, just 250 metres from where we stopped. Had Sonneville driven the jeep another three seconds further, we would all have been killed, too.

Marcel keeps the punctured British helmet as a grim souvenir.

8 September 1944

The sun is shining as I cycle slowly into Nieppe with my Sten gun over my shoulder. I feel a thousand years old. And I am sickened by the vision that greets me.

It is not the devastation. It is all the people wearing tricolour armbands, as if they have been fighting for freedom all these years. Suddenly every man in Nieppe is in the Resistance, and several of the women, too. Look: they even have a captured German rifle to prove it. France is being liberated, not by the armies of Britain and the United States, but by a bunch of puffballs who have not dared so much as to look at a German in the past four years.

Shameless smilers are having their photographs taken in front of the wrecked 88mm guns, or beside the remains of the bridge. Even Roger Rioual's mum is there, dragging poor Roger to the guns. As I watch, someone hands her a Sten gun to hang around her son's submissive neck. Others are arguing over which of them will escort the funeral procession of the dead heroes. So many strangers, crawling out of the woodwork on every side.

Elsewhere a group of men I do not recognise are driving a bunch of weeping women up the main road, like the SS with their human barricade. They claim these women have slept with German soldiers. They are taking them to the château in Nieppe.

It is a horrible scene. I see a girl I know being publicly slapped. Someone rips open her blouse. I turn away, but I can hear the jeers as she has her head shaved by some man I have never seen before.

I recognise another of the women. She is a distant relative of Maurice Leblon. And then I spot Maurice himself, at the front, trying to stop the man with the shears. But the angry mob will have their pound of flesh, or hair.

'They've been powerless for so long, that's the trouble,' says a man beside me. It is Marcel Lombard. He looks shell-shocked.

'Let's go, Lombard,' I reply. 'I can't take any more of this.'

As we walk away from the château towards the church, the spiteful baying of the crowd fades to a distant roar.

'Why are they doing it?' I ask.

'Shaving the women?' Marcel shrugs. 'Most of those men probably wish they were the ones who'd been in bed with them, instead of the Germans,' he says.

'But the women in the crowd are almost worse than the men. Did you see their faces?'

He nods. 'The war has made us hate ourselves.'

We pass the spot where we once sat: two scared boys in a German lorry with a broken Messerschmitt at our backs, and I wonder if Marcel is remembering, as I am. Our route takes us past *Au Petit Galopin*, too and past the little school where I learned my lessons from Ruckebusch's boot.

It is all so fresh. It is all so far away. How the world has changed since we were boys, yesterday.

Alone, I wander down to the river Lys. I need to see the place where my friends fell. But there is much here that I do not need to see: mangled weapons; blood-stained clothes; a swarm of flies eating someone's guts in the grass.

'Reflecting?' asks a gravelly voice behind me. It is Mayor Houcke, his eyes a little dimmer, his beard a whole lot longer, than I remember them. We shake hands, and I wish I could find the words to say how much it means that he is here. Beside him stands a British army officer. The officer introduces himself, in French, as Lieutenant Colonel Cargill of Civil Affairs.

'Pleased to meet you, sir,' I reply, in English. He smiles and gives me a long stare.

Together we survey the gory scene. Mayor Houcke says he has plans for a memorial. Cargill nods, visibly impressed at how much the men of the Nieppe Resistance managed to do, and at the bravery of their tragic last stand.

Now Mayor Houcke gives Colonel Cargill an embarrassing account of my own services to the Resistance. I just have to stand there, like a lemon.

'Jolly good show,' says Cargill. 'Who would have thought I'd find an English boy in the French Resistance? Is there anything I can do for you, young man?'

'I would like to join the British army, please, sir.'

He smiles. 'We can always use chaps like you. I'll see what I can do.'

'Thank you, sir.'

'So you work for the War Graves, do you?' he asks, lowering his voice. 'I'm afraid you'll find we've made a lot of new work for you, these last weeks.'

'I'm used to it, sir.'

'Really?' he sighs. 'How very sad.'

Houcke and Cargill are about to tour the local area with Sonneville in the captured *Kübelwagen*. They invite me to join them and ask if I'd like to bring one of my best men along for the ride.

I dash off, and come back with my father. They look as surprised as he is. My father is all dressed up in his Saturday night suit, complete with trilby and white silk scarf. And he keeps bursting into song, and kissing people, and running up and down the road, pumping his fists in the air. I almost don't recognise him. He surprises Mayor Houcke by kissing him on both cheeks. He even shakes Sonneville's hand. To Colonel Cargill, he gives a very stiff and soldierly salute.

'Reporting for duty, sah!'

'Jolly good show,' replies Cargill, cautiously. 'You must be awfully proud of your son, here, Mr Grady.'

'Ah, then you've already seen our cemeteries,' beams my father. 'Yes, I am.'

The five of us are the first Allies to enter the village of Ploegsteert in Belgium, and they welcome us as liberators. The atmosphere is electric. There are kisses and photographs, noisy rejoicing and Calvados all round.

'Plugstreet! Plugstreet!' roars my dad, his face wet with tears. He grabs me by the arm. 'Mr Churchill will be happy about this, Lightning. Did I ever tell you that his brother is buried here?'

'Yes, Dad. About fifteen times.'

Even in my sombre mood, I feel transported by the relief and jubilation all around me. I think of Capitaine Michel, staring up at the light streaming in through the window of a dark barn. How I wish he were with us today.

And then we are passing the road sign to Steenwerck, and my skin begins to prickle. Delbecque is here, marching up and down with his group in the square. You'd think they had just liberated Paris with their bare hands.

When Delbecque spots me, he strides straight over.

'Please come, Iroquois.' It's pathetic that he is still using my code name. He tells me that there is a collaborator he wants me to shoot for him.

In an upstairs room in the *mairie*, an old man is tied to a chair. I look Delbecque straight in the eye. 'How can I shoot a Frenchman in cold blood, without a trial?'

'Have you forgotten that you shot a German once?'

Something snaps in me. I clench my fist. But Delbecque ducks away and hurries from the room.

'I'm so sorry, old man,' I whisper, as I untie the suspected collaborator.

Confused, the terrified fellow sinks to his knees. He wants to thank me, he says, and to give thanks to God. I try to make him stand up, but his eyes are streaming. Everyone is crying today. And then I hear Sonneville tooting the jeep's horn outside, and I escape into the sunlight.

The next three months pass in a blur. There are celebrations and commemorations. Sonneville proposes that we gather up all the dangerous ammunition still lying around, and set it off in one giant explosion. His fireworks display rocks the village and must be visible from Lille. So Jean has his Spectacular after all.

With no police left after the German retreat, I and the other Resistants are tasked with keeping order. We walk around with our FFI armbands and our Sten guns. I feel like the sheriff in a Western. Conrad is in clover.

The threat of capture by the German police may have receded, but I still have to watch my back. For now, more than ever, Madame Houcke is doing her best to tie me down. I remind her that I want to join the British army.

'You've done enough,' she tells me, in the middle of the rue d'Armentières, picking an imaginary piece of fluff from the lapel of my jacket. 'You must get married and settle down. It's time to forget the war, Stéphane.'

What I really want to say in response is: 'If only I could.'

Yet I know that I have no hope of making her understand. No, the only ones who will understand are the men and boys who have lived through the last few years with me, with whom I have stared death in the face so many times that I do not fear it any more: Jean Sonneville; the brave Houcke brothers; Maurice Leblon and Francis André; Conrad Kersch; and, of course, good old Marcel.

Perhaps, in the end, it is only Marcel who can really understand. He and I have shared so much together, in Loos Prison and in the rue du Sac, in fields and haylofts and cemeteries, and in the glintingly sombre years since that summer's day when I scrawled a slogan on the side of a Messerschmitt, and the bottom fell out of our world.

* * *

Now the war will soon be over. The chaos of the past few years will be replaced with the old rhythms of the country-side, with that earthy, rustic order, in tune with the moon and the seasons, which characterises peasant life.

This is what I tell myself anyway: everything will soon be back to normal.

Yet, in my heart, I know that nothing will ever be the same again.

I sense that Marcel is in denial, too. After finally achieving his dream of joining the French air force, he returns to Bailleul. And there he spends the whole of the rest of his working life as a teacher, and then headmaster, and then inspector, in the very same school at which he spent his entire childhood.

My father is not so lucky. Free at last after his years in hiding, he travels to his beloved England, where he has inherited Briar Villa, my English grandmother's old house in Pegwell Bay. But when he gets there, all he finds is a heap of rubble. A V1 bomb has got there first.

Riding his old Royal Enfield to a motorcycle inspection in Ypres a few months later, my father swerves to avoid a little girl who has stepped out into the road. He crashes into a wall. Elizabeth and my mother visit him in hospital, and he is doing fine. He sings 'Ma'm'selle from Armentières' and asks Elizabeth to marry him. A few hours later he is dead, the victim of a double dose of tetanus vaccine administered by mistake.

In the midst of all this, Colonel Cargill has helped me to achieve my ambition of joining the British army. Armed with a letter of recommendation from Colonel Buckmaster of the SOE, I have been commissioned as a lieutenant in the Intelligence Corps. My dream is coming true.

I can hardly wait to see what the Boche look like as a beaten nation, especially when Maurice Leblon, now serving with the 43rd Regiment of French Infantry in occupied Germany, writes to me. Maurice triumphantly declares that he has just ordered the mayor of a small German town to clean out a lavatory pit with a toothbrush.

But instead of Germany, I am flown to Beirut, and then to Greece. As I swoop low in a Dakota over the Greek islands on my way to a posting in Salonika, I feel as if I have arrived in paradise.

My mother, now very ill, has other ideas about my future. She writes to me, begging me to leave the army. She wants me to come back and look after the family in Nieppe. So I resign my longed-for commission. I bury my military dream.

Rosemary gasps when I appear in the rue du Sac.

'You came back.'

'You know I always come back,' I reply.

She and Elizabeth have already buried their own dreams, and settled into the humdrum lives my mother always wanted for them.

On New Year's Day 1947, I arrive at Mayor Houcke's house at 11 a.m. to wish his family *bonne année*. This is the custom in France. But Madame Houcke is furious, railing at me on the doorstep for turning up so late. I explain that my mother is in a bad way. Madame Houcke is unmoved, accusing me of indifference and ingratitude. Do I not know how lucky I am?

This is the last straw. With ice in my veins, I tell her that she may henceforth consider my engagement to her daughter as broken. I walk away, and that's the end of it. A few months later, Andrée is married to someone else.

My mother dies in April 1947.

Kléber is killed shortly afterwards, riding my father's jinxed Royal Enfield too fast around Nieppe. He has taken a job in the cemeteries, working for the War Graves Commission. Marcel Houcke phones me from the hospital and tells me I must bring my brother home. So I bring Kléber back to the rue du Sac, one last time. I lay him in the front room, and sit beside him until the end. It is the worst day of my life.

With my future in tatters, I turn in desperation to the only job I know: as a gardener for the IWGC. But even for this I have no real qualifications. All they can offer me is a lowly job on the very bottom rung of the ladder, as a gardener's labourer, grade II, in one of the new war cemeteries.

I am to bury the victims of another war. I am home, once again, with the dead.

23 November 1979

A rainy, windswept day, and I am standing beside a grave in a forgotten corner of the municipal cemetery in south Lille.

This is not a British military cemetery. But among the hotchpotch of gothic monuments and curlicued tombs, one simple white tablet of Portland stone stands out.

The finely chiselled lettering is in English. The headstone matches those in every British military cemetery all over the world, to commemorate those who have died in battle. And as I stand before a large crowd in the rain, I feel as if I have finally done something in my life of which I can feel proud.

I take a step forward, peer down at the raindrops soaking into the typewritten pages in my hand and clear my throat.

Messieurs, Dames; Ladies and Gentlemen,

On Tuesday evening, it will be exactly thirty-six years since our chief, Captain Michael Trotobas – known to us as Capitaine Michel – met his death at the hands of the Germans.

The Gestapo must have celebrated that night, believing that they had destroyed an entire network, convinced they had shot a terrorist. How far they were from imagining that the example of courage and patriotism that Capitaine Michel set for us would propel his network to the very front rank in our victory and their defeat.

The way Capitaine Michel inspired us, thirty-six years ago, is still our inspiration, even now. It is impossible to forget the man who was our model of true courage.

And today, we have at last obtained the military headstone he has always deserved; a war grave for the warrior that he was. As far as men may assure it, this memorial will forever be protected, and the sacrifice of Capitaine Michel will ever be glorified here, under the guarantee of both the French and British nations.

May I dare to hope that this place will continue to be a sanctuary, visited regularly by those who come not only to honour the memory of Capitaine Michel, but to reaffirm their willingness to oppose aggression, no matter what the price; no matter how supreme the sacrifice required may be.

I take a step backwards. Everything is a bit of a blur. Someone shuffles forward and mutters a few words in my ear; someone else squeezes my arm. There are wreaths and bouquets. Later there will be a dinner, and we will swap stories about the old days. But I am not really listening. I am gazing at the white stone in our midst, remembering the bravest man I ever met, and hoping he would approve.

It is the very least I could do for Capitaine Michel.

July 2012 – Halkidiki, Greece

I sit out on the terrace with my papers and some of my treasures spread in front of me. It is a clear evening, and the sea looks calmer than usual tonight. I can hear the throbbing of the local nightclub in the distance, and then the sound of Father Vitali's footsteps approaching the house. He hesitates as he rounds the corner.

'You've taken away the tripwires,' he booms.

'I thought it was about time.'

I pull up a chair for him, and we sit in silence, watching the lighthouse flash in the darkness.

'You have stopped being afraid,' he says. 'That's good.'

I wish I'd put my photographs away. I would have done if I'd known he was going to drop in.

'And, you know, you never did tell me about these gravestones.' Vitali peers down at his feet. 'Are they significant?'

'They are to me.' I pause. 'There was a beautiful First World War cemetery here, badly damaged by a mortar attack in 1944. When the replacement headstones arrived, these fragments were going to be thrown out. I couldn't let that happen. So I rescued them.'

Vitali listens in silence. He looks at the table made for me by my son Francis, its surface inlaid with fragments of tile and coloured glass. He scans the battered typewriter; the half-finished bottle of Haig; the photos of me with the Queen; the drawings I made in Loos Prison; a letter from President Eisenhower.

'I thought you were a gardener,' he says at last.

'I was. All my life.'

415

Epilogue

Stephen Grady returned to the Gardens of Stone in 1947, after two and a half years in the British army. For his wartime service in the French Resistance, he was awarded the Croix de Guerre with Silver Star, and the American Medal of Freedom. He took up work as a gardener's labourer and served until 1984, when he retired as Director in charge of all Commonwealth War Graves Commission cemeteries in France, and was awarded the OBE.

Mayor Houcke had a distinguished political career, serving as a member of the chamber of deputies and later a senator. Under his directorship, the postwar *Voix du Nord* would become the most influential newspaper in the north of France.

Jean Sonneville went back to his smuggling after the war, until he was arrested for trafficking rabbit fur and sentenced to six months' imprisonment. Fortunately Mayor Houcke had not the forgotten the debt he owed, and secured Sonneville's early release.

Conrad Kersch returned to the USA, where he married Doris, the widow of his dead comrade. He brought her to Nieppe after the war, to try to help her to understand. Later, Conrad pursued a distinguished career in aviation and engineering.

Auntie Val stayed on in Nieppe, and never married.

Rosemary and Elisabeth Grady both live in the south of France.

Marcel Lombard lives with his wife at La Crèche, a stone's throw from Nieppe. He and Stephen Grady have remained life-long friends.

The Writing of *Gardens of Stone*

From my first meeting with Stephen Grady, at his remote home overlooking the sandy shoreline of Halkidiki, I had the impression that this was to be a book about forgetting, as much as about remembering.

With his son Francis's encouragement, Stephen wrote some fifty pages of factual memoir, which form the basis of this narrative. But there were clearly areas it was too painful or uncomfortable for him to revisit. He was still having nightmares and flashbacks about the German police.

Through conversations and interviews, I have attempted to flesh out the bare bones of his recollections, and to piece together the inner life of the man and boy who lived and breathed and did these things all those years ago. Or yesterday, as it sometimes seems.

One of the challenges has been that, like many men of his generation, Stephen Grady does not readily discuss his emotions. 'We didn't think about it too much,' he would tell me, again and again. 'We just got on with it.' So if at any point in the narrative he appears guilty of emotional excess, this is my fault, not his. And in those moments where some character or other tells him how brave he is, that comes from me, too, not him. He is a discreet and humble man.

I have been fortunate to be able to draw upon the unpublished wartime reminiscences of Stephen's sisters, Elizabeth and Rosemary. Visits to Nieppe and Steenwerck also helped. For the dialogue, I have followed Thucydides' approach of attempting to convey if not what people actually said, then what they ought to have said at the time. Several of the books listed in the bibliography have made it possible to enrich the backdrop of the Occupation against which Stephen's adventures are played out.

All of which is a long way of saying that the events in this book really did happen, and I have done my best to get as close to the truth, both historically and emotionally, as I possibly can. Some names and dates have been changed. Stephen has checked and rechecked the manuscript, and seems queasily satisfied with the result. I know he struggles with the idea that anybody will be interested in reading a book about him, but I am honoured to have had the chance to help him write it.

Michael Wright
La Folie, France
November 2012

Stephen Grady's Acknowledgements

I would like to thank my daughter Patricia, who typed the original draft of the memoir upon which this book is based, and my son Francis for his tireless work to see it published in the best possible way, including writing an initial book-length manuscript. Both of them are enormously supportive of me in my old age, and I don't know where I would be without Patricia's caring.

Peter Grimsdale, an old school friend of Patricia's, was a tremendous source of advice and encouragement in the project's early stages and, most significantly, put Francis in touch with Mark Lucas, a literary agent whose vision for the book took it on to a whole new level.

It was Mark's idea to bring on board Michael Wright, a wonderful writer and fluent French speaker, to turn my story into a full-length book. Michael's feeling for the locale of my youth and sympathetic understanding of the challenges of revisiting it gave me immediate comfort. I thank him for his assiduity as well as for his patience in dealing with many amendments and corrections.

After I left the army, I spent the next thirty-seven years in the service of the Commonwealth War Graves Commission, a praiseworthy organisation of which I remain deeply proud.

If this book has a future and serves any purpose beyond allowing people to experience a moment of history lived long ago, I hope it may draw attention to the bravery of many people in northern France, some eight thousand of whom were executed or suffered in German concentration camps for having resisted the brutal German occupation.

Stephen Grady

Picture Acknowledgements

Most of the photographs are from the author's collection. Additional sources: Getty Images p3 above, Rupert Lancaster p16, Ullsteinbild/TopFoto p3 below.

Michael Wright's Acknowledgements

I offer my deepest thanks to:

Stephen Grady, for trusting me with his story and welcoming me to stay with him at his house in Greece.

Francis Grady, Stephen's son, for reading the manuscript time after time, and always managing to come up with suggestions for improving or correcting it.

Patricia Grady, Stephen's daughter, for looking after me so beautifully in Greece and providing sensitive input into her father's story.

Elizabeth Grady, Stephen's sister, for her patience in answering all sorts of personal questions about her family life, and for allowing me to read her private reminiscences.

Madame Fach at the Mairie in Nieppe, for giving me so much useful background material and help with my research.

Rupert Lancaster at Hodder for his editorship of the book, with a touch at once firm and light.

Mark Lucas, my literary agent, who was instrumental in the early shaping of the narrative.

My friends and neighbours, James and Jilly Bernard, who allowed me the use of a quiet corner in their magnificent house in France, a haven of tranquillity which enabled me to write this book about war in peace. James proved a tremendous source of military and technical information, too.

My beloved wife, Alice, for taking care of our children and animals while I was enjoying the haven of tranquillity mentioned above. Alice also offered many useful improvements to the book, and generally made it a pleasure to write.

The current owners of number 6, rue du Sac, for allowing me to explore Stephen's old family home. The numbering of the houses in the rue du Sac has changed now, and it is not obvious which house is the old number 6. Perhaps this is just as well, for the new owners are private people. Cultural tourists, keen to explore the setting of this book, will find more to interest them in the centre of Nieppe and in the Pont d'Achelles cemetery, than at the Grady house itself. At Pont d'Achelles, the two bastions beneath one of which Stephen and Marcel dug their cache have been removed. In all other respects, the cemetery remains unchanged.

On this note, I would like to join Stephen in acknowledging the wonderful work of the Commonwealth War Graves Commission – formerly the IWGC – for treating our soldiers with a respect and dignity in death that one can only wish were similarly afforded them when they are still alive.

Michael Wright

Select Bibliography

Unpublished works

Grady, Elizabeth, *Ma famille*

Grady, Francis, *Dangerous Games*

Grady, Rosemary, *Jeunesse de Guerre*

Grady, Stephen, *No. 6 rue du Sac*

Kersch, Conrad, *The Albert de Groote Story*

Published works

Cobb, Matthew, *The Resistance: The French Fight Against the Nazis* (Pocket Books, 2010)

Dejonghe, Etienne et Laurent, Daniel, *Libération du Nord et du Pas-de-Calais* (Hachette, 1974)

Dejonghe, Etienne et Le Maner, Yves, *Le Nord-Pas-de-Calais dans la Main Allemande 1940–1944* (La Voix du Nord, 1999)

Duhamel, Jean-Marie, *La Voix du Nord Clandestine 1941–1944, vols 1 & 2* (Editions La Voix, 2011)

Fox, James and Elliott, Sue, *The Children who Fought Hitler* (John Murray, 2010)

Lheureux, Danièle, *Sylvestre-Farmer Avec le Capitaine Michel* (Geai Bleu, 2002)

Ousby, Ian, *Occupation: The Ordeal of France 1940–1944* (Pimlico, 1999)

Vinen, Richard, *The Unfree French: Life Under the Occupation* (Penguin, 2007)

Wallart, Claudine, *Le Nord Occupé 1940–1944* (Archives Départementales du Nord, 1990)

Index

Index

Index

An invitation from the publisher

Join us at www.hodder.co.uk, or follow us
on Twitter @hodderbooks to be a part of
our community of people who love the very
best in books and reading.

Whether you want to discover more about a book
or an author, watch trailers and interviews, have the
chance to win early limited editions, or simply browse
our expert readers' selection of the very best books,
we think you'll find what you're looking for.

And if you don't, that's the place to tell us what's missing.

We love what we do, and we'd love you to be a part of it.

www.hodder.co.uk

@hodderbooks

HodderBooks

HodderBooks